Africa

International Government & Politics Series

by
Edward Bever

ORYX PRESS

1996

The rare Arabian oryx is believed to have inspired the myth of the unicorn. This desert antelope became virtually extinct in the early 1960s. At that time several groups of international conservationists arranged to have 9 animals sent to the Phoenix Zoo to be the nucleus of a captive breeding herd. Today the oryx population is over 1,000, and over 500 have been returned to the Middle East.

© 1996 by Edward Bever
Published by The Oryx Press
4041 North Central at Indian School Road
Phoenix, Arizona 85012-3397

Published simultaneously in Canada
Printed and bound in the United States of America

♾ The paper used in this publication meets the minimum requirements of the American National Standard for Information Sciences—Permanence of Paper for Printed Library Materials, ANSI Z39.48-1984.

Library of Congress Cataloging-in-Publication Data
Bever, Edward
    Africa / by Edward Bever.
        p. cm. — (International government & politics series)
    Includes bibliographical references and index.
    ISBN 0-89774-954-5
    1. Africa—Politics and government. I. Title. II. Series.
DT31.B395 1996
320.96—dc20   96-43086
                                                        CIP

For Patricia
With Love and Appreciation

ORYX INTERNATIONAL GOVERNMENT & POLITICS SERIES

Central and Eastern Europe by John Dornberg
Western Europe by John Dornberg
The Middle East by Dilip Hiro
Africa by Edward Bever

CONTENTS

LIST OF MAPS

PREFACE

Africa provides an up-to-date introduction to contemporary African politics and a thorough presentation of its historical roots. The reader will get information about specific African countries, summary information about current political developments in the continent as a whole, and historical information to put current events into their larger context. The primary audience is students and other nonspecialists who have a need for or an interest in a more sophisticated presentation than can be found in general textbooks and journalistic surveys.

The book covers politics in all of Africa, including North Africa and nearby islands, from its roots in the distant past through the start of 1996. Part 1, "Historical Background to African Politics," contains three chapters that trace the course of the continent's political development from prehistoric times through the end of colonialism. Part 2, "The Nations of Africa," contains a discussion of the politics and government of each of the continent's 53 sovereign countries. Part 3, "Continental Perspectives," contains one chapter that explores Africa's international relations and another that examines broad economic, social, and political trends.

In Part 2, readers may be confused by the apparent disjunction between the names and the abbreviations of some political parties that have arisen in France's former African colonies. The reason is that the abbreviations are derived from the French, while the full names have been translated to English.

STATISTICAL PROFILES

The statistical information presented in the individual country profiles was drawn from the 1995 edition of *Keesing's Record of World Events* and the latest editions of *Lands and Peoples: Africa* and the *New African Yearbook*. All population and population growth rate estimates are from 1994, the most recent statistics available in these categories. GDP, per capita income, and foreign debt figures are the most recent available for each country; in most cases, this means figures from 1992 or 1993, but in some instances the most recent reliable figures come from the years 1989 to 1991. For ethnic groups and religions, the percentages in parentheses refer to a particular group's percentage of the overall population. They do not always add up to 100 percent, but they represent the best information available from the sources used. Official language refers to the language of government; other important languages spoken within a country are given where appropriate.

ACKNOWLEDGMENTS

I would like to thank Professor Robert Tignor of Princeton University, both for reading parts of this manuscript and for his support and encouragement in my graduate study of African history. I would also like to thank Professor Andrew Barnes of Carnegie-Mellon University and Professor Robert Whittmore of Western Connecticut State University for reading parts of the manuscript, and I would like to thank both for several stimulating conversations about African history and current affairs. In addition, I would like to thank my sister, Sarah Bever, who supplied me with a steady stream of clippings on African affairs from the *New York Times,* the *Financial Times,* and *The Wall Street Journal.* Finally, I want to thank the staff at Oryx Press for their excellent editorial work. All have helped tremendously with my effort. Responsibility for any flaws that remain, naturally, is entirely my own.

On a more personal level, I would like to thank my wife, Patricia, and my children, Noah, Tony, and Celia, for their patience and support while I worked on this book. I hope that its quality will justify the time lost with you.

PART

1

HISTORICAL BACKGROUND TO AFRICAN POLITICS

Introduction to Part 1

Until recently, the general consensus of educated opinion agreed with noted historian Hugh Trevor-Roper: before the Europeans arrived, Africa's political history was nothing but the "tale of barbarous tribal gyrations." This view justified European colonialism as "the introduction of order into blank, uninteresting, brutal barbarism," as the eminent Africanist H.E. Egerton put it. With the Europeans came the benefits of modern government: bureaucratic administration, democratic and socialist principles, and national consciousness. Today, this view underlies the assumption that Africa must look outside itself for models of political organization, an assumption that guides not only Africa's Western benefactors, from private foundations to the International Monetary Fund, but also most African leaders.

Recent scholarship has exposed this view of Africa's political past as a self-serving myth. Africans developed sophisticated and successful political institutions that made possible great empires in Egypt, the Sahel, and Zimbabwe. Until the very eve of European colonialism, Africans generally assimilated foreign influences, even the infamous slave trade, into their own institutions and on their own terms. European political control of Africa resulted from industrial Europe's sudden enormous jump in material power in the late nineteenth century rather than from any political backwardness in Africa.

Given the vitality of Africa's precolonial political institutions, colonial rule was not a beneficent gift but simply a means of furthering European interests. Colonialism distorted Africa's political development and left it ill-prepared for independence in the modern world. Colonialism's basic aim was to use political control to make Africa an economic appendage of Europe, and that accomplishment survived the end of colonial rule. The resulting poverty has hobbled independent Africa's political development.

CHAPTER

Early African Governments

Before European intrusion began in the fifteenth century, Africans created a tremendous variety of political systems—from bands of nomadic hunter-gatherers to bureaucratic structures governing great empires. Hunter-gatherers lived in small, impermanent groups, whose composition and size could vary greatly over time. People who lived by agriculture or herding generally developed more permanent and complex relationships based on lineage (descent from common ancestry) and, in the case of agriculturists, geographical proximity. These communities, sometimes called stateless societies, involved highly developed and intricately balanced political systems governing relations within and among clans (affiliated groups of lineages) and villages.

In areas where the population became particularly dense, territorially broader, more hierarchical political structures appeared. This process led to the world's first great empire in Egypt, and later to similar political developments further south. Still later, sub-Saharan Africans adopted new techniques of govern-ment from Arab traders and invaders. Through the end of the European Middle Ages, the empires in West Africa and the city-states along the Swahili Coast equaled or exceeded the kingdoms and cities of Europe in material power and cultural sophistication. Like Europe, they formed vital extensions of the belt of civilization across southern Asia, and vibrant outposts of the Islamic world.

This essentially evolutionary view of African government assumes that the more complex forms of government grew out of less complex forms as the societies they governed grew more complex. This chapter follows this approach because it is an economical way to survey the development of government in Africa before the coming of the Europeans. However, the reader needs to keep several important points in mind. First, more complex societies are not inherently better than less complex societies. Civilization has its advantages, but it also has its discontents. Second, not all less complex societies develop into more complex forms. Social stability is in most

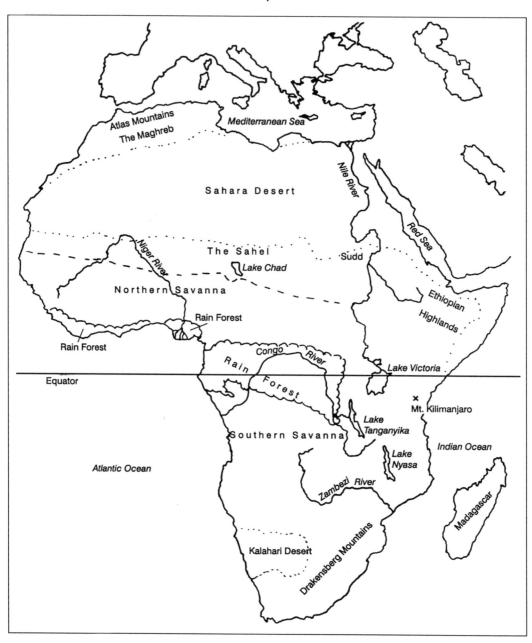

Africa: Geographical Features

circumstances a sign of strength, not weakness. Third, not all social change is toward greater complexity. Sometimes it makes sense for people to adopt a simpler way of life in the face of changing circumstances. In general, societies change or remain the same because of the interplay of environmental and internal factors. Groups of humans exist in a dynamic equilibrium with their surroundings. Social evolution occurs when people find new ways to adapt to a new reality resulting from internal developments or external changes.

THE ROOTS OF AFRICAN GOVERNMENT

The basic structure of pre-colonial African societies reflected their roots in the Mesolithic period (the middle Stone Age) when modern humans, *homo sapiens,* first appeared. *Homo sapiens* had the ability to create a variety of stone tools, make fire, find shelter in caves, and carry burdens. They lived in bands and survived by hunting animals and gathering edible plants. Supported by their advanced technology, their numbers increased steadily.

Nomadic hunter-gatherers generally coped with population pressures by migrating apart, but in certain circumstances the increasing number of people came to be supported by the adoption of agriculture. By planting, tending, and harvesting plants, as well as by domesticating animals, people were able to live in significantly greater numbers on a given amount of land. They might migrate from one plot to another when the soil became exhausted, but overall the agriculturists lived more settled lives than hunger-gatherers, and as agricultural techniques improved and populations became denser, some agricultural peoples became almost entirely sedentary. Living in the same place generation after generation, they accumulated considerable amounts of material goods, often developed an attachment to a particular plot of land, and almost invariably developed a social identity and political structure based on extended family relations. Among virtually all agricultural peoples, and also among pastoralists (herders), each lineage

group had a head who was chosen by custom according to some combination of age, maturity, and relationship to the ancestors.

These family ties—who you were descended from and who you were related to—were so important that people regarded them as part of the religious order. The ancestors might be dead, but their spirits remained nearby, and they were vitally interested in the ongoing life of the clan. Rituals to honor them and obedience to their will were part of the fabric of daily life, basic ingredients of the harmony of the universe. Respect for the ancestors and commitment to the traditions and structures of the clan did not prevent differences of opinion and even bitter disputes, but they did provide the framework for peaceful resolution of disputes and common actions for the greater good.

For some time, any particular location could support a group, but inevitably there came a point when the number of people exceeded the local food supply. When the population reached this point, a group from within the lineage group or clan would have to pack up and move away. The emigrants faced the question not only of deciding where to go, but also of how to govern themselves. Out of this process of fission and migration, which was repeated again and again over thousands of years, Africans developed a great variety of political and social systems. The two basic organizing principles for political and social systems were "stateless" societies or chiefdoms and kingdoms.

"STATELESS" SOCIETIES

The term "stateless" society is somewhat misleading because these societies had complex political arrangements governing relations between significant numbers of people over substantial territories. In this political arrangement, which characterized the Igbo, the Kru, the Tallensi, and many other groups, all clans were equal. A council of elders, consisting of the heads of each clan in the village, oversaw common activities and dispensed justice in ordinary circumstances. In reaching their decisions and deciding disputes, the members of this council sought unanimity, which was generally achieved through compromise. They generally could not force a decision on anyone because the resulting violence could escalate and tear a community to pieces. Alternatively, disgruntled lineage heads could simply pack up and move away.

In the case of an impasse among the elders or an important decision like war or peace, a more broadly based general assembly would be called. At this meeting, anyone could speak. Debate was often long and lively. The assembly would usually seek to reach a consensus, although in some societies the majority ruled if a consensus was not possible. The losers might not like the decision, but they could have no doubt that their voice had been heard and the outcome reflected the will of the community.

To preserve the autonomy of the clans, some stateless societies invested no individuals with general authority. No one had the right to impose a punishment on or compel an action by someone in another clan, even if such action represented the will of the whole community. Instead, responsibility for the execution of decisions or the imposition of penalties lay with the affected person's family.

Other stateless societies did have positions with general authority, but they carefully limited this authority and balanced it against the authority of other offices—judicial against military, for example, or religious against civil. Members of different lineages had to cooperate in handling community affairs, a system of checks and balances reminiscent of the checks and balances built into the American government.

One form of inequality that many traditional societies did recognize was clientage. A household or clan with relatively abundant resources might help out another that was not so well situated, and this relationship could become one of dependency. In political terms, the community recognized that members of the dependent household could not act autonomously from the patron, and therefore did not extend full political rights to them. This condition was theoretically temporary, but in practice it could lead to indefinite and substantial differences in wealth and power within a community. Patron-client relations continued to exist in more complex societies, and survived as an important aspect of contemporary African affairs.

No system could insure that abuses of power never occurred, but the "stateless" system of government proved remarkably resilient. Many African societies preserved their consensual, relatively open structure from ancient times all the way down to the European conquests of a few generations ago. Indeed, it is discouraging to think how much more secure in their rights many contemporary Africans would be had they been able to preserve their ancient liberties but a few decades longer. These stateless societies may not have constituted a modern liberal democracy, but they were closer to it than the racist authoritarianism of colonialism and the military despotisms that all too often followed them.

CHIEFDOMS AND KINGDOMS

In the chiefdom, all clans were not equal. Instead, the clan closest to the lineage that originally settled the area had the right to supply a chief. The position was not strictly hereditary because no particular member of the family had an automatic right to become the next chief, and occasionally someone outside the clan might gain the chiefdom due to extraordinary leadership abilities. However, the tendency in most societies was for the office to be dominated by one clan.

Details naturally varied from society to society, but usually the chief was a man who led the community's political, social, judicial, and religious life. He maintained order, oversaw community affairs, acted as a court of appeals, and provided a direct link to the ancestors. He collected tribute, fines, and tolls for the community, holding them in trust and using them to help clans in times of need and to entertain visitors. He also received from the winners of disputes he judged a portion of the settlement as compensation for his services.

The chief was generally assisted in his deliberations by an inner council made up of relatives and friends. He could consult these confidential advisors before initiating legislation or making important decisions. If they approved an idea, he would then take it to a council of elders drawn from all the clans. The elders would debate it with little or no input from him until they came to a unanimous decision. If they could not achieve unanimity, the chief called a general assembly that deliberated to reach a consensus or, failing that, a majority opinion.

At all levels of deliberation, debate was open, and the chief was no more a despot than is the president of the United States. In the first place, he was restrained by respect for political traditions and social customs, and by belief in the power of the ancestors to enforce them. Secondly, the inner council could depose him if he went against its will. The council of elders had the same power if it felt he was abusing his position. Although the inner council was made up of people the chief appointed, the position of the elders was hereditary, and thus they were beyond the chief's control. Finally, if all else failed, the people could give allegience to another chief, could go on strike by refusing to pay tribute, or could pack up and move away.

In recent times, chiefs almost always have ruled as subordinates of a king. Whether the position of chief or king came first cannot be known. Chiefs may always have been subordinates of a king; when a group moved away from a crowded area the leader of the original state may have retained a certain authority over the emigrants. Kingdoms may also have grown out of chiefdoms; the same desire for strong leadership and impartial arbitration that led villages to accept chiefs may have led chiefs in crowded areas to accept a king. Most likely, both processes took place in different circumstances.

As with chiefdoms, specific institutions in a kingdom varied from society to society. Kings generally had a limited but vital role in the life of the state, although as societies became more complex their role evolved and broadened. An electoral council chose the king from the royal family (the clan closest to the founding lineage). Chosen for his strength, generosity, humility, fierceness in war, devoutness in religion, and descent from the founding ancestors, the archaic king played mainly a ceremonial and religious role. He served as final court of appeal in judicial disputes and gave final approval to governmental policies, but left the details of ruling to his council of advisors and to councils of provincial chiefs. His ceremonial role involved the "theater of royalty," wearing special clothes, using special greetings, living in special quarters, eating special foods, and otherwise demonstrating the special nature of the bonds that held the state together. His religious duties centered on maintaining harmony between his people and the universal order. Regarded as divine, he had to maintain his own spiritual purity and potency, execute the magic rituals associated with his office, and oversee the activities of other cults.

Because of the importance of the king's role in securing the spiritual well-being of the people, he could be deposed if he proved unworthy. If he deviated from the rules of his office, acted arbitrarily, or otherwise broke the law, his council or the people had a variety of sanctions they could apply. Those closest to him could admonish him privately, while others could do so publicly at ceremonies or festivals, and could file formal grievances. If he refused to pay heed, the authorities that selected him could try to dethrone him (generally referred to as "destoolment" in the African context). Typically, they had to give him an opportunity to defend himself before a tribunal, and if the judgment went against him, he might have an opportunity to beg for forgiveness. If the aggrieved party refused to forgive, the destooled king would be banished. If the authorities failed to take action, or forgave too easily, the people themselves would protest, shunning the king, refusing to pay taxes or tribute, and ultimately rising up in rebellion.

Rarely seen or heard in public, bound by the rules and taboos of the office, the king was a distant presence in the affairs of the people and of the state. Nevertheless, by subsuming the ancestral powers of a large number of lineages, kingship made possible far larger political associations than did stateless societies. Stateless societies were almost inherently limited in their size and expanse, but kingdoms could expand indefinitely. As groups multiplied and moved, they did not necessarily break away, but often retained their ties to the original community, thus expanding the numbers and extent of the kingdom. Kingdoms also offered a level of government above villages and clans and therefore could arbitrate among them. Some stateless societies actually subordinated themselves to kings voluntarily in order to gain this valuable service.

THE KINGDOM OF THE NILE

The earliest known kingdom in Africa and the earliest great kingdom in the world grew up in the valley of the Nile. Egypt owed its life and its greatness to the Nile, the world's longest river. Every spring, the river spilled over its banks, leaving behind a new layer of fertile soil when the water receded. This rich gift supported a thriving agriculture, which in turn supported a rapid growth of population. There were around 100,000 Egyptians in 5000 B.C., 2 million (20 times more) in 2000 B.C., 4 million in 1000 B.C., and 5 million at the time of Christ.

Unlike the inhabitants of the forests and grasslands, the people of Egypt had nowhere to go as their numbers increased; they were hemmed in by deserts to the east and west, the Mediterranean Sea to the north, and rugged terrain in the far south. Consequently, Egypt became exceedingly crowded (its population density, 200 per square mile, was higher than in most modern nations). To cope, the Egyptians had to organize themselves more highly than any other society had done. At first, the large population led to the rise of towns and small cities, a process that had already occurred to the east in Palestine and Mesopotamia. However, the Egyptians forged larger and larger states, until King Menes of Upper (southern) Egypt conquered Lower (northern) Egypt around 3200 B.C. to become sole king, or pharaoh. The empire he established lasted over 2,000 years.

King Menes's accomplishment rested on two foundations. The first was Upper Egypt's copper and gold mines. Copper was the main ingredient in bronze, the metal then used for tools and weapons; gold was used in precious jewelry and ornaments. These resources gave him the power to conquer the North. The second foundation was the Nile itself. The river formed a central highway down the middle of Egypt. It flowed north and the wind blew south, so even a crude boat could float down and sail back up. Since virtually all the people lived within a few miles of the river, the king's officials and soldiers could easily collect taxes and maintain order. This lifeline made possible the extraordinarily long survival of the Egyptian state.

Just as the Egyptian people were natives of Africa, having moved up from the south and west millennia before, so too the Egyptian monarchy was an original African innovation, having no parallels in the older civilization of Mesopotamia. In some ways, it bore interesting similarities to the kingships described in the previous section. The Egyptian pharaoh wore a double crown symbolizing the union of the two halves of the valley, just as the traditional king unified diverse lineages in himself. The earliest images of the pharaoh show him with a tail while holding a crook and a flail— symbols of the hunter, herder, and farmer, the three main socioeconomic groups in the realm. Like other African kings, the pharaoh's prime responsibility was to maintain harmony between his people and the universe, in particular with the spirits of the ancestors who, in Egypt's case, were housed in magnificent tombs that were the centers of active cults and the source of oracular pronouncements. Like other African kings, the pharaohs were regarded as divine.

Since our records of Egypt long predate any knowledge of other African kingdoms, it is possible that the divinity of the kings elsewhere derived from the Egyptian model rather than from a common ancestral system. If that was the case, the other kingdoms totally missed another key element of the Egyptian system: bureaucracy. Unlike the relatively loose agglomerations of provinces that made up other indigenous African kingdoms (at least until the influence of Islam was felt), the Egyptian monarchy was a strongly centralized, bureaucratic state. Top officials were not large landholders owing a feudal allegiance to the king, but were instead officeholders charged with carrying out the will of the pharaoh. Royal officials collected all taxes and tribute and mobilized labor for civil and military purposes; all wealth flowed in to the center and all power flowed out from the center.

Because of the internal cohesion supplied by the river and the external protection afforded by the deserts and the sea, ancient Egypt enjoyed an exceptionally long and peaceful history. From 3200 B.C. to 2180 B.C. an unbroken succession of dynasties ruled a prosperous and dynamic civilization. A century of invasion and revolt ended this "Old Kingdom," but thereafter a "Middle Kingdom" reigned until 1640 B.C. A shorter interlude resulted from the Hyksos invasion, but in 1570 B.C. the "New Kingdom" emerged. It lasted until 1050 B.C., after which the Libyans, Nubians, Assyrians, Persians, Greeks, Romans, and Arabs seized the valley in turn, ruling it as just one province in their much larger empires.

THE ANCIENT STATES OF NORTHEAST AFRICA

From the Assyrians on, the foreign rulers drew Egypt into the orbit of other continents— Southwest Asia and Mediterranean Europe. But the Libyan and Nubian conquerors were fellow Africans, and they point to the further spread of large-scale government from its origins along the Nile. Of the two, the Libyans were the less significant. They came not as a conquering state, but as long troublesome nomadic raiders more interested in securing a position at the top of Egyptian society than in annexing it to their own.

The main civilization west of Egypt was the Phoenician colony of Carthage, founded as a trading outpost of the Palestinian city-state of Tyre in the seventh century B.C. The city grew into a substantial empire over the next 150 years, controlling parts of North Africa, Spain, Sardinia, and Sicily. In the fifth century B.C., Carthage collided with the expanding power of Rome, which led to the three Punic wars. Rome won them and destroyed Carthage in 146 B.C., bringing North Africa into a European orbit for the next 750 years.

The Nubian conquest of Egypt, in contrast, represented the humbling of the ancient kingdom by a rival upstart based up-river. Egypt had held the upper hand in its relationship with the peoples to the south since early in the Old Kingdom, setting the frontier as far south as was convenient, and regularly sending trading, mining, and punitive expeditions beyond. The frontier was initially the first cataract (the first rapids impassable to boats), and later the second. During the height of the Middle Kingdom, however, an indigenous civilization arose between the third and fourth cataracts, in a floodplain straddling a long, peaceful stretch of river similar to, although smaller than, Egypt itself. Strongly influenced by Egyptian beliefs and artistic styles, including royal divinity and monumental pyramids, this civilization, known as "Kush," expanded north to the first cataract during the collapse of the Middle Kingdom. The New Kingdom conquered Kush around 1500 B.C., and ruled it as a province for 500 years.

A renewed Kushite state based near the fourth cataract achieved independence during the decay of the New Kingdom around 1000 B.C., and conquered the area between the first and second cataracts around 900 B.C. Further conquests followed, and by 750 B.C. the Nubians controlled Upper Egypt. The

Nubian pharaoh, Piankhy, led a final assault on Lower Egypt in the third quarter of the century and became the founder of Egypt's twenty-fifth dynasty. He and his successors set about ruling as Egyptian pharaohs, undertaking ambitious building programs within Egypt as well as in their home territories to the south. They ruled Egypt until the arrival of the Assyrians in the 660s B.C. The Assyrians had already conquered Mesopotamia and Palestine, and their iron weapons gave them a decisive advantage over their bronze-equipped foes. They seized Egypt from the Nubians, pushing them back beyond the second cataract for good.

Frustrated in the north, Kush continued to rule a sizable and prosperous empire along the middle reaches of the Nile and slowly turned from Egyptian models to its own cultural traditions. This process was reinforced by the transfer of the seat of government southward to the city of Meroe, which was both geographically more central and the site of Nubia's burgeoning iron industry. Kush prospered for a time as a southern extension of the Mediterranean world, an entrepot between it and sub-Saharan Africa, but its power waned because the state was top-heavy. An aristocratic, bureaucratic edifice supported by exports of raw materials in exchange for imported luxuries rested on top of a primitive, disenfranchised peasantry. Kush became a tributary of the rising kingdom of Axum early in the fourth century A.D., which meant basically that it paid protection money to Axum to avoid conquest. When it later revolted, the armies of Axum destroyed it. The Axumite king Ezana declared:

> I made war on them . . . killing some and capturing others . . . I burnt their towns . . . and my army carried off their food and copper and iron . . . and destroyed the statues in their temples, their granaries, and cotton trees and cast them into the [Nile].

Nubian influence in Africa did not end with this defeat, however. Three successor states lived on, one until the end of the Middle Ages.

The demise of this state came just when the peoples of the savanna, the grasslands south of the Sahara and north of the tropical forests of central Africa, were ready to form large states. The Kushite royal family may have retreated to Kordofan or Darfur to the southwest, and its model of divine kingship and its ironworking may have lived on in the savanna. At any rate, most of the later West African states have myths of origins to the north and east, and the Yoruba kingship in present-day Nigeria traced its roots explicitly (if improbably) to Egypt and Arabia.

The state that destroyed Kush, Axum, originated with the migration of Semitic-speaking peoples from Yemen across the Red Sea in the early part of the first millennium B.C. They moved quickly from the narrow coastal strip along the sea's southwestern shore up the rugged escarpment onto the high Abyssinian plateau. There they mixed with the existing population of neolithic Kushite farmers. Ideally located at the crossroads of the trade routes linking the Mediterranean, the upper Nile, Arabia, East Africa, and India, Axum rapidly rose to great prosperity and power. Occupation of the principal port of Adulis by Greek-ruled Egypt in the last centuries before Christ helped Axum, for the Egyptian presence created strong ties to the vibrant commercial life of the Mediterranean. When Rome conquered Egypt, Axum retook Adulis. By the mid-fourth century A.D., Axum dominated both northeastern Africa and southwestern Arabia.

After his earlier campaigns, Ezana had thanked the gods, but when he crushed Kush he thanked God. The Axumite king had become a Christian. Most probably a political move designed to gain favor with the Roman Emperor Constantine, his act had an enduring impact on the region, for Axum evolved into Ethiopia, an isolated outpost of Christianity that has survived until today. Initially subordinate to the Alexandrian patriarchy and strongly influenced by Coptic missionaries, Abyssinian Christianity was cut off by the Arab conquests in the seventh century A.D., and at the same time was pushed back from the Red Sea coast onto the high plateau. Here the beleaguered Axumites ruled over the native Kushites for several centuries until they rebelled and forced the descendants of Axum to share power with their leading families and to leaven Christian doctrines with local beliefs. Thus renewed, Ethiopian civilization found the strength to resist repeated onslaughts from its Islamicized neighbors until help arrived from the Christian West in the sixteenth century. Ethiopia's fortunes continued to fluctuate thereafter, with the royal family retreating to a mountain stronghold and leaving the land to domination by a patchwork of provincial chiefs and nomadic intruders for two centuries. Both the creed and the national identity survived until circumstances in the nineteenth century favored a revival of the ancient state.

TOWNS, TRADE, AND EMPIRE IN WEST AFRICA

When the iron-wielding Assyrians chased the Nubians out of Egypt, they inaugurated a technological revolution in Africa that was to reverberate from one end of the continent to the other. The idea of ironsmelting spread rapidly to the southwest, and much of Africa went directly from the Stone Age to the Iron Age without passing through a Bronze Age at all. In particular, the Niger-Congo speakers of West Africa south of the Sahara picked up ironworking technology in the last centuries B.C. This technology then either created or accelerated a population explosion. The resulting demographic pressure caused revolutionary changes that brought West Africa into a new era.

One dramatic development was a massive migration of Bantu-speaking people out of eastern Nigeria. They spread eastward and southward, and over the course of centuries moved into every part of Africa south of the equator except for the Kalahari desert and the southern tip of the continent below the Fish River. They pushed the Pygmies into the depths of the Congo rainforest and the Khoi

into the Kalahari. This out-migration was one of the defining events in African history, but it did not have a revolutionary impact on African social and political institutions. It proceeded along the traditional lines of migration, settlement, population increase, and renewed migration, although on a much vaster scale.

The second consequence of the population pressure did change the way many Africans lived. Those peoples located farther west than the Bantu-speakers did not have the luxury of migrating outward; as their numbers increased, they were forced to settle more thickly. In the half-millennium before Christ, their pattern of settlement changed fundamentally. They began living in walled towns rather than small villages and dispersed settlements.

The earliest such settlements were relatively small fortified villages located in southern Mauritania. Dating from about 500 B.C., these communities encompassed an area about one kilometer square, suggesting a population of several thousand people. Developed too early to reflect the impact of ironworking, they probably housed people who had to concentrate around oases as the Sahara desert dried out, a process that had been going on for several thousand years. Nevertheless, these villages set a new pattern that was to be followed by their Iron Age descendants.

There can be no doubt about the connection of ironworking and urbanization at the next known site. Jenne Jeno was both one of the earliest areas of ironworking in West Africa and a region of sizable walled communities, and the two developments appeared at the same time. The largest center encompassed between 30 and 40 hectares and held between 5,000 and 10,000 people. Forty such communities lay within a 25-mile radius, and six were big enough to have been major centers in their own right. Most of the inhabitants were farmers, but a few were probably specialized artisans and traders who served the local population and the regional market along the middle Niger River.

The political structure of these communities was a variant of the chiefdom. The basic unit was the *kafu*, the walled town and its surrounding farmland, fallow land, and forest. Each lineage lived in its own compound within the walls and to a considerable extent managed its own affairs. Nevertheless, numerous lineages were living in close quarters, and so the community had a leader, called a *mansa*, whose functions included mediating inter-clan disputes, allocating land for farming and fallow, coordinating planting and harvesting, managing relations with other communities and strangers, and handling booty and prisoners. The last-named function gave the *mansa* his greatest power, for it gave him an independent source of income and, more importantly, an independent source of labor. Captives did not belong to any local lineage, and therefore made perfect police and soldiers.

A *kafu* was both partner and rival to its neighbors. Local trade and intermarriage created the conditions for partnership, while competition for land, herds, and foreign trade contributed to rivalry. Both partnership and competition laid the foundations for the growth of empires. The role of competition in the formation of large states is perhaps obvious: when communities fought, one would defeat the other and force it to pay tribute, which strengthened the victorious town, leading to further campaigns that yielded more booty in a self-perpetuating cycle of petty imperialism. Yet this process was not enough to create great empires. Two elements of cooperation were needed, one social and one economic.

The first element was the existence of lineage and age-grade ties. Lineages were defined by descent from common ancestors; age grades were a common institution in African societies of all types. Age grades linked people to others of their own age, bonding them through participation in initiation ceremonies and expecting them to cooperate in performing civic responsibilities appropriate to their age. Lineage and age-grade ties linked people in different towns together; the leaders who forged the great kingdoms were generally not *mansa*, but rather lineage or age-grade heads who used

this wider base of power to impose their authority and only later took the title of *mansa*. The states they forged reflected this basis, for each "had no boundaries; only spheres of influence . . . no name; only the title of its ruler . . . no body of law; only the fixed obligations based upon kinship or other inherited status."

The other element underlying the rise of empires was the growth of long-distance trade. All early African empires grew by controlling trade and the revenues it brought. The primary routes stretched across the Sahara to the Mediterranean, and carried gold, ivory, and slaves north in exchange for salt and exotic luxuries. Other routes stretched along an east-west axis, linking the peoples of the savanna to each other. And these long distance connections depended on the prior existence of extensive, dependable local and regional traffic.

If the *kafu* formed the skeleton of empire, lineage and age-grade ties were the muscle, local trade routes were the capillaries, and major trade routes were the arteries.

THE GREAT KINGDOMS OF MEDIEVAL AFRICA

Most of the great sub-Saharan kingdoms arose in the savanna; Ghana was the first. Berber traders from North Africa visited Ghana around 750 A.D., and their description indicates that it had already been in existence for a considerable time. The name "Ghana" meant "war chief, " which gives a fair indication of who founded it and how it was run. Its location between the Bambuk gold fields and the nearest route across the Sahara gives a fair indication of where it got its power. The Berbers took the gold in exchange for salt, a commodity valued so highly that chunks could be used as money. The trade supported a capital city of about 20,000 people and an army of about the same number. The state became so wealthy that the kings came to confiscate all gold but the dust in order to maintain the value of the currency. The empire lasted over 300 years, until 1076, and revived briefly around 1200.

Ghana did not control the only potential terminus of Saharan trade. In the century following their first visit to Ghana, the Berbers opened up two more routes, each of which supported another sub-Saharan empire: Songhai a few hundred miles to the east of Ghana, and Kanem on Lake Chad. Songhay drew its strength from both the Saharan trade running north and south and the trade along the Niger River, which ran east and west. The Songhay empire came into existence in the ninth century and survived for five centuries within the same general borders, with interludes of subordination to greater powers. In the mid-1400s, it grew dramatically, ruled a vast territory for about a century, and then collapsed, never to rise again.

Kanem enjoyed a longer life, although it never grew to the size Songhay achieved. Founded by nomadic immigrants from the desert, it was located in the floodplain of the two major rivers feeding Lake Chad. The area had supported a dense urban settlement since the time of Christ—as many as 600 towns that for centuries had no walls. Around 500 A.D., the number of towns diminished as their people concentrated in a smaller number of larger cities. These new concentrations had walls. The reason for this change was undoubtedly slave raiding, for the area's primary export was not gold but people. The rulers of Kanem began as a predatory warrior-aristocracy, and only gradually came to depend as much on local tribute as on the profits of long-distance traffic in slaves. Their state survived a series of ups and downs, including the transfer of the capital across the lake to Bornu, for a thousand years, until it was absorbed into the French colonial empire.

While these states grew up to the east of Ghana, Mali began to grow just south of it. Centering on the highly urbanized Jenne Jeno area, which contained fertile agricultural lands, rich gold fields, and extensive ironworking, Mali spilled far beyond its original Mandinke people to become sub-Saharan Africa's greatest state. A quiet backwater for its first few centuries, Mali came to the fore in

the early 1200s after Kaniaga, another ambitious vassal state, destroyed Ghana and conquered Mali. The Malian ruler, Sundiata, retook his realm, killed the Kaniagan leader, and embarked on a campaign of conquest that brought Mali control not only of the former territories of Ghana, but of Songhay as well. Ruler of the entire western savanna, Mali reached the height of its prosperity and power in the fourteenth century, declined in the fifteenth, and disappeared in the sixteenth. Because numerous chiefdoms that had been clients of the empire survived and flourished, Mali's heritage was well remembered.

While all the great kingdoms of the savanna were based on towns, not all towns in the savanna were part of kingdoms. Enjoying a great degree of autonomy even when subordinated to a larger state, most experienced periods of independence, and one major group remained independent until the nineteenth century. Hausa pastoralists (herders) settled in the land between the Niger River and Lake Chad and created large fortified towns from which they dominated the smaller towns occupied by the original inhabitants, a domination that took the form mainly of slave raiding. None of the seven principal Hausa city-states achieved primacy over the others, and they lasted as a loosely affiliated confederation until the nineteenth century, when they were conquered by a *jihad*, or Islamic holy war, undertaken by new nomadic people, the Fulani.

Two other major states arose far to the south of the savanna, in southern Africa. The first, Zimbabwe, was located near rich gold veins that had been worked since at least the ninth century and was just one of many capitals of small states that flourished in the eleventh and twelfth centuries. Great Zimbabwe, as it came to be known, became by the thirteenth century the largest settlement in pre-modern eastern and southern Africa, a metropolis containing at its height in the fifteenth century between 10,000 and 12,000 people. How it rose to greatness and how it was governed we do not know, for the only evidence we have comes from its mute walls. Consisting of a massive stone "acropolis" perched on a hilltop and a "temple" the size of a football field in the wooded valley below, the ruins testify to a thriving civilization that mobilized a huge labor force, executed fine stonework, and evolved a unique architectural style with no ties to Asia or Europe. The complex functioned as the royal residence for a series of kingdoms that added to and refined it until the last of them, the Changamire, was destroyed by invading Ngoni in the 1830s.

Somewhat to the north of Zimbabwe, the second major state gradually arose from the competition among 50 or 60 lesser states for control of the copper and ivory trade down the Zambesi River. At its height around 1500, Mutapa, the victor, encompassed a territory stretching from the Indian Ocean in the east to the Kahalari Desert in the west, and from the Zambesi River in the north to the Limpopo River to the south. Its king was revered as a god and lived in a secluded palace with his wives, concubines, and officials. He emerged only at lunar festivals to consult with his ancestors through mediums and to hold public audiences, at which he remained behind a screen and was approached by supplicants on their knees. He alone could dispense fire, and when he died all fires were extinguished until new flames were bestowed by the new king. His wives and some ministers accompanied him to the grave.

Despite this magnificence, the power of the king of Mutapa was limited. If he became seriously ill or deformed, he had to commit suicide. Isolated in his compound, he had little direct connection to affairs of state or to his subjects; much power was exercised by his ministers and queens. The empire was overly large for the existing communications, and it gradually lost power. Internal decay from court intrigue combined with external pressure not only from restive vassals, but also from the Portuguese, who installed themselves at the mouth of the Zambesi in the early sixteenth century. They reduced the kingdom to vassalage in 1629, a situation that lasted until the Changamire pushed the Portuguese out

and annexed Mutapa to their realm at the end of the seventeenth century.

THE ARABS AND ISLAM

After the Romans destroyed Carthage in 146 B.C. and conquered Egypt in 30 B.C., North Africa became a quiet backwater in the Mediterranean Empire. Egypt was vital to the Empire's political stability because of its annual export of grain, which fed the imperial capital. Otherwise, North Africa imported a trickle of tropical goods that made their way across the desert and up the Red Sea, added to them miscellaneous local products, and sold them to the rest of the Empire, taking in exchange items from all over the Mediterranean basin. Life was so good Rome needed but two or three of its 30 legions to garrison the region, and its borders did not change for over 400 years.

All good things come to an end, however, and so it was with Roman rule. As the barbarians from eastern Europe hammered the Empire in the north, the Roman hold on Mauritania (present-day Algeria and Morocco) melted away. Further east, the Vandals established themselves in the area around Carthage in the early 440s, and their kingdom lasted almost 100 years. The eastern half of the Empire, the Byzantine Empire centered on Constantinople, held on to Egypt, and in the 530s vanquished the Vandals, but the Byzantine resurgence was not to last.

On July 16, 622, in the heart of Arabia far to the east, an obscure self-proclaimed prophet named Mohammed led a handful of followers from his home town of Mecca, where his teachings had been scorned, to Medina, a journey immortalized as the *Hijra*. By the time he died 10 years later, most of Arabia had accepted his message: submission to the one true God, Allah. His successors, the caliphs, took command of armies fired with this faith and tempered by its discipline, and began one of the greatest campaigns of conquest in world history. To the north, they overran the Byzantine provinces in Palestine and Syria. To the east, they shattered and absorbed the Persian Empire. To the west, in Africa, they overran Egypt, Cyrenaica, and Tripolitania in just 15 years. Their first attempt on the Maghrib (present day Tunisia, Algeria, and Morocco) in the 670s failed, but a renewed effort at the turn of the century brought success. From there, the Arab armies crossed the straits of Gibraltar into Spain, subduing most of that country and raiding deep into France before being stopped. Their conquest of Spain would not be reversed until almost 800 years later; their accomplishments in Africa would endure. Islam took its place as one of the great world religions, and North Africa became an extension of the Arab world.

That world was characterized by cultural unity but political division, a state of affairs that began almost as soon as the tide of conquest peaked. Almost all Moslems acknowledged the spiritual supremacy of the caliphs of Bagdad, but the provincial governors rapidly established themselves as hereditary political rulers in their realms. By 900 A.D., North Africa was divided between three of them, and over the centuries the balance was to shift with regularity. For one brief period just before 1000, the entire Mediterranean coastline was reunited under the Fatimid dynasty (a minor clan that put together a big slave army), but when the dynasty collapsed, unity was gone for good.

The western end of Africa's Mediterranean coast, centered on the area that is today Morocco, remained stubbornly independent, tied into affairs along the Atlantic coast, in Iberia to the north, and across the Sahara to the south. It broke away from the Fatimids in 980; fell to the Almoravids, a militant reformist sect based in present-day Mauritania, a century later; and passed to the Almohads, a similar sect based locally, about 100 years after that. Almohad rule gave way in turn to the Marinid dynasty in 1269, which was followed by the Wattasids in 1465, the Sa'dids in 1510, and the Filalis in 1670. This last dynasty still rules Morocco today.

Egypt, at the eastern end of the Mediterranean, formed the other pole of Arab North Africa. Closely tied to affairs in the Middle East, it was ruled along with Palestine, Syria, and Western Arabia by the Tulunids, then the Fatimids, and afterwards by the Ayyubids (1171–1250), the Mamluks (1250–1517), and the Ottoman Turks (1517–1798).

The areas in between, modern day Libya, Tunisia, and Algeria, fluctuated between autonomy and dependence. They were invaded by the Arab tribes Benu Sulaym and Benu Hilal after they threw out the Fatimids, were then divided between the Almohads in the west and the Ayyubids in the east, and enjoyed independence under the Hafsid (Tunisia) and Ziyandid (Algeria) dynasties from the 1230s until they fell to the Ottomans in the mid-1500s. They remained under the Turks until the early 1700s, and then enjoyed independence until the coming of the French in the 1800s.

The Arabs came to Africa as a small conquering elite, and for decades they remained a distinct ruling class, separated by religion as well as background from the diverse Christian population, which included the descendants of the Romans, Greeks, and Germanic peoples who had ruled before the Arabs, as well as the Berber peasants and nomads who made up the majority of the population. The Arab dynasties ruled with increasing ostentation, rapidly transforming their rough edges as desert warriors into the polished urbanity of Near Eastern rulers. They settled in the middle of cities, creating monumental courts in which they lived apart, surrounded by their families, harem, slave guards, and high court officials (who were often also slaves). They emerged only on special occasions, royally bedecked and escorted by dozens of officials and flunkies with great pomp and ceremony.

Their power was based on the loyalty of professional slave armies, which they bought and supported with taxes and tolls. They acted as the highest court of appeals, and administered the state through an elaborate bureaucracy, which was generally divided into a chancery that prepared and stored official documents, a treasury that collected revenues and kept accounts, and a military bureau that oversaw the army. In early Arab governments, the ruler was seconded by a single vizier who effectively ran the bureaucracy, but in later dynasties the office was demoted so as to control only the treasury, or diluted by the appointment of separate viziers for each of the three departments. When the ruler had the power, he ran outlying provinces through appointed governors; when not, he worked with the traditional leaders.

The Arabs advanced by the sword, but Islam advanced by persuasion. Initially confined to the conquering elite, it gradually spread "from the garrisons to the slave soldiers, from the Arab governors to the locally recruited clerks and officials, from the masters to the servants, and from originally nomadic Arab pastoral migrants to their Christian farming neighbors." What began with military conquest became a far more profound cultural conversion, so that when Arab political unity fell away it left behind a cultural connection that not only survives but dominates to this day. Despite dynastic conflicts, Arab conquest brought a long period of relative peace for the ordinary people, prosperity based on burgeoning trade, and a cultural flowering that made the Medieval centuries in North Africa a Golden Age.

ISLAM SOUTH OF THE SAHARA

If the Arab conquests brought Islam to North Africa, they played little direct part in bringing it south of the Sahara. The only early instance of Arab rule in the region was the Almoravid Empire in the eleventh and twelfth centuries, which was actually a Berber state directed by Arab reformers. Around 1600, a brief expansion of Morocco brought Songhai under its rule for a short time; when the Moroccan empire collapsed, it left behind a rump Arab-run state centered on Timbuktu. Further east, around the same time, an Arab dynasty established a more lasting state, the Sultanate of Darfur, between Bornu and the upper Nile, and spawned a daughter state, Wadai, to the west a half-century later. Still further east, the Arabs controlled the African coast of the Red Sea and tried twice to found substantial states, but neither really took root. Along the east coast, the sultan of Oman established a loose suzerainty over the Swahili trading cities in the seventeenth century, but this was more a tributary than a governing arrangement. Except for the Almoravid conquest, all these Arab incursions came long after Islam was widely established south of the Sahara, and none advanced its boundaries by much.

Merchants and traders, rather than conquering armies, carried Islam south. The main contribution of the Arab conquests was ending the turmoil that had bedeviled North Africa since Rome collapsed. The cessation of turmoil created conditions for a dramatic upsurge in trade. The Berber nomads who traveled between the savanna and the Mediterranean had adopted the camel, an immigrant from Asia, centuries before, but only now did this new and improved mode of transportation come into its own. Islam suited the nomads who traveled to, and the merchants who later settled in, the savanna because its doctrine of the "umma," the brotherhood of all believers, made them part of a widespread community that transcended the narrow bonds of traditional clan and tribal relations. In the trading centers, they set up mosques, which gradually became the centers of Islamic neighborhoods, and they gradually converted some of the original inhabitants with whom they came into contact.

Far more important than religious conversion, however, was Islam's effect on commerce and government. It stimulated commerce by tying sub-Saharan Africa into the Arab trading network, by creating a community of traders across the continent who understood and accepted each other, and by providing a common body of law regulating business affairs. It affected government by providing a model of and the personnel for literate bureaucracy, by

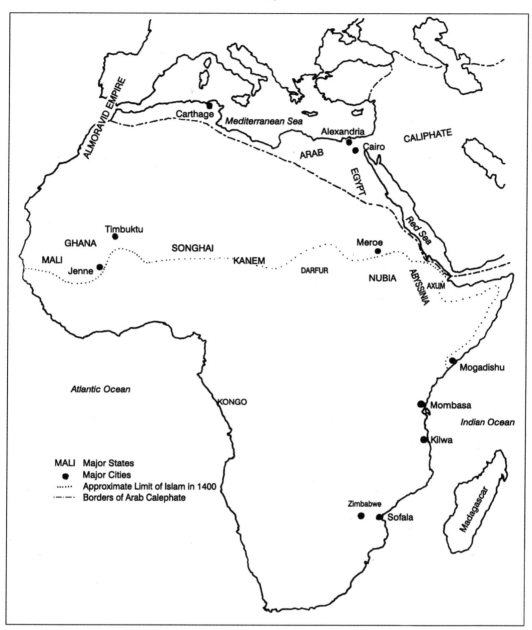

Africa to 1400

linking the Africans to the Islamic international community, and by supplying a creed that reinforced national unity. While the masses ignored or resisted Islam, rulers adopted it, at least as an additional form of worship. In 1010, the King of Gao became the first major ruler to convert; he was followed by the rulers of Kanem-Bornu in 1086. The biggest conversion was that of Mali in the thirteenth century, for it became the biggest state in the region, and ultimately one of the leading powers of Islam. King Mansa Musa (1312–1337) became caliph "of the western parts," and when he made his pilgrimage to Mecca he traveled with at least 500 slaves bearing gold staffs and 100 camels loaded with 300 pounds of gold each. He went on such a spending spree in Cairo that the value of gold on the local market fell 20 percent. Timbuktu became a center of Islamic learning, and Islam became the religion of progressive government. A final conversion came in the sixteenth century, when the animist Funj, who were migrating northwards into the Sudan, fought the Abdallabite Arabs, who were migrating southwards from Egypt, and then divided the territory with them and converted to Islam.

The mass of African peasants remained unmoved, perhaps because one of the chief commodities feeding the revival of the Saharan trade routes was slaves. Furthermore, the great African rulers bolstered their own power with slave labor on royal plantations, since captives were traditionally controlled by chiefs, and Islamic law accepted the enslavement of non-Moslems only. Moreover, the tributary system that held together these kingdoms was based on mystical ties grounded in traditional religion, so to have converted the people to Islam would have been to undercut the kingdoms' own foundations.

When members of the lower classes did convert, they found that Islam, despite its egalitarian ideology, had become the religion of rulers and elites who scorned the masses. As the medieval writer Ibn al-Faqih rather harshly put it, Moslem society was composed of

> the ruler, whom merit has placed in the foremost rank; the vizier, distinguished by wisdom and domination; the high-placed ones, whom wealth has placed aloft; and the middle classes, who are attached to the other three classes by their culture; while the rest of mankind is mere scum who know nothing but food and sleep.

The gulf between the Islamic elite and the peasantry led to a reaction against Islam in the seventeenth century that lasted well into the eighteenth. The frontiers of Islam in Africa ceased expanding, and even Islamic rulers de-emphasized Moslem practices in favor of traditional paganism.

In the late 1700s, the Fulani pastoralists at the western end of the savanna embarked on a series of jihads, campaigns of religious conquest. By the turn of the century, they established three theocratic states in present day Senegambia. Further east, in Hausaland, the Fulani religious leader Usman dan Fodio launched another jihad in 1804 that made him master of all the Hausa city states in a few short years. Before his death in 1817, he expanded his control to the rural areas between the cities and to the neighboring province of Ilorin. His son consolidated the family's hold on this new state, the Sultanate of Sokoto, and his disciple, Ahmadu Lobo, moved off to preach the jihad to the Fulani along the middle Niger. They responded enthusiastically, and soon the small kingdom of Masina had expanded to encompass much of the area previously ruled by neighboring pagan states. Another jihad around 1850 expanded Islamic rule further in the following decades. Late in the century, when the Europeans conquered the savanna, Islam was far more extensive and cohesive than it had been a century before.

The gulf between the Islamic upper classes and the mass of African peasants was even wider on the east coast, for here the traders were ensconced in coastal, often insular, city-states. These cities, established by nominally

Moslem Swahili peoples stimulated to maritime commerce by the activities of Arab merchants, grew from rude trading posts to magnificent cities in the late Middle Ages and evolved their own distinct variant of Islamic culture. Long independent, each city was governed by a merchant elite, much like the cities in Renaissance Italy and Hanseatic Germany. The wealth of these merchants came from trading the products of East Africa for merchandise from the Mediterranean, Middle East, and India. Travel into the interior was difficult, so they stayed on the coast, dealing only with chiefs and their agents from the interior. The peoples of the interior remained little influenced by the politics or religion of coastal peoples, until European railroads, governments, and labor policies brought the coast and the interior together.

CHAPTER

2

·········

The European Intrusion

When the Europeans first intruded on Africa, their primary advantages were oceangoing ships armed with numerous cannons' and handguns. The former gave them a decisive superiority in the world's sea-lanes, while the latter gave them a marginal superiority over indigenous peoples on land. Because the handguns were far less potent than the ships, the Europeans' primary influence on Africa before the late nineteenth century was indirect. They created plantation economies in the Americas and trade routes to connect them to Europe's industries and Africa's labor pool, thereby establishing a triangular trade route that would become the heart of the emerging world economy.

Africa's contribution to this system was millions of slaves shipped to work the plantations in the New World. The slave trade distorted Africa's political and economic development by encouraging war, enhancing the power of warlords, and debilitating Africa's economy while helping Europe's achieve unprecedented expansion. When the slave trade ended, Africa was much farther behind Europe than it

had been when the trade began. The slave trade was not the only cause of this situation, but it was an important one.

The gap between the two continents increased in the nineteenth century because Europe experienced an Industrial Revolution that gave it decisive material superiority over Africa and the rest of the world. Armed with spears and muskets against artillery and machine guns, the Africans, like virtually all other non-Europeans, were simply not equipped to effectively resist the Europeans. The Europeans also developed medicines that enabled them to survive African diseases.

PORTUGUESE EXPANSION ALONG THE WEST COAST

The Arab conquests in the seventh century ended the period of European rule in North Africa begun by the Romans and Greeks. For the next four centuries, Europe remained too poor and divided to contemplate overseas expansion, and thereafter directed its medieval resurgence, the Crusades, mainly towards the

Middle East. The fifth and seventh Crusades targeted Egypt and the eighth targeted Tunis, but none of these efforts achieved any success. Not until the early fifteenth century did European rule return to Africa.

The Portuguese came not across the Mediterranean but over the Atlantic Ocean. Through centuries of close contact, Portugal was familiar with the extent and wealth of the Islamic world. Portugal's rulers set out at the beginning of the 1400s to encroach on the lucrative Saharan trade. They seized the city of Ceuta in 1415; but instead of pushing farther inland, they wisely decided to use their rapidly improving seagoing ships to sail down the West African coast and outflank the Moslem-controlled caravan routes. They occupied Madeira Island in 1419, explored the mainland down to Cape Bojador in 1434, reached Cape Blanco in 1442, and Arguin Island in 1443. In 1441, the first ship bearing gold and slaves from the area returned to Portugal, and by 1448 the Portuguese had erected a fortified trading post on Arguin.

They were still not able to tap into the source of the Saharan trade, but between 1469 and 1475 their captains explored the Gulf of Guinea in hopes of finding a route to India as well as to the south side of the Sahara. In addition to the lure of trade, they also hoped to establish contact with the mythical Christian kingdom of "Prester John," which was rumored to lie beyond the lands of the Moslems (a myth based, undoubtedly, on the real survival of Christian Ethiopia). As they explored, they discovered a rich source of gold in the region that would come to be known as the Gold Coast. In 1482, they set up another fort, Elmina, to control the area, and in 1485 they established diplomatic relations with the kingdom of Benin to the east. This kingdom, the earliest to be based in the forest region south of the savanna, was a typical confederation of chiefdoms under a divine yet limited monarch. Trade with Benin and the rest of West Africa grew rapidly. The Portuguese were primarily interested in peppercorns, slaves from the "Windward Coast" (present day Guinea), and gold from Elmina.

The Portuguese successes in West Africa contrasted with their frustrations in trying to get around the continent to India. Their explorers discovered that the African coastline turned sharply south at the island of Fernando Po, and that it continued in that direction indefinitely. Diogo Cao led an expedition that discovered the mouth of the Congo River in 1483 and continued 600 miles farther before turning back. A second expedition reached Cape Cross in present-day Namibia, where Cao died in 1486. Two years later, Bartholomew Dias rounded the Cape of Good Hope at the southern end of the continent and sailed as far as the Fish River, but almost a decade passed before Columbus' stunning success in crossing the Atlantic spurred the Portuguese to send an expedition under Vasco da Gama into the Indian Ocean.

When Diogo Cao discovered the mouth of the Congo, he also learned of the kingdom of the Kongo, and on his second voyage he made a side trip up-river to visit the kingdom itself. The Portuguese crown followed up this contact in 1491 with a diplomatic mission to the court of Nzinga Kuwu, the *manikongo*, or paramount chief, of an extensive but loose confederation of chiefdoms. The *manikongo* and many in his court converted to Christianity, and he began a polite correspondence with his royal peer in Lisbon. Discouraged by Portuguese inattention (they became preoccupied with their quest for the Indian Ocean), the *manikongo* reverted to his traditional faith, but his heir, Afonso, not only converted but undertook to reform his kingdom along European lines after his accession to the throne in 1506. He refused to follow the traditional custom of eating in seclusion and promoted European fashions.

Unfortunately for Afonso, his reforms alienated an increasing proportion of his people, who were angered not only by the repudiation of traditional forms, but also by the increasing scale of Portuguese slaving to support their plantations on the nearby island of São

Tomé. The Portuguese planters, in turn, undercut Afonso's authority by cutting deals for slaves with local chiefs. The Portuguese king responded to Afonso's requests for help by dispatching a special agent armed with a *regimento*, or royal directive. This document stipulated that the Portuguese planters would be brought under control, but its main thrust was to impose Portuguese customs and law and to propagate the Christian faith in the kingdom. Afonso's attempts to introduce these reforms met with increasing resistance among his people, while local Portuguese machinations against him continued; by the time he died in 1545, the kingdom had fallen into disarray. It continued to deteriorate in the following decades, ravaged by invasion from the interior, slave raids from the coast, and steady depopulation as the hard-pressed inhabitants drifted away. The kingdom disappeared entirely in the seventeenth century, a victim in part of Portugal's mixed motives, but mostly of the futility of trying to impose a European-style monarchy on Africans, who expected consensual government and who could and did just move away when discontented.

A similar process characterized Portuguese relations with Africans farther down the coast in present-day Angola. Frustrated by the deteriorating situation in the Congo, Portuguese slavers moved south in the mid-1500s. In 1556, the Portuguese supported a breakaway chief, and in 1571 the Portuguese king claimed the area as a colony. Years of warfare ensued as the Europeans sought to impose control over the African communities, which were further disrupted by slave raiding. The Portuguese finally left Angola in 1975, but the colony had languished under first the burden, and then the legacy, of the insatiable slave system.

PORTUGUESE IMPERIALISM IN EAST AFRICA

When Vasco da Gama sailed into the Indian Ocean, he made his way up the East African coast before departing for India. At every port of call, the Portuguese explorers were surprised and impressed with the peaceful prosperity they encountered. They were so impressed that they soon returned to plunder and to conquer. In 1505 and 1506, Portuguese fleets sailed up the coast, sacking Kilwa, Mombasa, Hojo, and Brava. An eyewitness described how the Portuguese admiral at Mombasa "ordered that the town should be sacked. Then everyone started to plunder the town and to search the houses, forcing open the doors with axes and iron bars." Another remembered how Brava was

> . . . destroyed by the Portuguese, who slew many of its people and carried many into captivity, and took great spoil of gold and silver and goods. Thenceforth, many of them fled away towards the inland country, forsaking the town.

About the best that can be said for the Portuguese is that this was exactly the behavior of most conquerors at the time.

The Swahili cities probably could have recovered fairly quickly from these depredations, but their fortunes were further depressed by the Portuguese suzerainty that followed. The Portuguese took Kilwa as a tributary in 1502, Zanzibar in 1503, Sofala (the outlet for Mutapa's gold) in 1505, and the rest of the coast of Mozambique in 1507. In 1509, their tall ships, armed with dozens of cannon, destroyed a fleet of lighter Turkish, Arab, and Indian vessels and thereafter imposed their terms on trade in the Indian Ocean. Hoping to divert the riches that crossed those waters to their own coffers, the Portuguese established a system of tolls in ports and intercepted ships sailing without a permit. Unfortunately, they did not have the resources to supplant the shipping they suppressed, and the net effect was to stifle this once-thriving commercial network. Similarly, their heavy-handedness reduced gold shipments from the interior to a trickle, and their attempts to take control inland proved equally fruitless. It has been estimated that the cost of their empire outran the revenue it produced by some 40 percent as the trade they sought to control simply withered away.

The East Africans found Portuguese overlordship so onerous that they welcomed Turkish advances from Egypt and Arabia late in the sixteenth century. Turkish campaigns threatened Portugal's northern outposts, but did not conquer any of them. However, in the seventeenth century the Dutch, and later the French and British, broke Portugal's dominance of maritime trade, while the sultan of Oman attacked its possessions on land. Inspired by Oman's liberation of its own city of Muscat, which the Portuguese had seized in 1502, the Swahili called upon the Arabs to liberate them. The Omanis obliged in 1698, taking Mombasa, Portugal's main stronghold on the coast, after a 33-month siege.

Initially hailed by the Swahili as their savior, the sultan simply replaced Portuguese imperialism with his own. The Africans soon were as unhappy with Arab overlordship as they had been with European. They even tried calling the Portuguese back, but it was too late for that. East Africa continued to be troubled by struggles over and among the Swahili cities until the mid-nineteenth century, when the sultan of Oman transferred his capital to Zanzibar, inaugurating a period of peace and prosperity.

Farther north, the Portuguese scored a decisive success that brought them little profit. They had come to the Indian Ocean in part to find the Christian kingdom of Prester John, and in 1494 they found something pretty close in Ethiopia. In 1520, a Portuguese mission arrived at Massawa on the Red Sea to establish formal diplomatic relations. While distance and doctrinal differences discouraged further exchanges, increasing Moslem pressure from the surrounding states brought Ethiopia to a crisis point in the 1630s. Led by a gifted general, Ahmad ibn Ghazi of Adal, the Moslems beat the Ethiopian army in 1629, and followed up their success with a devastating invasion. The Ethiopians appealed to the Portuguese for help, and they responded by sending a contingent of musketeers. These arrived in 1642 just in time to turn the tide of battle against the Moslems at Lake Tana. Ibn Ghazi died in the engagement, and the Moslem threat to Ethiopia disappeared for good.

The battle marked the high point of Portugal's relations with Ethiopia. Grateful for Catholic Portugal's decisive help, the Ethiopians accepted a Jesuit mission, which succeeded in converting the emperors Za Dengel (1603–1604) and Susenyos (1607–1632). At first things went well, but when the zealous Alphonso Mendez replaced the patient and tactful Pedro Paez in 1626, his attempt to force immediate and thorough conformity to Catholic orthodoxy provoked a bloody backlash. Susenyos remained true to the Jesuits for a time, but in 1632 he expelled them, proclaiming the following to his people:

> We first gave you this faith believing that it was good. But innumerable people have been slain. . . . For which reason we restore to you the faith of your forefathers. Let the former clergy return to their churches. . . . And do ye rejoice.

Susenyos abdicated in favor of his son, and, still holding to Catholicism himself, died shortly thereafter.

SLAVERY AND AFRICAN POLITICS

Slavery was common in ancient and medieval Africa, just as it was in Europe, Asia, and America. When an army took prisoners in a war, the captors had the captives at their mercy. They could kill them if they wanted; they could let them go if they felt like it (or for a ransom); or they could put them to work. In small-scale societies feuding with their neighbors, the last option was often not practical because the captured enemies would run home at the first opportunity or their kinsmen would fight to get them back. As the scale of society grew, however, the possibilities for slaveholding increased. Town walls could keep captives in as well as enemies out, so prisoners became part of the booty handled by the *mansa*. He could distribute them as spoils to individual clans, but he could also put them to use for the community. Separated from the lineage links that structured the citizens' relations to each other and to the whole, slaves made excellent policemen and soldiers, loyal to the *mansa* rather than to a local family and supported by tribute and booty.

As kingdoms grew, they could shift captives to areas far from where they were taken and put them to work in gangs on plantations. These state-run farms provided food for the king and his court, which included a growing number of slaves. These slaves worked as domestics, soldiers, artisans, and even officials. Slavery thereby fed slavery: warriors captured field hands, who supported more warriors, who captured more field hands, and so on. Other slaves made farm tools and weapons, and some helped administer the whole operation. Slavery thus played a significant role in the growth and maintenance of many African empires.

Large kingdoms were not the only societies to hold large numbers of slaves. Trade routes enabled the movement of captives much farther from their homes than even empires did, and slaves became a staple item of trade both within and outside Africa. The Arabs initially enslaved the Berbers who had opposed them, but could not continue to do so when the Berbers converted to Islam because the Koran prohibited enslavement of believers. The Berbers then became the chief suppliers of slaves to the Arabs, capturing or buying them south of the Sahara and transporting them back across the desert. Sub-Saharan states sold slaves among themselves and supplied them to the Berbers as well. The profits further fueled the growth of kingdoms, but even weakly organized peoples participated. The proportion of slaves in society came to range in the 1800s from a low of 10–20 percent in the forest regions to 50 percent in the savanna and 80 or 90 percent among the Tuarg Berbers. To some extent, the high percentages represented the lingering status of people descended from slaves who had gradually acquired effective freedom, for the status of slave was generally less rigid in Africa than in the European colonies in America. Nevertheless, these proportions indicate how widespread slavery must have been.

The Portuguese used slaves long before they reached the Gulf of Guinea, and they did not hesitate to take Africans back with their first cargoes. They began using them on São Tomé and the Cape Verde Islands, and then on sugar plantations in Brazil. Africans proved far better than Native Americans for this kind of work, for they had nowhere to run and they could survive Eurasian diseases. They did die steadily from overwork, but in the Europeans' harsh calculations there were plenty more where they came from. The trade grew from about 1,000 per year in the mid-1500s to about 5,500 a year in the mid-1600s, surpassing the volume of the Saharan slave trade by around 1600.

The Spanish used African slaves in America as well, but the Portuguese dominated the slave trade for about a century. In the 1630s, the Dutch captured Brazil and Angola and spread sugar and slavery to the Caribbean Islands. The Portuguese eventually got their colonies back, but not their dominance of the slave and sugar trades. The English and French followed hard on Dutch heels, and by 1700 the four countries were transporting about 30,000 slaves from Africa to America each year. The number continued to increase in the eighteenth century, so that by 1800 about 80,000 slaves per year made the voyage. The British unilaterally prohibited the traffic in 1808 and set up a naval patrol off West Africa to enforce their decision; as a result, the trade began to fall off. By conservative estimate, a total of 10–12 million Africans had already been taken into slavery by that time. This number is roughly equal to the number of Native Americans who died as a result of the European intrusion into the New World.

While Europeans owned the ships that carried the slaves to America, they seldom went inland to procure them. Instead, they relied on a preexisting and increasingly extensive trade network that channeled captives from the interior to the coast. This network was fed in part by explicit slave-raiding, but more often by warfare brought on by the normal conflict and consolidation of states. Some peoples and regions organized themselves for slave exporting, but most of the time the slaves came out of areas in political upheaval.

When the Europeans arrived, the process of state formation that had begun in the savanna was spreading to the forest region along the coast. The kingdom of Benin that the Portuguese encountered in 1482 was the earliest, and it was followed by Oyo and Dahomey in the seventeenth and eighteenth centuries, and by Asante in the nineteenth. The rise of these states did not depend on the European slave trade. Oyo and Dahomey reflected the superiority of cavalry in warfare and the southward spread of its use. The king of Asante once bragged that neither he nor his ancestors ever waged wars "to catch slaves in the bush like a thief."

Nevertheless, the slave trade did have an impact on these states and on the lesser polities around them. During this period, political power began to come from the barrel of a gun. Since the Africans did not know how to manufacture guns, they had to get them from the Europeans. The Europeans wanted slaves in return, so every African state that wanted to expand, or simply survive, had to supply captives. Some bought them; others took them as tribute; some raided for them; others acquired them as a by-product of wars they would have fought anyway. All, however, had to get them, and in so doing contributed to the process by which Africa's own labor force became its biggest export by far.

Historians today tend to de-emphasize the demographic impact of the slave trade, pointing out that far more men than women were taken. In Africa's polygamous societies, the number of children produced would have remained the same, and indeed, the African population increased at a rate comparable to that of Europe. The economic impact was more important. The slave trade drained the continent of people in their most vigorous and productive stage of life and diverted those who

remained from capital accumulation toward raw materials production. This situation laid the foundations for a dependency that could not be overcome by the countervailing influence of a developing indigenous international trading class. Politically, the trade supported a process of consolidation that was taking place anyway, but it promoted warfare and violence for economic as well as political ends, and oriented the states that emerged towards raw-materials exporting at the expense of indigenous economic development.

SOUTH AFRICA'S ORIGINS

In 1652, the Dutch East India Company established a small colony at the Cape of Good Hope. Portuguese seamen had frequently stopped there during the long journey to and from the Indian Ocean to rest and to replenish their food supplies, particularly to buy fresh meat from the Khoikoi herders who inhabited the area. As the Dutch encroached on Portuguese domination of the Indian Ocean in the middle of the seventeenth century, they saw the strategic value of securing the place for themselves, and so South Africa was born.

The colonists made a modest effort at commercial farming, but soon gravitated to herding stock for meat. As their numbers and herds expanded, so did the colony's boundaries. This expansion caused conflicts over grazing land with the Khoikoi, who were pushed north or brought under the control of the Europeans. Those who moved north organized themselves for a hunting and cattle-trading existence, complete with horses, wagons, and ultimately guns, and put up a steady and often effective resistance to white encroachment. Those under European control fell into clientage relationships with the whites and gradually lost control of their herds. As their society dissolved, some Khoikoi established themselves as free farmers or townspeople, but most ended up as slaves working for the white herders or alongside other slaves imported from Mozambique, Madagascar, and Asia to work on the plantations set up near the Cape to resupply passing ships. South Africa quickly developed into a society in which the economic categories of slave and master corresponded to the racial categories of colored and white.

With only lukewarm support from home-country officials, who wanted to avoid the costs of warfare and extensive administration, the colony expanded slowly during its first hundred years. In 1760, the pioneer cattle farmers, called *Veeboers*, or Boers, reached the Great Fish River, where they first encountered the Xhosa. These iron-working Bantu speakers represented the southernmost extension of the great migration that had begun in West Africa around 500 A.D. and had led to the gradual replacement of Khoisan speakers, who relied on stone tools and weapons, across Central Africa and down the East Coast. Much more numerous, organized into typical small communities based on lineage, and equipped with iron-tipped spears (and soon with guns), the Bantu speakers proved a much tougher opponent for the Boers. The clashes between these two groups lasted well into the nineteenth century—a long series of raids and reprisals known as the "Kaffir Wars."

While the Xhosa gave a good account of themselves in these fights, the Boers gradually moved the frontier northeast, creating a domino effect as the retreating Xhosa pushed against other Bantu-speaking peoples behind them. Compounding the problem, slaving for Asian and African markets picked up in East Africa in the early nineteenth century, just as it began to die down in West Africa. Some peoples fled from the trade southward out of Mozambique, while others organized themselves to participate in it. The result was the rapid development of militarized kingships and chieftaincies, including two that would survive until today, the Swazi (Swaziland) and the Basuto (Lesotho).

It was the Zulu, however, who had the most profound effect on the region at the time. Shaka, who became their king in 1818, taught his warriors to hold onto their spears and use them for stabbing instead of throwing them

from a distance. He then launched these regiments against neighboring peoples in an irresistible campaign of conquest. The new tactics killed far more men in the defeated armies than heretofore. As word spread, anybody who could tried to get out of the way, a massive, rippling process of displacement called the *Mfecane*. Eventually, the displaced tribes found new homes to the north and west, mainly by subjugating the less organized peoples already there. In their wake, they left what a French missionary who passed through the area remembered as a "solitary and desolate . . . countryside. On every side we saw human bones whitening in the sun and rain, and more than once we had to turn our wagon out of its course so as to avoid passing over these sad remains."

Meanwhile, the European colony had grown to around 20,000 people and in 1806 passed from Dutch to British control. Relations between the Boers and the government went from bad to worse. The frontiersmen staged several rebellions against the colonial government between 1795 and 1815, and while the government suppressed them with increasing ease, the sources of tension steadily mounted. In the century and a half of the colony's existence, the colonists had begun to develop a sense of Afrikaner nationalism, based on their distinctive language, Afrikaans, the fundamentalist religion of their forefathers, and their collective experience in the harsh conditions of the frontier. Cosmopolitan English rule clashed with this incipient nationalism in many ways, but most critically on the issue of slavery. The British turned against the institution at the beginning of the nineteenth century. The Boers considered it fundamental to their social and economic position and repudiated British attempts to limit and ultimately abolish it.

SOUTH AFRICAN INDEPENDENCE

Matters came to a head in 1834, when the British outlawed slavery throughout their empire. Since resistance was obviously futile, the Boers looked beyond the frontier and saw a landscape made relatively empty by the *Mfecane*. Led by Louis Trichardt, almost 10,000 Boers embarked on the "Great Trek" in 1836. Driving wagons loaded with their families and household goods, they ventured over the Drakensberg Mountains and into the high velt of the far interior, the Transvaal. When the Bantu-speaking Ndebele attacked, the Boers formed the wagons into a circle, or *laager*, and shot from the intervals between the wagons with their muskets. These tactics enabled them to win a number of crucial victories that convinced the Ndebele to withdraw north, ceding the Transvaal to the Boers.

The main group of Boers turned east and descended into the coastal region near the sea, where they clashed with the Zulu. After initial reverses, the Boers won a stunning victory in which 500 men with 57 wagons killed 3,000 warriors without losing a single man. Following this victory, they set up an independent republic in 1839. The British were not far behind, however, intervening in the Boer's continuing warfare with the Zulu in 1842 and annexing the territory called Natal in 1845. Most of the Boers pulled up stakes and rejoined their brethren on the high velt. Here, beyond the reach of the British, they were able to set up two independent republics, the Orange Free State in 1852 and the Transvaal in 1860. And here they were able to set up the society they wanted. "I have myself been an eyewitness of Boers coming to a village," wrote David Livingstone,

> and, according to their usual custom, demanding twenty or thirty women to weed their gardens, and have seen these women proceed to the scene of unrequited toil. . . . Nor have the Boers any wish to conceal the meanness of thus employing unpaid labor; on the contrary, every one of them . . . lauded his own humanity and justice, saying 'We make the people work for us in consideration of allowing them to live in our country.'

The non-whites in the original Cape Colony (the descendants of the Khoikoi,

Asians, and mulattos) did considerably better, at least through the nineteenth century. Not only were they freed from slavery, but in 1853 the colony gained local self-rule based on a franchise that included modest property requirements but did not consider race at all. Colored freeholders regularly elected white liberals to represent them, which began the tradition of "Cape liberalism" that has continued to be a factor in South African politics down to today.

Natal, on the other hand, developed no such traditions because it developed a plantation economy with no room for liberal idealism. Commercial speculators imported indentured workers from India to harvest sugar cane, since they lacked the power to compel the natives to undertake this onerous labor. Natal confined the Africans to "native locations," where they were ruled indirectly via their chiefs. While the franchise granted in 1856 was theoretically nonracial, in practice it empowered whites only. Natal's chief political legacy to the later republic was the origin of segregation in general and the infamous homelands policy in particular.

Southern Africa might have settled down at this point with the British controlling the coast and the Boers ensconced inland, but the discovery of the Kimberly diamond mines in 1867 heightened British interest in the interior. The British immediately laid claim to the area and in 1868 annexed the nearby kingdom of Lesotho to keep it from being absorbed by the Orange Free State, which had just defeated it in war. The Boer republics naturally resented these British moves, yet found themselves in increasing administrative and financial disarray. In 1877, the British annexed the Transvaal Republic, "to the relief even of some in the South African republic itself."

In annexing the Transvaal, the British inherited the Boers' ongoing conflict with the Pedi to the north, and sent a strong force to settle affairs on this frontier. Encouraged by their success, they next turned on the Zulu, hoping to bring this kingdom into line. Instead, in 1879, they met their most stinging defeat at the hands of an African army when the Zulus overwhelmed a column and killed 1,600 out of 8,000 troops in the battle of Isandhlwana. The British got their revenge three months later at the battle of Ulundi, largely by using a new weapon called the "Maxim gun," a machine gun, to mow down the attacking warriors. Humorist Hilaire Belloc summed up its impact on Europe's relations with the rest of the world with the following couplet: "Whatever happens we have got/ The Maxim gun and they have not."

Even as the British subdued the Zulu, they lost their hold on the Boers. In 1881, the British established a protectorate over Zululand but in the same year lost control over the Transvaal. The Boers defeated a British force at Majuba, which strengthened the "Little Englanders" in the British Liberal Party, who criticized the cost of the African campaigns. Liberal Prime Minister William Gladstone restored the Transvaal's independence, with the sole condition that Great Britain retain veto power over the republic's foreign affairs.

Once again, southern Africa might have settled down, but for the discovery of a new precious mineral in 1884. Gold was found in the Witwatersrand in the Transvaal. The seams of gold were not rich, but they were huge and deep and would therefore require a massive investment of capital and labor to realize the immense profits they promised. A gold rush followed the discovery, and Johannesburg, the nearest town, rapidly grew into the region's largest city. The Boers of the Transvaal Republic found their newfound wealth to be a mixed blessing because the inrush of foreigners disturbed their conservative society. The great financial interests whose resources were needed to extract the mines' wealth found the Republic to be an unsatisfactory host, politically dominated by slaveholding farmers with little understanding of or sympathy for their needs.

The British moved gingerly at first. They annexed part and proclaimed a protectorate over the rest of Bechuanaland in 1885 to block any attempt to link the Transvaal to the colony

Germany had established in South-west Africa the year before. In 1890 Cecil Rhodes, who had made a fortune in the Kimberly diamond fields, sent a column north of the Transvaal and incorporated the lands of the Ndebele and Shona into a new colony named after himself, Rhodesia. This move encircled the Transvaal with British holdings. The British permitted the Boer Republic an outlet to the sea in 1895 by ceding them a protectorate over Swaziland, but revoked it upon learning of Boer overtures to Germany.

Rhodesia proved a disappointment to Rhodes, for it did not contain the expected gold fields. In collaboration with agents of a deep-level mining firm and the British government, he organized a small raid into the Transvaal in 1896, hoping thereby to spark an uprising by its numerous foreign residents, who were denied citizenship and the vote. When they did not rise, the "Jameson Raid" turned into a fiasco, ending Rhodes' career as a statesman. Suspecting official British involvement, the Orange Free State made a military alliance with the Transvaal, and the Transvaal moved closer to alliance with Germany.

The British government determined to take matters into its own hands, pushing unreasonable demands on the Boers and stationing troops along the border. Open war broke out in 1899. After some initial reverses, the British brought in reinforcements that broke the Boer armies by the middle of 1900. The Boers changed to guerrilla tactics. The British countered by bringing their troop strength up to 300,000, erecting chains of blockhouses, and then sweeping through each sector to herd the Boers' families into squalid "concentration camps" before burning their fields and demolishing their farms. These tactics succeeded in breaking Boer resistance by mid-1902, but at a cost of perhaps 10 percent of the Afrikaner population, mainly women and children, who died of disease and malnutrition.

If the Boers lost the war, they won the peace. At first the British attempted to anglicize the two former republics, but this effort only lasted a few years. In 1906 and 1907, they granted the Transvaal and the Orange Free State self-government, which led by 1908 to complete control by Afrikaner nationalist parties. In 1910, Great Britain completed its disengagement from South African internal politics by passing the Act of Union, which united the Transvaal and the Orange Free State with the Cape Colony and Natal to form the Union of South Africa, a self-governing dominion within the British Empire. Only whites could sit in the parliament of the new Union, and except in the Cape Colony, only whites could vote. Having gotten what they wanted—incorporation of South Africa into their international economic system—the British abandoned the 80 percent of South Africans who were black to the white minority. They thereby assured not only Afrikaner acceptance of the Union, but also a dependable supply of cheap labor for the British-owned mines.

LEGITIMATE COMMERCE AND INFORMAL EMPIRE

The nineteenth century began with only one substantial European colony north of the Cape Colony—the Portuguese holdings in Mozambique—and a dozen or so European trading forts scattered along the continent's north and west coasts. The century closed with all Africa save Ethiopia and Liberia partitioned among the European Powers (with Turkey holding Libya). For most of the century, the tide of colonialism flowed slowly; in fact, as the century began, it appeared that Europe was moving in the opposite direction. British abolition of the slave trade in 1808 severed the primary commercial link between Europe and Africa, and Great Britain's rejection of the mercantilist theories that underlay Europe's eighteenth century empires, coupled with its complete domination of the seas, led it to adopt a policy of free trade and informal empire. With the French colonial challenge defeated and no other competitor in sight, why pay to control the sources of wealth that could better be tapped (and would indeed be better

generated) through the effortless workings of the marketplace? The decline of the slave trade brought the rise of legitimate commerce, and mercantilist empire gave way to informal domination.

While Europe backed off during the early part of the century, Africa began to undergo a process of disruption that made it vulnerable to, and indeed in some ways invited, later European domination. At the root of this disruption was a growing disparity of power between the peoples along the coastline, be they European, Arab, or African, and the peoples of the interior. As the industrial revolution accelerated in Europe, military technology changed repeatedly. African craftsmen could repair and make ammunition for the smooth-bore iron musket in use at the beginning of the century, but they could do neither for the rifled musket that replaced it by mid-century. The gap became wider with the introduction of breech-loading steel rifles and ultimately the Maxim gun. Each innovation brought a significant increase in firepower: the rifle increased the effective range of fire dramatically; the breech-loader increased the rate of fire significantly; and the Maxim gun increased the rate of fire by a quantum jump.

This disparity of power between coastal and inland peoples accounts for the success of the Boers against the Bantu speakers and later of the British against both the Boers and the Bantu speakers in southern Africa, but it showed up in all other areas of Africa as well.

In Egypt, the century opened with the French briefly in control, having followed the romantic dreams of young Napoleon Bonaparte and shattered Mamluk power in 1798 in the battle of the Nile. Their hold on the country did not last, but they had broken the Mamluks' power for good. The Ottoman government sent an Albanian viceroy, Muhammad 'Ali, with a contingent of Albanian soldiers to help resist the French, and he stayed on after they left.

Muhammad 'Ali's formal reign began in 1805, but only in 1811 did he begin to take the dramatic steps necessary to create and

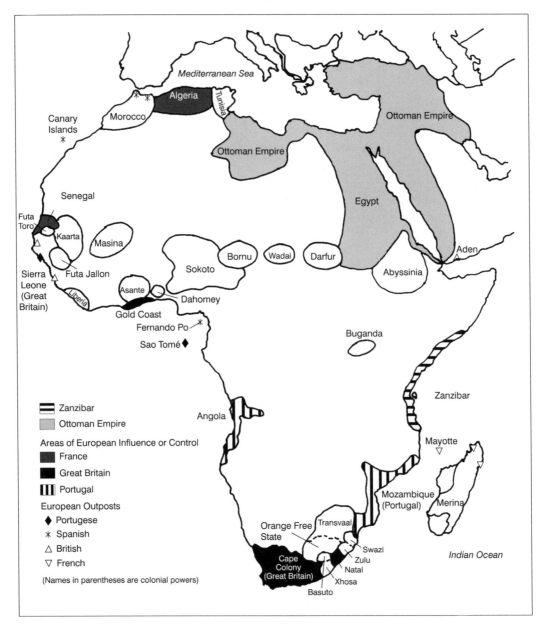

Africa in 1856

maintain a modern army. He began by invit-ing the surviving members of the Mamluk leadership to a banquet in Cairo at which he had them massacred. Having thus disposed of the old military elite, he began recruiting peas-ants into the army and contracted with French advisors to teach them Western infantry tac-tics. They learned to stand in line shoulder to shoulder, to fire in volleys, to form squares when attacked by cavalry, and to charge with the bayonet when ordered.

Realizing that the foundations of modern power lay deeper than this, he also embarked on an ambitious program of civil reform, build-ing hundreds of new schools, creating an ad-ministrative system organized into Western style departments under cabinet ministers, conducting a census, and setting up a gov-ernment printing press. To pay for these and his military reforms, he confiscated the land from its (now dead) feudal owners, national-ized it, and made the peasants virtual owners as long as they paid their taxes. In order to pay their taxes, they had to engage in com-mercial farming, which the government sup-ported by improving the irrigation works along the Nile. Because Europe's industrialization was being led by the textile industry, the mar-ket for cotton was assured, and the Egyptian state bought the farmers' output at a fixed price and then sold it on the world market for a substantial profit. These profits were plowed back into the economy in the form of invest-ment in Egypt's own textile mills, shipyards, and iron foundries, as well as the social and military initiatives. As a result, between 1800 and 1850 the amount of land under cultiva-tion increased by a third, government rev-enues multiplied by a factor of four, imports rose 10 times, and the population almost doubled.

In 1818, the Ottoman sultan requested Egyptian help in putting down a rebellion in Arabia, and the army's performance vindi-cated Muhammad 'Ali's reforms. In 1821, he turned south, sending his forces into the Sudan. They quickly defeated the warlike Shakiyya people and overran the Funj king-dom, a Westernized infantry force from the coast vanquishing a traditional cavalry army of the interior. Muhammad 'Ali now controlled an empire surpassing that of the pharaohs, and he aimed even higher, at the sultanate of the Ottoman Empire itself.

Unfortunately for Muhammad 'Ali, the Brit-ish did not want to see a strong power in the Middle East, and European merchants re-sented both state control of marketing and the tariffs that protected Egypt's nascent indus-tries. In 1838, Great Britain gained the right of virtual free trade with the Ottoman Em-pire, and three years later the Treaty of Lon-don compelled Muhammad 'Ali to abolish Egypt's protective tariff and also to reduce the size of his army. He remained in control of Egypt and the Sudan but lost Arabia and the economic underpinnings of Egypt's renais-sance. His last years in office saw the gradual abandonment of his Westernization program. All that was left of his economic program was the commercial farming, a situation that made Egypt an economic appendage of industrial Europe.

The Sudan never proved the economic boon that Muhammad 'Ali had hoped, for its gold mines were exhausted. His forces re-mained there to feed slaves and ivory north-ward, however, and in so doing they had a profound effect on the region. Furthermore, they were joined by armies hired by private merchants, which set up fortified encamp-ments across the savanna from which they raided for cattle and slaves. The slaves not sent northward were given to the soldiers, while the cattle were traded to other locals for ivory. The cumulative effect was to desta-bilize traditional society—devastating some villages, drawing others into commerce, and creating new communities dependent on the traders and disconnected from traditional structures.

A similar process was taking place to the south and east of the Sudan. The area had seen the gradual appearance of traditional states feeding off the growing trade with the coast, most notably the kingdom of Buganda in the heart of present-day Uganda. However, even as traditional states arose, they were challenged by the Islamic traders from the coast, who in the early nineteenth century moved for the first time from their coastal enclaves into the interior. Traveling at first in caravans, their armed retainers raided for slaves, hunted for ivory, and terrorized the locals into doing the same. Later, these Swahili merchants established fortified outposts deep in the interior, in which they lived in greater style and from which they commanded greater military power than any of the local chiefs. They might or might not give deference to a distant king; but in either case, with their comrades and slaves, they formed the nucleus of powerful communities divorced from and ultimately competitive with the traditional power structures. Their methods were often brutal, particularly in outlying areas; European travelers noted, however, that the centers of these new statelets were orderly and prosperous.

Behind this intrusion into the interior lay the consolidation of the Omani supremacy over the Swahili city-states along the east coast. Oman had dominated the area since it helped oust the Portuguese in the seventeenth century, but in the nineteenth century Sultan Sayyid of Oman turned his attention increasingly to the African coast, ultimately transferring his capital to the island of Zanzibar in 1840. (Oman itself went its separate way upon his death.) The basic reason for this change of emphasis was that the sultan got the bulk of his revenue from the African part of the empire, in particular from the customs duties on the ivory trade. It made sense to expand inland to the source of the goods.

Behind the revival of trade along the Swahili coast lay the French colonization of Mauritius and Reunion in the 1730s. The French turned these previously uninhabited islands far to the east of the African mainland into sugar plantations, drawing upon slave labor at first from Madagascar and later from the east coast of the mainland. Madagascar was a fertile source of slaves in the eighteenth century because of the warfare accompany-

ing the rise of its first significant states—Boina, Menabe, and Merina. Once the latter consolidated its hold on most of the island late in the century, the fighting fell off, and with it the supply of captives. The French had to look elsewhere for labor, which increased the demand on the east coast of the mainland. The resultant spread of slave raiding affected not only the hinterland of the Omani cities, but also the Portuguese holdings in Mozambique, and hence contributed to the squeeze on the Bantu north of the Cape Colony.

In the early nineteenth century, the French increased their presence on the African continent as well as in the Indian Ocean. They had an outpost on Madagascar as early as 1660, but withdrew it a few decades later in favor of the newer settlement on Reunion. They re-established a presence on Madagascar after the turn of the nineteenth century and garrisoned the nearby islands of Mayotte in the Comoros and Nosy Be in 1841. On the west coast of Africa, they had St. Louis at the mouth of the Senegal River, Goree down the coast, and commercial stations as far as 200 miles up the Senegal since the seventeenth century. In the nineteenth century, these stations were threatened by Islamic *jihads,* and one, Medina, was unsuccessfully besieged in 1857. The French then set about pacifying the interior along the river and organizing commercial agriculture, particularly groundnuts. They succeeded in both endeavors, establishing French control along the river for 300 miles and increasing groundnut exports from 3,000 tons in 1853 to 65,000 tons in 1894.

Along with this prosperity came a growing population—in the older centers, in the new towns of Dakar and Rufisque, and in the countryside. This growing population included an important sector of *compredores*, African and mixed-race merchants who formed a crucial link between the peasants in the interior and the European trading houses. Along with the growth in the towns came a growth in the colony's rights. In the 1870s, the French granted the "four communes" (St. Louis, Goree, Dakar, and Rufisque) both local self-government and representation in the Chamber of Deputies in Paris.

In 1830, almost by accident, the French began an even more extensive intrusion into Africa in Algeria on the northern coast of the continent. Piqued by a slight to their ambassador in Algiers, the French responded with an expeditionary force of 35,000 men. This force easily subdued the 15,000 Turkish troops garrisoning the coastal towns, but it was totally unable to cope with the Arabs and Berbers, who rose in the countryside against the European infidel. Unwilling to back out, the French went forward, ultimately deploying 100,000 troops to protect about an equal number of settlers. Given the nature of the opposition, the occupation could not be confined to the fertile (and profitable) coastal plain, but instead had to be extended into the mountains. The Arabs fought for almost 20 years under Abd el-Kader, and steady resistance only ceased in 1847, when the French finally forced him to surrender. Smaller scale, more sporadic fighting continued long after.

The British involvement with the northern end of the continent centered on the suppression of the slave trade and its replacement by other forms of commerce. The most obvious examples of this were the naval patrols Great Britain maintained in the Atlantic Ocean and the Mediterranean Sea after 1807 and the expansion of Sierra Leone. This colony had been set up in 1792 for loyalist slaves from the American Revolution, but only 1,000 ever came, and it really came into its own as the repository for slaves liberated by the Atlantic squadron. All told, about 80,000 "recaptives" entered Freetown harbor, and about half of them chose to settle in Sierra Leone. Many of them and their descendants went on to achieve wealth and prestige in business and the professions, making the colony a vibrant center of Anglophonic Africa. The ones who returned home had to have earned money in Freetown for the trip, so they brought with them an understanding of modern business and often a mission education and a firm belief in Christ as well.

The United States established a similar colony in West Africa, Liberia, founded by a charitable society as a homeland for freed slaves. Liberia's population included 16,000 slaves from the U.S. and another 6,000 brought by American anti-slavery patrols when Liberia became independent in 1847. These 22,000 people were a small minority within the territory, but from the beginning they formed an educated, Westernized business and political elite that dominated the indigenous peoples.

As in northern Africa, Great Britain also began to dominate the southern coast of West Africa as a consequence of its anti-slavery activities. At the beginning of the century, the British, the Danes, and the Dutch all had bases along the Gold Coast. In 1806, the Asante Empire began expanding toward the coast at the expense of the Fante Confederation. The British intervened to liberate the Fante, and after a typical initial disaster in 1824, helped them defeat the Asante in 1831 at the battle of Katamansu. British policy toward the Africans thereafter fluctuated between indifference and interference. The British bought out the Danes in 1850 and the Dutch in 1871. This last move infuriated the Asante, who favored the Dutch, and rekindled their desire to control the coast themselves. They invaded the coastal zone again, but in 1874 the British defeated the Asante and burned their capital. While they left the next day for the coast and annexed only the Fante territory near their forts, the British had humiliated the strongest African state in the area, loosening the Asante hold on their tributaries just as Europe was beginning to take a greater interest in Africa as a whole.

THE SCRAMBLE FOR AFRICA

During the last quarter of the nineteenth century, various European nations staked claims to almost all of Africa. Some of these were the old intruders expanding their footholds: Portugal, France, and Great Britain. Others were newcomers looking for a place in the sun: Belgium, Italy, and Germany. All took inspiration from the explorers and missionaries who had been penetrating the interior in increasing numbers since the turn of the century in search of knowledge and converts. All sought to secure raw materials and markets, and all looked jealously on each advance by the others. They all had better weapons than the Africans, and by late century they all had quinine, a medicine that prevents malaria, the disease that until mid-century had made tropical Africa the "white man's grave."

Historians disagree about when exactly the scramble for Africa began. Some date it to the expansion of French influence in Senegal and the British defeat of the Asante in the early 1870s. But the first *new* European player in African politics arrived a few years later in the person of King Leopold of Belgium. He knew that his subjects had no enthusiasm for empire, but he was determined to acquire one nevertheless. He personally funded expeditions by the famous explorer Henry Stanley. Stanley had traveled down the Congo River from its source to its mouth in 1876 and 1877, but the British did not show much interest in his achievement, so he accepted Leopold's backing. Stanley returned to the Congo basin in 1879 and spent the next five years signing concession treaties with the indigenous peoples and setting up trading posts along the river. By the mid-1880s, Leopold's Congo Free State had secure claim to the southern and eastern side of the river.

Leopold missed out on the northwestern side because the French did not sit idly by while Stanley was at work. From 1879 to 1882, the administrator and explorer Pierre de Brazza expanded Gabon, a small enclave for liberated slaves established by France in 1839, by traveling among and signing concession treaties with the Fang people along the Congo's north bank. Gabon and the French Congo had neither the size nor the economic potential of Leopold's portion of the Congo basin, but they formed the nucleus of French Equatorial Africa.

The Congo basin was not the only area of French expansionism. In 1881, the French established a protectorate over Tunisia on the North African coast. In Senegal, they embarked in 1879 on an ambitious project to build a railroad linking their coastal ports to the middle reaches of the Niger River. The project took several years, but was vindicated in 1883 when the French defeated the powerful Islamic state Kaarta and secured a foothold on the Niger. Years of fighting followed as the French expanded their thin strip of territory by absorbing Kaarta, the warlord Samori's recently consolidated holdings, and innumerable stateless societies.

The British took the next major step, one that some historians consider the real start of the scramble. In 1882, almost by accident, they took effective control of Egypt. That country had gone through boom and bust under Ismail, grandson of Muhammad 'Ali. The disruption of cotton exports from the United States during and after the Civil War in the 1860s had established Egypt as an alternative source, and the completion of the Suez Canal in 1869 promised still greater profits. Unfortunately, Ismail spent recklessly on projects both good and bad, and by 1879 he had brought the country to bankruptcy. His foreign creditors forced him from power and insisted on acting as economic advisors to his successor, Tawfiq. The austerity measures they implemented alienated the army, and in 1881 Colonel Urabi Pasha led an uprising. The British and French agreed to intervene together, but a cabinet crisis kept the French from participating at the last minute, so in 1882 the British found themselves de facto rulers of Egypt. Determined to secure their access to India via the Suez Canal as well as to protect their investments in Egypt itself, they resolved to stay.

Great Britain's windfall disturbed the careful balance among the European powers, or at least provided a convenient pretext for them to make further moves. In particular, Germany, which had never evinced the slightest interest in colonizing Africa, suddenly emerged as a major player. Concerned by a downturn in the economy and urged on by commercial in-

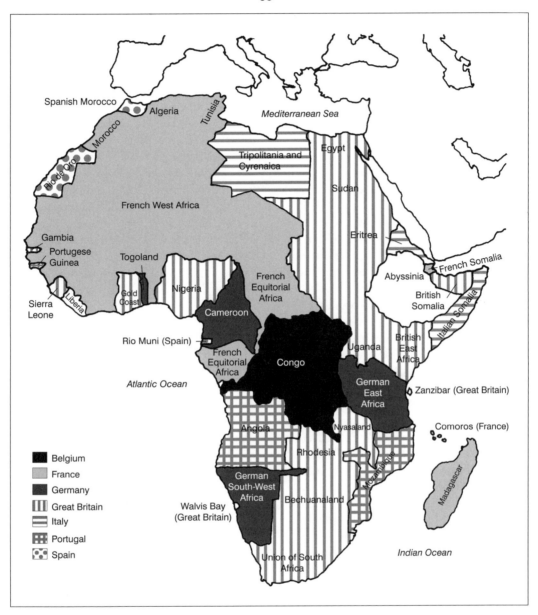

Africa in 1914

terests, Chancellor Otto von Bismarck reversed his long-standing rejection of colonialism. In 1884, he proclaimed protectorates over Togo and Cameroon on the West coast, Southwest Africa, and Tanganyika on the east coast, basing the claims on areas of missionary activity and "unofficial" empire-building by German explorers.

Because Germany's move created a number of overlapping and conflicting claims with other powers, Bismarck invited them to attend the Berlin Conference in late 1884. The gathering's ostensible purpose was to restrain rather than encourage expansionism, but its effect was to lay the ground rules for the subsequent partition of Africa. The participants agreed to freedom of navigation on the Niger and Congo rivers, recognized Leopold's realm in the Congo and Germany's new colonies, and agreed that further claims had to be based on "effective occupation" and followed up by notification to all the participant powers. The race was on.

Over the next 15 years, the European powers consolidated their coastal enclaves and expanded them into the interior. Basically, this involved pushing the borders along the coast until they butted into those of the nearest European neighbor, and drawing lines on a map from the point of contact inland. For the first 10 years the process proceeded relatively smoothly through a series of bilateral treaties between neighboring European claimants, brokered mostly by the British politician Lord Salisbury. The result was 33 coast-based spheres of influence, with France taking the lion's share of West Africa, Great Britain predominant in the East (except for Madagascar, which went to France), Germany's colonies sprinkled throughout, Italy given a place in the northeast, and Spain laying claim to a strip along the northwestern coast.

During this process, the only use of force by one European power against another was the British blockade of the Tagus River which was undertaken to compel Portugal to accept the separation of Angola and Mozambique by Northern Rhodesia. The last phase of the

scramble grew more tense as the Europeans adjusted their claims and hopes for the farthest interior. The main flashpoint was the Sudan, which had broken away from Egypt in 1881 under the leadership of the *Mahdi*, a religious prophet. For over 10 years the Moslem commonwealth enjoyed independence. But in the late 1890s it became the focus of the ambitions of Belgium's King Leopold, who hoped to extend his dominions from the Congo; the French, who approached it from West Africa; and the British, who feared the interruption of the Nile's water supply if Sudan were not under its control. A small French force got there first in 1898, but the British got there with an army of 20,000 men that devastated the Mahdists (killing 11,000 at the battle of Omdurman with negligible losses to the Europeans), and then moved upriver to confront the French. After a tense confrontation that almost brought war, the French withdrew.

The destruction of the Mahdists was an unusually violent episode in the scramble for Africa. In general, not only did the Europeans proceed peacefully with each other, but on the whole they fought relatively little with the Africans. There were certainly other violent episodes, like the French campaigns in Senegal and the British wars against the Asante. For the majority of Africans, however, the scramble was a caravan of whites that passed through, collected some food and a signature in exchange for some guns and a flag, and then disappeared again. The real violence came later when the Europeans began trying to make real the nominal sovereignty they had so easily gained.

The other main exception to this general picture was the Italian campaign against Ethiopia. Ethiopia had revived in the middle of the nineteenth century under the modernizing rule of Emperors Theodore II, John IV, and Melinik II, and, despite internal turmoil and conflicts with both the British and the Sudanese Mahdists, was strong enough to resist when Italy tried to establish its place as a major colonial power at Ethiopia's expense. Italy took over the coastal region of Eritrea in

1885 and Somalia in 1890, but its eye was really on the Ethiopian highlands. In 1896, it invaded with an army of 17,000 men. The Ethiopians assembled a force of 100,000 and routed the Italians at the battle of Adowa. This victory not only assured Ethiopian independence into the twentieth century, but also enabled it to stake its own claims to territories to the south and east. Ethiopia was thus the only traditional African state to survive the scramble (Libya and Morocco went to Italy and France, respectively, before World War I), as well as the only one to participate in it.

CHAPTER

3

The Colonial Interlude

The basic purpose of European colonialism was to transfer wealth from Africa to Europe. However, most of Africa's wealth was potential rather than actual—minerals, land, and human labor. In order to make a profit, the colonial powers had to restructure Africa's existing economy and society to adapt them to Europe's needs. Over the course of a half-century, the Europeans succeeded in doing this, setting up facilities to produce or extract raw materials, creating the infrastructure necessary to get them to the coast, and compelling Africans to do the actual work and to help pay for the administration of the enterprise.

In effecting this transformation, the colonial system uprooted Africans physically, culturally, socially, and politically. Physically, it compelled millions to migrate to where their labor was required, either by fiat or by the need to earn money to pay taxes. Culturally, it pushed them into new and unfamiliar circumstances, while offering alternatives like Christianity and European education that had no connection to their past. Socially, it pulled

traditional relationships apart, forcing men to abandon their families for months or years on end and bringing peoples from widely separated areas into contact. Politically, where it did not simply discard traditional institutions, it created new sources of wealth and power that competed with, and generally overwhelmed, the older sources of power and authority. Colonialism may have introduced aspects of the modern world that benefited Africans in different ways, but it did so without their consent and at great cost.

In transforming Africa, the colonial system also created the conditions for its own demise. Even as it overcame resistance from traditional groups in society, it created new groups that were opposed to it and able to work against it. The educated elite, urban workers, and peasant entrepreneurs chaffed at the restrictions placed on them by colonialism's racial preferences. Over the years, they gradually assimilated the concepts and techniques of modern politics, which enabled them to mount increasingly effective resistance by the middle third of the twentieth century. Helped by larger changes in the world's balance of economic and military power that weakened the colonial powers, Africans were generally able to gain independence by the third quarter of the century. The only hitch was that the colonial transformation had been so complete that the new nations had little alternative but to maintain the economic relationships that had been the Europeans' primary goal all along.

THE NEW REGIMES

Drawing lines on a map was one thing; asserting effective control over the hundreds of thousands of square miles and millions of people those lines enclosed was quite another. A concession treaty obtained through a hazy combination of purchase and fraud might signify "effective control" in the cabinets of Europe, but it meant little in the heart of Africa.

Yet, the Europeans needed to establish effective control over their new colonies, and to do so quickly. They staked their claims because of the colonies' perceived economic potential; until they began to realize that potential, the colonies would be nothing but a drain on their treasuries. Making the colonies self-supporting, let alone profitable, meant in most cases creating both the physical infrastructure needed to carry products from the interior to the coast and the socioeconomic infrastructure needed to harness millions of Africans to production for the world marketplace. Neither would take place within a time frame acceptable to the colonizers without substantial European intervention.

Creating the infrastructure necessary to open the interior would require a massive but relatively short-term application of African labor. In much of tropical Africa, pack animals could not be used because of the sleeping sickness carried by the tsetse fly, so all transport had to be done by human beings. One European official's camping gear typically required 40 porters, so carrying the whole panoply of colonial goods—from construction materials and heavy machinery to medicines and wines—from the coast to the interior required tens, and ultimately hundreds, of thousands of laborers. In addition, the actual construction projects required road gangs and rail gangs made up of tens of thousands more, with still more laborers needed to supply them. Since the work paid poorly, if at all, and was often dangerous, thousands of African soldiers and policemen were needed to enforce the recruitment system. The end result of all this effort was a transportation system linking the coast to the interior. Although this system would ultimately make much of this type of labor unnecessary—one small train could carry the loads of 15,000 porters—colonialism had a voracious appetite for labor during its first decades. It could only fill this need through forced labor on a monumental scale.

Reorienting African production to the world market required long-term, indeed permanent, changes in the African economy and society. To complicate matters, these changes were being undertaken at the very time that Europeans were ideologically committed to ending slavery, an institution that was central to much of the existing African commercial production. Thus, depending on the circumstances of the local economy, the colonial intrusion meant turning Africans from subsistence living or from slave-based production for export to a system of cash cropping or wage labor in European-owned plantations and mines. The problem was that few Africans saw any advantage in that transition, and so the Europeans had to compel them—either directly, through forcible recruitment, or indirectly, through the imposition of taxes or restriction to inadequate agricultural lands.

In some cases, the process of establishing a claim to an area entailed military conquest, which left the Europeans in a position to impose themselves directly on the people from the start of the colonial rule. This was the case as the French expanded out of Senegal to subdue the West African *jihad* states and when the British crushed the Mahdists in the Sudan;

it would have been the case had the Italians conquered Ethiopia.

More often, the Europeans established their initial claim to sovereignty peacefully and worked with the established rulers during the first years of colonial rule. Their primary motive was expediency. The home governments begrudged every penny sent to Africa and expected the colonial governors to do a great deal with very little. For example, Nyasaland (present day Malawi) got £10,000 per year starting in 1891, which, with locally raised funds, was enough to pay for 10 European civilians and two army officers, 70 Sikh soldiers from India, and 85 armed African porters. With these resources, the colonial government ruled an area 500 miles long and containing between one and two million people. The government of Uganda got £50,000 in 1894, enabling it to hire 200 Sudanese mercenaries to patrol a territory twice the size and population of Nyasaland. Northern Nigeria, with 10 million people organized in still vital Muslim states, got £100,000 in 1900 to help support six English administrators, 120 officers and NCOs, and 2,000 African soldiers. With such skimpy resources and such tremendous needs, especially for labor, the Europeans had little choice but to work through whatever emir, king, or chief could deliver the goods.

SUBJUGATION AND PACIFICATION

It did not take long for the new overlords to come into conflict with their new subjects. The cause might be their incessant demands for labor. It might be their prohibition of slavery. It might be their attempt to move beyond labor exactions, which hurt mainly the poor, to the imposition of taxes, which fell on everybody. Regardless of the reasons, the problem really boiled down to the sheer magnitude of the colonizers' ambitions. The Europeans were not just another tribute-taking conqueror. To realize their purpose, they would have to recast Africa altogether. Even they could not really comprehend the full implications of what they had begun.

Conflict usually came first with the larger states and established elites. Sometimes the Europeans precipitated the conflict. The British provoked confrontations with the Yoruba in 1892, the Asante in 1895, Benin in 1897, and Sokoto and Kano in 1903. The British won all these conflicts. The French invaded and conquered Dahomey after a series of provocations in 1894 and went on to subdue the Ivory Coast the next year and Guinea in 1896. In southern Africa, the British carefully built up their strength and then in 1896 attacked the Zanzabari slave trader, Mlozi, who was firmly established in an armed village at the northern end of Lake Malawi.

More often, the Africans precipitated a showdown as the full consequences of European rule became clear to them. The Swahili Arabs who effectively controlled the eastern Congo revolted against Leopold's rule in 1887, and it took a three-year campaign (from 1892 to 1895) costing tens of thousands of lives to crush them. Farther east, the Swahili Arabs along the coast of Tanganyika revolted against the Germans in 1888 for fear that the colonizers would outlaw slavery. Three years later, the Hehe began a five-year campaign of resistance to the Germans in the Tanganyikan interior. In 1893, the Nyamwezi chief Siki fought the Germans, and the next year Hasan bin Omari led a revolt against them in the Kilwa area.

In British East Africa, the king of Buganda joined with the king of Bunyoro in 1897 in an attempt to throw off the British yoke, but they succeeded only in losing their crowns. The Ngoni of Mpezeni took up arms the next year to repudiate a concession treaty that had been fraudulently obtained, but they succeeded only in losing their herds. In southern Africa, the Ndebele leader Lobengula finally stood up in 1893 against the gradual but insistent encroachments of the British, but he was defeated and his people were confined to two inadequate reserves. In West Africa in 1894, the Itsekiri trading chief Nana rejected a British protectorate and took refuge in his fortified headquarters, holding out against repeated shelling and ground attacks until the British brought up overwhelming forces. Similarly, the Brassmen attacked the Royal Niger Company post at Akassa in 1895 to protest the loss of their traditional markets to the company's new monopoly over inland trade, but the British overwhelmed them and destroyed Brass, their major town.

Resistance by major states and leaders ended by the turn of the century, but popular resistance intensified. If the last two decades of the nineteenth century were the era of conquest, then the first two decades of the twentieth were the era of pacification. Innumerable small columns of soldiers scoured the countryside, crushing armed resistance to forced labor and taxation. Where people fled instead of resisting, the soldiers resorted to scorched-earth tactics, burning the people's homes, destroying their fields, and stealing their animals. Occasionally, entire regions rose in revolt, which required wide-ranging operations to suppress and resulted in thousands and even tens of thousands of casualties from battle and from punitive actions.

All the European powers found it necessary to undertake these pacification campaigns, often repeatedly. The British had to put down scattered uprisings in Nyasaland in the early 1890s, suppress an uprising by the Ndebele and Shona in southern Africa in 1896, crush resistance to taxation in the hinterland of Sierra Leone in 1898, repeatedly assert their control of western Kenya, and send columns across southern Sudan. The French fought a series of small engagements in the central Ivory Coast, and found the nomads of the desert difficult to control. They did not break resistance in the zone stretching from Mauritania to Chad until the 1930s. Similarly, the Italians needed until the end of the 1920s to subdue the arid northern part of Somalia.

Of all the pacification campaigns, the most extensive and the most brutal were conducted by the Germans. In East Africa, the Germans decreed in 1905 that the Africans in the Kilwa region would have to cultivate cotton for export, which the Africans regarded as a threat to their ability to provide for their own subsistence. When religious leaders gave revolt their sanction by providing *maji*, magic water they claimed would give immunity to European bullets, the disturbance spread far and wide. Diverse peoples who had never cooperated before came together, showing a fanatical determination in battle that caught the Germans by surprise. The revolt raged for two years; the Germans could only bring it under control through a brutal scorched earth campaign that killed perhaps 200,000 Africans, including many women and children who succumbed to hunger and disease.

On the other side of the continent, the Germans conducted an even more heinous counterinsurgency campaign. In 1904, the Herero in Southwest Africa revolted against the steady confiscation of their cattle, their land, and their rights in favor of German settlers. A few months later, the Nama followed suit. "I know these African tribes," commented the German commander, General von Trotha. "They are all the same. They respect nothing but force." He resolved "to exercise this force with brute terror," to "wipe out [the] rebellious tribes with streams of blood." The Herero nation, he proclaimed, "must disappear."

Von Trotha set about this barbaric task with systematic and ruthless determination. When the Herero proved too tough to take on directly, he surrounded their main force on three sides, leaving open the way into the harsh Kalahari. As the Herero retreated into the desert, German troops occupied the waterholes along the fringes and shot down any who ventured near. The rest of the Herero died of thirst or exposure.

Those who remained behind fared no better. The Germans rounded them up and shot many on the spot. Others they put into "concentration camps" (as they were called in the records), where 45 percent died of disease and malnutrition. By the time it was over, the campaign had reduced the Nama population from 20,000 to under 10,000 and the Herero from 80,000 to 15,000.

RULE BY CONCESSION COMPANIES

If the Germans' punitive campaigns set a standard for military brutality, then King Leopold of Belgium's private empire in the Congo set a standard for administrative brutality. With far more limited resources than those of the state-backed colonial efforts, Leopold could not afford a 20- or 30-year lead time before his investment turned a profit. He had to find a way to bootstrap his operation. Economically, his solution was to force the inhabitants to harvest natural rubber in the rain forest, to expropriate the profits, and to use the funds to create the transportation facilities necessary to open the mines of the interior, which would provide the colony's long-term profitability. Politically, his solution was to give concession companies administrative control over the inhabitants for a percentage of the take. The concessionaires had both the motive and the power to exploit the people with reckless abandon.

Exploit them they did. They bought "freed slaves" from Swahili Arab traders and impressed them into a rural police force. Obliged to serve for seven years under the threat of execution for desertion, the gendarmes' primary function was to force the inhabitants to collect as much rubber as possible for a minimal price. This obligation inevitably meant that people would have to neglect their own food crops, a situation that naturally led to widespread resistance. The companies' response was a reign of terror in which armed expeditions scoured the countryside, taking women and children hostage, mutilating slackers, and killing resisters. "The more gendarmes," said the Europeans, "the more rubber." The situation became so scandalous that in 1908 the Belgian state took over the Congo, a transition Leopold had long hoped for, but for years afterwards the tactics stayed the same. As a consequence, the fertile bottomland was gradually depopulated as tens of thousands died and more fled the region. By 1919, the Congo region had only half as many people as in 1880. The reformer Joseph

Conrad summed up Leopold's rule in his novel *Heart of Darkness* as "the horror of it," the dark side of Europe's glittering civilization.

The horror of concession rule in the Congo was matched by the tactics of concession rule in the other forest regions of western central Africa. In Angola, the Portuguese depended on large-scale slave raiding by the Ovimbundu to deliver labor for their plantations on São Tomé and Príncipe, and in Mozambique they chartered over half the colony to concession companies. The French parceled out equatorial Africa among 40 such companies, under whose control, as the ordinance regulating them stated, "One idea dominates the system. All the products of the concerned territory, whatever they may be, are the property of the concession company." The people had to either turn in ivory or rubber to fulfill their poll-tax or provide direct labor. The dark side of the latter possibility was indicated by the record of the French Congo-Ocean railroad construction project: of 127,250 men recruited to work, approximately one in six—20,000—died. "The news of a recruitment . . . created a 'panic terror' for it signified . . . a probable condemnation to death."

German East Africa was initially ruled by the German East Africa Company; in the German Cameroons, the South Cameroons Company received in 1898 about 20 million acres from which it could collect rubber without payment forever. The next year, the Northwest Cameroons Company got control of 20 percent of the entire colony. Abuses mounted rapidly, creating scandals back home, which led in turn to the end of concession rule in all the German colonies before the First World War. Similarly, the British terminated rule by the International British East Africa Company in Kenya and Uganda and the Royal Niger Company in eastern Nigeria before the First World War, and took over administration of the Rhodesias from the British South Africa Company in 1924. The French concessionary system lasted well into the 1920s, when the contracts were not renewed. Concession rule in Portuguese Mozambique lasted longest, surviving in one section until 1942.

Concession rule came to an end in some places because the demand for the particular product it supplied declined, as when the market for natural rubber collapsed because of competition from synthetic rubber. In a larger sense, it collapsed both because of its weakness and, ironically, because of its success. It was weak because it was a parasitical system in which the companies leeched off the Africans and the European governments leeched off the companies, with both returning as little as possible in order to maximize their short-term gains. In some cases, the companies devastated the economy they were trying to milk; in other cases, they provoked outraged intervention by politicians back home. The success, however, was that once the colonial armies had done the honorable work of breaking organized resistance, the companies did the dirty work of breaking the peoples' spirit, of transforming them from independent farmers and herders into cowering laborers. Once the companies had accomplished this task, the colonial system could leave them behind like a snake shedding its skin.

COLONIAL ADMINISTRATION

Concession rule was not only cruel, it was inefficient. The unrestrained pursuit of profit required substantial coercive force, and concession rule slowly ate away at its own underpinnings. Consequently, the European powers gradually curtailed it in favor of various forms of government-run administration. The goal was still the same—maximum returns for minimum investment—but colonial administrations recognized that the optimum balance was not at the extremes. The Europeans' desire for profit had to be weighed against the social, economic, and political realities of Africa.

While the specific systems implemented by the European powers differed in detail,

they all reflected the same basic structure. A thin stratum of colonial officials at the top of the political hierarchy connected the colony to the metropolitan (home-country) government, receiving instructions, transmitting information, and coordinating administration across the colonial territory. Beneath the Europeans lay a much larger stratum of collaborationist Africans—"colonial chiefs" and clerks—who mediated between the Europeans and the mass of Africans. Initially, this governmental apparatus was thin and generalized, with a few Europeans assisted by a handful of Africans administering all aspects of vast territories. As time went by, the systems became more bureaucratized, with specialized services and personnel radiating out from the colonial capital.

The primary difference between the colonial systems was in how they regarded the colonial chiefs. The most common system was dubbed "direct rule," mainly to contrast it with the alternative, "indirect rule." Direct rule was used by the French, Germans, Belgians, Portuguese, and even, in some cases, the British. In this system, European administration penetrated as deeply into African society as the number of European personnel allowed in order to run administration directly in accordance with colonial policies. Traditional African rulers were deliberately excluded from the system, and the Africans involved in administrative service were merely low-level functionaries. The government paid as much or as little attention to the people's needs as the metropolitan authorities chose. After the scandals of their early pacification campaigns, the Germans did the most to improve their colonies' infrastructure, building hospitals, schools, and transportation systems, while the Portuguese and Belgians did the least.

A variant of direct rule was the French policy of "assimilation." This doctrine stemmed from the values of "liberty, equality, and brotherhood" espoused by French liberalism, and argued that Africans should be regarded as potentially equal to Frenchmen, and should therefore be given the chance to become Frenchmen. The policy was first instituted in the oldest French colony, Senegal. During the Revolution of 1789, the Senegalese were given French citizenship and encouraged to acquire French culture. The degree of autonomy and integration offered by France varied over the nineteenth century as its different governments rose and fell, but in the 1870s the colony gained the right to choose a representative to the Chamber of Deputies in Paris, the right to choose a territorial General Council with the same local legislative responsibility as general councils in metropolitan French departments, and, in the four largest towns, the right to democratically elect a town council.

No other territories gained this degree of political integration with France, and the French moved toward a policy of "association" as they acquired more extensive, less digestible territories in the Islamic Sahel and the tropical forests. Individual assimilation, however, was held open more widely, contingent on the individual African's acquisition of the veneer of French civilization. The Portuguese adopted a similar system of individual and collective assimilation in Angola from 1910 to 1926.

In one sense, assimilation diverged from the general model of direct rule in that it went against the rigid hierarchy that placed the colonial office at the top and the ordinary African at the bottom. In another sense, assimilation was the logical conclusion of direct rule, in that it completely separated Africans from traditional government and authority and placed them, individually or collectively, squarely within a Eurocentric political community.

In contrast, French "association" was closer to the British theory of "indirect rule." This policy was based on the conviction that Africans were fundamentally different from Europeans, and rather than attempting to integrate them into a European system, European rule should be placed as lightly as possible on top of traditional government,

enabling the Africans to develop naturally and autonomously. Championed by the famous Lord Lugard in northern Nigeria, indirect rule worked best where Africans already lived in large, bureaucratic states like Nigeria, Benin, and Ghana in West Africa; Swaziland and Basutoland in southern Africa; Barotseland in Northern Rhodesia; and Buganda in Uganda. Even in these, the British usually had to depose the current ruler and install a more pliable one. In less complex societies, they often misunderstood the role of kings and chiefs, investing them with far more authority than traditionally ascribed. In other cases they had to create the office of chief altogether, imposing it along with its first occupant. As a consequence, while British anthropologists spent a great deal of effort trying to identify the traditional legitimate chiefs of many peoples, the chiefs they ended up with were often neither traditional nor, in the eyes of the people, particularly legitimate.

Considering that other Europeans also sought to reduce the draw on European personnel and the likelihood of native insurrection by using traditional authorities where they were pliable, the difference between direct and indirect rule in Africa was far smaller than it seemed in Europe.

THE TRANSFORMATION OF AFRICA

Regardless of the theory of government, colonial rule changed Africa profoundly. By fair means and foul, through conscious effort and unintended consequences, the Europeans forced Africans out of their traditional economic, social, and political relationships, creating a situation in which—however they might go forward—the Africans could never go back. Colonial rule lasted for about 75 years, a little more than two generations, but in that time it uprooted Africa's traditional social and political structures, robbed the continent of its economic self-sufficiency, and substituted a precarious dependence on international markets to sustain a chaotic, corrupt, and often violent modernity.

The root cause of this radical transformation was the Europeans' desire to make good on their investment in creating their colonial empires. In order to unlock the continent's potential wealth for the benefit of their own economies, they had to reshape Africa's economy, and in so doing they revolutionized its social systems, cultural forms, population patterns, and even its basic geography. They set in motion political changes that were ultimately to undo their empires.

On a physical level, the Europeans recast Africa's geography to make the continent's resources more accessible. Their engineers reshaped the harbors along the coast, building breakwaters and dredging channels to make them suitable for oceangoing ships. Along the waterfront, they created new anchorages, piers, and docks. Inland, they constructed railways to connect navigable sections of inland waterways, and later constructed entire rail lines to connect mining and plantation centers to the coast. In so doing, they redirected the principal lines of communication from internal African routes to connections between the interior and the sea.

Far more profound in their effect than these physical engineering projects were the Europeans' social and demographic engineering projects. Demographically, they sponsored the introduction of entire new populations to the African continent, and they opened it to penetration by others as well.

First and foremost among the new groups were their own settlers, whom the colonial governments hoped would become the backbone of the export economy, and to whom they therefore gave favored treatment wherever the climate seemed suitable for them. From the "white highlands" of Kenya to the English and Portuguese colonies of southern Africa to French North Africa, the European colonists received favorable terms on land, taxes, and labor policies.

In addition to their own settlers, the English brought Indians to Natal to work on their plantations and to Kenya and Uganda to help build a railroad. Further north on the east coast, Indian traders took advantage of the colonial system to expand their position as merchants and shopkeepers. These Indians became a significant minority in a number of colonies. On the west coast, a similar process brought significant numbers of Greeks and Lebanese into Africa, where they played a similar role as middlemen and retailers.

The continent's most profound changes followed from an economic policy that was deliberately intended to remold the Africans' way of life. In order to force Africans to work for the Europeans' mines, plantations, and export monopolies, the colonial governments imposed taxes. No longer could the majority of Africans depend on subsistence farming for their livelihood, for individuals who did not pay their taxes were compelled to perform labor. Communities that resisted were subject to raids and reprisals by soldiers or police. This policy originated with the Glen Gray Act of 1894 in the Cape Province, which stipulated that Africans had to pay 10 shillings per year unless they could prove that they had been "in service or employment beyond the borders of the district" for three months or more during the year. The idea of using taxes to compel Africans to enter the cash economy spread rapidly; by 1900 it was used widely, and by the 1920s it was the principal means by which Africans were pried from their traditional subsistence economy.

At its most benign, the annual tax simply accelerated the movement of African producers into cash cropping, particularly in West Africa, which was already the most commercially oriented section of the continent. Many West Africans became dependent on export-oriented farming, either as small-to-medium-scale farmers or as farm laborers. However, the Africans who owned farms found themselves hobbled by restrictions that forced them to sell to European firms, which cooperated with each other so they could buy the Africans' products at well below world prices, sell them for a profit, and keep the difference (reinvesting relatively little in Africa). The farm laborers became a permanent lower class. From roughly egalitarian peasant communities in which most members were autonomous freeholders, cash cropping areas evolved into highly stratified class societies.

In other parts of Africa, the need to secure money for taxes had even more destabilizing effects. Africans in areas that had scarcely known money suddenly found they needed it, and the only potential sources were distant mines and plantations. The male populations of entire communities began embarking on annual migrations to work in unsafe mines (and live in unsanitary camps), leaving the women, children, and old folk to farm as best they could. The southern Rhodesian mines, for example, employed 40,000 African men per year in the 1920s. About 1,000 of them lost their lives to accidents and disease, and their home villages suffered as well. "The whole fabric of the old order of society is undermined," an official report on Nyasaland stated in 1935, "when thirty to sixty percent of the able-bodied men are absent at one time." Migration, "which destroys the old, offers nothing to take its place, and the family-community is threatened with complete dissolution."

Migrant work offered the local community some compensations for the disruption it caused, especially the gradual introduction of useful and desirable foreign commodities like steel hoes, pots and pans, sewing machines, and bicycles. Furthermore, it broadened the horizons of both the migrants and, to a lesser extent, the people they related their stories to. It made them aware of their membership in larger communities that would ultimately take the place of village and clan. In particular, the migrants in the camps and slums found they were members of larger communities defined by similarities of language and customs— the roots of tribalism. Tribes had existed as political units only in certain areas of Africa prior to European contact because Africans had organized themselves into villages, age grades, and lineages that might or might not be part of a larger kingdom or empire composed of similar or diverse peoples. The colo-

nial governments began the process of tribalization by grouping together similar stateless societies to simplify administration, creating the biggest "tribe" in Tanganyika, for example, out of the "Sukuma," who until the colonial period were merely a collection of peoples referred to as "south" by their northern neighbors. The migrants continued this process, as men surrounded by strangers forged bonds with others who spoke languages and followed customs similar to their own, thereby creating tribal or home-boy associations. Tribalism, often seen as the bane of modern Africa, does not primarily represent the survival of precolonial forms, but rather a relatively recent expansion of communal identity.

The displaced Africans created a variety of other new social organizations: dance clubs, football leagues, burial and lending societies, and independent Christian churches. On a larger scale, they began to be aware of colonywide interests, the concept of nationalism, and a larger brotherhood with all other Africans called pan-Africanism. These wider-scale identifications were weak at first, but came over time to represent the major challenge to the colonial system. All these new forms of community, from the local social clubs to the brotherhood of all Africans, represented adjustments to the profoundly destabilizing impact of European colonialism.

While the Europeans' economic policies had a wide-ranging impact on African society, they also had immediate and direct impact on the continent's traditional commerce and industry. Since the colonial powers sought to maximize profits from their colonies, they promoted development that favored their own citizens at the expense of Africans. Where European settlers started plantations, the government prohibited Africans from growing competitive crops. Where the Europeans engaged in mining, they imported heavy machinery that rapidly put independent African miners out of business. Where African businesses engaged in commerce, they competed against gigantic international firms with close ties to colonial and European governments.

Where European merchants sold Europe's manufactured goods, they undersold traditional producers and drove them out of business. Africans who sought to meet these challenges by modernizing their own operations found that they could not get help from the colonial government or credit from European banks, and those Africans who worked for Europeans were seldom in a position to learn technical skills or modern business practices. The colonial economies existed to transfer wealth from Africa to Europe, and the Europeans invested only the minimum and only in ways that furthered that process.

Despite European claims that their presence would help develop Africa, they drew wealth out of the continent, reinvested little, and increased the continent's relative backwardness and perhaps even its absolute poverty. People whose ancestors had been self-sufficient farmers became wage laborers; people whose ancestors had been prosperous merchants became marginal traders; people whose ancestors had been mighty rulers became minor officials. Even people whose ancestors had been slaves were often no better off; an Italian official in Somalia wrote in 1930 that the methods of forced labor were "a good deal worse than slavery." The reason, he said, was that a master had a stake in the health of a slave, but "when a Somali native dies after being given to an employer . . . the employer simply asks the government to give him another."

The process of impoverishment began in the first decades of the twentieth century, as the Europeans established their hold on their colonies, and was greatly accelerated by the Great Depression of the 1930s. The mass of Africans, so recently forced into the cash economy, were ill prepared for the collapse in world prices for their export goods, and the colonial governments gave none of the aid that they extended to their workers at home. They saw the colonies as a source of relief for the metropolitan economy, and imposed imperial protection schemes that raised prices on imported goods and drove small native producers out of the export market. As the Depression eased in the late 1930s, some of the colonizers began aid for development programs, but the development was targeted at European enterprises like railroads and ports, and the loans saddled the colonies with substantial debts.

The Second World War brought renewed hardships. As hundreds of thousands of men were drawn away to the armies, world trade was once again disrupted, and metropolitan governments strained to keep afloat. Peace brought new problems in the form of an accelerating population growth and uncontrolled migration to urban slums and shantytowns. The incipient population explosion was an ironic outcome of one of the Europeans' humanitarian successes, the introduction of public health measures. Unfortunately, the stagnant colonial economies could not support the increasing numbers of people, and the long-imposed policy of growing crops for export rather than for internal comsumption made the problem even worse. As Africa moved into the second half of the twentieth century, the debilitating effects of the colonial system were creating an explosive situation.

The colonial tinderboxes needed only a spark to blow off the lid, and that spark was provided by a final product of the colonial system—a small but influential educated elite. In large part, this elite was the product of the Christian missionary effort, which sought to lure converts by offering the rudimentary education that gave native youth entrée to the lower levels of the colonial bureaucracy. There were few members of the educated elite, for the proportion of children offered an education ranged from 1 in 10 in the advanced British and French colonies to less than 1 in 100 in the Portuguese areas. The education they received was scanty—mainly reading, writing, and religion, with a little European history and possibly one or two other subjects in the upper grades, which only a small fraction of native students ever reached.

And yet, despite the limited nature of the education, these "school-leavers," and the tiny minority who went on to secondary schools and even to universities in Europe and America, formed the new elite, the point of contact between the mass of Africans and the ideas of the modern world. And just as the mass of Africans had growing discontents with the colonial systems, so, too, did the educated elite. The Europeans either monopolized political power entirely or, where they permitted African institutions a role, conferred it on the traditional (or pseudo-traditional) upper class. The new elite's discontents proved to be the spark that eventually set off the powderkeg.

THE RISE OF AFRICAN NATIONALISM

African gropings for modern forms of political power date back even before the colonial era. Muhammad 'Ali in Egypt and the Husainid dynasty in Tunisia attempted to form modern states in the mid-nineteenth century; the Ethiopian emperors Theodore, John, and Melinik succeeded in reforming that medieval empire and making it capable of defeating a European power. The American freedmen in Liberia ruled an independent country after 1847, the Senegalese in the "four communes" came to regard themselves as part of the nation of France, and leaders in Sierra Leone began to look critically on the British and on their own society. A young Somali, the Sayyid Muhamad Abdille Hasan, united most of the Somali clans in a 20-year revolt against all the colonial occupiers in the first two decades of the twentieth century; a Moroccan, Abd al-Krim al-Khattabi, led a revolt against the Spanish and French in his country in 1920 that required six years and hundreds of thousands of men to put down. The Sayyid is remembered as the founder of independent Somalia, while Abd al-Krim consciously attempted to forge a modern state.

One of the earliest advocates of African nationalism was Edward Blyden, a West Indian scholar who emigrated to Liberia in 1851. He asserted that "I believe nationality to be an ordinance of nature" and argued that the Africans formed one of the principal peoples of the world, different from but equal to the others, and making their own special contributions to human progress. While not modern nationalism in the strictest sense, this perspective helped spawn a complementary ideology, pan-Africanism, which inspired a series of conferences from 1900 to 1945 that brought together African and African-American leaders and led ultimately to the Organization of African Unity. Founded in 1963, this organization of African states continues to provide an official forum for pan-African issues and activities today.

James Africanus Beale Horton, a native of Sierra Leone writing in the 1860s, called for a more focused African national development growing out of traditional kingdoms and ethnic groups. Asserting that differences between Europeans and Africans reflected historical and environmental circumstances rather than innate abilities, he argued that as Africans developed they would naturally transform their existing polities into modern nations. One group, the Fante Confederation, actually tried to put his ideas into practice, creating a formal constitution in 1871, but the state did not survive the rivalry between the Asante and the English.

The decisive movement, however, was a new nationalism, defined within the Europeans' colonial boundaries. This nationalism began not with a grand theory, but out of practical efforts to reform colonial administration. The Aboriginal Rights Protection Society, founded in 1897 in the Gold Coast, was the first African organization created for this purpose, and it succeeded in blocking the expropriation and sale of forestland to European companies. Only 14 years later, in 1911, S.R.B. Attoh Ahuma codified this political activism in *The Gold Coast Nation and National Consciousness*.

The next major African political success came in 1914, when Blaise Diagne became the first black to win a seat in the French Chamber of Deputies. He used this position to reverse the gradual erosion of the communes' political standing in exchange for his help in mobilizing Africans for service in the French army in World War I. However, he ceased to promote reforms after the war and became, in fact, a prominent defender of the French empire in exchange for a secure position in colonial politics. While his initial work advanced the Africans' political situation, he ended his career as an object of derision to many African nationalists.

Although Diagne's defection disillusioned many of his followers, World War I proved a watershed for African nationalism. Even as the colonial powers completed their subjugation of the rural hinterlands, the leading figures in the towns were imbibing the promises of national self-determination promoted by the victorious Allies. The pan-Africanists who met in Paris during the peace talks in 1919 succeeded in persuading the victors to treat the German colonies as League of Nations mandates, and a host of reformist and even radical organizations appeared in Africa during the next two decades.

In French West Africa, impatient rivals challenged Diagne throughout the 1920s. In Tunisia, the Destour Party, which called for a return to the pre-French constitution of 1860, took the initiative from the reformist Young Tunisian Party, which had been founded just six years before. To the east, three parties had existed in Egypt since 1906, and a new one, the Wafd, began calling for independence in 1918. The British, who had never been keen to rule Egypt anyway, granted the Wafd's desire in 1922, but they kept control of the Suez Canal, Egypt's defenses, and the Sudan (nominally ruled by Great Britain and Egypt jointly), and they took responsibility for protecting foreign interests in the country.

In British East Africa, the post-war years saw the rise of a series of political parties, particularly among the Kikuyu people, who were the most affected by the expropriation of land for white settlers. The Kikuyu Association appeared in 1920, and the next year Harry Thuku started the East Africa Association. He argued that the colonial government's role was just "to steal the property of the Kikuyu." The Young Kikuyu Association, formed in 1921, explicitly rejected white rule, as did the Young Kavirondo Association, formed in 1922. The latter group and the East Africa Association protested pass laws and other means of settler control inspired by South Africa. The police fired on a crowd demonstrating against the arrest of Harry Thuku in 1922, which led to the demise of his party. It was replaced in 1924 by the Kikuyu Central Association, which led a vigorous campaign starting in 1929 to retain the traditional rite of female circumcision against the opposition of European missionaries.

In British West Africa, Herbert Macaulay formed the first Nigerian political party, the Nigerian National Democratic Party, in 1923. He also led a movement that agitated from 1920 until 1932 for the reinstatement of the Eleko of Lagos, who had been dethroned by the British for refusing to cooperate with them in disputes over land usage and water rights. During the same years, J. E. Casely Hayford led the National Council of British West Africa in lobbying for African representation in the colonial legislative councils, opportunities for higher education, and employment in the civil service. These efforts scored some successes, for the British finally reinstated the Eleko, created Achimota College, increased African representation on some colonial and municipal councils, and promised civil-service reform.

The promised civil-service opportunities did not materialize, however, and the Africans on the councils remained isolated minorities; the frustration of the educated Africans involved in these reform movements increased as time went by. By the 1930s, at least some reformers were ready for more militant tactics. In 1935, I.T.A. Wallace-Johnson founded the West African Youth League on the principle of "new ideas and new vision; new determination and will." Three years later, the militant Nigerian Youth Movement beat Macauley's NNDP in elections, calling for "a complete take-over of the Government into the hands of the indigenous people of our country." In Tunisia, the New Destour arose in 1934 with a similar attitude, and like the other groups, it looked beyond the educated elite to the broad mass of people for support.

These educated reformers met opposition not only from colonial administrators, but also from traditional rulers, whose positions were threatened and who argued that they, not the new elite, were the legitimate voice of the people. Also, when the reformers became unruly, some of their more conservative peers turned against them as well. But the majority of Africans below them in the social order supported them. If anything, they wanted the reformers to be more assertive and more rebellious; for during the years that these "lawyer-merchants" pursued their polite reformism, the African masses began to flex their collective muscle. It was their support that in the end proved decisive.

Although popular resistance to colonialism went back to its earliest imposition, modern forms of collective action date from the years just after World War I. Workers began to organize trade unions and to strike in the Gold Coast, Senegal, and Tunisia in the 1920s, and in Kenya and the northern Rhodesian copperbelt in the 1930s. Riots against the rising costs of goods broke out in Sierra Leone in 1919 and in Dahomey in 1922. In 1929, Igbo market women in eastern Nigeria, incensed by rumors of a new tax during a time of declining commodity prices, attacked the canteens of the monopolies in a series of riots known as the "Women's War." The next year, Gold Coast cocoa producers tried to hold back production to force better prices from the buying firms; although this action failed initially, a second attempt in 1938 succeeded.

The most radical activity appeared in Algeria or, more properly, among Algerians in France. Unable to find work at home, over 18,000 Algerians had migrated to France by the mid-1920s, and in 1926 Messali Hadj began organizing a party called the *Étoile Nord-Africaine*, or North African Star. The first anticolonial party led by and composed of ordinary workers rather than lawyers and merchants, it was also the first to switch from a call for reforms to a call for independence. Membership grew in France and then in Algeria, beginning a process that would end only after a long and bitter struggle.

THE CONDITIONS OF DECOLONIZATION

World War II had a profound impact on colonizers and colonized alike, setting in train a series of developments that led to the rapid dismantling of the European empires.

The first effect actually occurred before the war began. As part of the lead-up to it, Fascist Italy invaded Ethiopia and conquered it in a brutal campaign marked by the use of aerial bombardment and poison gas. Africans across the continent were outraged by this revival of crass imperialism, and they were further incensed by the Western powers' refusal to help Ethiopia. Although the League of Nations imposed an embargo on Italy, the embargo did not include oil. Worse still, the British, who condemned the invasion, nonetheless allowed the Italians to move troops and supplies through the Suez Canal, and the Western powers recognized Italy's conquest within a year. The effect was "a new awareness of Europe's growing strangle-hold on Africa," and thus "to a great extent, the Ethiopian question played a part in awakening a new generation of West African nationalists."

Once the war began, the western Allies' claim that the basic issue was freedom versus tyranny had a meaning to Africans that the Allies had not entirely foreseen. In particular, the Atlantic Charter forged by American

President Franklin Roosevelt and British Prime Minister Winston Churchill promised self-determination for all peoples. Churchill later attempted to repudiate the implications of that promise, but Roosevelt insisted it meant what it said, and colonized peoples everywhere seized on it. As a Nigerian soldier wrote to Herbert Macaulay early in 1945, "We have been told what we fought for. That is 'freedom'. We want freedom, nothing but freedom."

Besides extracting promises from the Allies, the war also revealed and increased European weaknesses. In 1940, Nazi armies crushed France in a lightning campaign, occupying most of the country and reducing the rest to a dependency. Even more stunning, Japan inflicted a devastating series of defeats on British forces in the Far East the next year, shattering forever the Europeans' myth of their inherent superiority over the rest of humankind. These events emboldened the colonized peoples in Europe's empires and revealed the real limits to European power. Both France and Great Britain had been strategically overextended before the war, and the early defeats as well as the cost of final victory further weakened the colonizers.

By the end of the war, the European powers were shadows of their former selves, drained and devastated. Primacy in the postwar international world fell to the new superpowers, the United States and the Soviet Union. The latter opposed colonialism in an effort to weaken the capitalist states, while the former opposed it both as an affront to American ideals and as an obstacle to American commerce. The new United Nations also opposed colonialism, but continued and extended the League of Nations mandates over certain colonial territories. U.N. trusteeships contained explicit provisions requiring colonial powers to report annually, allowing colonized people to send delegations to the United Nations, and declaring the purpose of the trusteeships to be preparing colonized peoples for eventual independence.

At most immediate issue were the former Italian colonies. The victorious powers could not agree on which should get trusteeship of Libya, so it became independent in 1951. They agreed to let Italy have Somalia back, but only for 10 years, until 1960. Eritrea went to Ethiopia as an autonomous region, although after 10 years the Ethiopians reneged on the agreement and absorbed it as an ordinary province.

By the end of the war, both the British and the French realized they would have to treat their colonies differently. They changed from resisting labor unions to promoting them and began planning for African participation in politics. The French saw this new approach in terms of greater rights within the French empire, at least initially, but the British saw it in terms of eventual freedom. They began their retreat from empire in southern Asia, where India, Pakistan, Ceylon (which became Sri Lanka), and Burma became independent in 1947. With India gone, the reason for retaining de facto control of Egypt was gone as well. Although the British evacuated most of the country after the war, they insisted on keeping control of the Suez Canal. They also insisted on keeping control of the Sudan, believing that the Egyptians would annex it against the wishes of the Sudanese. Great Britain granted the Sudan independence in 1956 once Egypt agreed to give up its claims. As for the rest of the continent, the British saw independence as something that would come only after decades.

Developments within Africa threw over the plans of both the British and the French, bringing about decolonization over the course of years rather than decades. Ironically, one of the contributing factors was increased European investment, for the Europeans had huge wartime debts to the United States. The Americans had little interest in European goods, but much interest in African raw materials controlled by the Europeans. The Europeans' heightened hopes for Africa led to many salutary investments like tarmac roads, public health, and education, but also to less fortunate developments like the promotion of cash crops at the expense of foodstuffs, the accelerated flight of impoverished peasants to the already overcrowded cities, and the increased immigration of European settlers.

As a consequence, unrest among the African masses increased during the post-war period. Miners and railroad workers in Northern Rhodesia struck in 1945, and three years later they formed unions. Strikes by dockworkers in Lagos in Nigeria in 1945 and Dar es Salaam in Tanganyika in 1947 spread along the rail lines to become general strikes. African railroad workers in French West Africa struck for four months in 1947 against racist pay differentials and achieved their goal. A strike in Tunisia that same year ended with the death of 32 workers and defeat for the union that called it. A demonstration by ex-soldiers in the Gold Coast in 1948 also ended in bloodshed after police opened fire and was followed by days of rioting that shook British confidence in their policies in this "model colony."

A general strike brought Nairobi, Kenya, to a standstill in 1950, and in the same year a controversial plan by British agricultural officials to eradicate swollen shoot disease by destroying the entire cocoa crop provoked widespread resistance. Agricultural ordinances, no matter how modern and well-meaning, were opposed by African farmers—in Tanganyika, Rhodesia, and Nyasaland particularly. These areas also saw widespread resistance to administratively imposed chiefs and to taxes; by the late 1950s, the British were hardly able to collect any taxes in Tanganyika.

The most serious peasant unrest, however, was armed uprisings in Madagascar (1947–1948), Kenya (1952–1955), and the Cameroons (1955–1958). The troubles in Madagascar began in 1946 when the nationalist party MRDM won two seats in the French National Assembly and openly called for Madagascan self-government as a step towards independence. The French government, influenced by the island's large settler population, moved to suppress the party, but sparked a widespread rebellion in the countryside in 1947. The French had to dispatch a large army to re-establish control, at a cost of tens of thousands of African lives.

Similarly, the uprising in the Cameroons began when the French tried to suppress a popular and successful nationalist party, the UPC (Union of the Populations of Cameroons). Just as in Madagascar, the French settler population, which had grown rapidly after the war, pushed the government to destroy the nationalists. After six years of repression (1948–1954), the UPC retreated to the countryside and recruited a guerrilla army, which fought against the French into the late 1950s. The party's founder was killed in 1958 and his successor two years later, so the French were able to set up other, more pliable politicians as the benefactors of independence.

In Kenya, conflicts between Africans and settlers over land and long-term control of the colony brought escalating violence that culminated in 1952 in the proclamation of a state of emergency and the arrest of prominent nationalists. Thousands of young men and women thereupon fled into the mountains and launched a bitter guerrilla war that took the British four years and 100,000 troops to suppress. About 100 Europeans and 10,000 Africans lost their lives.

The most vicious and brutal decolonization struggle occurred in Algeria, where the French were determined to stay. Settlers, who numbered over one million, controlled one-third of the colony's arable land (while comprising about 10 percent of the population), and totally dominated the government, denying the Algerians not only political influence but cultural autonomy and economic security as well. In the 10 years after 1945, legal Algerian nationalist protests met nothing but ruthless repression, so young Algerians organized an armed insurgency in 1954. After initial successes against the 200,000 colonial forces, the rebels lost ground as the French adapted to counterinsurgency warfare and increased their forces to over 500,000. By 1960, the rebels had almost lost on the battlefield, but a series of massive demonstrations in cities and towns showed that they commanded the allegiance of the Algerian masses. As resolve in metropolitan France weakened, the settlers turned to a terrorist campaign in France that rapidly alienated French public opinion and led to Algerian independence in 1962. The struggle cost over one million Algerian lives, and left a bitter legacy in both Algeria and France.

In all these cases, strong links existed between the rural rebels and a nationalist party. This connection points up a larger fact about decolonization: mass political action played a crucial role. In virtually every colony, the postwar period saw the rise of broader-based nationalist parties out of or in place of the earlier parties formed by the "lawyer-merchant" elite. These parties were generally not true mass parties, but they adopted a populist tone that enabled them to position themselves as the representatives and leaders of the ordinary people. This new, apparently mass militancy served the elite nationalists in two ways. First, mass action provided political, and in some cases military, muscle to the nationalist cause, demonstrating that it was a growing force whose suppression would require a prohibitively expensive commitment of resources by the colonial powers. Second, the growth of mass action and the appearance of radicals prepared to lead it created the danger that the older, politically oriented nationalism would be superseded by newer movements with more radical social and economic programs that would pose a much graver danger to European economic and strategic interests than would independence. Viewed in this light, the political nationalists began to look like moderates, and where settler interests did not distort their vision, the colonial powers rapidly came to see their long-term interests as best served by accommodation with them.

Of course, this calculation revealed the long-term flaw in the anticolonial alliance. The elite nationalists generally aimed at political independence as an end in itself, as their opportunity to take their place at the head of their nations. The mass of people, in contrast, saw independence mainly as a means to an end, as a step along the road to achieving a better life. As long as opposition to the colonial power united them, this difference did not matter; but once independence came, it became an increasingly divisive factor in African political life.

In the short run, both before and after independence, the divergent goals of the masses and the elite were muted by the influence of a generation of charismatic leaders. In virtually every colony, the rise of a "mass" party occurred under the leadership of a single outstanding individual. In many cases, this same individual went on to become the newly independent state's first president. Jomo Kenyatta, for example, led the Kenya African Union (KAU) during the Mau Mau uprising and went on to become the first president of Kenya, ruling from 1963 until his death in 1978. In neighboring Tanganyika, Julius Nyerere founded the Tanganyika African National Union (TANU) in 1954, assumed the presidency of the new country upon its independence in 1961, and remained in that position until he voluntarily stepped down in 1985. Across the continent, Kwame Nkrumah founded the Convention People's Party in the Gold Coast to lead the struggles against the British and became the first president upon independence. Similarly, in French West Africa, Leopold Senghor of Senegal, Sekou Toure of Guinea, and Felix Houphouet-Boigny of the Ivory Coast led the anticolonial struggles and went on to preside over their newly independent countries, as did Habib Bourghiba of Tunisia and Ahmed Ben Bella of Algeria. Kenneth Kaunda of Zambia, H. K. Banda of Malawi, Agostinho Neto of Angola, and Robert Mugabe of Zimbabwe did the same in their countries.

THE PROCESS OF DECOLONIZATION

Against the background of metropolitan weakness, geo-political realignment, nationalist agitation, popular unrest, and nascent radicalism, Africa's outlook changed in a few short years from indefinite colonialism to imminent independence. The movement toward independence began in northeastern Africa, with Egypt, the Sudan, and the former Italian colonies of Libya and Somalia. In eastern North Africa, France granted both Tunisia and Morocco independence in 1956 in order to concentrate on the war in Algeria, but the sacrifice was in vain since France was forced to recognize Algerian independence in 1962.

South of the Sahara, the first crack appeared in the Gold Coast, where the British were shocked by the riots following the soldier's demonstration in 1948. By 1951, they had agreed to a process of gradual devolution leading to full independence in 1957. Elsewhere in British West Africa, a series of constitutions increased African participation in the government in Nigeria throughout the 1950s; independence came to Nigeria in 1960. A similar process brought independence to Sierra Leone in 1961 and the Gambia in 1965. The British calculated that it was better to grant political independence under conditions allowing continued economic domination than to hold on and risk losing everything, a policy which radicals dubbed "neo-colonialism."

Independence came more suddenly to French Africa, but at just about the same time. Liberalization began during the Second World War at the Brazzaville Conference, where de Gaulle's government-in-exile promised an end to forced labor and a beginning to wider African participation in government, albeit within the firm framework of a French Union, once the Allies won the war. The promise was fulfilled in the French constitution of 1946, which allowed many Africans to vote in elections for the French National Assembly and the Assembly of the French Union. The Africans used the opportunity to form political parties, which joined together in the interterritorial African Democratic Assembly (RDA). This organization began as a nationalist opposition movement but moved toward cooperation with the French as they moved toward acceptance of African nationalism. The first preparations for eventual independence came in 1956, when the French parliament passed the *loi-cadre*, which established 12 territorial assemblies responsible for local government in place of the two large units of French West Africa and French Equatorial Africa. The franchise was universal, a notable liberalization, but the most significant effect was to ensure that independence would come to 12 small and weak states rather than two large and potentially powerful ones.

Charles de Gaulle took the final step after he came to power, despite the fact that his mandate was to preserve the French empire in the face of the Algerian revolution. He quickly recognized the wisdom of accommodating the new nationalism south of the Sahara, and, even more than the British, consciously chose to cut France's political ties to Africa in order to preserve its economic and strategic ones. In 1958, he offered the French territories a choice between immediate, unconditional independence without further French technical or financial aid, or independence in two years as part of a larger French community that would maintain strong *de jure* French influence over the economy, defense, and foreign policy, and strong *de facto* French influence over national politics. Only Guinea, under Sekou Toure, opted for immediate independence, and the French responded by pulling out all their personnel, including the businessmen, teachers, technicians, and doctors, taking all the equipment and administrative records they could move, and destroying what they could not take. They even went so far as to burn the medicines they could not evacuate. The rest of the French empire—Cameroon, the Central African Republic, Chad, the Congo (Brazzaville), Benin, Gabon, Ivory Coast, Madagascar, Mali, Mauritania, Niger, Senegal, Togo, and Upper Volta—all became independent in 1960, leaving only Mauritius, the Comoros, and Djbouti to follow in 1968, 1975,

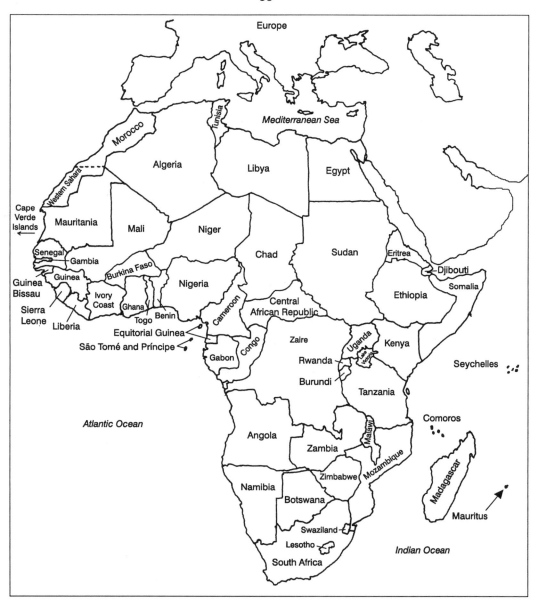

Africa in 1996

and 1977, respectively. The island of Mayotte in the Comoros broke away from the others to remain a dependency of France.

If independence came abruptly to French Africa, it came rudely to the Belgian Congo. Up until the mid-1950s, the Belgians maintained that they were in the Congo to stay, and they did virtually nothing to prepare the Congolese for self-rule or independence. In fact, aware of the corrosive effects of education on the British and French empires, they deliberately kept the Congolese down, denying all but a handful more than elementary instruction, and restricting them to the lowest levels of administration. In the mid-1950s, the Belgians began to make extremely modest changes, allowing African representation in local government and permitting elections for the councils of major cities. The winds of change blew hard through these cracks, and by 1959 the Belgian government faced widespread and vehement calls for democracy and early independence from an array of regional and national Congolese parties. Late that year, the Belgians announced that a conference would be held in January 1960 with the express purpose of setting the conditions for independence before the end of the year. It met as scheduled, drew up a constitution, and set elections for May and independence for June 30. The elections revealed that regionalism and tribalism far outweighed any sense of nationalism, and the weeks before independence saw the virtual breakdown of government authority. Less than two weeks after independence, tribal disorders broke out, the army mutinied, and the country's wealthiest province tried to secede. The beginning was inauspicious, setting the stage for even worse to come.

The same situation was true for the two trust territories, Rwanda and Burundi, which the Belgians had ruled since taking them from Germany in World War I. In these two tiny statelets, they had practiced "divide and rule" by setting up the Tutsi minority as the favored faction and ruling the Hutu majority through it. When the Belgians granted independence in 1962, they left behind political conditions that soon led to bloody cycles of repression and rebellion that have continued down to today.

If the Belgians left too quickly, the Portuguese held on too long. Afraid that they did not have the economic clout to ensure continued economic dominance without political control, strongly influenced by the settler lobby, and tied to the notion that colonies made them an important power, the Portuguese dug in against the tide of nationalism, refusing to budge until guerrilla wars in Angola and Mozambique exhausted the nation and discredited the dictatorship in Lisbon. An army coup in 1974 led to a republican government that granted independence to Guinea-Bissau that year and to Angola, Mozambique, the Cape Verde Islands, and São Tomé and Príncipe the next.

In contrast to this bitter struggle, most of Great Britain's colonies in eastern and southern Africa gained freedom relatively easily once the Mau Mau rebellion in Kenya had been crushed. Tanganyika was the first, in 1961, and Uganda followed the next year. Kenya and Zanzibar gained independence in 1963, with Zanzibar merging peacefully with Tanganyika to form Tanzania almost immediately. In the 1950s, nationalists in Northern Rhodesia and Nyasaland successfully staved off a regional union with Southern Rhodesia, which would have led to settler domination, and the two colonies emerged in 1964 as Zambia and Malawi. Botswana and Lesotho followed in 1966, Swaziland in 1967, Mauritius in 1968, and the Seychelles in 1976.

The exception to this peaceful transition was Rhodesia. The settler-dominated government issued a Unilateral Declaration of Independence with South African backing in 1965 in order to perpetuate the rule of 6 million blacks by 250,000 whites. A bitter guerrilla war ensued, tied in with the war against Portugal in neighboring Mozambique. The end of the war next door was the beginning of the end for white rule in Rhodesia. Now surrounded on three sides by black-ruled states, the whites tried to set up a joint government with an African party in 1978, but the guerrilla war continued. In 1980, the country officially returned to colonial status so that the British could administer an election, which swept in the two guerrilla parties and set the stage for the country's formal independence.

Spain gave up its small African empire gradually and without much bloodshed. When France left Morocco in 1956, Spain had no choice but to follow suit. A brief attempt to absorb the island of Fernando Po and the tiny enclave of Rio Muni into metropolitan Spain only led to increased nationalist agitation, so they were given independence as the Republic of Equatorial Guinea in 1968. Spain withdrew from its last major holding on the continent, the Western Sahara, in 1975, leaving it for Morocco, Mauritania, and the Western Saharans themselves to fight over. Today, Spain retains control of two ports, Ceuta and Melilla, on the Moroccan Mediterranean coast, and the Canary Islands off Morocco in the Atlantic Ocean.

The last colonial area to become independent was Namibia, the former German colony of Southwest Africa, which had been entrusted to South Africa by a League of Nations mandate after World War I. South Africa retained control of the area even though the International Court of Justice declared its occupation illegal in 1971, and used it as a base for intervention in Angola during that country's civil war. When Angola used Cuban aid to put an end to South Africa's interference in 1988, Cuba tied its own withdrawal to South African withdrawal from Namibia. Heavily pressured by the United States, South Africa agreed, and in 1989 the Cubans went home while the Namibians conducted a free and fair election. Namibia declared itself independent and joined the community of nations the next year. Although Eritrea and the Western Sahara remained occupied by African states claiming them as provinces, the continent's colonial interlude was clearly over by the start of the 1990s.

PART

2

THE NATIONS OF AFRICA

Introduction to Part 2

Africa contains 53 sovereign states, the largest number by far of any world region. In the early 1970s, when there were only 43, the American Secretary of State Henry Kissinger complained that it was impossible to form a coherent policy toward the continent because of its diversity. The same problem of diversity challenges anyone who tries to understand the African continent.

To ease this challenge, Part 2 considers each country separately, tracing its roots in the precolonial past, its colonial experience, and its trials and tribulations since independence. While each country has its own unique story, three almost universal themes emerge from the following discussions. One is increasing poverty, a difficulty almost all African economies are experiencing as they attempt to keep pace with population growth. The second is ethnic conflict, which bedevils almost every country to some degree. The third is multiparty democracy. Every African nation has experienced some pressure to institute a multiparty political system, and most have made some attempt to do so. The effects of these issues on each country can be seen in the discussions in Part 2, and are also explored more generally in Part 3 in Chapter 15.

CHAPTER

North Africa

INTRODUCTION

North Africa contains the five countries along the continent's northern coast: Egypt, Libya, Tunisia, Algeria, and Morocco. The bulk of the people in these countries live in the fertile strips along the Mediterranean coast, while the bulk of their territory consists of empty desert to the south. These countries are united by history and culture as well as geography, for the Arabs conquered them in the ninth century, converted them to Islam, and drew them into the larger Arab world. Today they are as much a part of the Middle East as of Africa. They have all felt the pressure of the democratization movement that has swept Africa, but none has made much progress toward multiparty democracy. They have also felt the pressure of the fundamentalist movement that has swept the Moslem world. None has a fundamentalist government. Algeria lacks one only because its military refused to honor an election won by a fundamentalist party and is currently in upheaval as a result. Egypt's authoritarian government is grappling with a fundamentalist insurgency, and Tunisia's government keeps tight control of the

country to avoid a resurgence of the troubles that arose in 1990. Libya remains under the tight control of its revolutionary leader, Muammar Gaddafy, and Morocco's King Hassan remains in firm control of his country. His annexation of Western Sahara is opposed by an armed movement there as well as by the world community, but he has gone a long way toward establishing it as a fact.

EGYPT
Statistical Profile

Capital:	Cairo
Area:	386,660 sq. miles
Population:	58,900,000 (1994 est.)
Density:	152 people/sq. mile
Growth Rate:	2.3% (1994 est.)
GDP:	$33,553,000,000
Per Capita Income:	$630
Foreign Debt:	$36,425,000,000
Life Expectancy:	46 (1960), 62 (1992)
Ethnic Groups:	Muslim Egyptian majority with Coptic Christian minority
Official Language:	Arabic
Religions:	Muslim (90%), Coptic Christian (7%)

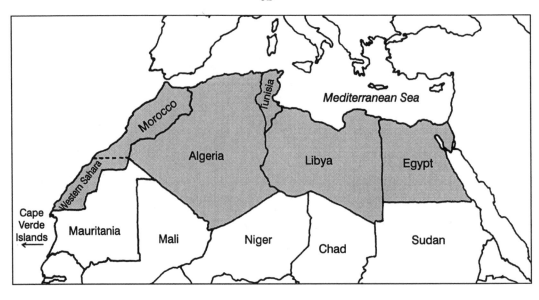

North Africa

Former Colonizer:	Great Britain
Date of Independence:	1922

History

Egypt's recorded history goes back farther than any other African country (see Chapter 1). In the nineteenth century, its failed modernization efforts and consequent slide into bankruptcy helped set off the scramble for Africa (Chapter 3), but ironically Great Britain never ruled Egypt in the way that it and the other European powers ruled the rest of Africa. A formal protectorate lasted only from 1914 to 1922, and both before and afterwards the Egyptians enjoyed most of the outward trappings of nationhood.

Nevertheless, both before and after the protectorate, British dominance was real, and the Egyptians knew it. In 1936, the two countries agreed to a 20-year treaty that reduced but by no means eliminated British control, as was demonstrated in 1941 when the British forced King Farouk to install a pro-British government against his wishes. Postwar economic problems coupled with royal profligacy, ministerial corruption, and constant British meddling fueled popular discontent, and the

Egyptian defeat at the hands of the Israelis in 1948 completed the discrediting of the old regime. Moslem conservatives and students openly agitated against the government, and a group of officers conspired secretly against it.

In 1952, bloody rioting in Cairo set the stage for a coup by the discontented army officers. They forced the king to abdicate, abolished the constitution, outlawed political parties, proclaimed a republic, and installed Brigadier General Muhammad Neguib as president and premier. Within two years, a younger officer, Gamal Abdel Nasser, forced Neguib out and took his place. Nasser then negotiated a phased withdrawal of British troops from their last bastions along the Suez Canal, ending British domination of Egypt for good.

Egypt's revolutionary rulers led the new republic in a leftward direction—implementing an agrarian reform program at the cost of the powerful landlord class, confiscating the king's estates outright, and pursuing a non-aligned foreign policy. The United States and Great Britain, thinking in terms of their global rivalry with the Soviet Union, perceived this neutralism as hostility. In mid-1956, they withdrew an offer to help finance a huge new dam at Aswan, which was the centerpiece of Egypt's economic development program. Humiliated, Nasser trumped them a week later by nationalizing the Suez Canal, saying that he needed its revenue to finance the dam. The British responded in turn by attempting to retake control of the Canal in concert with France, the other major shareholder, and Israel, which wanted to retaliate for guerrilla attacks from Egypt. The United States refused to back this revival of colonialism and the invaders had to withdraw.

Thereafter, Nasser moved closer to the Soviet Union in both internal and external policy, although he never formally renounced nonalignment, and he gradually emerged as the foremost leader of the Arab world. Within Egypt, he instituted further land reform in 1964 to combat rural poverty, gradually increased state dominance of the industrial and commercial sectors of the economy, enacted a series of social welfare measures to improve the lot of the working class, and created a new party of workers and peasants, the Arab Socialist Union, to solidify his political position. Abroad, he combined dependence on Soviet arms supplies with leadership of the Arabs, forming the United Arab Republic with Syria from 1958 until 1961, intervening in the Yemeni Civil War between 1962 and 1966, and promoting various pan-Arab schemes in the mid-1960s. These initiatives culminated in 1967 when he supported Syria and Jordan in a dispute with Israel by closing the Straits of Hormuz to Israeli shipping, thereby setting off the Six Day War.

Israel routed the Egyptians and the other Arab states. The defeat cost Egypt the Sinai Peninsula and threw its economy into a tailspin. Nasser reversed Egypt's previous policy by accepting UN Resolution 242, which recognized Israel's right to exist, because it also called for the return of the Sinai. However, he continued the military struggle through an undeclared "War of Attrition" in 1969 and 1970 even though Egypt could ill-afford the

continued drain on its economy. He had just accepted a peace plan advanced by American Secretary of State William Rogers when he suddenly died in September 1970.

Nasser's successor, Anwar Sadat, slowly reversed Egypt's direction in the years that followed. In foreign policy, he began by renewing the conflict with Israel, launching a surprise attack on Yom Kippur in 1973 that succeeded in throwing the Israelis back from the positions they had held along the Canal since 1967. A hastily contrived cease-fire barely prevented an Israeli counterattack from inflicting another crushing defeat. With Egyptian pride satisfied, Sadat after 1973 moved Egypt into the American orbit and toward peace with Israel. He negotiated the return of parts of the Sinai in 1974–1975, abrogated the treaty of friendship with the Soviet Union in 1976, flew to Jerusalem to appear before the Israeli parliament in 1977, negotiated the Camp David peace accords in 1978, and signed the resultant treaty with Israel that established relations and returned the remainder of the Sinai in 1979. The Arab world ostracized Egypt for Sadat's policy, expelling it from the Arab League and the Islamic Conference and cutting off financial subsidies, but 99.95 percent of Egyptians voted for peace in a referendum on the treaty. Sadat received the Nobel Peace Prize along with Israeli Prime Minister Menachim Begin in 1978.

Sadat similarly tried to reverse Egypt's domestic course, but here his record was far less complete. He launched an economic initiative labeled the "Open Door Policy," which emphasized foreign investment and de-emphasized state ownership and planning. This policy, along with peace, brought renewed economic growth, but it also brought a growing disparity between the rich and the poor, the Westernized elite and the traditional masses. Politically, Sadat relaxed restrictions on political parties in 1976 and held elections that year and again in 1980, but widespread poverty, conspicuous consumption by the elite, and growing criticism of social injustice and Western influences by Islamic fundamentalists fueled popular discontent, necessitating strong internal security measures and limiting political liberalization. Massive riots causing hundreds of deaths occurred in 1975 and 1977; reforms that allowed most political parties but disqualified the two primary opposition groups came in 1977; and Sadat's own National Democratic Party won all 140 elected seats on the new Advisory Council in 1980. Sadat appointed the remaining 70 Council members. Sadat's political and economic achievements were far less solid than his diplomatic successes. An Islamic fundamentalist assassin killed him as he watched a military parade on October 6, 1981.

Sadat's vice-president, Hosni Mubarak, suppressed the revolt that accompanied the assassination and was confirmed as Egypt's new president in a referendum held one week later. In the years since, Mubarak has followed the basic course charted by Sadat, although with greater finesse. In foreign policy, he has honored the peace treaty with Israel but taken a harder line on Palestinian rights, maintaining Egypt's close ties to the United States while reestablishing ties with the Arab world. In 1991, Egypt organized Arab resistance to Iraq's invasion of Kuwait, and Egyptian forces made up the third-largest contingent of the coalition force during the subsequent war. In gratitude, Egypt's creditors forgave half its foreign debt.

Internally, Mubarak continued to encourage free-market economic development and foreign investment while maintaining extensive state ownership and moving to alleviate widespread hunger. He released some political prisoners and broadened political participation, allowing the formation of two opposition parties, but he rigged the parliamentary elections of 1987 so blatantly that the Supreme Constitutional Court overturned the results in 1990. His policy towards Islam has been to emphasize the government's support for orthodoxy in law and public policy while cracking down hard on Islamic extremists. The government claims that 90 percent of the laws conform to Islamic codes and vigorously censors anti-Islamic publications. But the government has resisted imposing the Islamic criminal code and respects the rights of the country's Coptic Christian minority.

Egypt under Mubarak has seen a gradual rise in social tensions and occasional violence. In 1986, 17,000 conscripts in the Central Security Force rioted in Cairo for three days to protest rumors of an extension of their service, sparking similar violence in other cities later in the year. The 1990 elections resulting from the disqualification of the 1987 elections were marred by arrests and the assassination of the speaker of the National Assembly. Four of the main opposition parties boycotted them, and only 35 percent of voters turned out. Most opposition groups boycotted the municipal elections held in 1992, and the government disqualified so many of its opponents who did run that over two-thirds of government candidates won unopposed.

Most seriously, fundamentalist Moslems launched what amounted to a guerrilla war in 1992, attacking Coptic Christians and tourists, providing social services to impoverished neighborhoods in Cairo, and seizing control of villages and towns, where they exact taxes, dispense justice, and forbid the Copts from putting on public weddings and funerals. Street battles between Christians and Moslem militants became common, and in the worst violence since 1981, Moslems killed 13 Copts in May 1992. A month later, fundamentalists gunned down Farag Foda, an outspoken antifundamentalist, and threatened to do the same to others. In another incident, fundamentalists hijacked a Nile cruise ship, and on October 21 they killed a British tourist. As part of their civic action, they rushed relief supplies to poor neighborhoods after a devastating earthquake killed 500 people in Cairo, and established themselves as the de facto government in some areas. The government responded with a tough new anti-terrorist law that includes the death penalty and arrested hundreds of suspects in Cairo and the south.

In 1993, Mubarak won reelection to another six-year term, but the conflict between the fundamentalists and the government became worse. Islamic militants killed police, tourists, and outspoken cultural moderates, and attempted to assassinate high government officials. The government responded with continued arrests and executed several dozen suspects. Fighting continued throughout 1994 and into 1995, with no end in sight. Eighty people died in January 1995, 30 of them in just two days of fighting. The government claims to have the entire country under control, but security personnel are subject to frequent attacks in the south, and the violence has cost the country at least 30 percent of its tourist income.

Egypt's government combines constitutional and authoritarian elements, with the latter predominant. Enacted in 1971, the constitution vests executive authority in the president, who is nominated by the People's Assembly and elected by a national referendum for a term of six years. The president appoints the cabinet, military leaders, provincial governors, and other officials. Presidential decrees carry the power of law, and the Assembly approves rather than initiates policy. The ruling National Democratic Party maintains its hegemony through control of radio, television, and newspaper licenses; through its control of labor unions and state patronage; and through manipulation of the electoral process.

A state of emergency has been in effect since 1981, under which suspects can be detained for 90 days without charge and for six months more with a court order, the government can search people or property without judicial review, and a special Emergency State Security Court tries cases resulting from the Emergency Law. The only possible appeal is to the president, who can also order a defendant retried or rearrested without charge, even if he or she had been freed by a court order.

The judiciary has shown that it can act with independence, however, as evidenced by the invalidation of the 1987 elections. Egyptians freely criticize the government informally and in print, but even this freedom is limited by the government's ability to impose temporary news blackouts on sensitive subjects and its growing deference to Islamic sensibilities. Similarly, the country's tradition of respect for religious minorities is coming under increasing strain as the government reacts to fundamentalist pressures by resisting conversions out of Islam and denying applications to build or repair churches.

Citizens can travel freely within the country, but women must obtain permission—from their fathers if they are under 21 or from their husbands if they are married—to travel abroad. Workers can organize unions, but all unions must belong to the government-affiliated Egyptian Trade Union Federation, and strikes are illegal and heavily punished.

Egypt is a country in which ordinary people can live unobtrusively with relative freedom, but anyone who provokes controversy faces a formidable repressive apparatus.

LIBYA
Statistical Profile

Capital:	Tripoli
Area:	679,359 sq. miles
Population:	5,100,000 (1994 est.)
Density:	8 people/sq. mile
Growth Rate:	3.4% (1994 est.)
GDP:	$29,071,000,000
Per Capita Income:	$5,800
Foreign Debt:	$2,100,000,000
Life Expectancy:	47 (1960), 63 (1992)
Ethnic Groups:	Arab; Berber, including Tuareg and Tebu; migrant workers from various Arab countries
Official Language:	Arabic
Religions:	Muslim (97%), Christian (2.5%)
Former Colonizer:	Italy
Date of Independence:	1951

History

Libya consists of three provinces: Cyrenaica and Tripolitania on the Mediterranean coast and Fezzan in the southwest. Over the centuries, these provinces were sometimes united but more often divided until they were brought together under the Ottoman Empire. As that empire contracted in the first years of the twentieth century, the Italians attempted to claim the provinces, but Italian occupation in 1911 sparked fierce resistance by the Bedouin of the interior, led by the Islamic Sanusiyya brotherhood. Warfare lasted until 1928 and left a legacy of harsh rule by the Italians and festering resentment on the part of the Libyans. Idris Al-Senoussi, leader of the resistance, continued the struggle from exile, supporting the Allies in World War II. They liberated the country from Italy but squabbled over who would control it until 1949, when the United Nations defeated by one vote a plan to partition it between France, Great Britain, and Italy. Instead, the UN resolved that Libya would become independent in 1951.

Libya gained its independence as a federation of the three provinces under the rule of King Idris I. Elections the next year stimulated the formation of political parties, but they also brought out provincial animosities, for Tripolitania and Fezzan resented Idris' perceived favoritism toward his home province of Cyrenaica. As a result, the government quickly suppressed the new parties, and Libyan politics degenerated into a series of squabbles between the court and the government ministries.

Upon gaining independence, Libya was a poor, mostly desolate desert country whose few commercial farms along the coast were oriented almost entirely to producing exports to Italy. Most of the infrastructure that had existed had been destroyed during the war, and many economists wondered how the country could survive. The solution came when oil was discovered in the late 1950s, which transformed the country's fortunes dramatically. Exports began in 1961, with over a dozen smaller independent companies using Libyan oil to compete with the major companies that dominated most of the other oil producers.

Despite a new constitution that did away with the federal structure in 1963, Libya's corrupt and aging administration did not keep pace with the social changes unleashed by the oil wealth. By the late 1960s, the country was ripe for a coup. It came on September 1, 1969, when a group of young army officers overthrew King Idris while he was out of the country and installed a revolutionary regime.

The leader, Muammar Gaddafy, was a colonel from Fezzan and an ardent admirer of Egypt's President Nasser. In the next years, he established total domination over the country's government, gradually molding it to conform to the "Third Universal Theory" he expounded in his *Green Book* (1976–1979) as an alternative to Western capitalist democracy and Soviet totalitarian socialism. Insisting that "any form of government other than congresses of the whole population is undemocratic," he created a system in which all power theoretically originated in local People's Committees. These committees elected representatives to the General People's Congress, the national legislature. In accordance with his insistence that the country is not a *jumhuriya* (republic) but a *jamahiriya* (state of the masses), the government is run not by Cabinet ministers but by secretaries. In reality, the General Congress and the People's Committees acted from the beginning in Gaddafy's name and according to his will.

The revolutionary government was popular at first because it distributed the wealth from oil much more equitably than had the old regime. The $8 billion a year that oil was yielding by the mid-1970s brought the country's gross national product to $6,310 per person, making it the richest country in Africa by a wide margin and, in 1977, the fifteenth richest country in the world. The people benefited directly from improved wages and social services, and indirectly from the extensive development efforts undertaken by the government. These efforts included such mundane projects as providing electricity, running water, sewer systems, and housing as well as big-ticket items like massive irrigation works, huge industrial plants, and a nuclear power station. With oil prices high throughout the 1970s, the country and its people enjoyed a bounty, and although the weakening of the oil market in the 1980s frustrated ambitious development plans, the country continued to enjoy the highest standard of living in the area.

Gaddafy also used the oil wealth to pursue an aggressive, radical foreign policy. Ironically, Libya remained prudent in its external economic policies, not only maintaining good commercial relations with the United States, which bought 30 percent of the country's oil in the late 1970s, but also helping to support the economies of NATO's faltering "southern tier" states—Turkey, Greece, and Italy—along with independent-minded Romania and Yugoslavia. Nevertheless, in more visible ways, Gaddafy challenged the West, and became the *enfant terrible* of the late 1980s. He spent billions on Soviet arms to create one of the strongest armies in Africa. He asserted Libya's claim to the disputed, uranium-rich Aouzou Strip along the border with Chad, thereby becoming embroiled in that country's civil war, which eventually provoked countermoves by France. He similarly quarreled with Egypt over disputed border areas and the two countries fought a bitter four-day war in 1977. He also backed a coup attempt in the Sudan in 1976, and provoked a confrontation with U.S. Navy jets by asserting sovereignty over the entire Gulf of Sirte (which was considerably beyond the internationally recognized 12-mile limit).

The policy that gained Gaddafy worldwide notoriety, however, was his support for international terrorism. Starting with his steadfast support for the Palestine Liberation Organization, he became a chief source of financial and diplomatic backing for a variety of radical organizations. This stance led to a growing discord with the United States, compounded by the dispute over the Gulf of Sirte. The United States broke off all economic and commercial relations with Libya, and attacks by U.S. Navy planes on patrol vessels and shore installations apparently led to a Libyan-backed terrorist bombing of a bar in West Berlin in April 1986. This attack in turn provoked a U.S. bombing raid on the Libyan capital, which came close to killing Gaddafy

himself. Libya maintained a notably lower profile after that, but two years later several Libyan nationals, including Gaddafy's brother-in-law, were linked to the bombings of a U.S. commercial jet over Lockerbie, Scotland, and a French airliner over West Africa. Libya's refusal to extradite the nationals has kept tensions high, which resulted in an aerial dogfight between U.S. and Libyan planes in 1989 and the imposition of economic sanctions by the United Nations in 1992.

These sanctions, combined with the disappointing results of some development programs, have hurt Libya's economy. Public criticism of the regime has appeared in print and has even been voiced in the General People's Congress. In response, Gaddafy renounced terrorism and reorganized the government in 1992. Thirteen separate 1,500-member bodies containing one representative from each community were created to oversee the government's 13 ministries, and local elections were held in October 1992. Responding to complaints about corruption, inefficiency, and lack of basic services despite the high per capita GNP, Gaddafy loosened the economic system in 1993, allowing private ownership of banks and the holding of bank accounts denominated in foreign currencies. He survived an attempted coup by members of the armed forces loyal to a rival clan that opposed any cooperation with the West in the Lockerbie investigation, and in May 1994 he accepted an International Court of Justice ruling against Libya's claim to the Aouzou Strip by formally returning control of it to Chad.

Despite its reforms, Libya remains a state tightly under the control of one man, Muammar Gaddafy. Although he holds no official position, he, his aides, and committees acting in his name set public policies and appoint public officials. There is no free speech; the government owns and runs the media and criticism of the government is a criminal offense. Libyans do not have the right to free assembly for political purposes, the right to form independent trade unions, or the right to privacy. The security service maintains a network of informers throughout the country, and the judiciary is not independent. About 100 political prisoners are held in secret detention centers; detainees are often sentenced without a trial; many offenses are punishable by death. Although the country is overwhelmingly Moslem, the government tolerates a small Christian minority but bans the Islamic Sanusiyya sect and represses Islamic fundamentalists suspected of political activities. The Berber and Tuareg ethnic minorities suffer some forms of discrimination. Ironically, the government's attempts to promote women's rights have run into popular resistance.

Libya in the 1990s has become a country under siege, bolstered by its raw economic power but strained by the costs and consequences of its adventurous foreign policy.

TUNISIA
Statistical Profile

Capital:	Tunis
Area:	63,170 sq. miles
Population:	8,700,000 (1994 est.)
Density:	138 people/sq. mile
Growth Rate:	1.9% (1994 est.)
GDP:	$13,854,000,000
Per Capita Income:	$1,740
Foreign Debt:	$7,644,000,000
Life Expectancy:	48 (1960), 68 (1992)
Ethnic Groups:	Majority Arab; small number of Berbers; some Europeans (mainly French and Italian)
Official Language:	Arabic; French used widely in business, administration, and education
Religions:	Muslim (99%), Christian or Jewish (1%)
Former Colonizer:	France
Date of Independence:	1956

History

Tunisia's history as a distinct nation dates back to the thirteenth century, when the Hafsids established the first indigenous dynasty. The Ottomans conquered Tunisia in 1574, but it regained its independence in 1705. In the nineteenth century, the government fell into increasing debt, which gave France a chance to expand its influence until it occupied Tunisia and established a protectorate in 1881. France created an extensive network of roads and railroads, established commercial farms and mines, and stimulated the growth of new cities and towns, creating a classic colonial economy and society. In response, Tunisians began agitating for greater rights and representation in 1920 with the appearance of the Destour Party and a labor union, the General Congress of Tunisian Workers (CGTT). French repression destroyed the union but not the party, and in 1934 Habib Ben Ali Bourghiba led dissidents in forming a more radical party, New Destour. The party struggled against French colonialism both before and after the Second World War (although Bourghiba supported the Free French during the war), and it was joined by a new union formed in 1946, the General Union of Tunisian Workers (UGTT). The struggle reached a climax in 1956, when the French granted independence to Tunisia in order to avoid an armed struggle that would have distracted them from the growing conflict in Algeria next door.

New Destour consolidated its hold on the country, creating a one-party state. Bourghiba became president of the Republic while remaining head of the party, and party organs dominated the government at all levels, controlling elections and setting policies. The new government tried and executed numerous opposition figures; the most prominent, Ben Youssef, was assassinated in 1961. Thereafter, the government faced little overt opposition for over a decade.

There were, however, numerous struggles within the ruling party. In the early 1960s, the party embarked on a socialist course, changing its name to the Destour Socialist Party in 1964. The government implemented a socialist economic program, which led to a break with the more conservative UGTT. The program failed in the face of natural disasters, mismanagement, and growing opposition from powerful interests threatened by the reforms. Bourghiba, who had initially supported the policy, turned against it. In 1969, he expelled Ahmed Ben Salah, architect of the socialist program, from the party and the government, and had him arrested. In the early 1970s, the party and the government defined their policy as "pro-Western and pro-private sector but not pro-multiparty democracy." Emphasizing the last point, Bourghiba became life-president of both the party and the government a few years later.

The political frustration resulting from one-party rule was compounded by economic discontent as conditions of life for many Tunisians stagnated or declined in the 1970s. An escalating series of disturbances began with student demonstrations in 1974 and widened to labor actions in 1976, provoking increasingly strong government reaction. A general strike exploded into violence on January 26, 1978, "Black Thursday," with widespread rioting and army repression leaving scores dead. Although military courts sentenced numerous student and labor leaders to lengthy terms in prison, the government was clearly shaken. It reprieved the head of the UGTT and 263 lesser defendants, and embarked on a program of political reform. In 1978, it allowed one opposition party, the Socialist Democrats, to exist and to publish a weekly newspaper, and in July 1979 it amended the electoral code to allow two candidates to contest each seat. In September, the party resolved to open itself to a broader membership and new ideas.

These reforms provided only temporary relief, however, for in 1984 economic hardships led to a series of riots and strikes, and in 1986 opposition parties boycotted parliamentary elections. In the same year, the government launched a fierce crackdown on Islamic fundamentalists, swooping down on offices and homes, making dozens of arrests, and sentencing four to death.

By late 1987, Bourghiba's pronouncements and actions were becoming increasingly er-

ratic. Led by Prime Minister Ben Ali, the Cabinet called in doctors, who on November 7 pronounced the aging leader unfit. Ben Ali became president and quickly moved to liberalize the country's political system. Within a month, parliament approved a human-rights package that included a citizen's right to be charged within four days of arrest. A few months later, the government enacted extensive electoral reforms that abolished the post of life-president, limited the president to two five-year terms, and recognized six opposition parties. When the government party still managed to win 80 percent of the vote and all seats in parliament in elections in 1989, Ben Ali proposed changing to a system of proportional representation that would ensure at least some seats would go to the opposition. The government party again won all 144 contested seats in legislative elections in March 1994, but an additional 19 were reserved for opposition candidates. At the same time, Ben Ali won the unopposed presidential elections with 99 percent of the votes cast.

In the early 1990s, Islamic fundamentalism emerged as a serious challenge to the Tunisian government. While Islam is the state religion, with the state running the mosques and appointing the imams, the cosmopolitan elite that runs the country and the religious militants are deeply antagonistic. The minister of the interior has called the fundamentalists "sick minded people," and the government refuses to recognize their main party, Al-Nahda, or to conduct any dialogue with it. Disturbances in early 1991 led to massive arrests and the trials in 1992 of 171 members of Al-Nahda and 108 members of a splinter group, Talla el Fida (Commandos of Sacrifice). The government contended that the accused were trying to overthrow the government, while the defense claimed that the government was using the militants' threats of violence as an excuse to delay promised democratic reforms. Human-rights activists charged that the government used torture to extract confessions and interfered with some defendants' legal counsel, which apparently led the government both to adopt legislation that forced the dissolution of the Human Rights League, the oldest organization of its type in the Arab world, and to charge 74 security officers with abuses. Although the military tribunal trying the case returned surprising light sentences, the government continued its crackdown, and in late 1992 it claimed to have completely dismantled the network of fundamentalist groups in the country. Complaints of widespread abuses continued to be lodged by human rights groups, however, with Amnesty International publishing a report denouncing "the yawning chasm . . . between what the government appears to be doing for human rights and the reality of systematic human rights violations."

Tunisia today remains basically a one-party parliamentary state with constitutional protections in some areas but weak democratic institutions in others. The parliament is essentially a rubber-stamp for executive decisions, which themselves reflect policies set by the ruling party outside the framework of the national government. Opposition parties are allowed, but they must obtain government approval, and they must obtain separate approval to hold assemblies. The judicial branch is constitutionally independent, but the security forces can search without warrants, tap phones, make arbitrary arrests, and hold suspects incommunicado for 10 days. The press is both publicly and privately owned, but all publications require prior authorization, specific issues are routinely suppressed if they contain articles critical of the government, and writers, editors, and publishers are often arrested or fined for defamation. The major union is independent of the government, and counts about 20 percent of the workers as members.

Tunisia has a tradition of moderation, and the government permits the people considerable latitude in areas considered to be safe, but it clearly retains the right to repress movements that do not fit in. Islamic fundamentalists, in particular, feel the weight of stiff repression in a society that otherwise styles itself as relatively free.

ALGERIA
Statistical Profile

Capital:	Algiers
Area:	919,591 sq. miles
Population:	27,900,000 (1994 est.)
Density:	30 people/sq. mile
Growth Rate:	2.5% (1994 est.)
GDP:	$35,674,000,000
Per Capita Income:	$1,830
Foreign Debt:	$24,762,000,000
Life Expectancy:	47 (1960), 67 (1992)
Ethnic Groups:	Arab (80%); Berber, including Tuareg; 60,000 Europeans (mainly French)
Official Language:	Arabic
Religion:	Muslim (nearly 100%)
Former Colonizer:	France
Date of Independence:	1962

History

The oldest state in the area of present-day Algeria was Numidia, which arose around 200 B.C. The area was later ruled by Rome, the Vandals, Byzantium, and a succession of Arab and native Moslems states. The Ottomans ruled nominally from the early sixteenth century until the early eighteenth century, after which the area enjoyed independence until the French invaded in June 1830. The French took 30 years to consolidate their hold against bitter resistance. They confiscated most of the best land, brought in settlers who eventually numbered 750,000 out of a population of six million, and left only after a bitter guerrilla war that lasted seven years. Approximately three million Algerians perished from the campaigns and expropriations of the nineteenth century; another 1.5 million died in the conflict that ended French rule.

The leaders of the independence movement, the National Liberation Front (FLN), became the rulers of the country at independence in 1962. They, however, were divided into three major political factions, and the military was divided between the armies that had been based outside the country and the guerrilla forces that had worked from within. One of the faction leaders, Ben Bella, gained the backing of the army commander from Morocco, Houari Boumedienne, and emerged predominant, although at first he ruled in coalition with other nationalist leaders. Ben Bella implemented a socialist program of nationalization, worker self-management, and support for foreign anticolonial movements. Personally popular, he alienated his colleagues, and economic difficulties eroded mass support for his regime. To compensate for the loss of support, he steadily concentrated power in his own hands, taking the post of FLN general secretary in early 1963, getting himself elected president by holding a referendum in September of that year, and assuming the title of commander-in-chief shortly thereafter. His troubles mounted when armed rebellions arose in 1963 and 1964, and climaxed when he was ousted in a bloodless coup in mid-1965, which was caused by his purge of some of his closest associates.

The leader of the coup was the rumored target of Ben Bella's next move, his military backer Houari Boumedienne. Boumedienne suspended the constitution and consolidated his rule against a variety of opponents during the late 1960s. These opponents included former revolutionaries disgruntled with their lack of voice in the present or rewards for their struggles in the past; a former guerrilla leader who organized two assassination attempts and an armed uprising in 1967–1968 as well as several bomb attacks on Algerian offices abroad; former French colonists and intelligence officers who staged a number of attacks on Algerian installations and individuals; former FLN officials; and left-wing students and workers. Boumedienne survived all these threats but recognized the need to broaden the government's base. Consequently, he gradually demilitarized the government's image, adopted a National Charter in 1976, and revived the FLN, which had been inactive since shortly after independence. The latter move proved difficult in the face of both popular apathy and conflicts between local party officials and local government officials, who were still mainly military officers, but the effort was

moving forward slowly when Boumedienne died unexpectedly in 1978 from a rare blood cancer.

Boumedienne's reforms came together in the process of selecting a successor at a long-delayed FLN Party Congress in January 1979. The congress included representatives of all the major sectors of Algerian society, including local administrations, national corporations, the press, and the civil service. It elected a new central committee, politburo, and secretary-general. Colonel Benjedid Chadli, the army's choice, beat out politicians from leftist and rightist factions to become the new secretary-general, the party's candidate, and the country's new president.

Chadli expanded his power at an extraordinary congress of the FLN in June 1980 by gaining the authority to appoint rather than merely propose members of the politburo and by reducing the size of the politburo from 17 to 7 members, expelling his prime minister in the process. The next year he expelled his two chief rivals, and in 1984 he won a second five-year term, running unopposed. He used this power to lead a reform movement introducing greater competition into the economy and greater efficiency into the government. In December 1985, a special congress of the FLN proposed a new national charter, which allowed a greater role for the private sector in the national economy while calling for a policy combining socialism and Islam; the charter won 98 percent support in a referendum the next month. More reforms were introduced in December 1987 and in June 1988, and the slow response to them by the government led Chadli to declare a "war on bureaucracy." In another referendum, the reform measures were approved in November 1988 by 92 percent of the vote.

In the meantime, Chadli's economic reforms led to skyrocketing food prices, except in hard-currency outlets available only to the rich. On October 4, young people rioted and looted these shops, and Chadli had to call out the army to restore order. Civil unrest continued into 1989 with strikes, riots, and massive demonstrations in protest of further price increases. On July 2, a new law permitted the formation of opposition political parties, and almost immediately over a dozen new parties appeared. As local elections, postponed from December 1989 until June 1990, approached, the campaign narrowed to a contest between the FLN and the party of the Islamic fundamentalists, the Islamic Salvation Front (FIS). Some parties boycotted the election, but of the 75 percent of voters who went to the polls, 55 percent chose the FIS. The FLN refused to yield power, however, which provoked violence by the fundamentalists. This violence in turn led the government to impose a state of siege in mid-1991 and to arrest the fundamentalist leaders. The government tried elections again on December 26, 1991, this time for the national parliament. Against a background of $25 billion in foreign debt, 30 percent unemployment, 40 percent inflation, and inadequate health services, housing, and schools, the fundamentalists won again. They vowed to impose religious law, prohibit alcohol, and return women to the role of homemaker (blaming working women for high unemployment).

On January 2, 1992, 200,000 people, including trade unionists, women's rights advocates, and members of the secular parties demonstrated against the election results, calling for a cancellation of the second and final round of voting. Two weeks later, the army forced Chadli to resign, canceled the elections, and dissolved the National Assembly. It replaced the Constitutional Council with a High Security Council and then with the Higher State Council, an advisory body headed by Mohammed Boudiaf, a 72-year-old veteran of the independence war. The government imposed a state of emergency that suspended almost all constitutional rights, allowing it to detain citizens arbitrarily, impose curfews, censor the press, and ban public gatherings. It arrested many pro-FIS imams and replaced the rest, reasserting governmental control over the 8,000 (out of 10,000) mosques the fundamentalists had controlled. On March 4, 1992, an Algerian court banned the FIS outright on the grounds that the constitution forbids political parties based on race or religion, and the national government took over FIS-controlled local governments.

The fundamentalists resisted the government's repression in bloody street battles, and on June 29, 1992, a member of the security forces assassinated President Boudiaf. A special commission concluded that fundamentalists were behind the assassination, but the fundamentalists argued that members of the government itself had staged it to justify yet stronger measures. The government intensified its crackdown after the assassination, establishing special anti-terrorist courts with anonymous judges whose verdicts were final. On July 15, a military court sentenced the leaders of the 1991 disturbances to 4 to 12 years in prison, and in November the government executed two fundamentalist soldiers. It put 90 other soldiers on trial after a policeman was killed near Algiers, and in December it imposed an all-night curfew in the area.

The government tried to balance the repression with reforms, implementing an economic stability program, bringing opposition figures into the Cabinet, and investigating allegations of corruption among top officials. In 1993, it proposed a dialogue with the opposition about "imminent changes" in political direction, but the opposition refused on the grounds that the electorate had already spoken. Fighting between fundamentalists and security forces became an almost daily occurrence, and the rebels began targeting civilians—journalists, intellectuals, and foreigners. In January 1994, the Higher State Council handed power over to General Lamine Zeroual, as transitional president for three years, to prepare the country for new elections. Even as plans for these elections went forward, talks between the government and the opposition broke down, and the fighting continued. In March 1995, the government launched a concerted offensive against the most militant Islamic faction, the Armed Islamic Group (GIA), killing hundreds in ambushes and attacks. The government claims that some 20,000 fundamentalists and over 6,000 civilians have been killed since 1992.

Beyond its conflict with the fundamentalists, the Algerian government has been moving to restrict the Berber language and culture despite constitutional prohibitions against discrimination. The rights of women, while still protected by general provisions, do not in the current constitution have the specific guarantees they had previously. Women are still considered dependents of their husbands, fathers, or brothers, and cannot initiate a divorce. Algerians do have the right to form trade unions, but the unions cannot have connections abroad or with political parties, and the government closed the headquarters of the Islamic union. The state is officially Islamic, but it tolerates its tiny Christian and Jewish communities. Algerians can travel freely within the country, but are hampered in foreign travel by strict currency controls.

Algeria in the 1990s is an extremely troubled nation. The elite aspire to democracy in theory yet cannot live with its outcome in practice. Meanwhile, the general population is deeply divided between moderate modernists and fundamentalists.

MOROCCO AND THE WESTERN SAHARA
Statistical Profile

Capital:	Rabat
Area:	275,116 sq. miles
Population:	28,800,000 (1994 est.)
Density:	105 people/sq. mile
Growth Rate:	2.3% (1994 est.)
GDP:	$28,401,000,000
Per Capita Income:	$1,040
Foreign Debt:	$20,536,000,000
Life Expectancy:	47 (1960), 63 (1992)
Ethnic Groups:	Arabic speakers (65%); Berber speakers (35%)
Official Language:	Arabic; French used in business and academics
Religions:	Muslim (99%), Christian or Jewish (1%)
Former Colonizers:	France, Spain
Date of Independence:	1956

History

Although the Berbers have inhabited Morocco since at least the second millennium B.C., the first Moroccan state dates from about 808 A.D., about 100 years after the Arab conquest. The state, created by Idris Ibn Abdallah and his son Idris II, lasted only a century. Thereafter, a succession of foreign conquerors and weak, tribally based local dynasties ruled until the late sixteenth century. When Sultan Ahmad Al-Mansur defeated the invading Portugese at the Battle of Three Kings in 1578, Morocco gained so much wealth from ransoms that it was able to create a professional army and become a considerable power, destroying Songhai across the Sahara. The Alawite dynasty seized control in 1669 and continues to rule today.

During the nineteenth century, the dynasty was not able to create an economically viable modern state, and growing financial problems enabled the Europeans to steadily increase their presence, until the French and Spanish invaded in 1907 and established a protectorate in 1912. This intrusion met with bitter resistance that lasted until 1926 in the interior and cost 100,000 Moroccan and 30,000 French and Spanish lives. In the cosmopolitan coastal cities, resistance took a political form, as nationalists advanced a reformist platform in the 1920s and began calling for outright independence in the mid-1930s. After the Second World War, they intensified their campaign, allying with the sultan, who became a national hero when the French attempted to exile him in 1953. With the French defeat in Indochina and the growing insurrection in Algeria, the nationalists' bombing campaign in the cities and a growing guerrilla war in the countryside compelled France to promise independence in 1955. The Spanish followed suit, and modern Morocco began its history as an independent nation in 1956.

The legacy of the nationalist alliance with the sultan was a conservative regime, a constitutional monarchy in which the leaders of the Istiqlal Party accepted powerless cabinet positions in exchange for agreeing to the indefinite postponement of elections. Similarly, French acquiescence in formal independence allowed it to maintain most of its interests in the country. French officers held senior positions in the army, French capital still dominated the economy, and French settlers retained title to their agricultural estates. As a result, the Istiqulal Party split in 1959, with its more radical members founding the vaguely socialist National Union of Popular Forces (UNFP). The government responded with repression.

In 1961, Hassan II succeeded to the throne, which he still holds today. Initially, he tried liberalization, holding the country's first elections in 1963 under a constitution adopted in 1962. But the impotence of the parliament coupled with economic problems led to continued unrest, and he soon changed tack. The government arrested hundreds of UNFP activists and forced its leader, Ben Barka, into exile. In an attempt to dampen popular enthusiasm for the recent victory of socialism in Algeria, Hassan embarked on a war with the newly independent country over their ill-defined border region. Domestic discontent boiled over again in 1965 in a massive riot in the slums of Casablanca. The government had to call in the army, which killed about 400 people in the process of restoring order.

In the early 1970s, King Hassan again tried liberalization, again with poor results. His government drafted a new constitution in 1970, but the opposition boycotted elections because less than half the seats in parliament were to be filled by direct elections. In 1971, top army officers invaded the palace in an attempt to oust the king, and in the next year airforce officers tried to shoot down his plane. In 1973, Libyan-backed insurgents launched a guerrilla war in the mountains, while students and workers demonstrated in the cities. Hassan's government responded with a characteristic combination of repression, liberalization, and foreign adventure. Its repression consisted of banning the radical wing of the UNFP, detaining hundreds of its members and executing 22 of them. Its liberalization involved not only promising elections under a third constitution

drafted in 1972, but also moving to alleviate economic distress by expropriating the remaining settler lands. Its foreign adventures included sending troops against Israel in 1973 and launching in 1974 the diplomatic offensive that led Spain to cede most of the Western Sahara to Morocco in 1975. Riding the resultant wave of popularity, the government held the promised elections in 1976. The government party won a clear majority of the seats, while the opposition gained a substantial minority. The king appointed a coalition Cabinet in 1977.

If Hassan's success in the Western Sahara brought the expected popularity at home, it created unanticipated problems abroad that have continued into the 1990s. At first things went well. To press Morocco's claim to the Western Sahara, Hassan played on the succession crisis in Madrid after Spanish dictator Francisco Franco died in 1975. At the height of negotiations in 1975, he organized the "Green March" of 350,000 unarmed Moroccans into the Western Sahara. Spain soon agreed to divide it between Morocco and Mauritania, with the lion's share going to Hassan's realm. Most Moroccans were thrilled by this success. Western Saharans opposed to the partition began to fight back, organizing the Polisaro guerrilla group and the Sahraoui Arab Democratic Republic as a government in exile. Algeria gave the guerrillas extensive support, and until 1985, they appeared to have the upper hand. Militarily, they held their own, which for a guerrilla movement generally means they are winning, and indeed they scored many successes on the diplomatic front as well. By 1979, Mauritania abandoned its claims to the territory and a total of 34 states had recognized the Western Sahara's independence, including 20 African countries. By 1982, the latter number had risen to 26, and the Organization of African Unity (OAU), which contained 50 states, voted to admit the Sahraoui as a member. Morocco withdrew from the organization in protest, claiming that a two-thirds majority was needed to admit a new member whose existence was disputed.

On the ground, however, Morocco turned the tide in the Western Sahara in the late 1980s, creating a fortified wall across the desert that prevented the Polisario from moving into the populated and economically productive coastal areas (where there were valuable phosphate deposits). By the time the UN Security Council called for a cease-fire and referendum in 1991, Morocco controlled most of the territory and the Polisario began to fall apart. The cease-fire went into effect on September 6, 1991, but King Hassan made clear his opinion of the referendum when, two days later, he announced that a Moroccan "priority" was to "regionalize" the "Saharan provinces." Although Moroccan diplomats blocked the U.N. referendum by disputing the already agreed-upon formula for qualifying voters, Morocco went ahead with its own referendum in 1992 on yet another constitutional change and allowed residents of the Western Sahara to vote on it. Meanwhile, a number of top leaders of the Polisario defected, saying that the cause was lost and charging that the organization was diverting relief supplies intended for civilians for its own use.

Despite Security Council Resolution 809 calling for the UN referendum to take place before the end of 1993, Morocco managed to delay it not only through that year, but through 1994 and 1995 as well.

Western European countries and the United States are still formally at odds with Morocco over its actions in the Western Sahara and its human rights record, but it has proved such a reliable friend in the past—supporting Anwar Sadat's overtures to Israel and sending troops to prop up Mobutu in Zaire—that Hassan can be fairly confident that his policies will not lead to any serious diplomatic rupture.

The 1992 referendum in Morocco approved a new constitution that gives increased powers to the parliament while leaving final authority with the king. Parliament now has the power to approve ministers and government programs and to initiate inquiries; it can also subject the Cabinet to a vote of confidence. The king is the commander-in-chief of the armed forces, can declare a state of emergency, and appoints major officials. Parliament can oppose the government's economic policies, but not its foreign policy. Although there is significant freedom of speech, citizens cannot discuss three areas: the monarchy, the claim to the Western Sahara, and the sanctity of Islam. The government licenses, subsidizes, and censors publications, and it keeps a tight rein on public assembly and private organizations. Members of unauthorized groups are subject to political imprisonment, disappearances, and torture. Independent labor unions are permitted, but the government influences their selection of officers. Women are treated equally in work and public life, but they are subordinate to their husbands, brothers, or fathers in family life and need their permission to obtain a passport. The rights of the Christian, Jewish, and Berber minorities are generally well-respected, and the government has a dual judicial system with secular courts based on the French legal tradition and Islamic courts for family matters. So far, Hassan has held the fundamentalists at bay, allowing them to engage in only educational and charitable activities.

The government held municipal elections in October 1992, in which 90,000 candidates campaigned for 22,000 posts in 1,500 communes, including in the disputed Western Sahara. The campaign was marred by violence and by charges of fraud and corruption from the opposition. Nevertheless, the government proceeded with plans to hold parliamentary elections in June 1993, and a coalition of five center-right parties took 195 seats against 120 won by a coalition of center-left parties. The king was unable to come to agreement with either group on a Cabinet, so he appointed a nonpolitical government of technocrats, political independents, and royal allies.

In keeping with this liberalization, the government has recently released political prisoners and closed down prisons. It also has embarked on a privatization campaign, selling off 74 state-owned businesses and 34 state-owned hotels. Some Moroccans have questioned whether this would amount to more than transferring the assets from one part of the elite to another, and this skepticism seems to epitomize Morocco's political situation. Hassan's government strives for an appearance of constitutionality and democracy, and in comparison to many African countries Morocco is a relatively free and prosperous country. The government remains Hassan's, however—one of the few active monarchies that has survived, and indeed seems to thrive, in the modern world.

CHAPTER

5

The Sahel

INTRODUCTION

The countries of the Sahel form almost a mirror image of the North African countries, with narrow fertile regions in the south and the desert stretching northward. Like their neighbors to the north, their life is dominated by the desert, and in the 1970s and 1980s they suffered severely from drought. In contrast to the cultural unity characteristic of North Africa, the countries of the Sahel are deeply divided. Western observers have often cast the division in racial terms, as the "Arabs" in the north against the "Blacks" of the south, but in reality most of the people look similar, have intermarried for generations, and simply do not tend to think in the racial terms that Westerners take for granted. Instead, the divide is a much more complex cultural fissure, reflecting to varying degrees religion (Moslem vs. Christian and traditional animist), language (Afro-Asiatic vs. Congo-Kordofanian and Nilo-Saharan), and traditional lifestyle (pastoral vs. settled agriculture). In general, the first half of each of these pairs lives in the northern part of each country, while the second half lives in the southern part. For sim-

plicity, they will be refered to here as "Northerners" and "Southerners."

In Mauritania and Sudan, Northerners dominate the government and oppress the Southerners; in Mali, Niger, and Chad, Southerners dominate the government and at times oppress the Northerners. Burkina Faso has only small minorities in the north.

Mali and Cape Verde have successfully created multiparty systems, and Mali has reached a settlement with dissident Northerners. Chad achieved a stable peace for the first time in decades in 1990, and has begun political reforms. Niger, unfortunately, had a multiparty system, but lost it in early 1996 to a military coup. Although the economic outlook for the region is still difficult, its political fortunes have nonetheless risen in the 1990s.

MAURITANIA
Statistical Profile

Capital:	Nouakchott
Area:	397,953 sq. miles
Population:	2,300,000 (1994 est.)
Density:	6 people/sq. mile

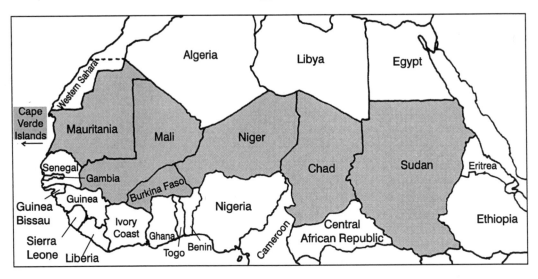

The Sahel

Growth Rate:	2.9% (1994 est.)
GDP:	$1,080,000,000
Per Capita Income:	$400
Foreign Debt:	$1,855,000,000
Life Expectancy:	35 (1960), 55 (1992)
Ethnic Groups:	Moors (75%), Pulaar (Fulani), Soininke, Wolof, Bambara
Official Language:	Arabic
Religion:	Muslim
Former Colonizer:	France
Date of Independence:	1960

History

People have lived since the Neolithic Age in Mauritania, certainly along the Senegal River in the south and probably farther north as well, since the climate was wetter. The Sanhadja Berbers moved in from the north in the third century A.D., and, after converting to Islam, launched a *jihad* that created the great Almoravid empire in the eleventh century. The empire lasted a century, and thereafter the area reverted to tribal independence, with an influx of Maqil Arab groups establishing dominance over the Sanhadja between the thirteenth and seventeenth centuries. The first European presence came in the fifteenth century, when the Portugese established a trading post on Arguin Island, but the main-

land was not reduced to colonial status until the early twentieth century, a process that took from 1902, when France established protectorates over the main coastal tribes, until 1934, when the last peoples in the interior were forced to acknowledge French overlordship.

The French ruled the territory as an appendage of Senegal, doing little to develop it and relying on a system of indirect rule. As a consequence, nationalism arose only after the Second World War, and the French successfully sponsored an alternative, conservative party based on the traditional chiefs. Its leader, Ould Daddah, became head of the Advisory Council established in 1957, and the party won all 40 seats in the parliament in uncontested elections in May 1959. In November 1960, France granted Mauritania political independence, while retaining virtually complete control over its economy.

Ould Daddah set out to solidify his control by establishing a one-party state. In 1961, he brought together representatives of all the existing parties and persuaded them to establish a single movement, the Party of the Mauritanian People (PPM). In 1964, a special congress at Kaedi made the party a state institution. These political successes, however, could not mask the economic and ethnic divisions of the country. Workers in foreign mines faced apartheid-like conditions under European expatriates. Southerners, who make up a third of the population, resisted the northern-controlled government's attempt to make Arabic the official language and to Arabize education. Non-Arabic Northerners also resented the Arabic Northerners' domination of politics and the economy. Southerners rioted against Arabization and discrimination in 1966, a miners' strike in 1968 left eight dead, a general strike in 1971 brought the country to a standstill, and in 1973, a clandestine Marxist group began forming.

Daddah responded effectively to this growing discontent with a number of nationalist moves that boosted his popularity. In 1973, he took Mauritania out of the Franc Zone and created a national currency, and the next year he nationalized the foreign-owned mining consortium. In 1975, he capped his successes by bringing most of the dissident Marxists into the PPM.

The same year, however, he began an initiative that squandered the goodwill he had gained and threw Mauritanian politics into turmoil for a decade. In November 1975, he signed the Madrid Agreement dividing the Western Sahara with Morocco and then violated his own constitution by absorbing the territory without submitting the matter to a referendum. The resultant war against the Polisario guerrillas proved disastrous economically, militarily, and politically. The country could not afford it, the army proved unable to fight it and a majority of both Southerners and Northerners opposed it. The French sent supplies and advisors and the Moroccans sent 10,000 troops in 1977, but Mauritanian disenchantment grew steadily until Lieutenant Colonel Mustapha Ould Mohamad Salek led a military coup in July 1978.

Salek promised peace, and the Polisario declared a cease-fire, but negotiations broke down over the guerrillas' demand that Mauritania unconditionally renounce its claim to its portion of the Western Sahara, while Morocco (with its 10,000 troops still inside Mauritania) opposed any treaty creating an autonomous zone. Salek compounded his problems by pushing forward with Arabization and reneging on his promise to move rapidly toward democratic elections. Popular demonstrations, a threatened strike by black teachers, and a boycott of the new National Consultative Council by the opposition prompted army leaders to depose Salek and to put Ould Bouceif and Ould Louly in his place as prime minister and president, respectively.

Bouceif took a hard line on both Arabization and the Western Sahara, but he died in a plane crash just one month after taking office. When the Polisario renewed the fighting in July, the new prime minister, Lieutenant Colonel Khouna Ould Heydalla moved quickly to make peace. Negotiations took just two days, and Mauritania renounced all territorial claims to the Western Sahara. Morocco immediately seized and annexed the territory.

Peace did not restore political stability. Heydalla replaced Louly as president in January 1980 and by early 1984 had survived three coup attempts. The first and third of these stemmed from continued controversy about the Western Sahara, the former resulting from an alleged Moroccan plot (and leading to a breakoff of diplomatic relations) and the latter reflecting discontent within the military over Mauritania's recognition of Western Saharan independence. Meanwhile, workers and students demonstrated to demand Mauritanian support for the Polisario, and Heydalla responded by personally assuming the posts of prime minister and minister of defense.

In December 1984, another coup attempt succeeded, and Lieutenant Colonel Maouya Ould Sid Ahmed Ould Taya replaced Heydalla. Taya immediately embarked on a policy of liberalization and reconciliation. Externally, he restored relations with Morocco without renouncing recognition of the Western Sahara, resolved a border dispute with Algeria, and resumed relations with Libya, which had been cut off in the face of allegations that Libya was bankrolling radical student movements. Internally, he amnestied many political prisoners arrested by Heydalla, endorsed a mass-education policy proposed but never implemented by his predecessors, and in 1986 began setting up democratically elected local councils. In 1991, a national referendum overwhelmingly endorsed a new constitution designed to pave the way for multiparty democracy.

Taya's liberalization policies did not end Mauritania's political troubles. Under him, ethnic tensions have increased markedly. In 1986, the government arrested 20 people for allegedly plotting rebellion, and since then it has arrested many more, particularly Southerners. In 1989, the government began expelling 60,000 Southerners, some of whom have responded by organizing guerrilla movements that have staged raids from neighboring Senegal. On March 3, 1992, 300,000 people demonstrated for racial justice. A new constitution came only after repeated demonstrations, and the elections that resulted were marred by significant irregularities. The government hindered voter registration, used violence to intimidate the opposition, and refused to allow neutral supervision of voting and ballot counting. After Taya won reelection with 63 percent of the vote, security police raided the main opposition's headquarters, injuring 22 people. Five people were killed and 160 arrested the next day in demonstrations protesting the raid, and civil liberties were suspended for several weeks. The opposition boycotted the subsequent elections to the legislature, and tens of thousands demonstrated on April 19, 1992, in protest against Taya's inauguration the day before. Municipal elections held in January 1994, in which the government won 172 of 208 councils, were similarly marred by charges of extensive fraud.

Mauritania's ostensibly democratic constitution is in reality window-dressing for continued rule by a narrow military elite. The courts in this overwhelmingly Moslem country apply Islamic law as national law, but they are subject to considerable manipulation by the government, which uses extralegal detention, torture, and execution when necessary. The victims are mainly Southerners. Arabic has replaced French as the country's official language, despite southern protests, as part of a larger campaign to extend the hegemony of Arabic Northerners throughout Mauritanian society. Slavery was legally abolished in 1980, but about 100,000 Mauritanians are still enslaved, generally Southerners owned by Arabic northern masters. The media include independent publications and government-owned radio and television and are legally free, but disseminating anything that promotes "national disharmony" or is "insulting to the President" can be punished by fines or imprisonment. Unions must be part of the Mauritanian Workers' Union, which is government controlled. The right to strike is limited, and political activity by unions is discouraged.

MALI
Statistical Profile

Capital:	Bamako
Area:	478,764 sq. miles
Population:	9,100,000 (1994 est.)
Density:	19 people/sq. mile
Growth Rate:	3.0% (1994 est.)
GDP:	$2,872,000,000
Per Capita Income:	$300
Foreign Debt:	$2,472,000,000
Life Expectancy :	35 (1960), 48 (1992)
Ethnic Groups:	Bambara, Songhai, Malinke, Senoufou, Dogon, Fulani, Tuareg
Official Language:	French
Religions:	Muslim (80%), Traditional (18%), Christian (1.2%)
Former Colonizer:	France
Date of Independence:	1960

History

Mali's roots are among the oldest of any sub-Saharan nation, for not only did the great medieval kingdom of Mali arise here, but Ghana, the first known state in West Africa,

Muslims pray before a mosque in Mopti, Mali. Islam dominates North Africa and has been steadily expanding south of the Sahara for centuries. *Source:* United Nations.

arose here as well. Furthermore, the Songhai empire, which succeeded the Kingdom of Mali, had its roots in the region straddling modern Mali and Burkina Faso. The Moroccans and their descendants ruled Timbuktu from the 1590s until the 1780s but the Bambara states which replaced them arose in the same area as ancient Mali.

Kaarta, one of the Bambera states, converted to Islam and conquered the region by the mid-nineteenth century. It bitterly contested French expansion up the Senegal River,

but the French vanquished Kaarta in the 1890s. They set up a colony they called "Soudan" but were not able to establish control of the northern part of the area they claimed until 1916. They set up a system of indirect rule involving a governor, 16 district officers, about 100 French civil servants, and 800 traditional chiefs. They did little to develop the country, only creating an office to oversee economic programs, the Office du Niger, in 1932.

Malian nationalism was correspondingly slow to develop, finding concrete expression in a party in 1946 with the founding of the African Democratic Assembly (RDA) in Bamako. After the Bandung Afro-Asian Congress in 1955, representatives of Sudan demanded immediate independence, and in 1958 France granted the "République Soudannaise" internal autonomy within the French Community. After the failure of attempts to create a broad West African federation, Soudan and Senegal tried for a more limited union, but French opposition made even that impossible. On September 22, 1960, the local branch of the RDA, the Soudanese Union, declared independence, adopting the venerable name of Mali.

Modibo Keita, leader of the Sudanese Union, who was also one of the founders of the RDA, became Mali's first president. A socialist opposed to French neocolonialism, he pulled Mali out of the Franc Zone and embarked on an ambitious program of state-sponsored industrialization with the help of the Eastern bloc. Unfortunately, his authoritarian and bureaucratic approach failed, and the austerity measures they necessitated rapidly alienated the people, particularly since the measures did not stop corruption at the top. The government responded to popular discontent with force, creating an armed people's militia in 1967, arresting civil servants and military officers, and dissolving the National Assembly. The army stepped in on November 19, 1968, in a bloodless coup that removed Keita. It set up the 13-member Military Commission of National Liberation (CMLN), and made Lieutenant Moussa Traore head of state.

Traore promised to set up new institutions, but he concentrated on consolidating his own power first. He dissolved Keita's Sudanese Union, suppressed the politicized National Union of Malian Workers, and survived coup attempts in 1969 and 1971. Not until 1974 did he create a new constitution, which institutionalized a new party, the Democratic Union of the Malian People (UDPM), as the sole legal party. He purged the bureaucracy of notably corrupt officials after three of them attempted a coup in 1978; installed a new, mostly civilian, cabinet; and held unopposed elections for president and parliament in June 1979. He called an extraordinary congress of the UDPM in February 1981 at which he increased his powers but failed to gain total control of the party, held more elections in June, survived another coup attempt at the end of the year, and won a second term as president in another uncontested election in 1985.

Popular discontent with Traore's rule mounted steadily during the late 1970s and 1980s. Spontaneous demonstrations broke out in 1977 upon the death in detention of the still-popular Keita, and in 1979 a strike by secondary and postsecondary students was met with arrests, torture, and executions of boys and girls. A pro-government rally in March 1980 attracted almost no support. Traore released all students and teachers a week later, but a new strike by teachers and exam proctors in July kept the upper schools closed for an entire year. He had to back out of a border war with Burkina Faso in 1985 after Burkinan forces attacked into Mali, and in the late 1980s opposition to his rule increased steadily. Demonstrations became endemic in 1990, beginning peacefully but becoming violent as security forces responded with furious repression. In one particularly brutal instance, soldiers shot and killed five women and then set fire to a building where other demonstrators had taken refuge, killing 80 more people and injuring hundreds.

In March 1991, a coup resulted in the removal of Traore and the installation of an interim government called the Transitional Committee for the Salvation of the People (CTSP). The government scheduled local, parliamentary, and presidential elections for late in the year, arrested Traore and five high-ranking officers of the armed forces, and began tracking down the $2 billion that Traore had embezzled from the treasury (about the same amount as the country's total foreign debt). Meanwhile, 36 parties registered for the elections, and in July a constitutional conference drafted a new, multiparty constitution guaranteeing basic civil rights. A referendum approved it overwhelmingly in January 1992. The elections took place in January and April, and were deemed free and fair by international observers. The victor in the presidential contest, Tieoule Konate, was inaugurated in June, and the provisional government stood down. Pressure from the International Monetary Fund for austerity measures generated continuing student unrest that forced two cabinets to resign in succession, but the instability did not undercut the basic viability of the democratic regime.

At the same time that the people of Mali went to the polls for their first real elections, the interim government attempted to settle another of the country's problems. Serious violence in the north had reflected not just disenchantment with Traore, but the Tuareg minority's disillusionment with southern rule. Hit-and-run attacks on army posts and government officials had sparked retaliatory raids by the army that all too often resulted in massacres, further fueling Tuareg discontent. In January 1992, the government arranged a cease-fire and negotiations, and in April the two sides agreed on a peace plan in which the Tuareg guerrillas were to be integrated into the national army. Negotiations relating to details of implementation continued over the next two years while sporadic violence continued, but the 100,000 refugees in neighboring states were able to begin returning in late 1993 as the level of violence died down. Unfortunately, violence escalated again in late 1994, and while it remained significantly less severe than before 1992, it indicated that the situation still was not settled.

Although Mali still faces substantial economic and social challenges of development and ethnic integration, its political liberalization marks it as one of African democracy's most promising success stories.

BURKINA FASO
Statistical Profile

Capital:	Ouagadougou
Area:	105,868 sq. miles
Population:	10,100,000 (1994 est.)
Density:	95 people/sq. mile
Growth Rate:	3.1% (1994 est.)
GDP:	$2,790,000,000
Per Capita Income:	$290
Foreign Debt:	$994,000,000
Life Expectancy:	36 (1960), 48 (1992)
Ethnic Groups:	Contains members of almost half the ethnic groups in West Africa, including Mossi (50%), Fulani, Gourmantche, Bobo, Lobi, Senoufou, Bissa.
Official Language:	French
Religions:	Traditional (60%), Muslim (28%), Catholic (10%)
Former Colonizer:	France
Date of Independence:	1960

History

The Mossi, who make up a majority of Burkina Faso's population, first entered the area in the tenth century A.D., but their first sizable states appeared in the fifteenth and sixteenth centuries. The French conquered them and the neighboring stateless societies in a bloody campaign in the late 1890s and made the area into a separate colony in 1919. In 1932, the French divided the colony between the Soudan (now Mali), Niger, and the Ivory Coast. In 1947, they made it into a whole colony again, at about the same time that a significant anticolonial movement appeared. The two main parties were a branch of the African Democratic Assembly (RDA), which was active throughout francophone Africa, and the Voltic Union (UDV). When the local leader of the RDA, Ouezzin Coulibaly, died in 1958, his rival, Maurice Yameogo, negotiated the union of the two parties under his leadership. The combined party won 64 of 75 seats in elections in April 1959, and Yameogo became president of the Republic of Upper Volta when the territory became independent a year later. The country adopted the same constitution as the Ivory Coast and joined the Council of the Entente with that country, Dahomey (now Benin), and Niger.

Yameogo won reelection handily in 1965, but his 99-percent margin was deceptive. His autocratic rule, ineffective economic policies, and open dependence on France alienated the army, students, and the powerful labor unions. In January 1966, a popular uprising forced Yameogo out, and he was succeeded by Lieutenant Colonel Sangoule Lamizana, whose regime began a steady alternation between military and civilian governments that would mark Voltic politics for the next 20 years. The government imprisoned Yameogo for embezzling over £1 million from the Entente's funds, and over the next four years it instituted an austerity program that underlay an economic upturn. Conditions seemed ripe for a return to civilian rule, as Lamizana had promised, but the civilian cabinet that he installed in 1970 was so riven by factionalism that the army took power again in 1974. Drought, famine, and a border dispute with Mali kept discontent high, as evidenced by a two-day general strike in December 1975. When concessions to the unions failed to curb opposition, a special commission recommended a return to multiparty civilian government in 1976. The old RDA/UDV party won a majority of seats in legislative elections in 1978, and Lamizana won the presidential election a year later. Both the economy and the government's relations with the unions deteriorated over the next year, however, and in November 1980 Colonel Saye Zerbo ended Lamizana's 14 year reign. Lamizana left a country that, despite the turmoil at the top and in the streets, had enjoyed a greater degree of civil liberty than most other African nations.

The military created a cabinet that included both officers and civilians and attempted to tighten the rules governing strikes. This policy led to increasing resistance by the unions that culminated in a widespread strike in January 1982 and another coup in November of the same year. This coup was different however, for it was conducted by young noncommissioned officers, and it instituted a revolutionary regime that marked a distinct break from the past. An obscure army doctor named Jean-Baptiste Ouedraogo headed the new government at first, but Captain Thomas Sankara, a popular 34-year-old officer who had distinguished himself in the conflict with Mali, won power in 1983. He changed the country's foreign policy from a pro-Western to a nonaligned stance, installed a new National Revolutionary Council (CNR), purged the army and the civil service, and arrested many older politicians. Inspired by Flight Lieutenant Jerry Rawlings of Ghana, he created popular Committees for the Defense of the Revolution (CDRs) which took over the functions of town councils and traditional chiefs. The Committees created "people's tribunals" to try former officials charged with abuses and corruption, and they also clashed with workers loyal to an established Marxist party. The tribunals acquitted former president Lamizana, but convicted Saye Zerbo and numerous lesser officials. Sankara and the Marxists forged an uneasy alliance that lasted into 1984, but in October Sankara arrested 11, including four who were serving as ministers.

In the same year, Sankara changed the name of the country from Upper Volta to Burkina Faso, meaning "land of incorruptible men." He also began a policy of political relaxation, releasing almost all political prisoners over the next few years and redirecting the CDR's efforts to civic improvements. He lost support because of an unsuccessful war with Mali, and even more so because of his attempts to curb the power of the unions. When he began advocating the creation of a single political party, his chief lieutenant, Captain Blaise Compaore, had a commando unit assassinate him and 13 of his associates. Compaore then took over and disbanded the CDRs, replacing them with Revolutionary Committees (CRs). He introduced an economic reform plan inviting foreign investment, encouraging private enterprise, and accepting negotiations with the International Monetary Fund, which Sankara had opposed.

Compaore also introduced political reforms leading to a new constitution in June 1991, a presidential election in December, and a legislative election in May 1992. The presidential election was marred by Compaore's refusal to create an independent administration to conduct the elections, violence and intimidation against opposition candidates, the withdrawal of all Compaore's opponents, and riots by the opposition that disrupted balloting. After the election, Compaore split the opposition by allying with one of its chief parties, and the subsequent legislative election was free and fair. Compaore's party gained 78 of the 107 seats, but the new government included representatives of seven parties. Youssouf Ouderaogo became prime minister, a post he held until student and civil service unrest caused by IMF-imposed austerity measures and the devaluation of the CFA franc in early 1994 forced him to resign.

Burkina Faso is one of the poorest countries on one of the poorest continents of the world, but its government is relatively benign. The courts are independent and generally fair, political prisoners are no longer being held, and the press is free and includes both independent publications and independent broadcasters. Freedom of religion is respected, as are the freedom to travel and freedom of association, including the right to organize unions and bargain collectively. The country remains in an economically precarious situation, but its political life is relatively blessed.

NIGER
Statistical Profile

Capital: Niamey
Area: 489,189 sq. miles
Population: 8,800,000 (1994 est.)
  Density: 18 people/sq. mile
  Growth Rate: 3.4% (1994 est.)
GDP: $2,345,000,000
Per Capita Income: $300
Foreign Debt: $1,567,000,000
Life Expectancy: 35 (1960), 46 (1992)
Ethnic Groups: Hausa, Zarma, Kanuri, Fulani, Tuareg
Official Language: French
Religions: Muslim (85%), Traditional (14.5%), Christian (.5%)

Former Colonizer: France
Date of Independence: 1960

History

Archaeological remains reveal human settlements in Niger dating back 4,000 years, and specialized activities like metalwork and trade date back to before Christ. No sizable states appeared until the sixteenth century, when the southwestern parts came under the sway of the Songhai Empire, the south-central area became northern Hausaland, and the southeastern area came under the Kingdom of Bornu. The upper classes in many regions had converted to Islam centuries before, but the religion took hold among the mass of people only in the nineteenth century, on the eve of colonial rule.

The first French expedition appeared in 1890, and the process of treaty-making and conquest took 20 years to complete. The French imposed a centralized bureaucratic administration in which reliable local chiefs formed the bottom layer of an otherwise white hierarchy and unreliable ones were replaced by those who were. With little of value to export, socioeconomic development was limited, and modern politics were correspondingly slow to develop. In 1946, administrative reforms and elections to assemblies stimulated the appearance of two political parties: the Niger Progressive Party (PPN), which was affiliated with the African Democratic Assembly (RDA) and the French Socialist Party and was backed by the French government, and the Niger Democratic Union (UND or Sawaba Party), a radical organization linked to the French Communist Party. The latter advocated immediate independence, rejected participation in the French Community, and looked likely to win the 1958 referendum, but administrative sleight-of-hand gave the victory to the PPN-RDA. Two years later, the country became fully independent. Hamani Diore, leader of the PPN-RDA, became president. The UND was outlawed and its leaders went into exile.

The first years of independence were marked by the struggle between Diore's government and the exiled opposition. In 1964 a small UND force tried to sneak across the border, and in 1965 an attempt was made on Diore's life. The latter incident cost the UND the support of Algeria, Libya, and China, and the threat from the exiles died down.

Trouble appeared on another front, however. The PPN-RDA established its agents in every village and urban district, but when it tried to enfranchise classes of people who had heretofore been vassals, it alienated members of the more privileged strata without winning over leftist students and intellectuals still bitter over the suppression of the UND. The massive drought and famine that began in 1973 compounded these problems, and on April 15, 1974, Lieutenant General Seyni Kountche seized power, arresting the leaders of the old government, dissolving the National Assembly and the PPN-RDA, and installing a Supreme Military Council.

Kountche's administration, which included more civilians than officers, weathered plots and coup attempts in 1974 and 1975 to enjoy a period of political tranquillity based on the rising price of uranium in the late 1970s. The value of uranium exports increased 10 times between 1975 and 1980, which paid for substantial development programs and temporarily removed the country from the French dole. Falling demand for uranium in the early 1980s hurt the country economically and perhaps contributed to an attempted coup in 1983, but the country continued to enjoy relative tranquillity. In 1983, Kountche created the National Council for Development (CND), which included 150 freely elected representatives from different social and professional groups in the country's seven regions. At the same time, he created seven regional councils, although their members were appointed rather than elected. One of the National Council's primary mandates was to set up a National Charter Commission to draw up a new constitution as part of a gradual process of returning the country to civilian rule.

Kountche continued the liberalization by freeing many political prisoners during the following year.

Kountche died in November 1987, but the country's chief of staff, Colonel Ali Saibou, filled in during the president's illness and assumed power peacefully upon his death. Within a month, Saibou granted a general amnesty, and in 1988 he moved the process of political reform into high gear. In July, he instructed the CND to draft a constitution, and in August he legalized political parties and founded one himself, the National Movement for the Development of Society (MNSD). In September 1989, Saibou won a seven-year term as president, and the MNSD won all the seats in the National Assembly in an election in which only MNSD candidates ran.

Three months later, a referendum confirmed the new constitution, making the MNSD the sole legal party, but dissatisfaction was so strong that in November 1990 Saibou announced that the country would adopt a multiparty system. In March 1991, the National Assembly approved a new constitution ending one-party rule, and in July a national conference convened for the purpose of organizing elections suspended the constitution and dissolved the national legislature, appointing Amadou Cheiffou to the post of transitional prime minister and creating a High Council of the Republic to act as an interim legislature. Despite complaints about the pace of reform, a mutiny by dissatisfied soldiers, a general strike to protest concessions to the mutineers, and a delay in the scheduled referendum and elections, the new constitution was approved before the end of 1992, and elections were held in 1993. The opposition coalition of eight parties, the Alliance of Forces of Change (AFC), bested the MNSD in the legislative contests held in February, and Mahamane Ousman, leader of one of the AFC parties, won the presidency in March.

Unfortunately, as Niger moved toward multiparty democracy, a new problem became acute: a rebellion by the Tuareg minority in the north. Trouble had been brewing since at least the early 1980s, when Libyan support for the Tuaregs, as well as for leftist insurgents, had led to a disruption of relations, but it became acute in the early 1990s after Libya expelled thousands of its own Tuaregs into Niger. The military mutiny of 1991 stemmed from disciplinary actions against an officer convicted of leading a massacre of 63 Tuareg civilians in 1990, and the Tuareg Front for the Liberation of Air and Azawad (FLAA) conducted attacks on soldiers and civilians across northern Niger. The government combined repression with negotiations and achieved a brief truce, but rebel attacks during and after the truce sparked reprisals by the army. Hostages were taken by both sides, and negotiations deadlocked. They resumed in 1994, and a formal end to hostilities was signed in April 1995.

Having resolved the Tuareg problem, Niger's government bestowed on the country substantial political freedom. Its courts functioned relatively free of political interference, except in regard to the insurgents, and the media was relatively independent. Religious freedom is respected, although the overwhelming majority of the people are Moslem, and freedom of association was respected as well, including the right to unionize.

Unfortunately, a military coup in January 1996 ousted Ousame. While the coup's leader, Colonel Ibrahim Barre, claimed he was acting to protect democracy and had "no intention" of remaining in power, the coup represented a definite setback for democratization and left Niger's freedoms in doubt.

CHAD
Statistical Profile

Capital:	N'Djamena
Area:	495,753 sq. miles
Population:	6,500,000 people/sq. mile
Density:	13 people/sq. mile
Growth Rate:	2.6%
GDP:	$1,247,000,000
Per Capita Income:	$230
Foreign Debt:	$667,000,000
Life Expectancy:	35 (1960), 47 (1992)

Ethnic Groups:	11 major groups (principally Sara, Bedouin Arab, Tuareg, Toubou)
Official Language:	French
Religions:	Muslim (50%), Traditional (40%), Christian (7%)
Former Colonizer:	France
Date of Independence:	1960

History

From the fourteenth century until the colonial period, the Islamic states of central Chad—the empire of Kanem-Bornu and the lesser kingdoms of Bagiurmi and Ouaddai—dominated the stateless peoples to their south. Those states reached their apogee in the last quarter of the nineteenth century, when Rabah Zobeir conquered Kanem and Bagiurmi and united them in a single large state. The French allied with the deposed rulers and vanquished Rabah in 1900, conquered Ouaddai in 1911, and secured the northern part of the country in 1916, absorbing it into French Equatorial Africa and making Chad a separate colony in 1920. Around the same time, the French began to promote cotton cultivation in the southern part of the country, and thereby began to reverse the old relationship between north and south in which the north dominated. The animist, stateless southerners proved more open to French cultural penetration than the Moslems in the north, and the introduction of commercial agriculture accelerated their integration into the colonial system. Drawn more quickly into modern political as well as economic relations, Southerners dominated the early anticolonial movement after the Second World War. Gabriel Lisette formed the Chadian Progressive Party (PPT) in 1947, and after a brief period of radicalism aligned it with the French decolonization program. He led the autonomous government that was created in 1957.

Francois Tombalbaye replaced Lisette at the head of the party in 1959, and thus became the head of state upon independence. He purged the party of Lisette's supporters in 1960 and made the PPT Chad's sole party in 1962, gradually tightening his personal hold on power in the process. Opposition to his despotism, to continuing ties to the French, and to the government's inability to improve the lot of the average Chadian, grew into a debilitating civil war that continued into the 1990s. Even before independence, workers, students, and intellectuals formed the Chadian National Union (UNT), which opposed the PPT's comfortable relationship with the French. The UNT spearheaded the opposition within Chad until Tombalbaye outlawed it along with other opposition parties, arresting many of its leaders and driving the rest into exile. The government responded to demonstrations in the capital of N'Djamena in September 1963 with violence, killing hundreds. The government's taxes provoked a peasant revolt in the south in 1965 that spread to the center and to the east. In June 1966, UNT and a conservative Islamic armed movement, the Chad Liberation Front (FLT), united to form the Chad National Liberation Front (FROLINAT), which was joined two years later by rebels in the northern region. Only French military intervention in 1968 and 1969 kept Tombalbaye in power, and French political advisors helped him split the opposition in the early 1970s. He survived an attack by FROLINAT on the capital in 1972, and the opposition was further weakened by internal splits and the loss of support from Sudan and Libya.

Just when Tombalbaye seemed victorious, he arrested the country's chief of staff, Felix Malloum, replaced the PPT with a new party, and sponsored a cultural revolution in which towns were renamed, Christian names were banned, and traditional ceremonies were revived. Instead of increasing his popularity, these measures increased discontent, and on April 13, 1975, he was killed in a coup d'état.

The new regime, led by former chief of staff Malloum, soon lost its popular support by guaranteeing foreign investments and prohibiting political activity. Strikes and an assassination attempt on Malloum followed, and over the next three years FROLINAT, with Libyan backing, united most of the opposition and led it to a series of military victories. France countered Libya's rising influence by arranging a new coalition government including Malloum as head of state and a dissident rebel, Hissene Habre, leader of a faction from the north, as prime minister.

As soon as the two took office in August 1978, they began to struggle with each other for power. Malloum's power was based on the Chadian Armed Forces (FAT), and his support came from the Christian and animist southerners. Habre's power was based on the Army Forces of the North (FAN), and his support came from the Islamic Arabs and Tuaregs. Habre gained the support of a breakaway faction of FROLINAT led by Goukouni Oueddi and of the French as well. Fighting between Habre and Malloum broke out in earnest in February 1979. The fighting lasted only a few months and led to a new "government of national unity" (GUNT), which took office in November with Goukouni as president. Goukouni and Habre began fighting the next March. Goukouni got the better of it at first with Libyan backing, by mid-1982 Habre had the upper hand. His army captured N'Djamena in June.

Habre proclaimed himself head of state, formed a government including both his supporters and former members of GUNT, and declared: "For the first time in 17 years the 14 Chadian administrative regions are under a single authority." Goukouni's forces attacked from Libya in 1983, and only U.S. aid and French troops kept them and a contingent of Libyans confined to the north. Troubles arose on another front in early 1985 when a guerrilla war broke out in the south and a variety of exiled parties pressed for alternatives to both Goukouni and Habre. Libya, which had agreed with France to a mutual withdrawal in 1984, invaded with a more powerful force of tanks and helicopters in February 1986, and French troops and planes had to intervene once again. In March, Habre brought several Southerners into his government, including two guerrilla leaders, and in the second half of 1986, several of Goukouni's allies broke with him and joined Habre, while Goukouni himself broke with Libya. In March 1987, Habre's forces defeated the Libyans at Ouadi Doum, and liberated almost the entire north except for the Aouzou Strip, a uranium-rich border area claimed by Libya. Once again, Habre could proclaim that he controlled the entire country.

Having finally secured power, Habre began political reforms, implementing a new constitution in 1989 and holding elections in which he won a seven-year term as president. In November 1990, however, Idriss Deby, who had fled to Sudan after an unsuccessful coup attempt in 1989, led an invasion that routed Habre's forces and drove him from the country. Deby suspended the constitution and promised a replacement that would include multiparty democracy as well as basic civil liberties. In February 1991, he formalized an interim government that would rule for 30 months and oversee a national conference to set up elections. His government legalized opposition parties during 1992, brought representatives of several of those parties into the cabinet, and, after repeated delays, held the national conference in 1993. Multiparty elections did not follow, however. The "transitional" period was extended for one year in April 1994, and in April 1995 elections were postponed again.

In addition to its difficulty in living up to its promise to create a multiparty democracy, Deby's government has a spotty record on civil liberties. As a result of attacks staged from outside the country by forces loyal to Habre and at least three coup attempts from within, special tribunals have usurped the role of the court system in security cases, and hundreds of people have been detained, tortured, and executed without trial. The official media voice the government's line, while independent journalists have been subject to harassment. The national journalists' union staged a protest strike in August 1992, while a new labor federation, created to replace one too closely associated with Habre, called a general strike to demand back pay and protest austerity measures. The fact that these groups could stage their protests at all showed the progress that Chad has made; the fact that they had to suggests how far Chad has to go. Perhaps epitomizing the mixed situation is the following contrasting set of events: in 1991, the Chadian Human Rights League appeared and publicly protested abuses by the Deby regime; in February 1992, "off duty" soldiers assassinated the League's vice president. Deby may still make good on his promises of democracy, but the civil war in Chad is not over yet.

SUDAN
Statistical Profile

Capital:	Khartoum
Area:	967,494 sq. miles
Population:	28,200,000 (1994 est.)
Density:	29 people/sq. mile
Growth Rate:	3.1% (1994 est.)
GDP:	$6,275,000,000
Per Capita Income:	$184
Foreign Debt:	$9,480,000,000
Life Expectancy:	39 (1960), 52 (1992)
Ethnic Groups:	Contains 570 groups, including Arabic speaking groups (50%); the Nuba, Beja, Fur, Dinka, Nuer, and Shilluk
Official Language:	Arabic
Religions:	Muslim (70%), Traditional (25%), Christian (5%)
Former Colonizer:	Great Britain
Date of Independence:	1956

History

Sudan was home to Africa's second-oldest civilization, and remained independent until the Mamluks of Egypt conquered it in the thirteenth century, bringing the northern parts into the Islamic world. The Arabs who settled there soon established their own independence, which lasted until the Egyptians, under Muhammad 'Ali, invaded in 1820 and brought the area into the modern world. As the British came to dominate Egypt, they also came to dominate the Sudan, which led to the Mahdist uprising that established an independent state between 1881 and 1898. The British crushed the Mahdists at Omdurman and established a joint government with the Egyptians, but this arrangement was really just a mask for British colonial rule. The British invested heavily in agriculture and infrastructure to transform the colony into a profitable cotton producer, and in the process they fostered the growth of modern middle and working classes who turned to nationalism and socialism between the 1920s and the 1940s. Great Britain granted the Sudan independence in 1956 to keep it out of the hands of radical Egypt. Sudan became the largest country in Africa in terms of territory; it contained a multiplicity of ethnic groups speaking over 150 languages and had the strongest communist party on the continent.

The deepest division by far was between the Moslems in the north and the Christians and animists in the south. Even before independence, the nascent government refused to consider autonomy for the south, and so a civil war began that plagued the country for three of the next four decades. The economy also began to deteriorate, and a junta headed by General Ibrahim Abboud seized control from the parliamentary regime left by the British. The junta failed to solve either the country's economic or its ethnic problems and a general strike and popular revolt brought a return to parliamentary rule in 1964. Neither the situation in the south nor the economy got better, and in 1969 a group of young officers led by Colonel Jaafar el-Nimeiry took power.

Nimeiry began as a radical—allying with the Communist Party, expropriating agricultural estates, and nationalizing large businesses. He created his own party, the Sudan Socialist Union, as the sole legal party, and survived a coup attempt by the Communists. His crowning achievement was to make peace with the rebels in the south in 1972. He moved steadily into the Western orbit, allying with Sadat's Egypt and supporting the Camp David agreements between Egypt and Israel. He moderated his rule at the same time, proclaiming an amnesty in August 1977, but austerity measures imposed by the International Monetary Fund fueled popular discontent, which erupted in strikes and street fighting in 1979.

Nimeiry compounded his problems in 1982 by adopting a plan to divide the heretofore unified south into three separate regions. Some Southerners advocated the measure to curb the power of the dominant Dinka tribe, but most saw it as an attempt to dilute the south's political power. Fighting broke out and escalated quickly; by September, the new Sudanese People's Liberation Army (SPLA) had about 6,000 men in the field, commanded by renegade Colonel John Garang. Nimeiry tried to boost his popularity in the north by adopting Islamic law in 1983, but the people were more concerned with the continuing deterioration of the economy. Nimeiry alternated between increased repressive measures and conciliatory gestures, but when he imposed a new austerity program in 1985, discontent boiled over in massive demonstrations that set the stage for another military coup.

The new military government, headed by General Swaredahab, suspended the constitution and imposed martial law, but promised elections for a civilian government within a year—and delivered. In April 1986, Sadiq al-Mahdi, great grandson of the great Mahdi, became president, promising to end the use of Islamic law and the civil war. Negotiations failed, and the economy continued to falter; in July 1989, another military coup brought Brigadier Omar Hassan Ahmed el-Beshir to power. Beshir abolished the elected constituent assembly, suspended the constitution, and himself made prime minister. He forged close ties with Libya in 1990; placed Islamic fundamentalists in control of the security forces, the judiciary, and the universities; and declared the Sudan to be an Islamic state, extending Islamic law (in theory anyway) over the entire country in 1991. In 1992, he created the Transitional National Assembly (TNA) to lead the country to democracy by the end of 1995.

At the same time, government forces mounted a massive campaign in the south that succeeded in pushing the rebels out of their headquarters and all but out of the country. In 1993, the military junta proclaimed el-Beshir president and dissolved itself. In April 1994, legislation was adopted that called for elections to take place later in the year, but they were postponed in November. Meanwhile, the conflict in the south continued.

Many regard the fundamentalist Hassan el-Turabi as the real leader of the country and see his goal as the creation of a theocratic state. Sudan remains under martial law and a state of emergency. The courts are completely subservient to the government, and extrajudicial detentions, torture, and executions are common. The government has set up a system of "popular committees" to supervise individual neighborhoods. Freedom of speech is limited, private publications are prohibited, and the government controls all electronic media. Nonreligious organizations, demonstrations, and strikes have all been banned. Although some political prisoners have been released recently, Sudan remains a country subjected to severe repression.

CAPE VERDE
Statistical Profile

Capital:	Praia
Area:	1,556 sq. miles
Population:	400,000 (1994 est.)
Density:	257 people/sq. mile
Growth Rate:	2.9% (1994 est.)
GDP:	$303,000,000
Per Capita Income:	$850
Foreign Debt:	$151,000,000
Life Expectancy:	52 (1960), 68 (1992)
Ethnic Group:	Crioulo, with no major subdivisions
Official Language:	Portuguese
Religion:	Catholic (97%)
Former Colonizer:	Portugal
Date of Independence:	1975

History

The Cape Verde Islands were uninhabited when the Portuguese discovered them in 1456. Settlers arrived in 1462 and the islands became a base for slave raiding on the mainland, the slaves being used initially in local agriculture and later for shipment to America. Interbreeding between masters and slaves led to the development of a distinct Cape Verdean nationality with its own culture and a language mixing old Portuguese with various African dialects. Because of their strategic position near the oceanic routes from Europe to both America and the Far East, the islands and São Vicente in particular—became important commercial centers. Severe droughts began in the mid-eighteenth century, and the resulting famines, plus the end of slavery, sent the islands into decline in the ninteenth century. Economic hardship, added to the fact that the Portuguese permitted Cape Verdeans greater educational opportunities than subjects in their other colonies, led many to leave for work in the administration of other colonies or for America.

In 1956, the Cape Verdean intellectual, Amilcar Cabral, started the African Party for the Independence of Guinea and Cape Verde (PAIGC), linking anticolonialism in Cape Verde with anticolonialism in Guinea. Cape Verdeans played a large role in the movement, but because of Cape Verde's isolated location, the main struggle was conducted in Guinea. PAIGC launched a guerrilla war there in 1963 that played an important part in bringing Portugal to its knees by 1974. When the Portuguese dictatorship fell, a mass movement arose on Cape Verde that forced the new Portuguese government to negotiate independence. The islands became independent on July 5, 1975.

Under the new country's constitution, called the "Organic Statute of the State of Cape Verde," the islands became a one-party state. The PAIGC was run by a 32-member National Council, which delegated executive powers to a small Permanent Committee, and decisions were passed down through party organizations at the regional and local levels. The party restricted membership to a small elite and involved the masses through auxillary organizations for women, youth, and workers. The party dominated the government, with many ministers drawn from the PAIGC National Council. The National Assembly met only a few days a year.

During the late 1970s, the PAIGC staved off challanges from both the right and the left, quashing a rightist coup plot in 1977 and purging dissident Trotskyites in 1979. During the same years, the leadership strove to unite Cape Verde and Guinea-Bissau, but economics, geography, and cultural traditions were against them. Furthermore, some Guineans resented Cape Verdeans because of their prominence in both the colonial administration and the PAIGC. After a coup in Guinea in 1981, relations between the two countries were broken off briefly, and the dream of unification died forever. The PAIGC changed its name to the African Party for the Independence of Cape Verde (PAICV), and the country adopted a new constitution recognizing the split.

For the rest of the 1980s, Cape Verdean politics remained stable. The PAICV under President Pereira held regular, if one-party, elections, and pursued moderate policies, at least in part because the arid country was heavily dependent on food and other aid from Western countries. In November 1988, the PAICV congress took up the issue of multiparty democracy, and two commissions were appointed in 1989 to consider electoral reforms. They moved too slowly for the opposition, so in February 1990 the PAICV held an emergency congress to consider the issue again. In April, the opposition groups abroad joined in the Movement for Democracy (MPD) to press for reform, and in July Pereira announced that multiparty legislative elections would be held in January 1991 and presidential elections in February. In September 1990, opposition parties were legalized. The MPD won 56 of 79 seats in the National Assembly in the January elections, and in February the MPD candidate, Antonio Monteiro, beat Pereira for the presidency. While elections in February 1996 were marred by an opposition boycott to protest MPD tactics, Cape Verdeans have nonetheless made the transition to become one of Africa's freer political systems.

CHAPTER
6
•••••••

Francophone West Africa

INTRODUCTION

The Francophone, or French-speaking, West African countries that are not in the Sahel are interspersed with Anglophone, or English-speaking, countries along the coast. They include Senegal, Guinea, Ivory Coast, Togo, and Benin. Guinea-Bissau is Lusophone, or Portuguese-speaking, but has gravitated to the French-speaking community since independence. The ecologies of these countries range from arid steppes to tropical forests, but savanna predominates. All except Guinea-Bissau were French colonies, all belong to regional institutions affiliated with France, and all have strong bilateral ties to France as well. Most of them are one-party states dominated by strongmen who have gone through the motions of democratization without actually instituting it. Benin and Guinea-Bissau are exceptions, having established multiparty democracies in the early 1990s.

SENEGAL
Statistical Profile

Capital:	Dakar
Area:	75,749 sq. miles
Population:	8,200,000 (1994 est.)
Density:	108 people/sq. mile
Growth Rate:	2.7% (1994 est.)
GDP:	$6,277,000,000
Per Capita Income:	$780
Foreign Debt:	$2,982,000,000
Life Expectancy:	37 (1960), 48 (1992)
Ethnic Groups:	Wolof (36%), Mende (30%), Serer (16%), Fulani (17%)
Official Language:	French
Religions:	Muslim (80%), Traditional (15%), Christian (5%)
Former Colonizer:	France
Date of Independence:	1960

History

The area that is now Senegal has been inhabited since Neolithic times at least, and the

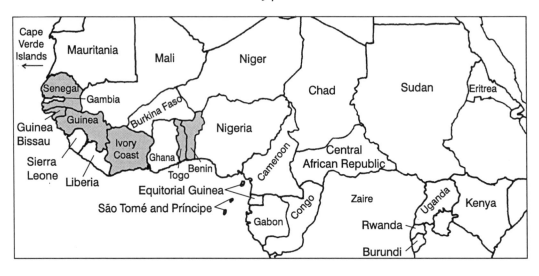

Francophone West Africa

inhabitants began organizing kingdoms during the first millennium after Christ at the latest. The Ghanaian empire ruled part of the area around 1000, and in the thirteenth or fourteenth century the Djolof kingdom established its suzerainty over two neighboring kingdoms to create a small, independent empire that lasted into the mid-sixteenth century. By the time the Djolof kingdom collapsed, the area had been in contact with Europeans for a century. The French established their first outpost in Africa at St. Louis in 1659. Their claim to the port survived the ups and downs of their overseas empire into the middle of the nineteenth century, when it became the base from which they undertook the systematic conquest of West Africa, a process that was not completed until 1892. In the meantime, France extended limited political rights to the citizens of St. Louis and the other old centers as part of their "assimilation" policy, and in 1914 the colony sent Blaise Diagne as the first black deputy to the French National Assembly. Diagne and his successors dominated Senegalese politics for the next two decades, until the appearance of Leopold Senghor in 1945. A Catholic and a renowned poet, Senghor nonetheless gained the support of both the Moslem leadership and the peasant masses, who elected him to the French National Assembly. He helped pass reforms like the abolition of forced labor; established his own party, the Senegalese Democratic Bloc (BDS), in 1948; and led the country to independence in June 1960 as part of a federation with Mali. In August 1960, the federation fell apart, and Senegal emerged as a separate country.

In the early years of independence, Senghor moved gradually to establish a one-party state. Even before independence, the BDS merged with several other parties to form the Senegalese Popular Bloc (BPS), which then merged with still other parties to form the Senegalese Progressive Union (UPS), both of which were dominated by Senghor and his BDS. In 1960, shortly after independence, the government banned the Marxist-oriented African Party of Independence (PAI), and in 1963 it dissolved and banned the opposition Bloc of the Senegalese Masses (BMS) as well. The same year, a national referendum approved a new constitution strengthening Senghor's presidential powers, and legislative elections gave the UPS a decisive majority, although there were widespread allegations of fraud. Thereafter, opposition groups lost heart; some were banned while the rest merged with the UPS. In 1966, the last legal opposition party, the Party of African Consolidation (PRA), joined with the UPS, which changed its name to the Senegalese Socialist Party (PSS) in 1976.

This consolidation of power did not go unopposed. As early as 1963, allegations of electoral fraud sparked riots and subsequent police repression that left 100 people dead. Political dissatisfaction plus austerity measures forced by economic problems culminated in a student strike in 1968 that led to a general strike. The strike was ended by a show of force that included putting French troops at Ouakam on alert and by promises of economic concessions and educational reforms. Further unrest at Dakar University broke out after another government electoral victory in 1973, which again sparked widespread labor actions. The upheaval ended with the expulsion of 55 students, the jailing of radical labor leaders, and the banning of the main trade union and the teachers' union.

Opposition to the government was not confined to students and organized labor. In 1969, peasants in Cabrouse resisted an attempt by the government to expropriate their land in order to give it to a tourist company. In 1976, peanut farmers went on strike to protest low prices and high equipment costs and taxes, planting food in place of export crops. When they continued the protest the next year, the government made concessions, but the peasants went ahead and formed a union with the backing of the National Democratic Assembly (RND), a party not recognized by the government.

These varied pressures led to a limited democratization in 1978. Under Senghor's guidance, a four-party system was codified, with each party assigned an ideological category. The governing PSS got the center "liberal and democratic" slot, the Senegalese Democratic Party (PDS) got the center-left "socialist and democratic" slot, the revived PAI received the "Marxist-Leninist" label, and the Senegalese Republican Movement (MRS) took the rightist "conservative" place. This labeling ensured

that the PDS and PAI would split the leftist vote. With the conservative party commanding little support, the net result of the "democratization" was continued dominance of Senegalese politics by Senghor and the PSS, which won the 1978 elections. Senghor's grip on power seemed secure.

During the next two years, corruption scandals led to anti-government agitation by workers, peasants, and students. In 1980, after the government successfully suppressed a series of demonstrations and riots, Senghor made perhaps his greatest contribution to African politics by becoming the first head of state to step down voluntarily. On December 31, 1980, he resigned and handed power to prime minister and heir apparent, Abdou Diouf, who formally took over on the first of the year. Diouf adopted a policy of "holding onto all that had been acquired by" Senghor, while making "some changes." Thus, he continued the economic policy of "severity and austerity," while moving to loosen the political system by allowing an unlimited number of opposition parties.

Once again, this liberalization had the practical effect of splintering the opposition and strengthening the government party. In elections in 1983, Diouf won the presidency, while the PSS retained overwhelming control of the legislature. The PSS won local elections in the following year, although 12 out of 15 opposition parties boycotted the vote. Opposition mounted in the mid-1980s with a political offensive by united opposition parties in 1985, student riots at the university in 1987, a police strike later that year, a strike by secondary-school students from 1987 to 1988, and widespread disturbances following disputed elections in 1988. Diouf's government responded with harsh measures at first, arresting opposition leaders and refusing to allow a union of opposition parties in 1985, calling in the police to suppress striking students and then soldiers to suppress striking policemen in 1987, and declaring a state of emergency after the disturbances sparked by the 1988 election. In the early 1990s, the government formed a coalition administration with two other parties and enacted electoral reforms, including secret ballots and opposition monitors at voting sites. Within this framework, Diouf and the PSS still won elections in 1993, although by a reduced margin.

Senegal faced other serious challenges both at home and abroad during the 1980s and early 1990s. An attempted coup in 1981 by leftists in Gambia, a smaller state strung along the Gambia River and entirely surrounded by Senegal, led to Senegalese intervention in support of the government and a troubled federation of the two countries that lasted from 1982 until 1989. Senegal's interest in suppressing the coup and promoting the partial union reflected its concern over separatist troubles in the southern region of Casamance, which is substantially isolated from the main part of the country by Gambia. Disturbances there first erupted in late 1982, and discontent simmered throughout the 1980s and flared again in 1992. Guerrilla fighters and the government's counterinsurgency forces both perpetrated atrocities, including kidnapping, torture, and execution of the others' supporters (and suspected supporters). Thousands were driven to flee. The two sides agreed to a cease-fire in July 1993, but clashes between their forces broke out within days, and fighting continued into 1996.

Senegal claims that Mauritania is supporting the Casamancian rebels, a claim that reflects continuing tension between the two countries. In 1989, their armies fought a number of brief border clashes, and riots broke out in each country against resident nationals from the other, leaving hundreds dead and leading to mass repatriations in both directions. The two countries did not restore diplomatic relations until 1992.

In 1994, the country was rocked by strikes and riots protesting the devaluation of the CFA franc. The devaluation made exports more competitive, but drove up the cost of imports, which include both luxuries and food. Additional violence resulted in 1994 when armed Islamic demonstrators and police clashed in Dakar. The government responded by arresting hundreds of demonstrators and banning a radical fundamentalist group known as the "Guides."

Senegal in the mid-1990s is something of a paradox. It is a parliamentary democracy in which the ruling party has never been seriously threatened at the polls. It is a country in which all the basic freedoms—speech, assembly, movement, and religion—are respected and an independent judiciary is maintained. It is also a country in which a bitter counterinsurgency is being conducted against one region and violent demonstrations have been breaking out elsewhere. It is a country that has pursued moderate development efforts in close collaboration with France and the IMF; yet it remains a country of peasants whose well-being depends primarily on the vicissitudes of its annual peanut crop. In some ways, Senegal has stood out as a bastion of democracy in Africa, but in other ways, it is a reminder of how limited such a haven can be.

GUINEA
Statistical Profile

Capital:	Conakry
Area:	94,927 sq. miles
Population:	6,400,000 (1994 est.)
Density:	67 people/sq. mile
Growth Rate:	2.5% (1994 est.)
GDP:	$3,233,000,000
Per Capita Income:	$510
Foreign Debt:	$2,466,000,000
Life Expectancy:	33 (1960), 44 (1992)
Ethnic Groups:	Susu (23%), Malinke (40%), Fulani (30%), Tenda, Kissi
Official Language:	French
Religions:	Muslim (85%), remainder Traditional and Christian
Former Colonizer:	France
Date of Independence:	1958

History

Inhabited since Neolithic times, the area of Guinea lay at the southern edge of the Ghanaian, Malian, and Songhai empires. Islamic pastoralists established small states between the fifteenth and eighteenth centuries, and in the second half of the nineteenth, Almamy Samori Toure created a militarized empire that resisted French encroachments until 1898. France had already declared the area a colony in 1891, and it formed part of French West Africa until 1946, when it became an overseas territory. The next year, Sekou Toure, a descendant of Samori and a militant trade unionist, founded the Democratic Party of Guinea (PDG) as part of the regional African Democratic Assembly (RDA). Toure's party scored decisive successes over two rival parties in elections to the French Assembly on January 2, 1956, in municipal elections on November 18 of that year, and in local territorial elections on March 31, 1957. When de Gaulle offered a choice of membership in the French Union or total independence the next year, Toure opted for the latter, as did the voters; Guinea was the only French colony in which the government and the voters agreed on this choice. France responded by cutting off all aid, pulling out all French personnel, and destroying all government property that could not be carted away.

Toure said "poverty in freedom" was preferable to "riches in slavery," and his people got what he preferred. Shunned by France's Western allies, Toure turned to the Soviet bloc. Ties to the Soviet Union reinforced Toure's leftist socioeconomic and political leanings, and he created a repressive, one-party state that presided over a crumbling economy. His PDG was a strongly hierarchical institution with a National Political Bureau overseeing 34 federations. At the local level, it ruled through 2,500 revolutionary village councils that controlled economic as well as political activity. Toure tightened his hold on the country by suppressing a series of alleged conspiracies: "reactionaries and feudalists" in 1960, intellectuals in 1961, merchants in 1964, the staffs of national enterprises in 1967, and leading civil servants and officers in 1969–1970. In 1970, dissidents and Portuguese mercenar-

ies mounted an unsuccessful attack on Conakry, which brought still more repression. In 1976, Toure had Diallo Telli, former head of the Organization of African Unity, jailed and executed for involvement in yet another alleged plot. In all, 17 of Toure's ministers were executed between 1958 and the late 1970s, 18 others were sentenced to life imprisonment, and thousands of ordinary Guineans suspected of opposing the government were imprisoned, tortured, and killed.

Along with the PDG's increasing control over the country's political life, there was a corresponding growth of its control over the country's economic life. Land reform was followed by the creation of agricultural production brigades, state control of wholesale and retail trade, and artificially low producer prices (to channel profits from agriculture to industrial development projects). While Soviet aid helped, it included such absurdities as snowplows, a military academy, and high school teachers who spoke only Russian, and the price was high. The cost of Soviet help in developing bauxite mines, the backbone of the export economy, was an agreement that the Soviet Union be able to buy 90 percent of the yield in rubles at below the world price and that all Guinea's income from the mine would go to repay its debt to the Soviet Union. The result of Toure's "development" program was reduced agricultural yields and inefficient industries, a steady decline in the standard of living, and the emigration of somewhere between 20 and 40 percent of the Guinean population (between one and two million people).

By the mid-1970s, even Toure had to acknowledge his country's problems. Declaring that the Soviets were "more capitalist than the capitalists," he performed a remarkable about-face in both his foreign and domestic policies. In July 1976, he attended the OAU for the first time in 10 years, and in 1977 he agreed to compensate French firms whose property had been nationalized. In March 1978, he attended the Monrovia Conference with Senegal and the Ivory Coast to patch up relations with these neighbors, and he succeeded—once he stopped demanding that they forcibly return opponents who had gone into exile within their borders. In November 1978, Toure called a PDG conference at which it reorganized itself and resolved to decentralize state power, form a new national assembly, and have elected rather than appointed regional governors. A month later, French President Valery Giscard d'Estang made a widely acclaimed state visit, and soon after the aid and investment taps began to flow. Toure expanded the pipeline through numerous visits to rich Arab oil producers between 1978 and 1981, and by 1980 Guinea was the largest recipient of Arab aid in sub-Saharan Africa.

In the early 1980s, Toure seemed to have made his transition successfully. The PDG won single-party elections in 1980, and he himself won reelection for another seven years in an uncontested election in May 1982. Later that year, he made a state visit to France despite opposition protests pointing to his human rights record. He was slated to become the next chairman of the OAU in the summer of 1984, but died of a heart ailment in April. Within a few days of Toure's funeral, Colonel Lansana Conte seized power, denouncing Toure's "bloody and ruthless dictatorship." Conte's Military Committee for National Recovery (CMNR) dissolved the PDG, detained its leaders, and promised political liberalization and economic development.

Conte has lived up to both promises to some degree, fulfilling the second more truly than the first. He has opened the country to foreign investment, and the per capita GNP has doubled. At over $510 per person, it is still below that of neighboring countries like Senegal and the Ivory Coast, but it is catching up fast and is already higher than that of many other African countries. Job cutbacks and high user fees for basic services have hurt the lower classes, but they are necessary to secure loans from international agencies. Given the spotty track record of similar programs elsewhere, it is by no means certain how far Conte's program will take the country. But

given the failure of Toure's socialism, it seems to offer the best chance available.

Conte's record on political reform has been weaker. He began by amnestying most of the former PDG leaders, but when some were implicated in a coup attempt in 1985 by his trusted associate and prime minister, Diara Traore, he had 20 summarily executed. Conte increasingly isolated himself from his cabinet and showed a marked reluctance to give up power, despite ostensible moves in that direction. In October 1989, he promised multiparty democracy and in December 1990 held a national referendum that approved a new constitution providing for a five-year transition period. In January 1991, the CMNR gave way to the Transitory Committee of National Recovery (CTRN), but Conte appointed all its members and served as its head. In April 1992, opposition parties became legal, and 40 soon emerged, but scheduled elections were delayed. Frustrated, the opposition became violent, with assassination attempts on Conte in February and October of that year. Violent clashes between supporters of the major parties took place repeatedly; in July political demonstrations were banned. The opposition continued to agitate for an independent transitional government, and in September 1993 the police killed 63 people while breaking up a demonstration. In the same month, Conte announced that presidential elections would take place in December and legislative elections would follow in February 1994. Conte won reelection amid violence and charges of fraud, and the legislative elections held in June 1995 were similarly marred. Opposition deputies only took their seats in September, when Conte made it clear he would not negotiate with them despite independent verification of their allegations about the elections.

Despite Conte's reforms, Guinea still suffers from the political and economic legacy of Toure. While the elections moved the country toward multiparty democracy, the courts remain corrupt and inefficient, the state maintains special security courts, and human rights abuses are common. There are numerous political parties, and religion and the press are relatively free, but the standard of living remains low and the future of political reform is uncertain.

IVORY COAST
Statistical Profile

Capital:	Abidjan
Area:	124,502 sq. miles
Population:	13,900,000 (1994 est.)
Density:	112 people/sq. mile
Growth Rate:	3.5% (1994 est.)
GDP:	$8,726,000,000
Per Capita Income:	$670
Foreign Debt:	$13,300,000,000
Life Expectancy:	39 (1960), 56 (1992)
Ethnic Groups:	60 groups in the following 4 major divisions: Akan, Mande, Kru, Voltaic
Official Language:	French
Religions:	Traditional (65%), Muslim (23%), Christian (12%)
Former Colonizer:	France
Date of Independence:	1960

History

The Mande people have inhabited the area of the Ivory Coast for a long time, but little is known of their history before the last few centuries, when the country's other main ethnic groups—the Kru, the Akan, and the Malinke—moved in and set up small kingdoms. The Europeans made early contact, but the coast was uninviting and visits were few until the French secured treaties of protection with the peoples near the Atlantic in the 1840s. France established a commercial monopoly and then, in the 1880s, a claim recognized by the other European powers. In 1893, the French declared the area a colony. Pacification campaigns lasted until 1917, but in the meantime the French set up a centralized bureaucracy connecting the colonial governor with local chiefs, imposed a head tax, and instituted forced labor. They succeeded in pushing the majority of Ivorians into the cash economy, and by the end of World War II the primary political force in the colony was prosperous native planters who resented the government's preferential treatment of French expatriates. Felix Houphouet-Boigny, a wealthy planter, emerged as their leader, transformed the African Agricultural Syndicate (SAA) into the Democratic Party of the Ivory Coast (PDCI), and affiliated it with the African Democratic Assembly (RDA). The PDCI's agitation for greater political participation and higher commodity prices led in 1948–1949 to mass demonstrations that left 52 people dead. But commodity prices did rise, and in the 1950s the party became more conservative. Although the PDCI scored big electoral successes as the French liberalized their colonial system, Houphouet-Boigny came by the late 1950s to oppose independence and resisted attempts to create regional federations that would have siphoned wealth from the Ivory Coast to its poorer neighbors in the interior.

When independence came, Houphouet-Boigny adapted quickly and, as the country's leading politician, assumed power. He made the Ivory Coast into a one-party state, occasionally suppressing but more often absorbing the opposition through a combination of political conciliation, personal persuasion, and government largesse. For example, he met repeatedly with the perpetrators of unsuccessful and eventually released them, even befriending one and taking him into the government as minister of health. In 1967, when university students went on strike, he met with them and persuaded them to return to their studies. Disturbances flared periodically—a regional revolt in Bete in 1973, discontent over inflation in 1978, and an abortive plot against the government in 1980—but as long as the economy grew, political stability seemed assured.

The Ivorian economy did grow steadily during the 1960s and 1970s; Houphouet-Boigny pursued a policy of agricultural, rather than industrial, development and maximum cooperation with foreign, particularly French, companies. The number of Frenchmen in the country actually increased several fold after independence, and they helped transform the Ivory Coast into a model of Third World development.

The miracle ended, however, in the early 1980s, when commodity prices plunged. Promise of political reforms, including the abolition of the one-party state, did not make up for the austerity measures the government imposed. Workers came close to staging a general strike in 1981, and in 1982 students at the university struck to protest censorship of an opposition lecturer. They were met this time by troops and police rather than conciliatory conversation. In 1983, university professors struck to protest corruption in the housing administration, and in 1984 dissidents distributed anti-government leaflets denouncing corruption and economic incompetence. At almost the same time, a government inquiry revealed widespread malpractices in three of the major state corporations, including the housing authority.

Running unopposed, Houphouet-Boigny won a sixth five-year term in 1985, and his party won the National Assembly, also unopposed. But discontent with his rule continued to fester and in 1990 focused on the new Catholic basilica he had built in his hometown of Yamoussoukro. He had already made the village into the nation's official capital in 1983, at a cost of millions of dollars (although most government offices remained in Abidjan). The cathedral he commissioned could hold 500,000 people, half the total number of Catholics in the entire country. Pope John Paul II dedicated the structure in January 1990, and in February and March students and civil servants began a wave of demonstrations and riots to protest the government's corruption and waste at a time when it was making cuts in salaries and services for ordinary Ivorians. Houphouet-Boigny responded by closing the university and schools and banning demonstrations.

On May 16, renegade soldiers took over the Abidjan airport. Loyal troops soon recaptured it, but Houphouet-Boigny changed tack and agreed to hold multiparty elections for the assembly and for president. Twenty-six parties soon registered, and 500 candidates ran for the 175 assembly seats. Laurent Gbagbo, a leading opposition figure, challenged Houphouet-Boigny for the presidency. The government party won 163 of the 175 seats, and Houphouet-Boigny won 81 percent of the presidential vote, but once again electoral victory did not end opposition to the regime. Claiming that the election was rigged, students protested in May and June 1991. This time the army crushed the protests brutally. When Houphouet-Boigny rejected the recommendation of a commission of inquiry that the soldiers and their commander be disciplined, opposition mounted, climaxing in mass demonstrations in Abidjan in February 1992, during which both Gbagbo and the president of the Ivorian Human Rights League were arrested. Pressure from the International Monetary Fund, to which the Ivory Coast was heavily indebted, forced the government to release the men, but Houphouet-Boigny coupled this act with a grant of immunity to the soldiers accused of crimes. Opposition to Houphouet-Boigny continued until his death in December 1993, at which time the president of the National Assembly, Konan Bedie, became the new president, as stipulated by the constitution. A dissident faction of the ruling party broke away in 1994 and the government passed a controversial election law that effectively disqualified its leader from becoming president, but these maneuvers did not derail the elections held in November 1995. Bedie won the presidency in his own right with 95 percent of the votes cast, and the ruling PDCI took 148 out of 175 seats. Two opposition parties split the remaining 25 seats.

Houphouet-Boigny's last years marred what was in many ways a magnificent legacy. Despite the country's economic problems, it maintained a relatively high standard of living, and it enjoyed remarkable political stability and relative freedom until the late 1980s. The judicial system is generally efficient and fair in criminal and civil cases, and security cases are relatively rare. The government respects freedom of assembly, movement, and religion, and in 1990 it authorized private publications. Workers can organize unions, although most belong to government-controlled ones that seldom authorize strikes. While the Ivory Coast is hardly a paragon of democracy, Houphouet-Boigny did create the foundations on which a stable democracy may well arise.

TOGO
Statistical Profile

Capital:	Lomé
Area:	21,927 sq. miles
Population:	4,300,000 (1994 est.)
Density:	196 people/sq. mile
Growth Rate:	3.6% (1994 est.)
GDP:	$1,611,000,000
Per Capita Income:	$400
Foreign Debt:	$1,138,000,000
Life Expectancy:	39 (1960), 54 (1992)
Ethnic Groups:	More than 36 groups: the largest are Ewe and Kabiye, others include Aja, Kem, Mina, Krachi, and Gurensi
Official Language:	French
Religions:	Traditional (75%), Christian (20%), Muslim (5%)
Former Colonizers:	Germany, France
Date of Independence:	1960

History

The Ewe, Togo's largest ethnic group, moved into the country's central region from the east between the twelfth and the eighteenth centuries. Legend has it that an early would-be king attempted to impose his rule on other clans but they dispersed to avoid his domination. At the end of the nineteenth century, when the Germans staked their claim to the area, the Ewe, like most of their neighbors, lived in stateless societies; only in the north were there larger states.

The German colony was just a sliver between the British colony of the Gold Coast (Ghana) to the west and the French territory in Dahomey (Benin) to the east, but it followed an existing north-south trade axis established by mulattos from Brazil. They had settled on the coast and made themselves into a commercial aristocracy through trade first in slaves and later in cattle. Before the First World War, the German colony was widely regarded as a model because the Germans invested extensively in agriculture, transportation, education, and public health. However, the victorious Allies took the territory from them and divided it among themselves as League of Nations mandates, with France getting the eastern part and Great Britain the western part.

The victorious powers invested little in the area, and had geographically divided the Ewe, a circumstance that became the focal point of nationalist agitation between the world wars. After the Second World War, this agitation intensified in the French portion, led by the wealthy merchant Sylvanus Olympio, head of the Committee of Togolese Unity (CUT). French repression only intensified the nationalists' resolve, which survived even the western region's 1956 decision by plebiscite to remain part of Ghana. (English-controlled Ghana was then on the verge of independence; French-controlled Togo was not.) The French tried to defuse the nationalist movement by enacting administrative reforms and making Nicolas Grunitky, the head of the Togolese Progress Party (PTP), prime minister, but the moves only led to violent demonstrations. CUT swept new elections in 1958, winning 33 seats to the PTP's three. Olympio became prime minister and then president upon independence two years later.

CUT's youth group launched a radical social program that the peasants still refer to as "the Revolution," but this program brought increasing conflict with Olympio, who was a member of the wealthy elite. In 1963, black Africa's first military coup toppled Olympio and replaced him with Grunitky, who was himself toppled by a coup in 1967. The new leader,

General Gnassingbe Eyadema, was both head of the army and a member of the northern Kabiye tribe; he set about consolidating a regime that has lasted into the 1990s. His party, Rally of the Togolese People (RPT), organized down to the village level, and in 1969 he made it the sole legal party in the country. Similarly, he replaced the old trade unions with the National Confederation of Togolese Workers (CNTT), brutally repressing both old activists and opponents of the new organization.

In 1972, Eyadema's new order was endorsed by 99 percent of the votes cast in a national referendum, signifying his iron grip on power. An unsuccessful coup in 1977 only strengthened his hand, allowing him to vilify Olympio's relatives and another elite family in a trial that branded them enemies of the state. In 1978, a congress of the RPT denounced corruption, raised producer prices, inaugurated land reform, and extended state control over commerce, and in 1979, Eyadema felt strong enough to free a number of political prisoners and to enact a new constitution. Under it, he ran unopposed for president, and won.

In the early 1980s, Eyadema played the role of statesman. He peacefully resolved tensions with Ghana over the activities of Ghanaian exiles in 1983, and a year later he invited neighboring countries to a two-day conference to discuss the problem of refugees, of which Togo had more than its share. He further liberalized the Togolese political system by allowing contested elections in March 1985. Although all candidates had to be from the ruling party, the elections did result in most incumbents losing to younger challengers.

The liberalization did not have the desired effect, however, for opposition to the regime increased. A series of bomb explosions in August 1985 led to a government crackdown, allegations of human rights abuses, and an attempted invasion by exiles from Ghana. France sent 250 troops to Eyadema's aid, allowing him to defeat the invaders. He won another seven-year term as president in 1986. In 1990, he held another round of single-party legislative elections, but the clamor for reform continued as massive demonstrations called for multiparty elections. In March 1991, after violent student protests, Eyadema agreed to legalize opposition parties, amnesty arrested protesters, and allow a national conference to chart a course to multiparty democracy. Ten opposition parties emerged, and a conference convened in July set up a transitional High Council of the Republic (HCR). It appointed Kokou Koffigoh transitional prime minister.

The army, however, remained unreconciled to the changes. It surrounded the conference hall, seized the state radio station, tried to kidnap Koffigoh, and fought a series of street battles with protesters that continued through the rest of the year. In December, army units attacked the prime minister's office, seizing Koffigoh and forcing him to dissolve the transitional government in favor of a new government of national unity that included a number of Eyadema's supporters.

The struggle continued in 1992 in both the halls of government and the streets. The opposition gradually lost ground politically as the HCR was forced to reverse itself and let Eyadema run in elections and to accept a proposed constitution that set the minimum age so high that Koffigoh was ineligible to run. Furthermore, the HCR agreed to provisions that guaranteed significant Kabiye representation in the future parliament (Eyadema and most of the army were Kabiye; most of the protesters were Ewe). In the streets, Eyadema's soldiers attacked a number of opposition figures, most prominently Tavio Amorin, the leader of the Pan-African Socialist Party and a harsh critic of the president. Amorin was gunned down in broad daylight in the center of the capital. The violence forced repeated postponements of both the referendum on the constitution and the promised elections.

After voters finally approved the new constitution in late September 1992, soldiers took the HCR members hostage until a strike and moves by France and the United States to cut off aid forced the government to give them up. In November, Koffigoh tried to dismiss two of Eyadema's supporters from the cabinet, but the president refused to accept his action and the army moved to protect them. Another strike was called to protest this interference by the army in the political process, but the transition to democracy had broken down. Opposition parties refused to participate when elections were finally held in August 1993, and Eyadema won an unopposed victory. He then survived an attempted coup by dissidents based in Ghana in January 1994.

Eyadema accommodated enough of the opposition's demands to win their agreement to participate in legislative elections held in February 1994. However, when an opposition party appeared to have won more seats than the government party, Eyadema had the Supreme Court order by-elections in three constituencies that gave his supporters a plurality, and he then split the opposition coalition by making the head of its junior partner the prime minister. These maneuvers enabled him to remain in control behind a veneer of legality.

Not only does Eyadema still control the political system, but he controls the judicial system and much of the economy as well. Although his rule has not been as spectacularly despotic as some others', the Togolese are subject to arbitrary arrest, detention, torture, and execution; they cannot assemble to protest without risk of police repression; their access to information is censored; and they do not have a meaningful right to strike. Eyadema has survived the challenges to his rule because of the support of the army, which is composed largely of his fellow Kabiye. Togo is one African country in which the winds of change in the early 1990s bent but could not break the old regime.

BENIN
Statistical Profile

Capital:	Porto-Novo
Area:	43,483 sq. miles
Population:	5,300,000
Density:	122 people/sq. mile
Growth Rate:	3.1%
GDP:	$2,181,000,000
Per Capita Income:	$410
Foreign Debt:	$1,322,000,000
Life Expectancy:	35 (1960), 51 (1992)
Ethnic Groups:	Fon (47%), Adja (12%), Bariba (10%), Yoruba (9%), Aizo (5%)
Official Language:	French
Religions:	Traditional (68%), Christian (17%), Muslim (15%)
Former Colonizer:	France
Date of Independence:	1960

History

If Togo is one of democracy's recent failures in Africa, Benin is one of its success stories. The country's history is rooted in the kingdom of Dahomey, which came into existence in the sixteenth or early seventeenth century and became an empire in the early eighteenth when it conquered its neighbors Allada and Porto-Novo. Dahomey's power was rooted in the export of slaves (and its obverse, the import of guns), and when that ended in the nineteenth century, in the export of palm oil. A French trading company established a fort at Ouidah in 1842 and obtained the right to exploit the Grand-Popo region. In 1863, the king of Porto-Novo sought French protection after an English bombardment. Five years later, the French also took control of the area around Cotonou through a treaty with the king of Dahomey, thus securing control of the entire coast. After defeating an 1890 attempt by his successor to reclaim the area, France established a protectorate in 1892. In 1894, the French consolidated their holdings in the area into the colony of Dahomey and in 1899 incorporated them into French West Africa.

Parts of the colony resisted French rule until 1914, however, and frequent rebellions occurred during the interwar years. The period after World War I also saw the first stirrings of modern politics, as the small group of French-educated Beninois began agitating for social and political equality with French colonists. Political action intensified after World War II, when Benin became an overseas territory of France and sent representatives to France's three assemblies and to its own local General

Council. Several parties emerged, and the two most successful ones, the Dahomian Republican Party (PRD) and the Dahomian Democratic Movement (MDD), joined and formed the colony's first government. They supported continued association with France in the referendum of 1958 and went on to form the first government upon independence in 1960.

Three men—Migan Apithy of the PRD (from the Porto-Novo), Hubert Maga of the MDD (representing the north), and Justin Ahomadegbe, also from the MDD (representing the core area of the former kingdom of Dahomey)—formed a triumvirate whose shifting alliances of two against one dominated national politics until the military imposed a provisional government in 1963. The leader of the coup, Colonel Christophe Soglo, took power himself in 1965, but he was overthrown in 1967 by Lieutenant-Colonel Alphonse Alley and Major Maurice Kouandete. The military junta set up a civilian government under Emile Zinsou in 1968, but Kouandete overthrew it in 1969. In an attempt to end the country's chronic instability, Kouandete set up a system of "revolutionary presidencies" in which a three-man council ruled, taking turns as president for two years each. Apithy, Maga, and Ahomadegbe were made the three members of the council. This unstable arrangement lasted until October 26, 1972, when Major Mathieu Kerekou and a group of young "modernist" officers staged another coup. The junta established a National Council of the Revolution on November 20, and ten days later Kerekou announced that the council intended to create a socialist society based on Marxist-Leninism.

The new regime enjoyed two years of relative calm, but in 1975 it faced a number of challenges—an attempted coup, the assassination of the minister of the interior, a series of strikes for higher salaries in the capital, and unrest in several provinces over shortages. The government responded by setting up a Popular Militia, arresting opponents, and soliciting support from Guinea and communist governments in Eastern Europe and the Far East. At the same time, Kerekou distanced the country from France and the moderate nations of West Africa, changing the name of the country to the People's Republic of Benin.

In 1976, the regime moved to improve relations with its neighbors and France while continuing to cultivate good relations with the Eastern bloc. It intensified its reformation of society by instituting a new educational system emphasizing ideology and agriculture, inculcating a more militant spirit in the army, launching a campaign against religious sects and witchdoctors, and increasing the number of national enterprises.

Kerekou's government survived another coup attempt in January 1977, when a force of mercenaries connected to France, Morocco, and Gabon attacked the capital. The incident lead to a serious breach with Gabon that culminated with the expulsion of 9,000 Benin nationals from Gabon in 1978. Internally, the government combined a new pragmatism in economic policy with intensified revolutionary social and political actions, as codified in the "Fundamental Law" of August 1977. This document reaffirmed Marxist-Leninism as the official ideology, instituted a "revolutionary dictatorship," vested almost all power in the Party of the Popular Revolution of Benin (PRPB), reorganized the trade unions, and instituted new labor laws and a system of social welfare.

In November 1979, the government held single-party elections for the 336-member Revolutionary National Assembly, which unanimously elected Kerekou president in February 1980. In February 1983, the assembly extended its own tenure from three to five years, and in July 1984 Kerekou won another term as president, running unopposed. Thereafter, he felt secure enough to release almost all political prisoners, but in reality the revolutionary regime was already in deep trouble. Students at the University of Cotonou went on strike to protest cutbacks in civil-service recruiting, their main hope for good jobs, and the strike led to violence. Although security forces quelled the disturbance and the university expelled 18 students, these measures did not address the economic problems that lay behind the government cutbacks that had sparked the disorders in the first place.

The trouble resurfaced in January 1989, when teachers, students, and civil servants went on strike to protest nonpayment of salaries. The government sent in paratroopers with orders to shoot demonstrators, but work stoppages continued, and in December Kerekou agreed to hold a national conference to create a multiparty state. The conference was held in April 1990, and 71 political groups attended. They elected Nicephore Soglo, a former executive director of the World Bank, transitional prime minister; set February 17, 1991, as the date for elections; and proposed a new multiparty constitutional system balancing a president eligible for two five-year terms, a national assembly, a high council, a constitutional court, and a mediator. The people approved the new constitution in a referendum on December 2, 1990, and the elections were held as scheduled on February 17. The results were fragmentary, with just 52 percent of the electorate voting and the largest single bloc—just 12 seats out of 64—gained by a coalition of three parties, the Democratic Union of Forces of Progress (UDFP), the Movement for Democracy and Social Progress (MDPS), and the Union for Liberty and Development (ULD). The results of the presidential election overshadowed all else: of 13 candidates who stood in the first round of balloting on March 10 , two, Kerekou and Soglo, went on to the second round. When Soglo emerged the victor, Kerekou became the first incumbent African president to yield power as a result of a democratic election.

Multiparty democracy has not solved Benin's economic problems. It remains one of the poorest countries on the African continent, and the new government's IMF-imposed austerity program has not made it popular. It faced one attempted coup just a few months after coming to power, and Soglo's support in parliament slipped so much in 1994 that he had to impose the budget by decree. The country's constitutional court validated the

move, but the parties opposed to his policies got their revenge in March 1995 by winning a clear majority in legislative elections. Corruption trials of Kerekou's associates did not yield satisfactory results, perhaps because Kerekou himself was granted immunity. In March 1996, Kerekou was actually returned to power in the presidential elections by voters disenchanted with Soglo's austerity measures.

Meanwhile, the government is forging ahead with liberalizing reforms. The law enforcement establishment is being retrained to respect the rule of law; the government respects freedom of assembly, freedom of religion, and the right to strike; and a large and diverse range of opinions is expressed in print and through broadcasts. While the government reserves the right to limit disruptive assemblies and pressures both official and private media to avoid "irresponsible journalism" (meaning strong criticism of the government), Benin is one African country where the winds of change of the 1990s blew the old order away.

GUINEA-BISSAU
Statistical Profile

Capital:	Bissau
Area:	13,946 sq. miles
Population:	1,100,000 (1994 est.)
Density:	79 people/sq. mile
Growth Rate:	2.1% (1994 est.)
GDP:	$220,000,000
Per Capita Income:	$210
Foreign Debt:	$580,000,000
Life Expectancy:	n.a. (1960), 39 (1992)
Ethnic Groups:	Balante (32%), Mandinka (13%), Fulani (22%), Mandjak (14%), Pepel (7%); a few thousand Europeans, Asians, and Cape Verdeans
Official Languages:	Portuguese; Cape Verdean Crioulo
Religions:	Traditional (54%), Muslim (30%), Christian (8%)
Former Colonizer:	Portugal
Date of Independence:	1974

History

The first of the present-day inhabitants of Guinea-Bissau immigrated during the turmoil that accompanied the collapse of Ghana. They later came under the domination of the Mali empire and then ruled themselves until the European intrusion. The Portuguese first arrived in the 1440s, and the French and British followed in the seventeenth and eighteenth centuries. The Europeans did not attempt to exert control beyond the coast until the late 1800s. Portugal declared the territory a colony in 1879, and the other European powers recognized the claim in 1884, but the large-scale military campaigns needed to impose colonialism on the Africans raged until 1915, and scattered resistance lasted until 1936.

Because Portugal was economically weaker than the other colonial powers, it was not able to do as much to develop its colonies. Portugal also could not contemplate decolonization, for it could not hope to compete in a free market. Therefore, the Portuguese government adamantly refused to consider letting its colonies go in the 1950s and 1960s. As a result, nationalist movements were slow to appear, but when they did, they were more militant and more strongly infused with socialism than in the French and British colonies. In Guinea and Cape Verde, the African Party for the Independence of Guinea and Cape Verde (PAIGC) began organizing urban workers and small shopkeepers in the 1950s. Led by Amilcar Cabral and other *mestico* (mixed race) Cape Verdeans, who were better educated than the mainland blacks, the movement organized strikes that met implacable resistance from the authorities.

In 1959, after more than 50 striking dock workers were killed by the police, the PAIGC leadership moved to Conakry in independent Guinea, and in August 1961 the party declared the beginning of an armed struggle against Portuguese colonialism. By 1963, the party controlled enough of the countryside to hold a conference within the colony. Forty thousand Portuguese troops proved unable to put the rebellion down, and it evolved into a textbook war of national liberation. Passively or actively, the people supported the rebels and the authorities gradually lost control over everything but the capital and a handful of outposts. The rebels worked closely in international forums with their counterparts in the other Portuguese African colonies, Angola and Mozambique, and when they declared independence and held national elections in 1973 over 80 countries recognized the new governments almost immediately. Soon thereafter, the Salazar dictatorship in Portugal fell, and the Portuguese themselves recognized Guinea-Bissau's independence on September 10, 1974.

For the first decade, the victorious PAIGC ruled almost unchallenged. Amilcar Cabral had been assassinated in 1973, but his brother Luiz took on the task of governing, which meant creating a one-party state and coping with the economic devastation left by a decade of war. The government was one of the most stable in 1970s Africa, but it was not one of the most free. Party congresses, the country's ultimate authority, met only once every four years. In the interim, the 90-member Supreme Council of the Struggle met once a year and elected a 26-member Executive Council of the Struggle that met quarterly. An eight-member Permanent Commission ran the party from day to day—and held real power. It dominated not only the PAIGC (which ran Cape Verde as well), but also the local party organs in Guinea-Bissau, the 50-member National Council, and the small executive Permanent Committee. The government itself had a similar structure: nine directly elected regional councils elected 150 representatives to the National People's Assembly, which met once a year and left day-to-day administration in the hands of a 15-member Council of State. In addition to these structures, three mass organizations linked various population groups to the government: a youth movement, a national union, and a women's movement.

Criticism of the PAIGC leadership grew in the late 1970s, evidenced by an attempted coup by a cashiered officer in 1978 and agitation by leftists disillusioned with the government's pragmatic, Western-oriented economic policies. Serious political strife only appeared in 1980, when disgruntlement in the army engendered by demobilization of soldiers and the introduction of ranks, a struggle over a constitutional change that would have enhanced the power of the president at the cost of the prime minister, and mainlanders' resentment of Cape Verdean domination came together in a coup against President Cabral led by Joao Bernando Vieira, the prime minister. The new government temporarily broke relations with Cape Verde and moved closer to Guinea, which immediately recognized the rebels in hopes of avoiding a conflict that had been brewing over offshore oil. The government also cooled relations with the Soviet Union and gradually pushed leftists out of the government. In 1983, Vieira's government purged corrupt officials; in 1984, it pushed through a constitutional change that strengthened the president at the cost of the prime minister; and in 1985 it survived a serious coup attempt sparked by the government's IMF-imposed economic stabilization policy. Major purges, trials, and some executions followed.

In 1989, Vieira won another five-year term as president in an unopposed election, but the opposition began pressing for a transition to multiparty democracy. In 1991, the PAIGC decided to bow to this pressure, mainly to satisfy international lenders looking for political reform. At first, Vieira proposed a three-year transition controlled entirely by the government, but in 1992 the opposition forced an accelerated pace and the formation of a multiparty electoral commission. The government postponed the elections repeatedly, but they were finally held in 1994. The PAIGC won an absolute majority in the legislative elections, but Vieira retained the presidency only after a run-off election.

The PAIGC has managed successfully to move Guinea-Bissau from one-party rule to multiparty democracy. The judiciary is still dominated by the regime, but the press is relatively free, the party's hold on the national labor union has relaxed, and the people enjoy freedom of religion. This formerly revolutionary Marxist party has managed to do what many Western-backed regimes have singularly failed to accomplish.

CHAPTER

Anglophone West Africa

INTRODUCTION

Like the Francophone countries discussed in the previous chapter, the Anglophone West African countries—Nigeria, Ghana, Liberia, Sierra Leone, and Gambia—are strung out along the coast. Their ecologies include savanna and tropical forests. All but Liberia were colonies of Great Britain. In comparison to their Francophone neighbors, they retain relatively few strong ties to their former colonizer. One of them, Liberia, is essentially a wreck because of civil war. One Sierra Leone has instituted multiparty democracy, and it is still recovering from its own civil war. Gambia recently lost its long-standing democratic institutions to a coup. Nigeria almost made the transition to democracy, but a military coup aborted the process on the eve of success. Ghana has the most auspicious situation of the lot, for while its leader, Jerry Rawlings, manipulated its supposed democratization process, its economy is growing robustly.

NIGERIA
Statistical Profile

Capital:	Lagos
Area:	356,668 sq. miles
Population:	98,100,000 (1994 est.)
Density:	275 people/sq. mile
Growth Rate:	3.1% (1994 est.)
GDP:	$29,667,000,000
Per Capita Income:	$320
Foreign Debt:	$28,789,000,000
Life Expectancy:	40 (1960), 52 (1992)
Ethnic Groups:	Over 250 groups; the largest, comprising at most 58% of the population, are: Hausa, Fulani, Kanuri, Tiv (in the north); Yoruba, Edo (southwest); Igbo, Ijaw, Ibibio (southeast)
Official Language:	English
Religions:	Muslim (47%), Christian (35%), Traditional (18%)
Former Colonizer:	Great Britain
Date of Independence:	1960

Anglophone West Africa

History

With its population of 88 million people, Nigeria is the tenth largest country in the world and the largest in Africa. With its extensive oil reserves, it is a potential player on the world stage.

The oldest agricultural settlements in present-day Nigeria date back at least 7,000 years, while Africa's first ironworking culture flourished there in the last centuries B.C. The oldest centralized state in the area, Kanem, arose in the eighth century A.D. around Lake Chad, and over the next millennium it was joined (and eventually replaced) by Bornu and the Hausa states in the savanna and, in the last few centuries, by Oyo, Benin, and Iife in the forest belt along the coast. In the early nineteenth century, the Fulani united Hausaland under their control as the sultanate of Sokoto and expanded it to include most of the northern two-thirds of present-day Nigeria.

The Fulani achievement was overshadowed by the expansion of British power in the latter part of the century, as British commercial interests—in particular the Royal Niger Company—penetrated into the interior. The British government established a small colony at Lagos in 1861 and extended its power into the hinterland in the decades after the Berlin conference. The British declared protectorates in the south and the north of the future colony in 1900, amalgamated the southern protectorate and the Lagos colony in 1906, and consolidated the northern and the southern territories into a single colony in 1914.

Looking to minimize the cost of ruling the huge colony, the first governor, Lord Lugard, pioneered the policy of "indirect rule," or rule through traditional institutions. His approach worked well in the north, which had a long tradition of political centralization. It did not work so well in the southwest, where the Yoruba kings, while powerful, had never actually collected taxes. It did not work at all in the southeast, where the Igbo had no tradition of centralized government.

All regions had resisted the initial British conquest to some degree, but calls for political rights and independence grew especially in the two southern regions, and particularly the eastern one, between the two world wars. After the Second World War, the National Council for Nigeria and the Cameroons (NCNC), led by Dr. Nnamdi Azikiwe and dominated by the Igbo, and the Action Group (AG), led by Obafemi Awolowo and dominated by the Yoruba, took the fore in the anticolonial movement. Pressured by the United States as well as these indigenous movements, the British decided to end their political dominance in a way that maintained their economic interests. They introduced the Richards constitution, creating separate assemblies for each of the three regions. In 1952, they imposed the Macpherson constitution which created a central House of Representatives and a Council of Ministers and planned for independence in 1956. The first nationwide elections were held in 1952 under this constitution, but the Northern People's Congress (NPC), resisted the Macpherson plan because it feared that the Southerners (particularly the Igbo), who had the benefit of two generations of modern Western education, would dominate the Northerners, who did not. At their insistence, the civil service, the judiciary, and the marketing boards controlling exports were regionalized, so that when independence came in 1960, Nigeria was in many ways three countries: the North, predominately Moslem Hausa-Fulani; the East, predominately Catholic Igbo; and the West, dominated by a mixture of Anglican and Moslem Yoruba. Each of these regions contained numerous minorities. The country as a whole contained approximately 250 distinct ethnic groups.

The national elections in 1959 that preceded independence confirmed this three-way split, with the NPC carrying the North, the NCNC the East, and the AG the West. The NCNC and the NPC formed a coalition government and set out to destroy the opposition AG. First, they used minority grievances in the West as a pretext to split that region in two, creating a fourth state, the Midwest. This power play caused a split in AG ranks between

conservatives, who favored continued accommodation with the government, and progressives, who advocated more radical action. The resulting disturbances gave the government cause to declare a state of emergency in the region, suppress the progressives, investigate Western state finances, and arrest opposition leaders for allegedly plotting to overthrow the government. At this point, the victorious coalition split, with the NPC seeking to ally with the conservative wing of the Action Group. This pushed the NCNC to court the progressive faction of the AG.

The object of this intense power struggle was not political power for its own sake, but the wealth and patronage that the government controlled. While the country's elite vied to feed at the public trough, the public at large became more and more discontented with the corruption and growing inequity in the country. With prices rising faster than wages, workers staged a general strike in 1963. The government set up a commission of inquiry but then rejected its recommendation to raise the minimum wage, so a strike occurred again in 1964. The economic problems remained.

The two crises, the political and the socioeconomic, came together in the general elections of 1964. Opposition groups disputed the validity of the census upon which districts were based and boycotted the election. The crucial vote in the West, which would determine which other regions would be in the government and which would go into opposition, was rigged and marred by open violence. By late 1965, demonstrations and riots had brought the country to the verge of anarchy. On January 15, 1966, hoping to bring order and to end corruption, a group of army officers, mainly Igbo, staged a coup in which they killed the prime minister (a Northerner), the premiers of the North and West, two cabinet ministers, and most of the senior army officers, but spared the Igbo premiers of the East and Midwest. The head of the army, General Ironsi (an Igbo), led the resistance and defeated the coup. The remaining members of the cabinet met and handed power over to General Ironsi.

The majority of Nigerians were hopeful at Ironsi's ascension to power, but he was not a skilled politician and rapidly alienated the North. On May 24, 1996, he announced the unification of the civil service—a move that threatened Northerners with an influx of more qualified Southerners. Within days, anti-Igbo riots broke out in the North. A month later, Northern officers staged another coup, killing General Ironsi and installing Lieutenant Colonel Yakubu Gowon, a Christian Northerner from a minority tribe. More anti-Igbo riots in the North turned into massacres, which caused a massive exodus of Igbos and ruined any chance of a national reconciliation. Attempts in early 1967 to heal the breach failed, and on May 30 the army commander in the East, Lieutenant Colonel Chukwuemeka Ojukwu, announced the region's secession and the formation of the Republic of Biafra.

Just before secession, Gowon had declared a new, 12-state structure for the country, which came too late to avoid war but managed to secure the loyalty of several minority groups in the East that would otherwise have joined the rebellion. From the first, the government forces had the upper hand militarily, but the Biafran leadership managed to convince both its own people and influential members of the world community that the Nigerians were bent on genocide, which stiffened resistance within and rallied support outside the beleaguered republic. The Biafran people fought tenaciously, and a strange combination of countries, including South Africa, France, Zambia, and Tanzania supported them, but all the Biafrans could accomplish was prolongation of the agony. With the aid of British and Soviet arms and Egyptian and East German pilots, the 250,000-man Nigerian army gradually ground down the Biafran forces while Igbo civilians starved and the rest of the world wrung its hands. After three years and 600,000 deaths, Biafra went down in defeat in 1970.

Giving the lie to wartime propaganda, Gowon's government imposed a remarkably conciliatory peace. Igbos, even those who had fought as rebels, were rapidly reintegrated into national life, and development aid poured into the ravaged region. Buoyed by a sudden inflow of oil wealth, the country as a whole entered a period of prosperity that helped it quickly revive. Unfortunately, Gowon proved less able as an economic planner than as a wartime leader or a peacemaker, and he failed to channel the oil wealth into improving the lives of the mass of people or into long-term economic development. Instead, the wealth fueled corruption, inflation, an increasing disparity between rich and poor, and general discontent with his rule. His increasing reluctance to honor his pledge to return the country to civilian rule created yet more dissatisfaction, and on July 29, 1976, a group of army officers staged a peaceful coup d'état while he was attending an OAU summit meeting in Uganda.

The man who replaced Gowon, General Murtala Muhammed, immediately set 1979 as the year for transition to civilian rule, announced the creation of a new national capital at Abuju in the center of the country, redivided the country to add seven more states, and launched a campaign against corruption that resulted in the dismissal or retirement of 10,000 civil servants. Muhammed also realigned Nigeria's foreign policy to a self-consciously Afrocentric orientation, strongly supporting the anticolonial struggles in Angola, Zimbabwe, and Namibia. Unfortunately, this dynamic and popular leader was killed in an inept coup attempt just six months after taking office, before his true abilities could be tested. His successor, Chief of Staff Olusegun Obasanjo, proved unable to reverse the country's deteriorating economic situation as oil revenues fell and the cost of food imports soared. Public dissatisfaction grew steadily, and in April 1978 a tripling of university fees as part of an austerity budget sparked riots, arson, and looting that left at least 20 people dead. Later in the year, a restructuring of the trade unions that increased government control led to widespread strikes.

Obasanjo stuck to his timetable for democracy, fulfilling his promise in 1979. A constitutional drafting committee created a system modeled on the U.S. government, with a powerful president, a two-house legislature, and an independent judiciary. To promote the formation of national rather than regional or ethnically based parties, the constitution stipulated that the president had to win at least 25 percent of the votes in two-thirds of the states and required him to appoint at least one cabinet member from each of the 19 states. Fifty-three political parties attempted to register, but to avoid fragmented parliamentary politics the electoral commission restricted the contest to five. The elections followed a complex progression of votes at weekly intervals for the Senate, the Federal House of Representatives, state assemblies and governors, and the president. The results revealed that four of the five parties were still essentially regional; but as the framers of the constitution had hoped, the party with truly national scope, the National Party of Nigeria (NPN), emerged as the victor. It won its 36 (of 95 total) Senate seats in 12 different states, seven governorships from across the nation, and state assembly seats in 17 of the 19 states. Its leader, Alhaji Shehu Shagari, won the presidency by gaining 25 percent or more of the vote in 12 states and 20 percent of the vote in one; his closest rival, Nnamdi Azikiwe of the Nigeria People's Party (NPP), won four states by an overwhelming margin.

Shagari's first term in office was marked by a number of disputes between the federal government and the states, a gradual tightening of restrictions on the press, and a poorly organized coup attempt in 1983. The most serious domestic problem was unrest in the North, which resulted in riots by Moslem fundamentalists in December 1980 that left over 4,000 people dead. Deteriorating economic conditions and a wave of violent crime created more pervasive dissatisfaction, which the government attempted to assuage in January 1983 by expelling all unskilled foreign workers on two weeks notice. This heartless act cruelly

affected several million people, including over a million from Ghana and 500,000 from Niger.

Despite these problems and continued corruption at all levels of public life, Shagari and the NPN won reelection with a larger majority than before. However, just three months later, the military staged another coup, citing widespread electoral fraud as well as economic mismanagement and corruption as the justification. Major General Muhammadu Buhari emerged as the leader of the Supreme Military Council (SMC) and quickly cracked down on corruption and street crime, putting former politicians on trial for venality and making armed robbery a capital offense. The government perhaps overplayed the anticorruption campaign when it sponsored an unsuccessful attempt to kidnap Umaru Dikko, a former minister of transportation, in England, but it did recover over 110 million naira (Nigerian dollars) and handed out over 1,000 years of prison sentences. It also made good on its threat to execute armed robbers, putting an average of three to death every week in 1984, and it used the army to restore order after the outbreak of more fundamentalist rioting in the North.

As resistance to its draconian policies grew, the military government cracked down on its critics. It harassed journalists and dismissed doctors who struck to protest the banning of their professional association. It attempted to deflect anger by expelling foreign workers again, but when criticism continued it forbade all political debate. Even members of the military became disaffected with the regime, and on August 27, 1985, Major General Ibrahim Babangida led a peaceful coup that replaced the hard-line faction with a group of officers inclined toward a milder, more consultative approach to government. Babangida announced a more liberal policy toward the economy and human rights, repealed the decree limiting press freedom, and promised a return to democratic civilian rule by October 1, 1990. He brought opponents of the former regime into government, encouraged open debate on public issues, settled a clash between students and police in 1986 with a compromise, and abolished the death penalty except for murder.

Religious violence periodically flared in the North, and two coup attempts challenged the government, but Babangida maintained the goal of a return to civilian rule, even though he delayed the transition twice, first to 1992 and eventually to 1993. The government created a new constitution in 1989 that formed the basis for local elections between two parties in 1990, state elections in 1991, and national legislative elections in mid-1992. Unfortunately, allegations of widespread fraud marred the presidential primaries held in September 1992, so the government suspended political activity, announced that the transition to civilian rule would be further delayed, and changed the electoral process. The election finally took place in June 1993, but when the candidate Babangida favored appeared to be losing, he annulled the result. He appointed instead Ernest Shonekan to replace him when he stepped down in August, but General Sani Abacha seized power on November 17, returning the country to military rule.

Abacha rules by decree, censors the press, has dissolved labor unions and jailed their leaders, has purged army officers and bureaucrats, and regularly has opponents arrested, detained, tortured, and executed without due process of law. Nigeria was suspended from the Commonwealth in November 1995 because of the regime's execution of a prominent opponent, the writer Saro-Wiwa. Abacha reshuffles his cabinet frequently, most probably because every change forces businesses to ante up a new round of bribes, and he has exhibited a mania for security. Abacha claims to be working to keep the country together and return it to civilian rule, but he has squelched attempts to heal the rift between Igbos and Yorubas, which he sees as a threat to continued rule by the northern-dominated army. He delayed the promised return to civilian rule from 1996 to 1998. The opposition has refused to cooperate with Abacha, demanding instead that he recognize the results of the 1993 election and restore civilian government immediately.

With its huge population and rich natural resources, Nigeria is potentially Africa's powerhouse. But in the mid-1990s it continues to languish in the hands of a corrupt elite that has squandered its oil wealth and let slip its latest opportunity to advance to the ranks of democratic nations governed by the rule of law.

GHANA
Statistical Profile

Capital:	Accra
Area:	92,100 sq. miles
Population Size:	16,900,000 (1994 est.)
Density:	183 people/sq. mile
Growth Rate:	3.0% (1994 est.)
GDP:	$6,884,000,000
Per Capita Income:	$450
Foreign Debt:	$3,131,000,000
Life Expectancy:	45 (1960), 55 (1992)
Ethnic Groups:	Contains over 50 groups. The major divide is between Gur-speakers in the north (principally Guan and Moshi-Dagomba) and Kwa-speakers in the south (principally Akan); Ga, Ewe, and Adangme are also significant.
Official Language:	English
Religions:	Christian (43%), Traditional (38%), Muslim (19%)
Former Colonizer:	Great Britain
Date of Independence:	1957

History

Despite its name, the modern nation of Ghana does not encompass the territory of the oldest West African empire, although it is possible that emigrants from ancient Ghana did move there. Small states grew up between the thirteenth and seventeenth centuries, but the most significant pre-colonial political development came in the late nineteenth century with an attempt to form a state along modern European constitutional lines, the Fante confederation. While the attempt failed, it created a forward-looking political tradition that survived British annexation in 1874 and colonial rule. The Aboriginal Rights Protection Society began lobbying for African rights as early as 1890, a time when most African resistance took the form of traditional warfare. The Gold Coast Youth Conference took up the banner of African rights in the interwar years, and the United Gold Coast Convention (UGCC), founded in 1947, began calling for "self-government in the shortest possible time." It also began organizing in the rural hinterland as well as the coastal towns. Kwame Nkrumah kept this national focus when he split from the UGCC the next year to found the Convention People's Party (CPP), but he went farther by appealing to the mass of ordinary people instead of just to the educated elite. He adopted the slogan "independence now" and called for "positive action" and a general strike. The British jailed him, but while he was incarcerated, the CPP won the general elections of 1951, so the British released him and asked him to form a government. The CPP won two more elections in 1954 and 1956, so Nkrumah was still at the helm when the country became the first sub-Saharan African country to gain independence on March 6, 1957.

Unfortunately, Nkrumah was a better agitator than administrator. He adopted a socialist program that focused on large-scale development projects at the expense of agriculture and that created a large and increasingly corrupt public sector. Faced with strong opposition from both economic and regional interest groups, he steadily transformed the country into a repressive one-party state. Because his economic and political policies alienated Western countries, he turned increasingly to the Soviet bloc for aid, a tendency that reinforced both his socialistic and his autocratic tendencies. The CPP's dominance of the national union, the Trades Union Congress (TUC), alienated the workers, while

Nkrumah's expansion of his personal bodyguard into a regiment alienated the military. When a group of senior officers deposed him in February 1966, the people pulled down his statue in Accra and sent his portrait to Interpol (the international police agency), charging him with extortion and corruption.

The military sought to repair Ghana's relations with the West, in part by promising a swift transition to democratic civilian rule. It created a 150-member constituent assembly in 1968 and promulgated a new constitution in August 1969. Kofi Busia, leader of the Progress Party (PP), became the head of the new civilian government, which was dominated by self-styled technocrats. He purged the government of 1,000 civil servants and expelled tens of thousands of foreign workers, but the disruption this caused, plus the collapse of world prices for cocoa, Ghana's chief export, hurt the economy. Busia's increasingly stringent austerity measures alienated both workers, who went on strike in 1971, and the military, who threw him out in 1972.

Colonel Ignatius Acheampong emerged as the country's new leader. He enjoyed an initial period of popularity because of his partial renunciation of foreign debts incurred under Nkrumah, his concessions to organized labor, and his "Feed Yourself" campaign promoting local food production. However, in dismantling the constitution of 1969, he ended the rule of law, banned all political activity, and replaced the judicial system with military tribunals against which there was no appeal. While luxury and corruption flourished among the elite, workers found they could not live on their wages. When they protested, the government cracked down on them. Record cocoa prices brought increased smuggling and corruption rather than an increased standard of living for the people. By 1976, professionals had joined students and workers in strikes and demonstrations calling for an end to military rule. Repression by the regime sparked even greater protests, so on July 5, 1978, the Military Advisory Council forced Acheampong to resign.

The new ruler, General Frederick Akuffo, proposed a four-year interim period of civilian government before new elections, but workers continued to strike, and junior civil servants joined them in November. Declaring a state of emergency, the government stepped up the pace of transition to democracy, appointing a constitution drafting committee, holding district council elections, and lifting the ban on political parties at the beginning of 1979.

On May 15, 1979, just two weeks before the scheduled elections, junior officers led by Flight Lieutenant Jerry Rawlings staged a coup. In a virtually unprecedented move, the new ruler allowed the elections to continue. The winner, Hilla Limann of the People's National Party (PNP), took office in late September. Rawlings and his companions continued to lead the armed forces. They staged a vigorous purge in which they executed Acheampong, Akuffo, and six other leading officers; tried 100 others; and collected millions of dollars in back taxes. Meanwhile, Limann's government rapidly lost popularity when it imposed austerity measures, attempted to remove the chief justice through parliamentary action, and harassed critics in the press. Rawlings himself became increasingly critical of Limann's government, which led the government to harass him and his associates. The political opposition came together as the All People's Party in September 1981, and on December 31 Rawlings' supporters staged another coup.

Rawlings made it clear from the start that his coup was not going to be just "another opportunity for some soldiers and their allies" to get rich at the public's expense. He set up the Provisional National Defense Council (PNDC), which consisted mainly of soldiers, but soon appointed a civilian cabinet consisting of "secretaries" who were given the opportunity to "serve the people sacrificially." He forged links with Libya, established people's tribunals to try corrupt politicians, and set up people's defense committees (PDCs), modeled on Cuba's committees for the defense of the

revolution, to run local government by exposing corruption, combating counterrevolutionaries, and promoting self-help programs.

Rawlings' revolution met fierce resistance from the established elite, which was supported by neighboring Togo and the Ivory Coast and probably by France and the United States as well. At least four internal coup attempts and two invasions by exiles occurred in his first three years in office. Ghanaian intervention in the politics of neighboring countries included Rawlings' aid to Captain Thomas Sankara in taking power in Burkina Faso to the north and the backing of an unsuccessful coup against the Togo government. Relations with the Ivory Coast remained tense despite an Ivorian promise to curb Ghanaian rebels on its soil. Conspiracies, trials, and border crossings continued through the mid-1980s, and several dozen people were executed as a consequence.

Rawlings did not rely on repression alone. Instead, he adopted a pragmatic approach to Ghana's situation, imposing austerity budgets in 1983 and 1984 that hurt his popularity at home but reassured international lenders, who restored the flow of aid. In late 1984, he abolished the PDCs, whose zealousness had alienated middle-class Ghanaians, and replaced them with committees for the defense of the revolution, stressing that these committees should include all citizens. His National Mobilization Program helped redirect workers into new jobs and was particularly successful in helping the more than one million Ghanaian migrant workers who were abruptly expelled from Nigeria in 1983. In 1988, the regime held elections for local district assemblies, and in May 1991 it created the Consultative Assembly, which issued a new constitution in March 1992 providing for multiparty elections. Presidential elections, which Rawlings won, were held in November, and legislative elections took place in December.

Because the campaign and the process of creating the constitution had been so strongly manipulated by the regime, the opposition parties boycotted the legislative elections. The regime had appointed the Consultative Assembly, pushed into the constitution at the last minute provisions protecting its members from prosecution, staffed the interim electoral commission that oversaw the elections, and used that commission to hinder voter registration. While international observers judged the actual balloting to have been relatively free and fair, the government's manipulation of the constitutional transition tainted the election's outcome. Ghana is freer than it was before 1992, but as of the mid-1990s it is still not really democratic.

LIBERIA
Statistical Profile

Capital:	Monrovia
Area:	43,000 sq. miles
Population:	2,900,000 (1994 est.)
Density:	67 people/sq. mile
Growth Rate:	3.3% (1994 est.)
GDP:	$2,000,000,000
Per Capita Income:	$400
Foreign Debt:	$1,101,000,000
Life Expectancy:	41 (1960), 53 (1992)
Ethnic Groups:	Americo-Liberians (5%), Kpella, Dey, Bassa, Kru, Mandingo, Dan, Mende, Loma, eight other groups
Official Language:	English
Religions:	Christian (68%), Traditional (18%), Muslim (14%)
Date of Independence:	1847

History

The ancestors of most of Liberia's inhabitants migrated into the area between the twelfth and sixteenth centuries. The modern political history of the country began in 1816 in the United States with the founding of the American Colonization Society (ACS) to promote the emigration of freed slaves to Africa. In 1822, the first group of these freed slaves arrived and founded Monrovia (named for U.S. President James Monroe). Other groups followed and set up separate enclaves, which were governed by the ACS until they amal-gamated in 1847 to form the independent Republic of Liberia.

For the first two decades, a small group of mulattos ruled the country, but in 1869 the party of the darker skinned settlers, the True Whig Party, ousted them. This party represented the 300 or so leading Americo-Liberian families; it ruled the coastal area directly and dominated the interior through tribal chiefs in a form of indirect rule. The Liberian government appeared on the surface to be a small version of American democracy, complete with a constitution providing for a president, two houses of congress, and a supreme court. Similarly, the Americo-Liberians created in Africa a small version of the society that the founders had known in the American South, with colonial-style mansions, Masonic lodges, and elaborate public ceremonies involving formal western clothing, brass bands, and honor guards. Beneath the surface, the True Whigs ruled as an autocratic oligarchy, and along with the antebellum atmosphere came a caste system and forced labor practices that were reminiscent of the dark side of the old American South. The main difference was that now the descendants of the slaves were on top; the indigenous African population—the vast majority of the country's people—found themselves in a situation similar to that of the neighboring peoples under European colonial rule. The principal difference for them was that they got virtually no benefit from modern education or infrastructure, for Americo-Liberian rule was so corrupt and inefficient that the country always wavered on the verge of insolvency. Aid and investment from the United States kept it afloat, and the quid pro quo was a favorable climate for foreign business and a foreign policy closely aligned to that of its benefactor.

President William Tubman, who took office in 1944, brought the country into the modern age. His "open door" policy created extremely favorable conditions for foreign investment. His "unification" policy took the first steps toward incorporating the people of the interior into the country's political system by giving the vote to those who met property qualifications. He also gave them representation in the House of Representatives and even confiscated and redistributed property, although never on a scale to threaten foreign investors or the domestic elite. Similarly, representation for the hinterland did not seriously challenge the power of the Americo-Liberian True Whigs, and because the terms were so favorable to the lenders, foreign investment did not lead to indigenous economic development. Liberia, in fact, became a model of "growth without development," as an official American study put it, and political reform did not lead to political change.

When Tubman died in 1971, Vice President William Tolbert succeeded to the presidency. Tolbert introduced a new, more open style of government. He appeared in public in casual clothes, brought non-Americo-Liberians into government, introduced universal suffrage, and amended the constitution to allow him to serve more than one term. In foreign policy, he was one of a handful of African leaders to denounce Uganda's murderous dictator Idi Amin. He cultivated good relations with the Communist bloc (without disrupting rapport with the United States), and increased Liberia's cooperation with its neighbors, creating a customs union with Sierra Leone and a commission of cooperation with the Ivory Coast. Confident in his country's long history of stability, he tolerated a level of political organization and opposition that would have been unthinkable under his predecessors. Rural communities and urban workers formed self-help organizations that ventured into political issues, a radical faction appeared in the university students' union, and publications critical of the government circulated. Most significant of all, a nascent opposition party, the Progressive Alliance of Liberia (PAL), emerged and, in 1978, petitioned for permission to transform itself into a political party.

As political restraints weakened, long-dormant resentments against Americo-Liberian domination began to simmer. They boiled over in April 1979. On Easter Saturday, the PAL called for a rally to protest a proposed increase in the price of rice; the government refused to allow the rally. People began to gather anyway, and the police responded with force, shooting into the crowd and killing at least 40. A night and a day of uncontrolled rioting ravaged Monrovia's business district. Because of insubordination in the army, Guinean troops were needed to help restore order. The illusion of Liberian stability was shattered, and so was the illusion of consensual democracy. Tolbert rescinded the price increase and raised the pay of soldiers, but also assumed emergency powers. He imposed a dusk-to-dawn curfew, suspended the right of *habeas corpus* for a year, and arrested numerous opponents.

Calm had returned by the time Tolbert hosted the OAU in August 1979, but another political challenge arose when an independent candidate, Dr. Amos Sawyer, stood for election as mayor of Monrovia. The government postponed the election but then faced a greater challenge when the PAL registered as the Progressive People's Party (PPP). After a few months of wary coexistence, the government arrested the new party's leaders for treason.

Two days before they were to be executed, Master Sergeant Samuel Doe led a coup that overthrew the True Whigs and sent the country into upheaval. The insurgents captured Tolbert in bed, killed him, mutilated his body, and threw it into a mass grave. They went on to execute 13 other leading members of the old elite, shooting them on a beach in front of a cheering crowd; they killed about 200 other people as well. The new government, the People's Redemption Council (PRC), suspended the constitution, imposed martial law, set a new minimum wage, and replaced the Supreme Court with the Supreme Tribunal of the People. The soldiers brought prominent civilians into the government but forced them to take military ranks and accept military discipline. Doe opened relations with Libya and appeared to be leading the country down a radical path.

However, both the constraints on Liberia's freedom of action and the limits of Doe's vision quickly made themselves apparent. The coup sparked a flight of capital from the country, the wage increase created inflationary pressures and a budget deficit, the Economic Community of West African States (ECOWAS) set up a commission to monitor events in the country, and the United States pressed for the release of political prisoners and a timetable for the restoration of democracy. Since Doe had nothing more in mind than the destruction of the old regime and the enrichment of himself and his fellow Kran tribesmen, he had no problem moderating his government's actions, courting moderate African leaders, and moving his foreign policy away from Libya and the Soviet Union and back into line with American interests.

In 1981, he promised elections by 1985. He had a constitutional committee led by Amos Sawyer prepare a new constitution, which turned out to be remarkably like the old constitution. He submitted it to a referendum in 1983 (it passed), legalized opposition parties in 1984, and held the elections in 1985. However, the process of registering opposition parties was used to delay the operations of some and to keep others out of the race completely. The government also imposed censorship on the press and detained opposition figures. The voting itself was marred by gross irregularities: when Doe appeared to be losing, the ballot boxes were trucked to an army base where they were tallied and Doe was declared the winner. Liberia's election had been a sham.

Opposition to Doe intensified, and he survived a total of eight coup attempts in the course of the 1980s (although some of them may have been fabricated to justify the arrest of opposition figures). The last one, in December 1989, was more of an uprising than a coup; Doe's forces crushed it easily, but the movement behind it, the National Patriotic Front of Liberia (NPFL), survived. During 1990, the NPFL revived and seized control of most of the country. Its leader, Charles Taylor, then made the mistake of pausing outside Monrovia to avoid causing civilian casualties. While Doe held out in his fortified executive mansion, Prince Yormie Johnson split from the NPFL, and the ECOWAS countries dispatched to Monrovia a multinational force that set up an Interim Government of National Reconciliation (IGNR) led by Amos Sawyer.

Johnson's men captured Doe and tortured him to death, but the dictator's end came too late for his country. Taylor, with the backing of the Ivory Coast, controlled most of the country, but the ECOWAS force controlled the capital to protect the IGNR. The two sides honored a cease-fire during 1992 in order to negotiate, but the talks came to nothing. In the meantime, another faction, the United Liberation Movement for Democracy (ULIMO), began attacking Taylor's forces from Sierra Leone. Taylor responded by backing rebels in Sierra Leone and Gambia (which contributed troops to ECOWAS), but was unable to prevent ULIMO from taking control of two western counties. In October 1992, he renewed the fight with ECOWAS for Monrovia but lost ground around the capital. In July 1993, the different factions agreed to a UN peace plan, but the agreement broke down. Both fighting and negotiations continued through 1994, and peace was finally restored in the summer of 1995. Taylor entered Monrovia to participate in the government, and the armies began to demobilize.

Estimates place the number of people killed in the civil war at 150,000 or more. At least a million Liberians fled to neighboring countries, and another 500,000 were displaced within the country. Civil order broke down completely in many places. Where the rebel armies exerted control, they ruled with an iron fist. The IGNR in the capital adhered more to the rule of law and allowed a greater measure of freedom than did the rebels, but the circumstances inevitably prevented anything approaching normal life.

Long a bastion of stability, Liberia has become one of Africa's most troubled states. The end of the fighting in mid-1995 was a hopeful step, but fighting broke out again in April 1996. While the country did not descend once more into anarchy, its future remains in doubt.

SIERRA LEONE
Statistical Profile

Capital:	Freetown
Area:	27,699 sq. miles
Population:	4,600,000 (1994 est.)
Density:	166 people/sq. mile
Growth Rate:	2.7% (1994 est.)
GDP:	$634,000,000
Per Capita Income:	$170
Foreign Debt:	$680,000,000
Life Expectancy:	32 (1960), 43 (1992)
Ethnic Groups:	Temne and Mende (30%), Krios (2%), Lokko, Sherbo, Limba, Susu, Fulani, Kono
Official Language:	English
Religions:	Traditional (45%), Muslim (30%), Christian (25%)
Former Colonizer:	Great Britain
Date of Independence:	1961

History

As in Liberia, the indigenous peoples of Sierra Leone trace their roots back to the twelfth century, but the people who defined the modern nation were refugees from the European slave system. In 1787, the British established a small colony at Freetown, and over the next century it became the point of return for captives liberated by the Royal Navy's antislavery patrols. Many slaves returned home as soon as they could, but others remained, imbibed missionary religion and education, and joined the elite "Creole" society that held itself above both the native peoples and the immigrants from the hinterland who came to the colony looking for work. The Creoles used their educational advantages to establish themselves in the professions and the civil service, which served as bastions against both the growth of European and Lebanese commercial interests and the gradual enfranchisement of the indigenous people in the late nineteenth and early twentieth centuries.

Wallace Johnson's West African Youth League, the colony's first modern political movement, included members from all segments of Sierra Leone's diverse society, but the British administration and conservative Creoles used the outbreak of war in 1939 to repress it. The parties that emerged during the transition to independence after the war were regional and tribal, with the Sierra Leone People's Party (SLPP) representing the Mende in the southeast and the All People's Congress (APC) representing the Temne of the northwest. During the 1950s, the SLPP, under Milton Margai, dominated politics, and its predominance continued after independence in 1961 until Margai's death in 1964. Margai's successor began to replace Creoles, who had heretofore supported the SLPP, with southern "provincials." In response, the Creoles supported the APC in the 1967 elections, and the northern party won. Almost immediately, two military coups installed a southern-dominated military government, which ruled until a third coup in 1969.

This last coup finally brought the APC, led by Siaka Stevens, into power. Because the nation's politics had become so embittered, the new regime continued the formal state of emergency and used its powers to try SLPP supporters of the initial coup, suppress breakaway factions of the APC, and detain other opponents. The opposition resorted to increasingly violent means, attempting to assassinate Stevens twice in one day in 1971. The regime responded by executing suspected plotters and signing a mutual defense agreement with Guinea, which sent troops to protect Stevens. The Western powers, worried by the "leftist" tilt to Sierra Leone's foreign policy, supported the opposition, and the tenor of political life became even more violent. The 1973 elections, which the APC won, were marred by violence and widespread fraud. In the next year, a bomb went off at the residence of the finance minister, and the ensuing trials led to the execution of eight alleged plotters. The government brutally suppressed student riots in 1977, and violence accompanying the elections that year left more than 100 people dead.

Perturbed that the SLPP won 15 out of 41 seats, Stevens moved to solidify the APC's hold on the country. He had already transformed it into a republic with himself as president in 1971, but in 1978 the parliament passed a new constitution making the APC the sole legal party. The SLPP representatives crossed over to the APC and Stevens became president for another seven-year term.

In 1980, Stevens garnered the dual honors of hosting the annual OAU summit meeting and being knighted by the Queen of England. The next year, however, the government was rocked by a corruption scandal dubbed "vouchergate" because it centered on government payments for fictious invoices. The magnitude of the scandal reflected an economy rife with irregularities; for instance, an estimated 90 percent of annual diamond exports were smuggled out of the country. Workers expressed their dissatisfaction through a general strike late in 1980. Students rioted late in 1981, an opposition party was formed in exile in 1984, and students rioted again in early 1985 when Stevens appeared to waffle on his announced intention to retire.

Faced with this mounting public pressure, Stevens arranged in August 1985 for General Joseph Momoh, commander of the armed forces since 1971, to become the APC's (and the only) candidate for president. Enthusiastically elected in October by a populace anxious to be rid of Stevens, Momoh was soon characterized as "new man, same jacket." In 1986, dissatisfaction with the regime took the form of an abortive mercenary invasion and legislative elections in which many of the APC old guard lost their seats. Thereafter, political life seemed to settle down for several years, but corruption remained rampant. In one government ministry, for instance, 75 percent of the employees were found to be fictitious in 1988. In 1990, another major scandal broke out.

Late in the year, Momoh yielded to public pressure and appointed a constitutional committee to review the 1978 constitution. In March 1991, the committee recommended a return to multiparty democracy, and in October 1991 the constitution was amended accordingly. Unfortunately, that same year saw ULIMO forces from Liberia set up camps in Sierra Leone from which to strike at their NPFL enemies in Liberia. NPFL forces promptly invaded Sierra Leone to attack the ULIMO bases. Sierra Leone's army, supported by forces from Nigeria and Guinea, fought the NPFL, which itself was supported by the Revolutionary United Front (RUF) of Sierra Leone. The Liberian civil war thus spawned civil war in Sierra Leone, and soon brought the democratic transition to a halt. Momoh announced that the transition would have to be put off as long as the conflict raged, and proposed a state of emergency. A protest against supply shortages by troops from the front then turned into a coup.

The leader of the coup, Captain Valentine Strasser, proclaimed that he had acted because

> the nation as a whole was in a state of virtual collapse. Corruption, indiscipline, mismanagement, tribalism, nepotism, injustice, and thuggery were rampant. . . . Infant and under-5 mortality rates are among the highest in the world [and] life expectancy . . . is among the lowest.

Strasser promised an end to corruption and a speedy transition to multiparty civilian rule, but his government suspended civil liberties along with the constitution, set up special military tribunals for political cases, censored the press, and inhibited free assembly and association. The regime respected freedom of religion, allowed widespread trade-union activity, and embarked on a transition to democracy in 1995. Despite a coup that overthrew Strasser in January 1996, elections took place in February. The government and rebels agreed to a cease-fire and negotiations, and the military returned the country to civilian rule in April. Sierra Leone has joined the ranks of Africa's democracies.

GAMBIA
Statistical Profile

Capital:	Banjul
Area:	4,363 sq. miles
Population:	1,100,000 (1994 est.)
Density:	252 people/sq. mile

Growth Rate:	2.7% (1994 est.)
GDP:	$5,913,000,000
Per Capita, Income:	$390
Foreign Debt:	$2,998,000,000
Life Expectancy:	n.a. (1960), 45 (1992)
Ethnic Groups:	Mandingo, Fula, Wolof, Jola, Serahuli, Aku
Official Language:	English
Religions:	Muslim (90%), Christian and Traditional
Former Colonizer:	Great Britain
Date of Independence:	1965

History

Inhabited since before 1000 A.D., the area along the lower Gambia River came under the Mali Empire in the 1200s and was ruled by minor successor states after that empire fell. The Portuguese first came in 1455, and the English followed in 1588 and built a fortified trading post in 1660. The small enclave passed back and forth between them and the French, who controlled neighboring Senegal, until Great Britain gained control for good in 1787. During the nineteenth century, the British extended their control upriver and divided the whole territory between a coastal colony, which they ruled directly, and an inland protectorate, which they ruled indirectly through traditional chiefs.

The people of the coastal colony gained the right to elect a member of the British parliament just after World War II, but the people who lived in the protectorate—the majority—only got the vote in 1960. As they did, a new political party, the People's Progressive Party (PPP) under Dawda Jawara, took up the cause of the rural inlanders and challenged the older, urban-based parties, the United Party (UP) and the Democratic Congress Alliance (DCA). The PPP won 9 of 12 seats and joined an all-party government. It withdrew from the government, however, when the colonial administration did not name Jawara as chief minister. The British relented only when the PPP won another set of elections in 1962, and Jawara formed a government that steered Gambia to self-government in 1963 and independence in 1965.

During the period before independence, the country's future status was uncertain because it seemed too small to stand on its own. Since it was surrounded on three sides by Senegal, union with that country seemed logical, but differences in the two political and cultural traditions made that problematic. Although long-term economic factors favored the union, specific economic interests stood to lose from it in the short run. Consequently, several early plans fell through and a UN recommendation in 1963 for a loose federation was only partially implemented by a treaty of association signed in 1967. The two countries agreed on foreign affairs, defense, and some other matters, but they did not take the crucial step of establishing a customs union, which would have ended Gambia's lucrative role as conduit for goods being smuggled into Senegal.

Gambia became a republic and Jawara became its first president in 1970. His political power survived the breakaway in 1975 of Sherif Dibba to form the National Convention Party (NCP). In 1980, radical agitation increased with the formation of two Marxist parties; in October, the commander of the republic's small army was assassinated. A threatened mutiny was forestalled only by the arrival of 150 Senegalese troops, and when evidence suggested that Libya was supporting fundamentalists bent on establishing an Islamic republic, Gambia broke off relations with that country. This move failed to end the trouble, however, for it was rooted in the widespread perception that the ruling party was little more than a complacent patronage machine. In July 1981, a group of junior officers staged a coup attempt while Jawara was out of the country, and the president had to call in 3,000 Senegalese troops to put them down. The fight lasted two days, cost over 600 lives, and left the country, heretofore a model African democracy, shaken.

Jawara immediately put into motion a plan for confederation with Senegal. The armed forces of the two countries were integrated within two months of the coup, and the terms of confederation were worked out by February 1982. The two countries would remain sovereign but would run joint foreign, defense, and economic matters. The Senegalese president would also be the president of Senegambia, the Gambian president would be vice president of the confederation. They would be assisted by a general secretariat and a council of ministers, and there was to be an assembly with one-third of its 60 members chosen by the Gambian parliament and two-thirds by the Senegalese parliament. Jawara and the PPP won elections in May 1982, and the Gambian parliament went on to pass the first protocol of confederation on August 18, 1982. The Senegambian council of ministers met for the first time on January 12, 1983.

The two countries signed most of the protocols of confederation in 1983 and 1984, but the economic provisions remained a stumbling block. Gambia still didn't want a customs union, and it also didn't want to unite its relatively strong currency with the relatively weak Senegalese currency. The confederation lasted less than a decade, being formally dissolved in September 1989.

In the meantime, Gambian politics settled down for the rest of the 1980s. Jawara and the PPP won the elections of 1987 despite challenges from a new party that split off from the PPP, the Gambian People's Party (GPP), and from the People's Democratic Organization for Independence and Socialism (PDOIS). Shortly before the 1992 elections, 30 Gambian soldiers left their camp without permission and marched to protest the lack of pay for their service with the Economic Community of West African States (ECOWAS) forces in Liberia. More seriously, the government announced the next month that a Libyan-trained force of Gambian dissidents with ties to the National Patriotic Front of Liberia, ECOWAS' main opponent, had assembled in Burkina Faso and was preparing to invade. While the publicity apparently forestalled the attack, and Jawara's PPP went on to win the 1992 elections, the respite was only temporary. On July 23, 1994, a group of junior officers overthrew Jawara, ending his 30-year reign and Gambia's 30 years of democracy.

The new government under Lieutenant Yahya Jameh suspended the constitution, banned political parties, and arrested members of the old government who remained in the country. It announced a plan for a four-year transitional period leading to a restoration of democracy in October 1994, and it survived one coup attempt in November and another in January 1995. Under pressure from international aid donors, the new government moved the date for elections forward to July 1996.

Gambia under Jawara suffered from corruption, but its elections had been free and fair and its government bound by law and a respect for human rights. Whether Gambians will be as fortunate under their new rulers remains in 1996 an open question.

CHAPTER

Central Africa

INTRODUCTION

The countries of central Africa are clustered on the western side of the continent where it narrows just north of the equator. The region includes Cameroon, the Central African Republic, Zaire, Congo, Gabon, Equatorial Guinea, and São Tomé and Príncipe. The region encompasses savanna and forest, with the latter predominating in the Congo basin and along the coast. Most of the countries were French colonies, but Equatorial Guinea was Spanish and São Tomé and Príncipe were Portuguese. Most countries in the region now belong to regional organizations with ties to France, and also have strong bilateral ties to France. Three of the seven—Congo, São Tomé and Príncipe, and the Central African Republic—have implemented multiparty democracy. Cameroon, Gabon, and Equatorial Guinea have gone through the motions of democratization without actually implementing it, and the government of Zaire has repeatedly blocked the democratization process.

CAMEROON
Statistical Profile

Capital:	Yaoundé
Area:	183,568 sq. miles
Population:	13,100,000 (1994 est.)
Density:	71 people/sq. mile
Growth Rate:	2.9% (1994 est.)
GDP:	$10,397,000,000
Per Capita Income:	$820
Foreign Debt:	$5,759,000,000
Life Expectancy:	40 (1960), 56 (1992)
Ethnic Groups:	Fulani, Kirdi, Bamileke, Bulu, Bamoun, Ewondo, Beti, Bassa, Douala
Official Languages:	French and English
Religions:	Christian (40%), Traditional (39%), Muslim (21%)
Former Colonizers:	Germany, France
Date of Independence:	1961

History

Located at the "hinge" between West and Central Africa, the area that became Cameroon stretches from the tropical forests

Central Africa

of the coastal region to the arid shores of Lake Chad. Before colonial rule, the 150 or so ethnic groups contained within it ranged from stateless lineage societies in the south through independent chiefdoms in the center to feudal chiefdoms subordinated to great empires based in the savanna.

The coastal people had exported slaves since the sixteenth century, turned to tropical products in the early nineteenth century, and in 1856 signed their first commercial treaty with the British. Some years later, they invited the British to establish a protectorate; but when their letter to Queen Victoria went unanswered, they turned to Germany, which staked its claim in 1884. The Germans subdued the interior and started creating a modern infrastructure before the First World War, but afterwards the victorious French and British split the colony under a League of Nations mandate, with the French getting the lion's share.

The UN confirmed the arrangement after the Second World War, but by then the colonial system was already beginning to unravel. In 1948, the Union of the People of Cameroon (UPC) raised the call for "unification and immediate independence." The French moved forcefully to suppress it, but also began steps that would lead to self-rule and independence for Cameroon. In 1952, they allowed the people to elect representatives to a territorial assembly and to the French parliament. In 1955, the UPC staged a series of anticolonial demonstrations, which the French crushed ruthlessly, driving the UPC underground. The next year, under the loi cadre, Cameroon gained local self-rule and a parliament, which first met in May 1957. Power was divided between four main parties. After a political scandal involving the prime minister picked by the colonial administration, Ahmadou Ahidjo, leader of the northern-based Cameroonian Union (UC), became the leader of the government in early 1958. He led the French portion of the country to independence on January 1, 1960, and was elected president by the new National Assembly, in which his UC held 51 of 100 seats. The English-speaking section voted to join Cameroon rather than Nigeria in October 1961.

The new country entered upon independence amidst great turmoil, for the UPC had been waging a bitter guerrilla war against the French and their Cameroonian allies since the mid-1950s. French troops and aircraft continued their ruthless counterinsurgency for the first year after independence, and the French had one of the guerrilla leaders assassinated in Geneva, Switzerland, in November 1960. Sporadic fighting continued until 1970, when the last rebel leader was captured and executed.

Meanwhile, Ahidjo gradually tightened his hold on the rest of the country. In September 1966, he amalgamated the six largest political parties into one under his control, and in 1971 he combined the country's three trade unions. In 1972, he transformed the country from a federal state with three assemblies and three governing bodies into the United Republic of Cameroon. He was reelected to the presidency in 1975 and again in 1980 in unopposed contests. His autocratic rule was vindicated in the eyes of many, however, by impressive economic growth based on conservative policies emphasizing agricultural development and cooperation with France. His longevity in office reflected genuine popular support.

Ahidjo resigned unexpectedly in November 1982 for reasons of health in favor of his prime minister and designated successor, Paul Biya. He soon regretted his decision, however, for Biya moved with deliberation to put his own stamp on the government. Biya also refused to let Ahidjo remove his considerable fortune from the country to support his retirement in France. Ahidjo let it be known that he had "made a bad mistake," observing that the man who had been his protégé for 15 years "is weak, a hypocrite who allows himself to be led by those around him." He was also a southerner and a Christian, while Ahidjo's supporters were mainly Moslems from the north. A small group of officers plotted a coup, which was discovered in August 1983 before it got under way, but the next April most of the elite Republican Guard rose up in an attempt to overthrow the government.

Troops loyal to Biya were able to crush the uprising after two days of heavy fighting, but the attempt changed the course of Biya's administration. Earlier, he had promised demo-

cratic reforms and a more open society, but in the wake of the revolt some participants were executed summarily, and hundreds of suspects were tried in secret and imprisoned or executed. Biya quickly purged suspected coup sympathizers from the government, and at the fourth UC party congress in March 1985 purged the old guard and replaced them with young technocrats. He also changed the name of the party to the Democratic Assembly of the Cameroonian People (RDPC) and announced that the country would remain a one-party state.

Biya did promise to make the party more democratic internally, and in early 1986 the first local elections in which voters had a real choice took place. At the same time, the government launched a major campaign against opponents in the perennially dissatisfied Anglophone areas in the west. Two years later, Biya stood for election unopposed, and the accompanying legislative elections were only competitive among RDPC-approved candidates.

These half measures did not satisfy the regime's growing opposition. The UPC had reemerged in 1985, and Biya had rebuffed its attempt to legally participate in the country's politics. In response, the UPC began agitating for multiparty democracy, and by 1990 students and workers were supporting its call in the streets. The government responded with force, and many protesters were killed in the ensuing violence. The demonstrations continued, and Biya met with the opposition in November 1991 and agreed to legalize opposition parties and hold multiparty elections. Sixty parties soon emerged, and 32 participated in legislative elections held in March 1992. The RDPC won the most seats but fell three short of an outright majority. It formed a coalition government with the Democratic Movement for the Defense of the Republic, one of the small parties. International observers judged that the elections were marred by poor administration rather than deliberate fraud, but only 15 percent of the eligible voters participated.

Twenty-seven opposition parties met in July 1992 in an attempt to unite on a single candidate to oppose Biya in the elections scheduled for April 1993, but they were unable to settle on one. The government pressed its advantage by moving the polling date forward to October 11, 1992. It refused to reopen voter registration and thereby froze out everyone who boycotted the legislative elections. It also rejected calls for independent supervision of the election process. The result was a vote marred by massive fraud in which Biya won a plurality of 39 percent of the votes cast. Since he had promulgated a law limiting the election to one round, Biya was declared the victor. The opposition cried foul, and the runner-up claimed victory, but the government declared a state of emergency, swept up protesters, and ignored a judicial order to let them go. The United States responded by cutting off foreign aid. The opposition continued to protest the election results throughout 1993 and 1994, but the uproar had no effect.

Cameroon remains a country whose people cannot change the government democratically. While the courts function relatively fairly in ordinary matters, the security apparatus dominates in political matters, and torture and abusive neglect of political prisoners is routine. Human rights activists have been singled out for arrest and beatings and then have been denied medical attention. The government must approve, and sporadically censors, publications, and it frequently breaks up opposition meetings by force. Strikes are forbidden, and union activity is controlled by the government. Cameroon had moved to the brink of democracy, but at the last minute pulled back.

CENTRAL AFRICAN REPUBLIC
Statistical Profile

Capital:	Bangui
Area:	240,533 sq. miles
Population:	3,100,000 (1994 est.)
Density:	13 people/sq. mile
Growth Rate:	2.4% (1994 est.)
GDP:	$1,251,000,000
Per Capita Income:	$410
Foreign Debt:	$808,000,000
Life Expectancy:	37 (1960), 47 (1992)
Ethnic Groups:	Baya and Banda (50%), Baka, Zande, Yakoma, Banziri, Sango, Sara
Official Language:	French; Sango is a common language used in the country; Swahili and Hausa are used by traders
Religions:	Traditional (60%), Christian (35%), Muslim (5%)
Former Colonizer:	France
Date of Independence:	1960

History

The Central African Republic straddles the watershed dividing the Congo River, the Nile River, and the basin around Lake Chad. It has consequently been influenced by forces as diverse as the ancient civilization of Meroe, the Bantu migrations of around 500 A.D., the medieval kingdoms of the eastern savanna, and the European slave trade along the Atlantic coast. Before the eighteenth century, it formed a refuge for peoples fleeing from slave raiders, but then it became a major source of slaves. In the early nineteenth century, it was losing 20,000 people a year as slaves to Egypt and thousands more to Brazil. The trade caused the area to become underpopulated, and in the mid-nineteenth century new groups moved in, the now-dominant Banda, Baya, and Zande.

During the "scramble for Africa," the French staked a claim to the territory and in 1894 settled its borders with the British Sudan to the east and the Belgian Congo to the south. France carved the area up into 17 huge concessions, giving them over to agents and managers charged with milking them for maximum profit. Forcible labor recruitment and open warfare resulted in famines and epidemics that brought the colony of Oubangui-Chari, as it came to be known in 1903, to a state of anarchy. The French government ostensibly took over administration, but the army had to stage a series of campaigns from 1909 to 1931 to overcome the people's resistance. In the process, they began creating the infrastructure for systematic exploitation of the country's resources—building roads, establishing plantations, and digging mines.

They also allowed the Catholic Church to set up mission schools, and in 1949, one graduate of these schools, Barthelemy Boganda, established the Movement for the Social Evolution of Black Africa (MESAN). He called not only for a rejection of colonial rule, but also for a social revolution. He garnered widespread support in elections in 1956, 1957, and 1958, but died in a mysterious plane crash in 1959. His nephew, David Dacko, took over the party and immediately ousted its progressive members.

Dacko became president upon independence in 1960. He quickly transformed the country into a one-party state, banning his rival Abel Goumba's Movement for the Evolution of Central Africa (MEDAC) before the end of the year and arresting or driving into exile its leaders. His rule became increasingly arbitrary and repressive, even though, with no army until 1962 and chronically inadequate financial resources, his government depended completely on French military and economic support. The French backed him until 1965; but when the government's inability to pay its own employees threatened to precipitate a general strike, they persuaded him to yield power to Jean Izamo, the head of the police.

On January 1, 1966, before the transition could take place, Colonel Jean-Bedel Bokassa staged a coup, forcing Dacko to resign immediately and murdering Izamo. Backed by the army and soon by the French, Bokassa promised reforms but instead created one of the most bizarre despotisms in Africa. He began by imprisoning and executing opponents, both real and imagined, promulgating decrees of increasing arbitrariness, and enriching himself and his clique of supporters at the expense of the rest of the country. In 1972, he became president-for-life, but in 1976, shortly after declaring a Libyan-style "revolution," he de-

cided to become an emperor, like Napoleon. The coronation cost the country a quarter of its foreign earnings, even though the ever-indulgent French and the country's leading diamond mining companies picked up most of the tab.

Opposition to His Highness grew steadily. In September 1978, the first of many strikes broke out. Four months later, school children demonstrated against a decree compelling them to wear uniforms manufactured by a factory Bokassa owned. When the protests turned violent, the emperor brought in Zairian troops who killed somewhere between 50 and 400 protesters. Three months later, with opposition still simmering, Bokassa had his Imperial Guard arrest several hundred "ringleaders." He then ordered that about 100 of the imprisoned children be beaten to death, and he killed a few himself. This atrocity caused an international scandal that spurred his French patrons to cut off financial aid. When he went to Libya seeking funds, they flew David Dacko and 1,000 French troops into the capital. The French set up a major base, and Dacko set up a new government.

Dacko's new order got off to a shaky start and never found firm footing. He alienated the people by declaring that the French troops would remain for 10 years (they were still there in 1996, 18 years later) and announcing that his government would recognize South Africa. His government tried and executed six of Bokassa's closest associates, and in February 1981 it introduced a new constitution establishing multiparty democracy. When he won with 50.23 percent of the vote in March, however, the opposition cried foul, and rioting broke out. Dacko postponed the scheduled legislative elections, which caused further disturbances, including a grenade attack on a cinema in June. On September 1, 1981, chief of staff Andre Kolingba announced that he had obtained Dacko's resignation and was taking over.

Kolingba immediately suspended the constitution and outlawed political parties. He formed the Military Committee for National

Recovery (CMRN), survived a coup attempt by the runner up in the disputed election, and kept a firm lid on opposition political activity. In 1982, he promised a return to democratic rule by 1985, issued a new constitution, and began drawing a limited number of civilians into the government, but he resisted real democratic reforms. In 1985, he replaced the CMRN with a mixed military and civilian government based on a new party, the Central African Democratic Assembly (RCD). He continued to rule into the 1990s.

The challenge to his regime intensified in the new decade, however. In September 1990 an opposition coordinating committee to promote democracy met. Although the police suppressed it, the RDC met in an extraordinary session the next month to consider reforms. The party congress rejected multipartyism, but the opposition began calling for a sovereign national conference to lead a transition to democracy. Strikes and demonstrations continued into the summer of 1991, so the national parliament approved a bill introducing multiparty democracy. The protests continued, tying together demands for political reform with those for economic relief, and the government negotiated fitfully with the opposition into 1992. The stumbling block was the mandate for a national conference: the opposition wanted the conference to be able to make binding decisions, while Kolingba wanted only a "broad national debate" that the government would presumably heed in creating a new electoral code.

Negotiations broke down entirely in May 1992, so Kolingba went ahead with his national debate in August. On September 7, he announced that legislative and presidential elections would take place on October 25 and November 8, respectively. Five candidates vied for the presidency and hundreds ran for the 84 parliamentary seats. However, fraud by the government and violence by the opposition marred the October contests, so the Supreme Court annulled the results and the government suspended the November contest. Kolingba extended his own term in office and rescheduled the elections for February 1993. When the elections were finally held in August, Kolingba and his party lost. When Kolingba tried to repudiate the results, France immediately suspended aid. Ange-Felix Patasse became president, and his Central African People's Liberation Party (MPLC) took a plurality of seats in parliament.

The Central African Republic has made a fragile transition to multiparty democracy. Until the 1993 election, its governments had been among the most consistent violators of human rights on the continent of Africa. In late 1994, Patasse sought and gained adoption of a new constitution allowing him to run for a second term and strengthening his powers, but the new document does not change the democratic nature of the government. The current situation is hopeful, but establishing a truly free and democratic society from this legacy and in the midst of the country's chronic economic troubles remains a formidable challenge.

ZAIRE
Statistical Profile

Capital:	Kinshasa
Area:	905,563 sq. miles
Population Size:	42,500,000 (1994 est.)
Density:	47 people/sq. mile
Growth Rate:	3.3% (1994 est.)
GDP:	$7,540,000,000
Per Capita Income:	$235
Foreign Debt:	$8,895,000,000
Life Expectancy:	42 (1960), 52 (1992)
Ethnic Groups:	Includes over 200 groups. The majority belong to the Bwaka, Kongo, Kwangu-Kwilu, Lunda, Tshokwe, Luba, Lulua, Mongo, Ngala, Songe, and Zande groups
Official Language:	French
Religions:	Christian (50%), Traditional (50%)
Former Colonizer:	Belgium
Date of Independence:	1960

History

The original Khoisan-speaking inhabitants of the Congo basin, the Pygmies, lived in small bands as nomadic hunters and gatherers. Bantu-speakers immigrated during the great migrations of the first millennium A.D., bringing agriculture, ironworking, lineage-based village settlements, and the kernel of more complex political structures. By the fourteenth century, chiefdoms had grown into kingdoms among the Kongo, Luba, Kuba, and Lunda peoples of the southern savanna. When the Portuguese arrived at the end of the fifteenth century, they found these kingdoms to be extensive domains with provincial governors and regular systems of taxation. Portuguese meddling and the growth of the slave trade undermined these native kingdoms, leading to several centuries of political regression and eventual domination by Arab slavers, whose forays and later rule gained them the title of *wamaliza*, or "the exterminators." Native rulers emulated and ultimately outdid them; M'Siri of the Yeke tribe created a huge slave-based empire in the Shaba region in the south.

The European explorers who penetrated the area in the mid-nineteenth century and the financiers who hired them claimed that their work was inspired at least in part by the desire to liberate Africa from the slavers and the slave trade. But the regime they created in the Congo practiced the slavers' cruelty on a much grander scale. In 1879, Henry Stanley began a five-year process of securing treaties giving King Leopold of Belgium title to the Congo basin. Leopold thereupon created a "free state" based on military force and forced labor. The Belgian government took over the colony in 1908 because of international outrage over the wanton inhumanity of Leopold's personal rule, but it curbed only the worst excesses. The trinity of the government, business, and the Catholic Church (which ran the schools) dominated the Congo until independence. The Belgians ruled indirectly for the most part, but their hand was heavy nonetheless. They imposed economic roles (forcing some peoples to work in mines, others to grow food, and so on), restricted movement, censored expression, and consciously obstructed the emergence of a modern, educated leadership.

Many peoples in the hinterlands resisted the Belgians stubbornly, some into the 1930s, but the first modern Congolese anticolonialism took the form of messianic Christian movements. When the Belgians reacted with bitter persecution, anticolonialism became more radical and more political. Peasants in the east revolted in 1944, and a nationalist party of the Bakongo, the Alliance of Bakongo (ABAKO) led by Joseph Kasavubu, emerged in the 1950s. Other parties appeared later in the decade, including the National Congolese Movement (MNC) led by Patrice Lumumba, the first party with truly national scope. The Belgians, however, stubbornly refused to consider even limited moves towards independence until riots in the capital of Leopoldville (now Kinshasa) on January 4, 1959 brought a sudden about-face. The government organized the colony's first elections before the end of the year, and Belgium granted the Congo independence on June 30, 1960. Lumumba became the prime minister, and Kasavubu became the president.

The Congolese embraced independence joyfully, but they were woefully unprepared for it. The huge, populous country contained over 200 major ethnic groups speaking over 700 different languages and dialects, and it was hobbled by the resistance of the Belgian expatriates, whose help it desperately needed. Even before independence, a split developed between Lumumba's "nationalists," who favored a strong central government and an independent foreign policy, and the "moderates," who were discretely backed by the Belgians and not surprisingly favored a loose federation and strong ties to Belgium. Within a week of independence, the Belgian-led army mutinied, most of the Europeans fled, and the government and the economy faltered. Moise Tshombe, backed by Belgian settlers and financial interests, declared the independence of Katanga, a mineral-rich region in the south that was economically vital to the new state.

Lumumba called for assistance from the United Nations, and when that proved ineffective, he turned to the Soviet Union. This move aroused American fears, so the CIA worked against Lumumba with Belgian intelligence and local opponents. Kasavubu dismissed him from office on September 5, but when Lumumba claimed to still represent the government, Colonel Joseph Mobutu, the CIA's man, seized control in Leopoldville. Lumumba retreated to his base of support in Stanleyville (now Kisangani) in the east. On December 2, government troops captured him and turned him over to the Katangese rebels, who killed him in January 1961. This martyrdom gained him an enduring place as a symbol of independence throughout Africa.

After Lumumba's death, his followers gained control over the eastern half of the country, but they came to terms with the government at the Lovanium Conclave in August 1961. The resulting government of national union under Cyrille Adoula crushed the rebels in Katanga by early 1963 with the help of UN forces. However, when Kasavubu dissolved parliament in September, the nationalists formed the Committee of National Liberation (CNL), took control of the east again, and in 1964 proclaimed the People's Republic of the Congo. The new state lasted only a few months before being defeated by government forces led by Belgian officers, buttressed by European mercenaries, and assisted by Belgian paratroopers. A series of uprisings in succeeding years fared no better, and the movement split—with moderates reconciling with the government once again and radicals waging a protracted guerrilla war as the People's Revolutionary Party (PRP).

Meanwhile, Moise Tschombe, former leader of the Katanganese rebels and now prime minister of the Congolese government, ran against Kasavubu in a presidential election in 1965. Unfortunately, Western governments feared that Kasavubu's support of an OAU resolution against the use of mercenaries signaled a turn to the left, so they supported another coup by Colonel Mobutu. This time, instead of al-lowing the ongoing political game to continue, he established himself as dictator. In 1967, he organized the Popular Movement of the Revolution (MPR), which became the sole legal party in 1970. In 1974, he subordinated all public institutions, including the army and the universities, to the party. He reduced the number of provinces in the country from 21 to 8 and reduced their power from near independence to strict subordination. He sponsored an ill-fated "Zaireanisation" economic policy in the early 1970s that involved expropriation of foreign companies and expulsion of Asian merchants. He expounded an ideology, which he originally called "authenticity" and later renamed "Mobutuism," that called for the rejection of Western cultural artifacts, including Christian names, in favor of African forms. This ideology inspired him to change the country's name to Zaire, to change many city names, and to change his own name to Mobutu Sese Seko. He had his people change what they called him to "Messiah."

At first, Zaireans found Mobutu's rule a welcome relief from the turmoil of the early 1960s. For the first 10 years, high prices for copper and other mineral exports kept the economy strong. Mobutu appeared to be solidly in control, and the country enjoyed the stability for which the United States, France, and Belgium had backed him. Despite rampant corruption and repression, the opposition remained quiescent.

In 1975, world copper prices began a long, steep slide and the Zairean army was humiliated when it intervened in the Angolan civil war. These events gave heart to Mobutu's enemies. Prominent politicians began to form illicit political parties. Army officers plotted against Mobutu in 1975 and again in 1978. PRP rebels in the east, who had been quietly recuperating since the CNL's defeats in the mid-1960s, went on the offensive and tried to coordinate with exile armies that invaded Shaba (Katanga) from Angola in 1977 and 1978. Only Western intervention—troops from Morocco, Belgium, and France; pilots from Egypt; transport planes from France; and supplies from West Germany and the United

States—enabled Mobutu to weather this last crisis. In addition to the casualties of the fighting, hundreds of thousands of people fled the country.

The end of political stability, coupled with a debt crisis resulting from the country's extravagant borrowing in the good years, brought a crisis of confidence among Mobutu's foreign backers. After the first invasion of Shaba in 1977, they began urging him to make political reforms, and after the second invasion, the United States, France, Great Britain, and West Germany held an international conference on Zaire in Paris. In response to the pressure to liberalize, Mobutu held parliamentary elections near the end of 1977, and he gave the parliament an increased role in national affairs. In conjunction with his foreign backers, he reformed his security apparatus, dissolving part of the army and replacing it with three brigades trained by France, Belgium, and Red China. An international African force kept the peace in Shaba in the meantime. Mobutu's new forces suppressed the PRP in the east in late 1978 and forcibly resettled the Lunda people, who straddled the border between Shaba and Angola and who provided the backbone of the exile army. Mobutu also reorganized the MPR to increase his control, brutally suppressed student uprisings, and arrested lawyers who refused to become state functionaries. Despite his army's weakness, he sent troops to the Central African Empire, where they killed scores of antigovernment demonstrators.

Excepting a brief invasion of Shaba, a series of bomb explosions in Kinshasa, and an army mutiny at Moba in the far east, all in 1984, opposition to Mobutu in the 1980s was more political than military. Both within Zaire and abroad, criticism of his regime steadily increased. Abroad, Amnesty International began publicizing the regime's abysmal human rights record—pointing to arbitrary arrests, indefinite detentions, widespread use of torture, and hundreds of deaths in captivity. The Belgian press revealed that Mobutu had amassed a vast personal fortune, around $8 billion, which made him by his own estima-

tion the second richest man in the world. Mobutu's reaction to these criticisms fluctuated between accommodation and bullying: he amnestied political prisoners to improve his human rights record, but he provoked an international confrontation with Belgium over the exposés of his corruption, suspending air service and moving the headquarters of parastatial corporations out of the country. (Parastatials are business enterprises in which the government owns a controlling interest.)

Mobutu was unable to get the Belgian government to muzzle its press, but he did succeed in getting the Belgians to curb the pronouncements of Zairean exiles living in Belgium. Nevertheless, the exile community played a vital role in fanning the flames of opposition to his rule. In 1979, four parties in exile united to coordinate their actions. In 1981, one of Mobutu's leading allies, Nguza Karl I Bond, fled to Belgium, denouncing the regime's corruption and economic incompetence. Mobutu got the Belgian government to silence him. In 1982, Professor Dikonda wa Lumanyisha, a prominent dissident, fled after being released from detention, and the Belgian government called off a visit by Mobutu planned for two weeks later because of the likelihood of disturbances by exiles. A few months later, Dikonda's party, the Union for Democracy and Social Progress (UDPS), joined with the PRP and another party to create the Congolese Front for the Restoration of Democracy (FCD).

Dikonda had been detained because he was one of a number of prominent politicians, including members of the parliament elected in 1977, who called for political reform. This group formed the UDPS, and in 1982 tried to negotiate with the government to have the UDPS become a legal second party. After Dikonda fled, other members of the party remained in Zaire to continue agitating against Mobutu. In the spring of 1985, thousands of pamphlets critical of Mobutu were distributed, and shortly thereafter the president of the party disappeared mysteriously and seven other members were arrested and exiled to their home villages. In the same year, students rioted against IMF-imposed austerity measures. They rose again in 1989.

This latter disturbance combined with other domestic and foreign political pressure to induce Mobutu to announce a commitment to multipartyism in April 1990, a commitment he has neither been willing to live up to nor able to live down. Over 200 political groups quickly formed, and in July 1991, they came together to form the "Sacred Union" opposed to Mobutu's rule. Their chief demand was the convocation of a sovereign national conference to pave the way for establishment of a democratic regime. Mobutu agreed to this quickly but then tried to pack the assembly with his own supporters. The opposition parties walked out two weeks later, and the assembly did not reconvene until December, after the opposition made sure that Mobutu could count on less than half the delegates. They then elected Monsignor Laurent Monsengo Pasinya president of the conference over Mobutu's nominee.

Mobutu responded by suspending the conference indefinitely on January 19, 1992, which brought condemnation from the United States, France, and Belgium, and massive protests at home. When soldiers killed 40 peaceful protesters in February, pressure from abroad increased, and in April Mobutu allowed the conference to resume. It quickly declared its decisions to be sovereign, and in the following months it changed the name of the country back to the Congo, readopted the former national flag, and elected Etienne Tshisekedi of the UDPS as prime minister. Before it adjourned on December 6, it drafted a transitional charter to replace Mobutu's constitution and dissolved the old parliament, replacing it with a new legislature, the High Council of the Republic (HCR), with Pasinya as its president.

Mobutu refused to recognize the conference's authority to make such sweeping changes and refused to relinquish control of the nation's treasury and armed forces. In October 1992, he used troops and tanks to block Tshisekedi from replacing the governor of the central bank, and in December he used the military to protect members of the old parliament as they sat in defiance of the conference's decision. The dictator ordered top civil servants to take control of the ministries and then suspended the HCR. In March 1993, he created a parallel government, and then, with Western backing, forced a "compromise" that merged his government with the HCR in January 1994. The new High Council of the Republic–Parliament of Transition (HCR-PT) set a 15-month timeframe for the transition to democracy in April. The deadline for elections was July 1995; but in May 1995, the government postponed them indefinitely.

While the politicians wrangled in the capital, the central government's authority over the country slipped badly. Shaba, which had refused to recognize Tshisekedi in 1992, declared its autonomy in December 1993 and changed its name back to Katanga. This move was just the most obvious manifestation of the country's general collapse. Amidst the political turmoil, the economy ground to a halt. In 1993 and 1994, hyperinflation pushed the value of the currency to a fraction of its former value, unemployment ran to 75 percent, and real wages fell to just 10 percent of their value at independence. Meanwhile, corruption remained rampant, with Mobutu and his entourage living in ostentatious splendor, secured by his security forces' wanton disregard of human rights.

No election has been held since the beginning of Zaire's "transition" to democracy. The government controls the judiciary, and extralegal arrests, detentions, and executions are still common. The government does not respect the people's right to assemble peaceably. Although an independent press has appeared, its members are subject to harassment and its facilities to damage by security forces. Churches need government approval to operate, travel is restricted, and the MPR formally controls the national labor union. Although stability was the main justification for

Mobutu's dictatorial rule for a quarter-century, his refusal to step down is now the main cause of Zaire's ongoing upheaval.

CONGO
Statistical Profile

Capital:	Brazzaville
Area:	132,046 sq. miles
Population:	2,400,000 (1994 est.)
Density:	18 people/sq. mile
Growth Rate:	2.6% (1994 est.)
GDP:	$2,816,000,000
Per Capita Income:	$1,030
Foreign Debt:	$3,878,000,000
Life Expectancy:	38 (1960), 51 (1992)
Ethnic Groups:	Total of 70 groups: (principally Kongo, Teke, Mboshi, Vili, Sanga); significant numbers of Gabonese and Europeans, mainly French
Official Language:	French
Religions:	Christian (50%), Traditional (47%), Muslim (2%)
Former Colonizer:	France
Date of Independence:	1960

History

As elsewhere in central Africa, the earliest inhabitants of the Congo were Khoisan-speaking hunter-gatherers, many of whom became dependents of the Bantu-speakers who migrated into the area around 1000 A.D. Over the centuries, the Bantu in the area established polities ranging from stateless societies to strong kingdoms, with the key feature distinguishing them the extent of judicial power exercised by the central authorities. In most of these societies, population pressures forced some men to move onto land belonging to other clans and to accept a subordinate status in which they were not slaves but their rights were not equal to those of their neighbors. Their status changed to that of slaves when the Europeans appeared, however, and the area became a major source of slaves without needing to resort to the wars and hunts

that occurred elsewhere. Several small kingdoms centered on trading posts grew up along the coast, prospering when the trade boomed and declining when it ended.

French traders visited the coast frequently in the seventeenth and eighteenth centuries, and the French established their antislaving station and resettlement community on the coast of Gabon in the early nineteenth century, but they did not penetrate the interior until the late nineteenth century. The explorer Pierre de Brazza founded Brazzaville in 1880, signing treaties of protection with the peoples in the area. French control along the northwestern banks of the Congo River was recognized at the Berlin Conference of 1884–1885. The colony of the French Congo was formally proclaimed in 1891, and in 1910 it became part of French Equatorial Africa. Extensive areas of the colony resisted French rule into the 1920s, and the campaigns of conquest and the famines that accompanied them cost some areas two-thirds of their population between 1914 and 1924. Meanwhile, de Brazza's hope that generous concessions would attract major international companies to develop the area proved vain. Instead, only smaller companies showed an interest, and they focused exclusively on extraction of easily acquired resources. Their ruthless exploitation and minimal reinvestment impoverished the inhabitants without fostering significant development. As late as 1925, the colony had no roads. The death rate of forced laborers on the Congo-Ocean Railroad was a major scandal, but the forced labor system did not disappear entirely until 1946.

Messianic religious movements like Matswanismhe formed the transition from traditional to modern anticolonialism, and after World War II explicitly political organizations linked to the French Communist Party took the lead. The French moved to increase the colony's political rights, making it an overseas territory in 1946, but the pressure for independence increased in the 1950s. In 1958, the Congo voted for autonomy as part of the French Union. Fulbert Youlou's Democratic Union for the Defense of African Interests

(UDDIA) and Jacques Opangault's African Social Movement (MSA) clashed violently for the right to take over upon independence, with the UDDIA gaining the upper hand.

Youlou became the country's first president, but his close ties to France and his open enjoyment of the perks of office steadily alienated the people. When he attempted to make UDDIA the sole legal party and to curb the power of the unions, "three glorious days," as the people called them, of street demonstrations forced him from office. The French stood by and let him fall, figuring that they could control his successor through their many agents in the army.

Alphonse Massemba-Debat took over in place of Youlou, but he proved less subject to French control than they had calculated. He made the National Movement of the Revolution (MNR) the country's sole party. With his approval, the party's youth movement, the JMNR, took a radical line, establishing its own armed groups, setting up a journal, and running cooperatives. He organized a popular militia that challenged the position of the armed forces and police, at times violently, and he arranged for a Cuban palace guard to protect him from pro-French elements in the army. His anti-Western policies led to a diplomatic break with the United States, and he established close relations with Communist China.

A coup by pro-French army officers in 1966 failed, but Massemba's attempts to increase his own power alienated the militia and the JMNR. They came to an agreement with the army to replace him with the leading leftist officer, Captain Marien Ngouabi. The militia was integrated into the army while retaining its own officers, and the MNR and JMNR were replaced by the new Congolese Workers' Party (PCT).

The Congo under Ngouabi moved further left, explicitly adopting Marxist-Leninism as its official ideology and changing its name to the People's Republic of the Congo. Behind the scenes, leftist civilians and rightist military officers struggled for dominance. The left-

ists staged an abortive coup in 1972 and then resorted to a clumsy guerrilla war that lasted into 1973. These developments pushed Ngouabi into the arms of the pro-French officers, who let him continue to rule until 1977. When he refused to help Zaire seize the enclave of Cabinda from Angola because of mass protests in Brazzaville, he was assassinated and replaced by the army chief of staff, Joachim Yhombi-Opango.

Yhombi's attempts to reduce the power of the PCT sparked more street demonstrations and led the party's central committee to oust him in early 1979. Pro-Soviet army officers, the militia, and the unions all backed his successor, Colonel Sassou-Nguesso. The party moved further to the left, reaffirming its socialist and anti-imperialist position, expelling Yhombi, and putting a pro-Soviet politician in charge of the foreign affairs department. The country got a new constitution, and in July it held elections for local, district, and regional councils and for the National Assembly. Although Sassou's government maintained Marxist-Leninism and even signed a treaty of friendship and cooperation with the Soviet Union in 1981, it showed increasing respect for human rights and pragmatism in economic affairs. Sassou survived a plot to overthrow the government in 1982 and was reelected president by the central committee in 1984. In 1985, his government met violent student riots with force, but also staged counterdemonstrations to rally popular support. Regional tensions appeared when only Southerners were tried for the 1982 coup attempt, and were intensified by economic development plans that favored the north, Sassou's base of support, over the south. Economic discontent increased still further when the IMF imposed an austerity program in the late 1980s.

The PCT central committee reelected Sassou to the presidency in 1989, but, under domestic and foreign pressure, began a transition to democracy in 1990. In the middle of the year, the central committee issued a communiqué promising that the party would renounce Marxist-Leninism, guarantee civil rights, end one-party rule, and organize a national conference to lay the groundwork for the transition. A few months later, it legalized other parties, and in March 1991 the transitional commission began its meetings. This body abolished the PCT-dominated legislature, began work on a new constitution, scheduled elections for 1992, created the Supreme Council of the Republic (CSR) to run the country during the transition, and elected Andre Milongo as the transitional prime minister. After the transitional commission adjourned in June, a number of prominent exiles returned home to found opposition parties, which joined together in an anti-PCT coalition, the Coordinated Forces for Change.

In January 1992, mutinous soldiers threatened the transition, but when tens of thousands of civilians took to the streets against them, the army high command refused to support the mutiny. Municipal elections took place on May 3, and Pascal Lissouba's Pan African Union for Social Development (UPADS) emerged as the strongest, although not the majority, party. The National Assembly elections in June and July had a similar result, and Lissouba won the presidency in a two-round election in August. Charges that Sassou endorsed him in the second round in exchange for a promise of immunity led to a governmental crisis when the National Assembly voted no-confidence in the government. Lissouba refused to replace his party's prime minister with a leader of the opposition, instead dissolving the assembly and calling for new elections. Opposition supporters took to the streets in protest. After the police killed several, Lissouba and his opponents came to a compromise in which Claude Antoine da Costa became head of a cabinet including 60 percent opposition members and 40 percent government supporters, with elections scheduled for March 1993.

When the first round of voting finally took place in May, the opposition charged that the voting had been "tarnished by monstrous irregularities" and refused to participate in the second round unless voting in 11 constituencies was repeated. The government went ahead with the second round on June 6 and gained an absolute majority in the National Assembly. The opposition took to the streets, and fighting escalated while the two sides talked. In July, they agreed to repeat the elections in the 11 contested constituencies in October and to submit other disagreements to international arbitration. The results of the October elections reduced but did not eliminate the government's majority. Meanwhile, violence costing dozens of lives continued into early 1994, and sporadic incidents broke out throughout the year. Nevertheless, the democratic system survived, albeit just barely.

The citizens of the Congo now have the ability to replace their government democratically, to speak and assemble freely, and to be tried by an impartial court when charged with a crime. They can travel and worship freely, and the labor unions, once dominated by the PCT, are now independent. The country has succeeded in making the transition from a one-party state to a full multiparty democracy.

GABON
Statistical Profile

Capital:	Libreville
Area:	103,347 sq. miles
Population:	1,100,000 (1994 est.)
Density:	11 people/sq. mile
Growth Rate:	2.7% (1994 est.)
GDP:	$5,913,000,000
Per Capita Income:	$4,450
Foreign Debt:	$2,998,000,000
Life Expectancy:	41 (1960), 54 (1992)
Ethnic Groups:	Fang (30%), Eshira, Mbeda, Bakota, Omyene, approximately 35 others; approximately 50,000 Europeans, mainly French
Official Language:	French
Religions:	Christian (60%, mainly Catholic), Traditional (40%)
Former Colonizer:	France
Date of Independence:	1960

History

Khoisan-speaking hunter-gatherers were the earliest inhabitants of present-day Gabon. Despite its proximity to their original home-land, Bantu-speakers came to the area rela-tively late, perhaps in the thirteenth century. Another migration brought the Fang into the north in the eighteenth century, and by as-similation and conquest they gradually estab-lished dominance over the earlier arrivals. Before long, they were reduced to subordina-tion by the Europeans, who had been trading along the coast since the fifteenth century, and who began settling in earnest in the early nine-teenth century. The French established a na-val base in 1843 in the Gabon estuary and set up a colony for free slaves, Libreville, in 1849. French commercial interests increased in the following decades, and in 1879 the explorer-administrator de Brazza used Libreville as the base for expansion into the interior. The French made the area into a colony in 1886 and three years later made Libreville the capi-tal of the "French Congo." For the next 25 years, the French Congo suffered some of the most severe depredations of any European colony under concession company rule. Com-pany rule was replaced by direct colonial rule in 1911, a year after Gabon became a sepa-rate colony within French Equatorial Africa.

During World War II, the Free French in the neighboring Congo seized Gabon from its Vichy governor, and in 1946 Gabon became an overseas department with its own elected council. In the same year, Leon M'Ba founded the United Gabonese Movement (MGM) as the local affiliate of the African Democratic Assembly (RDA). His rival, Jean-Hilaire Aubame, Gabon's deputy to the French par-liament, formed the Gabonese Democratic and Social Union (UDSG) two years later. M'Ba's party, renamed the Gabonese Demo-cratic Bloc (BDG) in 1957, won elections held that year. The colony voted for independence within the French Union in 1958 and became independent in 1960. M'Ba won the presi-dency in 1961 and created a coalition gov-ernment with Aubame.

Over the next years, the partnership slowly deteriorated. In January 1964, M'Ba decided to dissolve the parliament and hold new elec-tions. Before they could take place, the mili-tary staged a coup and invited Aubame to form a government. However, Aubame had the reputation of being further to the left than M'Ba, so French paratroopers intervened to restore the president. The BDG won 31 of 47 seats in the election, and M'Ba governed un-til his death in 1967.

Upon M'Ba's death, his hand-picked suc-cessor, Albert Bongo, took over. In 1968, he transformed the country into a one-party state under his own new Gabonese Democratic Party (PDG), creating one of the most stable regimes in Africa. A member of a small tribe, Bongo was accepted as protector of all the small tribes. As Bongo's vice president and prime minister, Leon Mebiame, a Fang, reas-sured the dominant ethnic group. Further-more, oil revenues gave Gabon the highest standard of living in sub-Saharan Africa, which definitely helped promote stability. Just in case, Bongo maintained a presidential guard of European mercenaries and Moroccan troops, and the French stationed aircraft and 550 elite paratroopers in the country, along with a host of French military, administrative, and business advisors. Libreville developed a reputation as a center of French covert op-erations, and Bongo openly supported France's role as policeman of Africa. He contributed forces to the French intervention in Zaire's Shaba province in 1978, and in the same year expelled 10,000 migrant workers from Benin because that country's leftist president charged that mercenaries who invaded in 1977 had used Gabon as a base.

Solidly entrenched, Bongo concentrated power in his own hands and in the hands of his family and fellow tribesmen. During the 1970s, prosperity and foreign support kept the political scene calm, and he won reelection in uncontested contests in 1973 and 1979. In the late 1970s, the economy soured, and op-position began to appear in the 1980s. In 1981, students and teachers at the University of

A worker in Owendo, Gabon, sorts logs for export. Most African countries remain dependent on exports of a limited number of primary products whose value on world markets has been depressed since the 1970s. *Source:* United Nations

Libreville went on strike, and a dozen of them were arrested. In the same year, opponents founded the clandestine Movement for National Recovery (MORENA) . It issued a 13-page manifesto calling for multiparty democracy and denouncing Bongo for tribalism, nepotism, and corruption. The government reacted harshly, detaining without charge the editor of the state newspaper, the head of the national radio station, and a former education minister, among others. In November 1982, 13 people were sentenced to 20 years' hard labor, and another 16 were fined or sentenced to lesser terms in prison.

Bongo remained firm in his opposition to multipartyism and felt secure enough to amnesty most of the people convicted in the MORENA trials in 1985–1986. The government easily quashed a plot by junior officers and soldiers in May 1985, and Bongo won another unopposed term as president in 1986.

In the same year, however, MORENA formed a government-in-exile in Paris, and in May 1989 its leader met with Bongo in Gabon. Bongo agreed that political exiles could return home, but a year later the secretary-general of the opposition Gabonese Progress Party (PGP) died under suspicious circumstances and soldiers took the party's president into custody. A week of riots ensued. Although the army suppressed them harshly, Bongo agreed to hold multiparty elections. Elections to the National Assembly were held in October 1990 and March 1991, and were judged by outside observers to be reasonably fair, although eight seats had to be recontested due to irregularities. The PDG emerged with 66 seats in the 120-member house. The PGP took 18, the National Rally of Woodsmen took 17, and a coalition of three small parties, the African Forum for Reconstruction (FAR), gained 7. Presidential elections were scheduled for 1993.

The political scene in 1992 was dominated by pressure from the opposition to ensure a fair presidential election. The government survived no-confidence votes in December 1991 and June 1992 but agreed to many opposition demands after numerous strikes and demonstrations. A new crisis arose when a striking teacher was killed by a rubber bullet; this crisis was defused only when President Bongo met with teacher representatives and accepted many of their demands and expressed regret over the incident. The move eased the immediate situation, but did not placate the political opposition. When presidential elections were finally held in December 1993, Bongo's opponents refused to recognize his victory. His defeated rival formed a rival government, and the opposition's supporters rioted in the streets. Demonstrations and police repression continued in early 1994, and the controversy died down only when the government and opposition leaders came to agreement in September on measures to ensure fairer elections in the future and a place for the opposition in the present government.

It is uncertain whether the citizens of Gabon will truly be able to enjoy the fruits of freedom under their new constitution. They can vote in elections, but the results of the most recent presidential election were clouded by allegations of fraud, violent demonstrations, and police repression. The Gabonese can express their views relatively freely in print and through peaceful demonstrations. They can also worship and travel freely, and form both political and nonpolitical associations, but the executive branch continues to dominate the judicial system in political cases, and detention without charges and torture still occur. Gabon has tried but has not yet fully succeeded in making the transition to true multiparty democracy.

EQUATORIAL GUINEA
Statistical Profile

Capital:	Malabo
Area:	10,830 sq. miles
Population:	400,000 (1994 est.)
Density:	37 people/sq. mile
Growth Rate:	2.6% (1994 est.)
GDP:	$140,000,000
Per Capita Income:	$330
Foreign Debt:	$206,000,000
Life Expectancy:	n.a. (1960), 48 (1992)
Ethnic Groups:	Rio Muni: Fang (80%), Kombe, Balengue, Bujeba; Bioko: Bubi, Fernandinos, Fang
Official Language:	Spanish; a dialect mixing English and local languages is also commonly used on Bioko
Religions:	Christian (94%, mostly Catholic), Traditional
Former Colonizer:	Spain
Date of Independence:	1968

History

Equatorial Guinea is composed of two territories, an area on the African mainland known as Rio Muni and the island of Bioko (formerly Fernando Po). They are united mainly because they once comprised Spain's equatorial possessions. The island was originally settled by the Bubi, a Bantu-speaking people, who crossed over from the mainland in the thirteenth century. The Portuguese first visited it in 1472 and claimed it until 1778, when they traded it to Spain for some land in America. From 1827 to 1843, the British leased the port of Malabo as a base for their antislavery patrols and settled recaptive slaves on the island. Late in the century, the Spanish established plantations, for which they needed labor from the mainland. With this in mind, they laid claim to the small enclave of Rio Muni with its Fang inhabitants in 1885. Spain reached agreement with neighboring European powers on Rio Muni's borders between 1900 and 1902, but Spanish rule did not extend into the interior until the 1920s, and its control was not complete until after the Second World War. In the meantime, most of the migrant laborers on the island's plantations actually came from Nigeria.

The Spanish ruled paternally at first, entrusting African communities to Catholic missionaries, forbidding political activity, and creating roads and schools. During the 1950s, nationalist sentiment began to grow among the Fang, and in 1959 Spain switched to an assimilationist policy, making Equatorial Guinea a part of Spain and giving it representation in the Spanish parliament. In 1962, two nationalist parties-in-exile, the National Movement of Equatorial Guinean Liberation (MONALIGE) and the Popular Idea of Equatorial Guinea (IPGE), appealed to the United Nations for independence. The next year, Spain granted the territories autonomy, with a president, cabinet, and local legislature under a Spanish high commissioner, and installed the head of a new pro-Spanish party, the Movement of National Union of Equatorial Guinea (MUNGE), as president. The head of IPGE, Francisco Macias Nguema, became vice president.

In 1967, the Spanish began to consider complete disengagement and convened a series of meetings to create an independent government. The constitution that emerged guaranteed Bioko disproportionate representation because its inhabitants feared domination by the more populous mainland, but otherwise it created a model democracy. Most political leaders supported it, but Macias denounced it as a neocolonialist cover for continued Spanish domination. Elections took place in September. Macias won the presidency, and the country became independent on October 12.

Macias rapidly transformed the government into one of the most repressive and ruthless dictatorships on the continent. In 1969, he drove the 7,000 remaining Spanish out of the country and killed a number of prominent politicians who tried to mediate. He founded a new political party, the Party of National Unity (PUN), later renamed the National Unity Party of Workers (PUNT). He made the country into a one-party state in 1970. In 1972 and 1973, he made himself president-for-life and commander of the army and imposed a new constitution that gave him the power to appoint judges and dissolve the National Assembly. Backed by the Soviet Union and China and protected by a force of Cuban soldiers, he crushed all opposition, killing 10 of 12 of his original cabinet members and half of the members of the House of Representatives elected in 1968. He persecuted intellectuals, purged the civil service, and harassed the Catholic Church. Between 1969 and 1972, his government killed about 50,000 of the country's 300,000 people and drove another 100,000 into exile. He and his cronies looted the national treasury and crippled the economy. Cocoa and timber exports dropped over 80 percent and coffee production ceased altogether. Relations with neighboring African and Western countries deteriorated rapidly. Nigeria withdrew its 20,000 workers from Bioko in 1976 (Macias tried to compensate by resorting to forced labor), and Spain broke relations in 1977. Macias remained in power because of the fear of the masses and the self-interest of his small circle of supporters.

In 1979, Macias turned on members of his inner circle, so they turned on him. He quashed an attempted coup in June, but his cousin, Teodoro Obiang Nguema Mbasogo, led another in August. Rebel troops chased Macias to his hometown and then into the bush, where they caught and arrested him. The new government tried him and six associates for murder and corruption, and executed them on September 29.

The new military government quickly released all political prisoners, removed restrictions on the Catholic Church, and restored relations with Western countries. It reestablished diplomatic ties with Spain, which had supported the coup, and with the United States. It obtained aid from Spain, the European Community, and the International Monetary Fund. The country broke off relations with the Soviet Union in 1980, and Moroccan soldiers replaced Cubans as the presidential bodyguard. Crowds in Malabo harassed Soviet technicians, and the government barred the Soviet fishing fleet, which it said "had scraped the ocean beds dry" through earlier treaties. The country joined the francophone Central African Customs and Economic Union (UDEAC) in 1983, adopted the French Union's CFA franc in place of its own currency in 1985, and replaced its Spanish-founded bank with the Franco-African International Bank of West Africa between 1986 and 1988. These latter moves were part of a shift in primary economic dependence from Spain to France, which were made because France promised to be a stronger aid to economic development.

Internally, the new president banned all political parties and created a cabinet containing only military officers. Although a Fang like Macias, and member of the same clan, he moved to establish a broader-based regime. He appointed a Bubi as governor of Bioko and brought the first civilian into the cabinet in 1981. He survived a coup attempt in April, and in August 1982 he submitted to a referendum a new constitution establishing an elected presidency with a seven-year term and a legislature with a five-year term. The referendum was approved and Obiang won the presidency in an uncontested election. After a second coup attempt in May 1983, the people elected 41 representatives to the National Assembly from a field of candidates nominated by Obiang. In 1987, he formally created a new political organization, the Democratic Party of Equatorial Guinea (PDGE), to be the country's sole legal party.

Obiang foiled another coup attempt in 1986, but opposition to the undemocratic regime grew throughout the 1980s. The first opposition group in exile appeared in 1981, and a government-in-exile was formed in 1983. The two main opposition groups merged to form the Social Democratic Convergence (CSD) in 1984. In 1989, Obiang won another term as president in another unopposed election, but pressure for multipartyism continued to mount. Fearing the loss of foreign economic support, the PDGE came out in favor of multipartyism in mid-1991.

Later in the year, Spain threatened to end economic aid unless the government began actual reforms, so on November 17, 1991, it held a referendum to ratify a new constitution setting up a transitional government. The government also scheduled elections for 1996. It required all candidates to have been resident in the country for 10 years, thus barring the exile opposition, and granted Obiang immunity for any acts committed before, during, and after his term in office. The government legalized new parties a month later but required a $160,000 security deposit and approval by the president's council of ministers.

Obiang began what he called his new "era of pluralism" in January 1992 by creating a new transitional government. The opposition organized itself into the Civic Negotiating Committee for Equatorial Guinea and called for a sovereign national conference to create a transitional government and set up internationally supervised elections. Security forces arrested and beat members of the opposition, one to death, while some exiles who accepted an amnesty were imprisoned when they returned. Obiang's government held legislative elections, but 80 percent of the electorate heeded the opposition's call for a boycott. The results were, in the words of the U.S. State Department, a "parody of democracy." Presidential elections in May 1996 were similarly marred by an opposition boycott and allegations of massive fraud.

Equatorial Guinea has clearly not made the transition to multiparty democracy. The people cannot change the government democratically. The regime controls the courts and detains, tortures, and executes its opponents. The people continue to enjoy only those civil rights the government allows them. The new constitution was supposed to usher in a new era, but the government continues to act much as it did before.

SÃO TOMÉ AND PRÍNCIPE
Statistical Profile

Capital:	São Tomé
Area:	371 sq. miles
Population:	100,000 (1994 est.)
Density:	270 people/sq. mile
Growth Rate:	2.5% (1994 est.)
GDP:	$52,000,000
Per Capita Income:	$5,480
Foreign Debt:	$169,000,000
Life Expectancy:	n.a. (1960), 71 (1992)
Ethnic Groups:	Six major groups: *filhos da terra, angolares, forros, servicais, tongas,* and Europeans
Official Languages:	Portuguese; *Crioulo* is generally spoken
Religions:	Christian (90%)
Former Colonizer:	Portugal
Date of Independence:	1975

History

The Portuguese first sighted these islands around 1470 and began settling them in 1485. They set up sugar plantations worked by slaves imported from the mainland, but a massive slave revolt in 1530 scared the planters off to Brazil. The islands continued to act as an important staging post for the slave trade, and in the eighteenth century slaves were again employed on plantations, this time growing coffee and cocoa. The Portuguese abolished slavery on the islands around 1870 but replaced it with a system of contract labor that scarcely differed. An exposé of working conditions by the reformer Henry Nevinson at the turn of the century led to an international boycott of São Tomé cocoa.

The São Toménses struggled against the oppressive system from the revolt of 1530 on. In 1953, the most dramatic protest ended with a massacre of 1,032 striking plantation workers by Portuguese troops. São Tomé's first modern nationalist party, the Committee for the Liberation of São Tomé and Príncipe (CLSTP), was organized in 1960. In 1963, it led a general strike, and in 1972 it changed its name to the Movement for the Liberation of São Tomé and Príncipe (MLSTP) and established its headquarters in nearby Gabon. When the democratic government that replaced the Portuguese dictatorship in 1974 balked at negotiating with the MLSTP, a movement called the Civic Association led a series of protests that climaxed in September with a mutiny by black troops. The Portuguese agreed to meet with the MLSTP in November, and on December 21, 1974, they established a transitional government dominated by the MLSTP. On July 12, 1975, the small country became independent, with Manuel Pinto da Costa, leader of the MLSTP, as president.

Even before independence, radical members of the Civic Association had challenged the head of the MLSTP, demanding nationalization of the cocoa estates and demobilization of the army. Da Costa purged them from the party in March, but their main goal was accomplished after independence when most Portuguese left, abandoning their plantations, which da Costa then nationalized. Rightist opponents led by the minister of health, Carlos da Graca, went into exile in Gabon and began plotting an invasion by mercenaries to topple da Costa. Although the invasion never took place, Angola, Guinea-Bissau, and Cuba sent troops and military advisors to support da Costa, and the MLSTP set up a People's Militia to supplement the small regular army. The government detained suspected opponents after an invasion scare in 1978, and the party held its first regular congress in August to better define its goals and its organization. In addition to the general political organization, the party created affiliated organizations for women and youth.

During the early 1980s, da Costa gradually expanded his powers as president. In 1980, he took over the powers of the prime minister, and in 1981 he took charge of the ministry of defense and national security. Minor disturbances on Príncipe in the same year led to increased security measures, and in February 1985 da Costa took over the ministries of foreign affairs and planning. On September 30, he won reelection to a third five-year term.

In March 1986, two exile groups in Portugal formed the Democratic Opposition Coalition (CDO) with the goal of establishing "a free and democratic regime" and achieving "free and honest general elections."

Even before the CDO formed, da Costa proclaimed his goal of "opening up the country on an economic and political level." In October 1987, an MLSTP congress endorsed a democratization program. In March 1988, as a gesture of reconciliation, da Costa made the former opposition leader, da Graca, foreign minister. The democratization movement survived an invasion attempt by a small group of dissident members of the CDO, and in December 1989 da Costa committed his government to multiparty democracy. In 1990, former Prime Minister Miguel Trovoada, who had been in exile since 1981, returned, assumed leadership of the Democratic Convergence Party–Group of Reflection (PCD-GR), and led it to victory in multiparty elections in 1991. The party won 33 of 55 seats in the National Assembly in January, and Trovoada won 81 percent of the votes and the presidency in March.

As part of democratization, the government was restructured so that the president is head of state and commander-in-chief of the armed forces, but the prime minister is head of the government. In 1992, relations between Trovoada and the prime minister, Daniel Daio, broke down, and Trovoada publicly accused Daio of abusing his power and forced him out of office. More seriously, the army and the paramilitary police fought a gunbattle in a dispute over jurisdiction. The gunplay did not escalate, however, and the political dispute was handled within the structures of the democratic government.

Disagreements between the president and subsequent prime ministers were similarly handled within the system, with the president ultimately dissolving parliament and calling new elections that returned the MLSTP to power in October 1994. The government also loosened the bonds tying Príncipe to São Tomé, by creating an autonomous administration that took control of Príncipe's internal affairs in April 1995. The government still contains remnants of the former one-party system, like government-owned media and executive interference in judicial matters, but leaders of the new regime have demonstrated their commitment to respect parliamentary forms, free speech, free association, free religion, and the independence of the judiciary.

CHAPTER

9

East Africa

INTRODUCTION

Five countries in the central part of the east side of the continent make up East Africa. The region includes arid deserts in the northeast, dry scrub and thorn forests, stretches of steppe and savanna, monsoon forest, and mountainous uplands. Three of the countries—Kenya, Tanzania, and Uganda—are former British colonies, while two—Rwanda and Burundi—are former Belgian colonies. The latter were based on precolonial kingdoms, while Uganda was made from a number of similar traditional units. Kenya and Tanzania, in contrast, unite a great variety of peoples drawn together haphazardly during the colonization process. Tanzania is the only East African country that has achieved multiparty democracy. Rwanda and Burundi are in the throes of ethnic upheaval, while Uganda and Kenya remain under the control of strongmen and their parties.

KENYA
Statistical Profile

Capital:	Nairobi
Area:	224,961 sq. miles

Population:	27,000,000 (1994 est.)
Density:	120 people/sq. mile
Growth Rate:	3.3% (1994 est.)
GDP:	$6,884,000,000
Per Capita Income:	$330
Foreign Debt:	$5,214,000,000
Life Expectancy:	45 (1960), 59 (1992)
Ethnic Groups:	Kikuyu, Mere, Embu, Kamba (39%); Luo (14%); Luhya and Kisii (21%); Masai, Samburu, Turkana, Kalenjin (11%); Somali and Oromo (3%); Mijikenda, Pokomo, Taita, Taveta (6%)
Official Languages:	Swahili and English
Religions:	Christian (66%), Traditional (26%), Muslim (6%)
Former Colonizer:	Great Britain
Date of Independence:	1963

History

Archeological evidence suggests that some of the earliest human beings lived in Kenya, but the present-day inhabitants trace their origins to migrations of Kushites from the northeast,

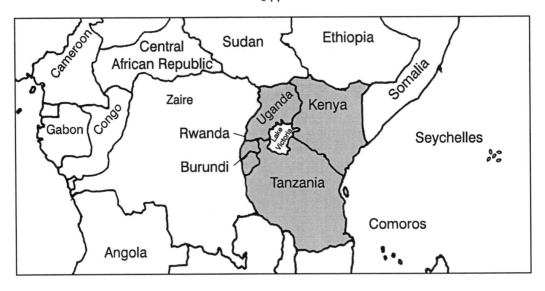

East Africa

Nilo-Saharans from the northwest, and Bantu from the west. Arab traders came down the coast, and the trading cities Pate, Malindi, and Mombasa grew up as part of the coastal Swahili civilization. Indian and Chinese merchants visited during the Middle Ages, and the Portuguese arrived at the end of the fifteenth century. They ravaged the coastal cities and then ruled them for the next 200 years, until the Omanis replaced them. Inland, the people lived in small and dispersed groups as farmers or herders, with only the Luo in the west organized into a substantial kingdom.

The British became interested in the area in the late nineteenth century—partly to counter Germany's commercial and imperial moves in the area, partly because it lay between Uganda and the sea (Uganda contained states that were both large and prosperous and the strategic headwaters of the Nile River), and partly because the territory contained an area of temperate highlands favorable to European settlement. In 1884, the British East Africa Company obtained a trading concession from the sultan of Zanzibar for the territory that is now Kenya and Uganda, and it proceeded to acquire territory in the interior through treaties with local chiefs. In 1895, the royal government declared Kenya an imperial

protectorate, and in 1920 it changed Kenya's status to a crown colony. The British imported Indian laborers to build a railroad from Mombasa to Uganda in the 1890s and began granting land in the highlands to European settlers in the next decade. Despite an official policy of holding "native" interests paramount, the colonial administration in fact favored the settlers, establishing in 1915 a system of racial preference in the "White Highlands." By 1922, 1,715 settlers had grabbed over 11,375 square miles of the country's best land. Needing African laborers to do the work, they got the government to impose taxes that forced 87,000 Africans into their employ by 1924. Fearing African competition, they got the government to prohibit the indigenous inhabitants from cultivating the same crops on their own.

These developments naturally alienated the Africans who already lived in the highlands, particularly members of the Kikuyu tribe. They became early leaders of the anticolonial struggle, forming the reformist Kikuyu Association in 1920 and the more radical East Africa Association in 1921. When the British broke the latter, a new organization, the Kikuyu Central Association, soon assumed leadership. In 1944, one of its leaders, Jomo

Kenyatta, founded the Kenya African Union (KAU), the first truly nationalist party. Kikuyu similarly dominated the Mau Mau movement, which waged a guerrilla war in the 1950s.

Defeated militarily, the Mau Mau insurgency won politically. It helped convince the British government that it could no longer afford the empire, and it doomed the settlers' hopes of creating a white-dominated state. The colonial administration began to honor the "native paramountcy" policy by promoting African participation in both commercial farming and political life. In the late 1950s, it increased African representation in government councils and extended limited voting rights to Africans. In 1960, the British held a conference with African leaders to set the stage for independence, which was granted in 1963.

Despite a lack of evidence tying KAU leader Jomo Kenyatta to the Mau Mau movement, the British imprisoned him in 1952; he was still in custody in 1960. Nevertheless, the Kenya African Union chose him to be its president when it transformed itself into the Kenya African National Union (KANU). After his release in 1961, he led it to victory in parliamentary elections in 1963. In 1964, the country became a republic, and Kenyatta became its president.

Putting economic pragmatism above political posturing, Kenyatta adopted a conciliatory policy towards the white settlers, a capitalist economic policy, and a staunchly pro-Western foreign policy. He convinced most of the settlers to stay and made Kenya into a center of Western business. He used British financial help to buy up land for African peasants, which bolstered the government without alienating the Europeans. The economy prospered, and, by positioning himself above factionalism and parliamentary politics, Kenyatta was able to establish himself as the undisputed father of his country. He remained in office until his death in 1978. During his rule, Kenyans enjoyed economic prosperity and a relatively free and open society.

During Kenyatta's reign, two trends began that bedevil Kenya today. The first was the growth of corruption, and the second was an intolerance of opposition. Kenyatta's capitalist economic policy would have benefited the well-educated Kikuyu in any case, but he allowed an inner circle of family, fellow tribesmen, and members of tribes related to the Kikuyu to shamelessly take advantage of their knowledge and connections. Their behavior set an example that became standard practice throughout Kenyan society. Similarly, the country's unitary, parliamentary system of government favored the larger tribes like the Kikuyu, which was why KANU, before independence, had lobbied for it versus the federal system proposed by the party of the smaller tribes, the Kenya African Democratic Union (KADU). Kenyatta bolstered KANU's position and stifled dissent. In 1964, KANU absorbed KADU. Oginga Odinga and other leftist dissidents (mainly members of the Luo tribe) left to form a new opposition party, the Kenya People's Union (KPU), in 1966. But the government banned the KPU and imprisoned most of its leaders in 1969 after the assassination of a prominent Luo member of KANU led to ethnic violence. In the early 1970s a small group of critics emerged within KANU, denouncing economic inequality, corruption, and dominance of the economy by foreign firms, but in 1975 their leader, J. M. Kariuki, was murdered after a series of bomb explosions rocked Nairobi. A select committee appointed by the government to investigate the murder included some of the most outspoken opponents of the regime, and its findings implicated the heads of the army and the security police and the minister of state, but Kenyatta's government did nothing but arrest all the country's prominent dissidents over the next two years.

Foreign affairs dominated the last two years of Kenyatta's reign. In 1977, the East African Community, which Kenya had formed with Uganda and Tanzania 10 years earlier, broke down. Tanzania then closed its border with Kenya until 1983. More seriously, Somalia's attempt to seize the Ogaden region of Ethiopia in late 1977 put Kenya at odds with its Cold War allies because Kenya feared Somali claims to northwestern Kenya more than it feared Soviet influence in Ethiopia. When Tanzania invaded Uganda in 1979 to bring down the notorious dictator Idi Amin, Kenya, with a weak army and absorbed by its own internal changes after Kenyatta's death, avoided the fighting.

The country's new president, former Vice-President Daniel Arap Moi, took over promising reform within continuity. He delivered on the "reform" part of that promise in the short run by punishing some minor officials for corruption, appointing officials on merit rather than tribal affiliation, releasing all political prisoners, and letting former KPU members rejoin KANU and run in the parliamentary elections of 1979. He delivered on the "continuity" part in the long run by ignoring, and indeed participating in, the corruption at the top of society and by gradually tightening his hold on the political system.

Although all candidates in the elections of 1979 were nominally from KANU, a high voter turnout resulted in a high turnover of office-holders, with seven cabinet members and 15 assistant ministers losing their seats. Soon thereafter, Moi and KANU moved to increase their power. In mid-1980, the government banned tribal organizations, which most hurt Gema, the powerful Kikuyu-dominated tribal association (Gema had opposed Moi's succession because he was a member of the small Kalenjin tribe). In 1982, KANU expelled Oginga Odinga once again, and called for the formal creation of a one-party state. Despite student riots in protest, parliament passed the necessary legislation in June, and shortly thereafter the government began detaining critics.

Soaring inflation and rising unemployment heightened political discontent, and in August 1980 members of the air force attempted a coup. Rioting broke out in Nairobi. Although the government rapidly restored order, over 150 people were killed, $200 million in prop-

erty damage was done, the air force was abolished, and hundreds of people were detained. The resulting trials lasted into 1984, and 12 leaders were executed in 1985. Most of the other detainees were gradually pardoned.

After handling the coup emergency, Moi returned to consolidating his power. In 1983, he turned on Charles Njonjo, who had been one of his closest and most powerful political allies. He accused Njonjo of "serious irregularities" and put him through an inquiry that concluded Njonjo had been involved in the coup attemp. Moi pardoned him in December 1984. In the meantime, Moi won another term as president in an unopposed election, and 40 percent of the sitting members of parliament were replaced by other members of KANU. In 1986, the government revised the voting procedure so that voters would have to stand publicly in a queue behind their candidate of choice. Later that year, the president gained the power to dismiss the attorney general and the auditor general without convening the special tribunal that had previously protected them. In 1988, the National Assembly gave the president the power to dismiss judges at will and to detain people for 14 days without charges. International human rights organizations reported that beatings, detention, and torture of critics had became commonplace.

During this same period, opposition to the government increased steadily. Student protests in 1985 and 1986 met with brutal repression. A movement called *Mwakenya* ("Of Kenya") appeared and became the object of an intense police investigation. Moslems rioted in October 1987 when Moi banned a public meeting, and students demonstrated against the government again in December. Moi publicly denounced his opponents but attempted to mollify discontent by sacking some corrupt police officials and restructuring his cabinet several times.

The festering situation came to a head in February 1990 when the eminent elder statesman Dr. Robert Ouko was murdered. While detectives from Scotland Yard were unable to solve the crime, public opinion ascribed it to the government's security forces. Massive demonstrations in Nairobi and Kisumu in March resulted in scores of arrests, including that of Reverend Lawford Ndege Imande, a leader of the Presbyterian Church. When prominent citizens began calling for multiparty elections, Moi detained them, and when violent riots ensued, the security forces cracked down hard. When the U.S. ambassador announced that the United States would concentrate its aid on countries that "nourish democratic institutions, defend human rights, and practice multiparty democracy," Moi agreed to abolish the system of queue voting, restored the independence of the judiciary, and readmitted expelled members of KANU. He refused, however, to consider a multiparty system until Western governments made additional aid conditional on multiparty reforms. Within days of these conditions, Moi announced the end of the one-party system, which was worth an additional $38 million from the United States alone.

Having established a multiparty system, Moi's government then did everything it could to subvert it. To give KANU the element of surprise, the government refused to publicize the date of the upcoming election. When in late October 1992 it finally announced that the date was December 7, 1992, the High Court found that it had been set early to benefit the established party and put the date back three weeks, to December 29. In the meantime, Moi ordered civil servants to support KANU. They complied by refusing to issue permits for rallies to opposition parties, closing down their offices, registering only KANU supporters, and denying the opposition access to state-owned broadcast media. The president also picked the electoral commission, which the opposition denounced as biased. Unidentified men assaulted opposition supporters and burglarized opposition offices.

Three opposition parties contested the election: the small Democratic Party and two factions of the Forum for the Restoration of Democracy (FORD): one led by the Luo Oginga Odinga (FORD-Kenya) and the other led by the Kikuyu Kenneth Matibu (FORD-Asili. Between the government's manipulation during the campaign, the opposition's disunity, and widespread irregularities on election day, Moi and KANU carried the elections. Moi won 37 percent of the vote, against 28 percent for Matiba and 17 percent for Odinga. KANU won 95 of 188 seats in parliament, with another 12 to be appointed by Moi.

Commonwealth observers assessed the elections as neither free nor fair, and opposition denunciations of the regime continued. Ethnic violence which had started shortly after Moi announced the transition to multiparty democracy, increased in 1993. In January 1992, rumors had circulated that Moi planned to foment ethnic conflict to justify calling out the army. The government arrested four opposition figures for spreading the rumors, but in March gangs of Kalenjin, Moi's tribesmen, attacked Luo and Kikuyu in the western part of the country, which led to counterattacks on Kalenjin in Nairobi. By late 1993, over 1,500 people had been killed and over 300,000 displaced. The U.S.-based human rights group Africa Watch placed responsibility squarely on the government, saying it had "deliberately manipulated" tensions "in order to undermine . . . political pluralism." The violence died down in 1994, but the government launched a renewed campaign of harassment against its political opponents in 1995.

Kenya has a multiparty system, but in reality it remains under the tight control of the president and his clique. The country has the reputation of being a relatively free society, but that is more a reflection of the past than of present reality. Moi has stated that the concept of "constructive opposition" is foreign to Africa, and dissidents are frequently beaten and can be detained indefinitely. The government can and does curb freedom of assembly for political purposes, and the police make free use of force in breaking up unauthorized demonstrations. The president does not have the power to hire and fire judges directly, but the panel that does have this power answers directly to him. The government controls the broadcast media, and the law forbids expression that might "excite disaffection against the government." The regime harasses critical publications by pressuring printers not to print them, confiscating objectionable issues, arresting editors for sedition, and beating journalists covering opposition activities. The government also harasses members of the Protestant churches, and the only legally recognized trade union has close ties to the government. Western pressure may have pushed Moi into making gestures toward democracy and respect for human rights, but these gestures are clearly just a facade covering up continued corruption and repression.

TANZANIA
Statistical Profile

Capital:	Dar es Salaam
Area:	364,900 sq. miles
Population:	29,800,000 (1994 est.)
Density:	82 people/sq. mile
Growth Rate:	3.4% (1994 est.)
GDP:	$2,345,000,000
Per Capita Income:	$110
Foreign Debt:	$6,060,000,000
Life Expectancy:	41 (1960), 51 (1992)
Ethnic Groups:	Contains over 120 different groups, including Ngoni, Ngindo, Hehe, Kimbu, Nyamwezi, Masai, Sandawe, Kindiga, Hadimu
Official Languages:	Swahili and English
Religions:	Traditional (42%), Muslim (31%), Christian (25%), Hindu
Former Colonizers:	Germany, Great Britain
Date of Independence:	Tanganyika 1961, Zanzibar 1963, Creation of Tanzania 1964

History

Archeological finds suggest that the oldest human beings originated in the area that is today Tanzania. Khoisan-speaking peoples have inhabited the area since antiquity, and Bantu-speakers migrated in during the first centuries after Christ. Middle Eastern traders have visited the coast since the Hellenistic era at least, and Arab traders settled and intermarried during the first millennium A.D. In the ninth and tenth centuries, the Swahili cities rose to new importance, with Kilwa in the south controlling access to gold routes into the interior. The Portuguese favored Mombasa in Kenya during the sixteenth and seventeenth centuries. The Omanis, who replaced the Portuguese in the eighteenth century, eventually made the island of Zanzibar their capital. Omani power was based on the export of slaves and ivory from the interior and cloves from Zanzibar itself.

British influence in Zanzibar increased steadily in the nineteenth century as Great Britain attempted to simultaneously end slavery and expand the island's trade. Late in the century, Great Britain vied with Germany for control of East Africa, and in the 1880s agents of both competed to sign concession treaties with the sultan on the island and local chiefs on the mainland. In 1890, they settled their affairs between themselves, with the British getting a protectorate over Zanzibar (along with Uganda and Kenya), and the Germans getting Tanganyika.

On Zanzibar, the British had only to install a governor and establish new courts, and let the sultan continue to rule. On the mainland, the Germans had to impose themselves on over 120 different ethnic groups ranging from docile Bantu farmers to warlike Nilo-Saharan herders. The Germans waged a series of wars of pacification that climaxed with the widespread *Maji Maji* rebellion in 1905–1906. The German administration ruled indirectly through a hierarchy of chiefs, even when this meant enhancing their power, or even creating them. They made substantial investments in economic development, but did not see them come to fruition because they lost control of the territory as a consequence of World War I.

The British took over the mainland under a League of Nations mandate and invested little. After World War II the mandate became a United Nations trusteeship, and Great Britain both increased its investment and began preparing the territory for independence. Legislative councils had existed in both Tanganyika and Zanzibar since 1926, but the British widened their membership to include Africans in 1945. They opened the civil service to Africans, Arabs, and Indians, and conducted local elections. At first, they resisted the nationalist Tanganyika African National Union (TANU) when it replaced the reformist Tanganyika African Association at the forefront of African politics in 1954, but under the leadership of Julius Nyerere, the new organization proved itself to be both essentially moderate and widely popular. It won the general elections of 1958 and worked with the authorities on a smooth transition to independence, which came in 1961. The country became a republic in 1962, and Nyerere became its president.

In contrast to Tanganyika's smooth transition to independence, Zanzibar's was marked by factionalism and violence. A radical party, the Zanzibar Nationalist Party (ZNP), represented Arab interests, while the more moderate Africans were split between the Afro-Shirazi Party (ASP) and the Zanzibar and Pemba People's Party (ZPPP). Elections in January 1961 resulted in an even split between the three parties, and a second election led to fighting that left 68 dead. The ASP won a plurality, but the ZNP and ASP formed a coalition government that remained in office when the island became independent in 1963. Supporters of ASP seized power at the beginning of 1964, and requested union with the mainland. Nyerere quickly agreed, and negotiations led to a consolidated state with a federal structure in which a joint government controlled military and diplomatic affairs but Zanzibar otherwise ruled itself. Nyerere was the president of the union government; the leader of Zanzibar became one of its two vice presidents, and the prime minister of Tanganyika became the other. The state took the name Tanzania.

The new state got off to a rocky start. The leaders of the Tanganyika Federation of Labor

(TFL) opposed Nyerere's gradualist approach to Africanization of the economy and civil service, and staged a series of strikes. The government responded by dissolving the TFL and replacing it with the government-controlled National Union of Tanganyika Workers (NUTA). The army mutinied in early 1964, and Nyerere had to call in British troops to put it down. The army was subsequently reorganized and led by new officers drawn from TANU's Youth League.

In 1964, Tanganyika became a one-party state, although the high turnover of officeholders in subsequent elections testified to a vigorous political life within TANU. In 1967, Nyerere issued the Arusha Declaration, which laid out a policy of "socialism and self-reliance" that was widely hailed as the defining statement of "African socialism." The centerpiece of his program was the creation of *ujamaa* villages, a two-step process involving first "villagization" of the dispersed peasantry and then collectivization of agricultural production. After an unsuccessful attempt at achieving voluntary compliance, Nyerere decreed in 1973 that "to live in villages is an order," justifying the move as necessary for provision of services like education, medical care, and clean water. The main purpose, however, was to raise agricultural productivity through a combination of technical assistance and political oversight. The *ujamaa* villages received improved seeds, fertilizers, and equipment, but were subject to bureaucratic supervision of acreage planted, hours worked, and job performance. Between sporadic resistance to the mandatory policy, disruption caused by resettlement itself, inefficient management of the new collectives, the disincentive effect of low producer prices, drought, the collapse of the transportation system, and the insufficiency of storage facilities, the policy was an utter failure. Production of most crops declined steadily in the late 1970s, and output of food crops failed to increase in step with the population. The country, heretofore self-sufficient in foodstuffs, faced a crisis in 1981 and became a food importer. A program aiming at socialism and self-sufficiency had produced instead dependence on the charity of the capitalist West.

Nyerere was aware of the potential for abuse by state officials, and sought to combat it through a combination of personal example, moral exhortation, and legal actions. He conspicuously refrained from enjoying the perks of office routinely flaunted by other African heads of state. He created a leadership code for party officials that prohibited them from renting out property or engaging in entrepreneurial activity. In 1972, he issued *mwongozo* (party guidelines) that encouraged the people to resist "commandism" by government and party leaders. The government conducted a widespread anticorruption campaign in 1984, arresting over 4,000 suspects, including some senior civil servants and police officials. Despite some notable lapses, corruption and authoritarianism are far smaller problems in Tanzanian public life than elsewhere in Africa today.

Because of its internal autonomy, Zanzibar had a different experience than the mainland in its first decade of independence. Abeid Karume, the leader of ASP, brooked no opposition to his rule, holding no elections and repressing all dissent. He nationalized over two-thirds of the island's economy, instituted forced marriages between Asians and Africans to promote integration, abolished the British-style courts, and compiled a notorious record on human rights. He was assassinated in 1972, and the treason trial that followed curbed the power of the leftists. Karume's successor, Aboud Jumbe, moved the island's politics closer to those of the mainland, agreeing in 1975 to a merger of ASP with TANU. A joint conference in January 1977 created a new Party of the Revolution (CCM, its initials in Swahili). Nyerere became the first chairman and Jumbe became the first vice chairman. The new party registered new members and elected new leaders at all levels. It absorbed TANU's ancillary organizations for women, youth, workers, peasants, and parents, and extended them to Zanzibar. A new union constitution went into effect in April, and in December, Zanzibaris went to the polls for the first time since independence to select their representatives to parliament.

After the 1975 merger, foreign policy dominated Tanzanian affairs. Differences over trade policies led to the breakup of the East African Community with Uganda and Kenya and a closing of the border with the latter that lasted until 1983. The rift hurt both, but Tanzania more, since Kenya was a regional entry-point for Western businesses and tourists. In a more serious matter, Uganda's erratic leader, Idi Amin, seized a disputed province along the border, and Tanzania's counterattack became a general offensive that brought down the Ugandan dictator. Even though his despotic rule made Amin an international embarrassment, African leaders criticized Tanzania's use of force to overthrow a neighboring government, and the indiscipline of some Tanzanian soldiers created another source of criticism. The cost of mounting the offensive and then sustaining an occupation force for the next two years drove up the government's debt to $200 billion, four times the planned level, and disrupted normal economic activity. The heightened economic problems generated increasing criticism within Tanzania, and two members of parliament were expelled from the party in 1980 for opposing the continued occupation.

An official report by Professor Rene Dumont the same year looked beyond the war effort to criticize the growth of the bureaucracy and the inefficiency of state corporations. Newspapers repeated and expanded his critique, pointing to the failure of *ujamaa* in particular. Voters reflected this discontent in elections on October 26, 1980 by returning only 37 percent of the incumbents. Although Nyerere won a second five-year term as president in an uncontested election with a 93 percent "yes" vote, the country was shaken by two serious disturbances aimed at him in the early 1980s. In February 1982, dissidents hijacked an Air Tanzania jet to underscore their demand that Nyerere resign. That incident ended peacefully, but a coup attempt was uncovered in January 1983. Twenty-eight suspects were taken into custody, two of whom escaped to Kenya. When the two countries reestablished open relations in 1983, they were exchanged for Kenyan plotters who had taken refuge in Tanzania. The treason trials of the 28 suspects dragged on into late 1985. Nine plotters were sentenced to life imprisonment.

In 1984, trouble broke out in Zanzibar because of fears that the island was becoming too subordinate to the mainland. Specifically, a proposal to empower the CCM's central committee to nominate candidates for office in Zanzibar generated intense debate and even calls for secession. Four dissident ministers were arrested. President Aboud Jumbe resigned over the matter, and Ali Hassan Mwinyi took over. He shepherded the constitutional change through, reduced the Supreme Revolutionary Council from 15 to 10 members, and appointed a new team of loyalists to it. In October, more constitutional changes brought the administration and judicial system further into line with the mainland.

In 1985, Nyerere kept his promise to step down from the presidency of Tanzania at the end of his second term, although he remained head of the party for another five years. On August 15, the CCM Central Committee nominated Zanzibari president Ali Hassan Mwinyi to be the sole candidate, and he was duly elected on October 27. The Zanzibari Salim Salim had to resign as prime minister so that Zanzibaris would not hold two of the three top posts in the union. Mwinyi focused on economic matters in his first years in power, concluding a deal with the IMF that Nyerere had resisted. The deal devalued the currency, reduced the public sector, and encouraged the growth of private businesses. He also sponsored a major reexamination of the Arusha Declaration on its twentieth anniversary. This study noted that the population had grown faster than the economy, but it also recognized the program's important successes in education and public health. Mwinyi's economic moves generated considerable tension within the CCM between old-guard and youth fac-

tions on the one side and middle-aged pragmatists on the other, but the tension did not lead to any open ruptures.

In 1990, Mwinyi won a second five-year term as president in unopposed elections, but Tanzania began to feel the effects of the multiparty democracy movement. The CCM held a symposium that year to discuss the end of Communist Party rule in Eastern Europe, and the next year Mwinyi appointed a presidential commission to study the single-party system formally. Despite opposition suspicions that its purpose was to reiterate the ruling party's justification that single-party rule was needed to maintain stability, the commission in fact recommended the legalization of multiple parties. In 1992, the CCM executive committee endorsed a transition to multipartyism, although it rejected a call to create a sovereign national commission to oversee it. It also recommended that elections take place in 1995 as scheduled. Opposition parties were legalized in June 1992, and 22 soon registered. The CCM adjusted to the new situation by launching widespread recruiting drives.

While the transition to multipartyism went far to satisfy the regime's critics on the mainland, it held less promise for those on Zanzibar. Secessionist feelings had grown since the mid-1980s, but the law required that opposition parties be national rather than regional in scope. Dissidents refused to cease their activities despite government warnings, which led to the brief detention of 15 in early 1992. Another group, *Kamahuru*, took a more promising tack later in the year by merging with the Civic Movement on the mainland to form the Civic United Front. Islamic fundamentalists became increasingly active in 1992 and 1993. For a few months, Zanzibar belonged to the Islamic Conference, but constitutional concerns about its position in the union led it to withdraw. On the mainland, one reaction to Zanzibari separatism was a proposal to form a Tanganyikan administration within the union.

The promised multiparty elections were held in October and November 1995. The CCM won 80 percent of the seats in parliament, the CCM candidate, Benjamin Mkapa, won the presidency, and the party retained power on Zanzibar. Most importantly, Tanzania joined the ranks of Africa's multiparty democracies. The country as presently constituted does not have a perfect human rights record, for opponents can be detained and exiled, local police have been known to use torture, freedom of assembly is sometimes difficult to exercise, and all unions belong to the government-controlled Organization of Tanzanian Trade unions. On the other hand, the judiciary, modeled on the British system and modified to reflect Islamic and customary law, is independent in most matters, and preventive detention is in fact seldom and moderately used. Similarly, while the president theoretically has the right to censor publications, the press in practice is free and active. In the same way, restrictions on internal travel are used to keep rural peasants from flooding into urban shantytowns as they have elsewhere on the continent, not to enforce political repression. Freedom of religion is respected, although conflicts between Moslem fundamentalists and Christian evangelists have led to some restrictions on public preaching. Tanzania has long had an exemplary reputation, and despite economic problems and political restrictions, its long-term outlook is promising.

UGANDA
Statistical Profile

Capital:	Kampala
Area:	91,135 sq. miles
Population:	19,800,000 (1994 est.)
Density:	217 people/sq. mile
Growth Rate:	3.0% (1994 est.)
GDP:	$2,998,000,000
Per Capita Income:	$170
Foreign Debt:	$2,495,000,000
Life Expectancy:	43 (1960), 46 (1992)
Ethnic Groups:	Bantu-speakers are the single largest group (65%), including Gan-

da Nkole, Toro, Nyoro, Soga, Gisu, Chiga; eastern Sudanic-speakers include Langi, Teso, Acholi, Karamojong, Alur; the Lugbara are central Sudanic-speakers

Official Language:	English; Swahili is also widely spoken
Religions:	Christian (50%), Traditional (44%), Muslim (6%)
Former Colonizer:	Great Britain
Date of Independence:	1962

History

Bantu-speaking peoples entered Uganda early in the first millennium after Christ. Some settled along the shores of Lake Victoria, and others continued to the south and east into present day Kenya and Tanzania. They were joined in the fourteenth to sixteenth centuries by Nilo-Saharan immigrants, Luo speakers who founded feudal kingdoms to the northwest based on military power and ownership of cattle. Bunyoro was the most powerful kingdom at first, but in the nineteenth century the more strongly centralized Bantu kingdom of Buganda eclipsed it.

Early European explorers found the Nyoro hostile and the Ganda receptive, and so Catholic, Protestant, and soon Moslem missionaries vied to convert them, with the Ganda vacillating between tolerance and rejection. The missionaries were soon joined by secular agents of German and British imperialism vying for their secular allegiance until the two European governments agreed in 1890 that Uganda would go to Great Britain. The British East Africa Company represented that country's interests at first, but when it teetered on the verge of bankruptcy in 1894, the British government feared losing control of the headwaters of the Nile and so declared a protectorate.

The Africans did not immediately accept this new status, but the British practiced "divide and conquer." Buganda cooperated in a campaign against Bunyoro and received for its help several border counties and considerable internal autonomy. In addition, the royal family and officials received salaries while the chiefs received title to land, an arrangement that both bound them to British rule and intensified the hierarchical structure of their society. In three other kingdoms, the British ruled indirectly through the existing elites, but they left them far fewer powers. In most other districts, they sent Ganda chiefs to set things up for them (and allowed them to profit from their efforts), which ingrained anti-Ganda feelings in the people.

Indirect rule, the favoritism shown the dominant Ganda, plentiful jobs for the educated elite, and commercial opportunities for the peasantry kept nationalism from developing in Uganda until quite late. In 1953, the kabaka of Buganda called for an independent Bugandan state and was exiled, but his vision did not extend beyond his own domain. Ignatius Musazi had founded the Uganda National Congress (UNC) in 1952 but it did not really focus on the national level either. The West German Christian Democratic Party sponsored the creation of a Catholic Democratic Party (DP) in 1956, but its vision also was limited. Only in 1958, when Milton Obote split from the UNC to found his own UNC, did Ugandan nationalism truly appear. Obote became the most forceful voice in the Legislative Council, a body that had been in existence since 1921 and had almost 50-percent African membership by the late 1950s. Two Africans sat on the Governor's Executive Council, and in 1958 Africans voted for their representatives on the Legislative Council for the first time. Despite its belated nationalism, Uganda was moving rapidly towards nationhood.

In 1960, Obote merged the UNC with the Uganda People's Union (UPU) to form the Uganda People's Congress (UPC), and in preindependence parliamentary elections the UPC won 37 of 80 seats, with the DP gaining 22 and the Kabaka Yekka (KY), the party of the Bugandan monarch, 21. These latter par-

liamentary members represented nominees appointed by the Bugandan Royal Council, which refused to allow its subjects to participate in politics. Nevertheless, Obote forged an alliance with the KY, and when independence came on October 9, 1962, he became prime minister and the kabaka of Buganda became the ceremonial head of state.

The coalition hid a deep conflict between the two parties' programs, for the UPC favored a unitary government, while the KY favored federalism to preserve Buganda's traditionalist form of government. The two split when Obote staged a referendum to decide the fate of the "lost counties," which chose to return to Bunyoro. Idi Amin appeared on the national stage in 1964, when an army mutiny demanding that Africans be made officers led to his rapid promotion. In 1966, he and Obote were both implicated in a complex plot to support Congolese insurgents by smuggling gold and ivory into Uganda, and the outcome was a military coup in which Obote arrested five dissident ministers and Amin stormed the kabaka's palace and drove him into exile. A new constitution did away with Bugandan autonomy and made Obote president of the new republic. Proclaiming a "move to the left" and the "Common Man's Charter," Obote embarked on the eradication of feudalism in 1967, and in 1969 he proclaimed that the government would take a 60-percent stake in all major foreign-owned firms.

Obote's relationship with Amin deteriorated in 1969 and 1970 because of a financial scandal involving Amin, an assassination attempt on Obote, and the murder of a young officer who denounced Amin as the author of the plot. For some reason, Obote hesitated to arrest Amin, who staged a coup with British and Israeli backing while the president was out of the country. Amin quickly consolidated his power by executing real, potential, and imagined opponents, individually and in groups—creating a reign of terror that ultimately cost about 200,000 Ugandans their lives. He expelled the country's 32,000 Asians on 90-days' notice in 1972, confiscating their considerable property and dividing it up among his cronies. They soon ran the expropriated businesses into the ground, which added to the growing economic decay caused by the regime's brutality, arbitrary policies, and corruption. Amin turned on the Israelis in 1972, closing their embassy and giving the building to the Palestine Liberation Organization; he turned on the British early the next year, nationalizing their remaining investments in the country.

Amin defeated an attempted invasion by exiles in late 1972 and came to rely ever more heavily on the army. He dismissed his civilian cabinet and passed a law absolving members of the armed forces for any crimes committed since the coup. He reorganized the country into 38 districts, which he then gave over to his leading officers in an almost feudal arrangement. This arrangement promoted economic decentralization, however, as each district's governor contrived to export its products without accounting for it to the central government. Amin soon found himself in increasingly dire financial straits. His unpaid soldiers became restive, staging a number of abortive coups and mutinies. To distract them, he sought foreign adventures. He tried to bully Kenya in 1976 but had to back off when it threatened an economic boycott. Military discontent continued to grow, so in October 1978 he sent his forces to seize territory in Tanzania. Unfortunately for Amin, a Tanzanian counterattack routed his army and rolled on to Kampala, his capital. A coalition of 26 opposition groups, organized as the Uganda National Liberation Front (UNLF), worked with the Tanzanians, and when the dictator fled to a comfortable exile in Saudi Arabia, the UNLF leader Yusufu Lule became president.

The UNLF coalition was united only by its opposition to Amin, and the politically inexperienced Lule proved unable to hold it together. He soon fell out with the interim parliament, the National Consultative Council (NCC), which deposed him just 68 days after he took power. Godfrey Binaisa replaced

him on June 21, 1979, and after putting down riots protesting Lule's ouster, began the difficult task of national reconstruction.

In this, Binaisa faced an almost insurmountable task, with tens of thousands of refugees returning to the country, more than a million people homeless, the economy in a shambles, and armed bands roaming the countryside. He tried to attract foreign aid through a nonaligned foreign policy and a liberal investment code. To reduce tribalism, he reorganized the country into 33 districts, and he committed his government to elections by the middle of 1981. His relations with the fractious NCC deteriorated steadily, and he survived mainly because of the backing of the Tanzanians, who still had 10,000 troops in the country at the end of 1980. In 1981, he split with Obote's backers, and when he tried to dismiss one of them, David Oyite Ojok, from the army, Ojok led a coup that toppled Binaisa instead. A military commission dominated by Obote's supporters took power, and the ex-president returned from his nine-year exile to lead his old UPC in elections scheduled for December. The UPC won 72 seats in the new National Assembly, the old DP took 52, the Uganda People's Movement (UPM) gained one, and Obote became president once more.

The campaign had been marred by gross irregularities, and opposition to the new regime soon became violent. One faction of the DP refused to recognize the results of the election and formed the militant Uganda Freedom Movement. Troops loyal to Amin remained in the north, while soldiers in the west mutinied in order to exact revenge on groups there that had supported Amin. Yoweri Museveni, leader of a party that had been shut out in the elections, went underground and emerged as the leader of a guerrilla force, the National Resistance Movement (NRM). His group conducted a classic insurgency, combining terrorism, political mobilization, guerrilla raids, and, ultimately, conventional operations. The military responded with brutal repression that fell on innocent civilians more often than on armed foes. Its excesses included widespread looting, detention without charges, torture, summary executions, and massacres, all of which fueled support for the rebels. By the middle of 1985, the army's tactics had claimed over 200,000 victims and helped the NRM push the government to the brink of defeat.

On July 27, 1985, northern army leaders staged a brief offensive that drove Obote from the capital and established themselves as the country's new leaders. Their government retained prominent Obote supporters but kept Museveni at arms length, so, after a brief truce, the NRM renewed its offensive. It expanded its control over the countryside while reconciliation talks under Kenyan auspices dragged on. After another brief truce in December, the NRM seized Kampala on January 26, 1986. The NRM's army quickly secured the rest of the country. Banditry and sporadic guerrilla raids continued for several years, but the Ugandan civil war was over.

Museveni became the new head of state, and he appointed a cabinet containing five members of the DP, three from the just-defeated UPC, and representatives of smaller parties. On March 20, he hosted a one-day summit attended by the leaders of Kenya, Tanzania, Zaire, Sudan, Rwanda, and Burundi to put an international seal of approval on his new regime, and he launched a 10-point program emphasizing grass-roots democracy and economic self-reliance. He survived two coup attempts by Bugandans in late 1986 and two by members of the UPC in 1987. He agreed to IMF economic reforms and held local and regional elections later that year. In 1988, the NRM's supreme body, the National Resistance Council, transformed itself into a parliament. Elections to it were held the next year, and local elections took place again in 1992.

In 1992, the government outlawed political activity, although it allowed political parties to exist. It continued to resist opposition calls for a sovereign national assembly to oversee a transition to multiparty democracy, and it held nonparty elections on March 28, 1994, for a constituent assembly to discuss a draft constitution. The NRM took 114 of 214 elected seats, with 10 more appointed by the president and another 56 assigned to special-interest groups. The chairman of the assembly unilaterally proclaimed that the NRM would continue to rule for five years after the adoption of the constitution and that the ban on political activity would continue. In response, on November 9, 1994, 36 opposition representatives walked out.

Uganda under the NRM remains an undemocratic country in which the rights to choose the government, to be tried by an impartial court, to speak without fear of reprisal, to associate freely, and to organize independent labor unions have not yet been secured. It also remains one of the poorest countries in the world. Without doubt it is better off than it was at any time back into the 1960s, but equally without doubt it has a long way to go.

RWANDA
Statistical Profile

Capital:	Kigali
Area:	10,170 sq. miles
Population:	7,700,000 (1994 est.)
Density:	757 people/sq. mile
Growth Rate:	2.3% (1994 est.)
GDP:	$1,552,000,000
Per Capita Income:	$250
Foreign Debt:	$804,000,000
Life Expectancy:	42 (1960), 46 (1992)
Ethnic Groups:	Hutu (90%), Tutsi (9%), Twa (1%)
Official Languages:	Kinyarwanda and French; Swahili (commercial)
Religions:	Traditional (50%), Catholic, Muslim (small minority)
Former Colonizer:	Germany, Belgium
Date of Independence:	1962

History

Rwanda's original inhabitants were Khoisan speakers, who hunted and gathered to survive, but their descendants now make up only about one percent of the country's population. The ancestors of the majority, the agricultural Bantu-speaking peoples called the Hutu, immigrated around the year 1000. The cattle-herding Tutsi followed around 1400, and while they were numerically inferior, they were militarily superior. They imposed on the Hutu a system of feudal overlordship that bordered on a caste system, not only monopolizing military and political power and controlling land and labor, but also claiming to have come from a different world than the Hutu and refusing to eat the same kinds of foods.

The Tutsi aristocracy was itself firmly subordinate to the king, or *mwami*, who ruled absolutely as supreme leader, legislator, and judge. The Rwandan kingdom reached its zenith in the mid-nineteenth century but then succumbed to German imperialism in 1890. The Germans succumbed in turn to the Allies in World War I, and Belgium took charge under a League of Nations mandate. To the Rwandans, the difference between the two European powers was minor, since both practiced indirect rule and both favored the dominant Tutsi. Not only did they rely on the Tutsi for day-to-day administration, they also gave them the keys to the future: missionary education and jobs in the colonial administration.

The disenfranchised Hutu fell into increasing poverty until, in the late 1950s, their spokesmen began calling for an end to Tutsi dominance and radical reforms in the government. Upon the death of *Mwami* Matari III in 1959, radical Tutsi seized power and tried to eliminate Hutu leaders, but the Hutu countered with a widespread uprising in which they killed uncounted numbers of Tutsi. The king and thousands of other Tutsi fled, while the Belgians began a transition to an independence in which the Hutu would clearly be dominant. They held communal elections in October 1960, and a UN-supervised referendum in September 1961 approved a republican constitution. Parliamentary elections brought Parmehutu, the Hutu party, to power, and Gregoire Kayibanda became the country's first president when it became independent on July 1, 1962.

Ethnic violence flared again in 1963–1964 when Tutsi guerrillas conducted vicious raids that provoked Hutu reprisals costing thousands of Tutsi their lives and driving tens of thousands of others into exile. By the end of the 1960s, some 200,000 Tutsi had fled, but the Hutu still sporadically persecuted the ones who remained. Their anger was kept alive by Tutsi atrocities against Hutus in neighboring Burundi. These disturbances led General Juvenal Habyarimana to stage a coup in 1973 against Kayibanda, who had been reelected in 1965 and 1969. He replaced Parmehutu with the Revolutionary National Movement for Development (MRND), making it the sole legal party in the state. In 1978, a new constitution replaced military with civilian rule, but Habyarimana remained head of state, and he was reelected in 1983 and 1988. He ruled in concert with the National Development Council, which had 70 members elected from the ranks of the MRND for terms of five years.

In a move to help ease Rwanda's ethnic conflicts, Tanzania naturalized 36,000 Rwandan Tutsi refugees in a mass ceremony. Indeed, in the 1980s, Habyarimana's government ruled without serious challenge—from the Tutsi or from other Hutu groups. In 1990, a new Tutsi guerrilla group, the Rwanda Patriotic Front (FRP), began launching attacks from Uganda, setting off a bloody civil war. Their proclaimed goal was political reform and the repatriation of Tutsi refugees. Habyarimana responded with a new constitution in June 1991 that allowed more than one party, limited the number of times the president could be reelected, and prohibited political activity by the army and the judiciary. He appointed Dismas Nsengiyaremye of the Democratic Republican Party (DRP, the old Parmehutu) to the new post of prime minister. Nsengiyaremye created a transitional government that included representatives of four parties.

This government did not include the FRP, however, so the civil war continued until Habyarimana negotiated a peace accord with its leader, Colonel Alex Kanyarengwe, in Au-

President Kayibanda of Rwanda and Ambassador Guillaume of Belgium during ceremonies in 1962 marking Rwanda's independence. *Source:* United Nations.

gust 1993. A new transitional government including the FRP was to take office, but in April 1994 Habyarimana was killed before it could take power when a surface-to-air missile brought down the plane carrying him and the president of Burundi from a conference on ending the ethnic strife in their countries. The ethnic violence that followed reached genocidal proportions by May, with an estimated 500,000 Tutsi slaughtered. It was not a mindless massacre, as often portrayed in the American press, but a calculated attempt by conservative members of the Hutu-dominated military to eliminate the Tutsi minority and Hutu moderates once and for all.

The FRP fought back, and by the beginning of July it had captured Kigali, the capital. Promising to institute a multiparty democracy, it installed moderate Hutus as president and prime minister. Nevertheless, Hutus fearful of Tutsi reprisals for the earlier bloodbath fled Rwanda by the hundreds of thousands, so by the end of July 1994 over 2 million Rwandans had fled the country, half of them Hutu. Just as peace seemed to have arrived, a virulent cholera epidemic broke out in the refugee camps. Unrest continued, as some refugees returned to their bitterly divided communities while others refused to budge from the camps. Some Tutsi did take revenge on returning Hutus, although not on the scale of the earlier massacres of Tutsi, and Hutu militia continued to exploit the confusion to battle the FRP government's troops. The UN set up a tribunal to prosecute those guilty of genocide. It will clearly be years before the reverberations from the recent holocaust die down.

BURUNDI
Statistical Profile

Capital:	Bujumbura
Area:	10,745 sq. miles
Population:	6,000,000 (1994 est.)

Density:	558 people/sq. mile
Growth Rate:	2.9% (1994 est.)
GDP:	$986,000,000
Per Capita Income:	$210
Foreign Debt:	$947,000,000
Life Expectancy:	48 (1960), 48 (1992)
Ethnic Groups:	Hutu (86%), Tutsi (12%), Twa (1%)
Official Languages:	French and Kirundi; Swahili (commercial)
Religions:	Christian (66%), Traditional (32%), Muslim (2%)
Former Colonizers:	Germany, Belgium
Date of Independence:	1962

History

Like Rwanda, Burundi contains a small number of people descended from the original Khoisan-speaking inhabitants of the area, a majority population of Hutu whose ancestors immigrated around 1000 A.D., and a sizable minority of Tutsi whose presence dates from the fifteenth century and who dominated the Hutu until the present century. Unlike Rwanda, however, the Tutsi in Burundi did not create a strongly centralized state, but ruled as a loose feudal network in which a small number of families, the *ganwa* class, vied for primacy. Burundi, like Rwanda, fell first under German and then under Belgian rule, and the Europeans favored the Tutsi here as well. The Hutu of Burundi were not able, however, to throw off Tutsi hegemony as their brethren did in Rwanda during the transition to independence. Instead, the two primary Tutsi clans became leaders of the two main nationalist parties. One of them, the Union for National Progress (UPRONA), reached out to include prominent Hutus and thereby became the colony's dominant political force.

Unfortunately, on October 13, 1961, just two weeks after UPRONA's leader, Prince Louis Rwagasore, became prime minister, a European acting on behalf of Belgian interests (which were threatened by his success at uniting the Burundi) assassinated him. Thereafter, Tutsi fanatics took control of UPRONA. They pushed the Hutu representatives out of

the party and then fell out among themselves. When independence came, the king, *Mwami* Mwambutsa IV, took personal control of the government and tried to reconcile Hutu and Tutsi by including representatives from both groups in it. He was unable to create a stable coalition, however, and on January 15, 1965, Prime Minister Pierre Ngendandunwe, a Hutu, was assassinated. In parliamentary elections in May, Hutu candidates won 23 of 33 seats, but the *mwami* appointed a Tutsi as prime minister. Hutu leaders responded by attempting a coup in October, and Hutu peasants killed hundreds of Tutsi around the country.

The *mwami* fled to Switzerland, but a group of Tutsi gained control of the government and purged the Hutu from the army and bureaucracy. The Tutsi leader, Colonel Michel Micombero, created a "government of public safety" in July 1966, in alliance with the *mwami's* son and successor, Ntare V. This alliance lasted only a few months, and then Micombero became president of a newly proclaimed republic. Micombero transformed the nation into a one-party state, and encouraged the Tutsi to take revenge on the Hutu. This policy culminated in tragedy in 1972. A Hutu uprising killed 10,000 Tutsi before the army put it down. Thereupon, the army embarked on a campaign of "selective genocide," in which it killed all Hutu with any formal education. Approximately 200,000 Hutu died, and another 100,000 fled to neighboring countries.

In 1976, Colonel Jean-Baptiste Bagaza overthrew Micombero. Although the new leader was also a Tutsi, he adopted a more conciliatory policy. He abolished the feudal services Hutu peasants owed Tutsi landlords and transferred some land to Hutu ownership. He encouraged Hutu refugees to return and reclaim their land, and he brought some Hutu into the government. A number of Hutu won seats in the National Assembly in elections in 1982. At the same time, Bagaza clamped down on anyone suspected of stirring up Hutu discontent. In 1985, his government expelled 90 Catholic missionaries and put two on trial.

Bagaza won reelection in the same year in an unopposed election, but his associate, Major Pierre Buyoya, overthrew him two years later. After Buyoya had been in office for only 11 months, another Hutu uprising killed 600 Tutsis. Buyoya sent in the army, which killed 20,000 Hutu and sent a further 60,000 across the border into Rwanda. Within months, Buyoya announced his intention to implement radical changes to promote social justice, appointed a majority of Hutus to his council of ministers, and named a Hutu prime minister. In December 1990, UPRONA approved a draft National Unity Charter intended to abolish ethnic discrimination and lay the groundwork for a democratic constitution. Buyoya created a constitutional commission in March 1991 that released a draft document in early 1992. The document was approved by 90 percent of Burundians in a referendum.

The new constitution permits multiple parties so long as they are not ethically, regionally, or religiously based. The president and members of the National Assembly are elected for five-year terms, and the prime minister, appointed by the president, must be approved, along with his cabinet choices, by the Assembly.

In the same month as the constitutional referendum, Buyoya resigned from UPRONA to make the presidency nonpartisan. He refused calls for an all-party transitional government. Militant Hutus staged repeated raids in 1991 and 1992, while radical Tutsi soldiers attempted to derail reform by starting an uprising in 1992. Nevertheless, Buyoya kept the transition to democracy on track. Elections were held in June 1993, and Buyoya lost the presidency in a surprise upset to a Hutu, Melchior Ndadaye. Ndadaye's party, the Front for Democracy in Burundi (Frodebu), gained 80 percent of the seats in the National Assembly.

Sadly, Tutsi soldiers killed Ndadaye four months later, and bloody ethnic violence broke out once more. Tens of thousands of people died, and over ten percent of the population fled. The National Assembly elected Cyprien Ntaryamira president in January 1994, but he died just three months later in the same plane crash that killed Rwandan president Habyarimana as the two returned from a conference in Tanzania on ending the violence. The violence intensified instead, as the Tutsi-dominated army battled armed Hutu across the country. In September, representatives of the major parties worked out an interim power-sharing arrangement under Sylvestre Ntibantunganya, the speaker of the National Assembly who became temporary president upon Ntaryamira's death. The two major parties, Frodebu and UPRONA, maintained a tempestuous collaboration into 1995, while fighting and massacres brought the country, in the words of the president, "to the brink of genocide."

Burundi almost made the transition from an ethnically dominated, one-party dictatorship to a multiethnic, multiparty democracy, but it foundered on the intransigence of Tutsi reactionaries unwilling to yield power to the Hutu majority. Instead of choosing political reform and social reconciliation, the country has fallen into a crippling state of ethnic conflict that has devastated the government, civil society, and human rights, and that plagues the lives of the vast majority of the people.

CHAPTER

The Horn of Africa

INTRODUCTION

The Horn of Africa contains four countries, one of which (Ethiopia), is the oldest in Africa, while another (Eritrea), is the youngest. The other two are Somalia and Djibouti. The region's ecology is predominantly desert, dry scrub, and thorn forests, with some savanna, broadleaf forest, and extensive mountains in Ethiopia. Somalia was divided among three European colonial powers and Ethiopia. Ethiopia remained independent and actually absorbed not only the Ogaden region of Somalia but also Eritrea. Eritrea won its independence in 1993 as part of the same upheaval that ended communist-military rule in Ethiopia, and both are currently dominated by single parties and strong leaders who claim to be moving toward multiparty democracy. Djibouti also has recently ended a civil conflict and has proclaimed multiparty democracy as a goal, while Somalia has been in a state of collapse, dominated by clan-based warlords, since the late 1980s.

ETHIOPIA
Statistical Profile

Capital:	Addis Ababa
Area:	435,186 sq. miles
Population:	55,200,000 (1994 est.)
Density:	127 people/sq. mile
Growth Rate:	3.1% (1994 est.)
GDP:	$6,257,000,000
Per Capita Income:	$110
Debt:	$4,168,000,000
Life Expectancy:	36 (1960), 49 (1992)
Ethnic Groups:	Over 100 groups, principally Amhara (25%), Tigreans (12%), Oromo (40%), Sidamo (9%), and Gurage, Somali, Afar, Saho, Beni Amer, Baria, Kunama, Beni Shangul, Annuak
Official Languages:	Amharic; English used in commerce
Religions:	Ethiopian Orthodox Christian (40%), Muslim (40%)

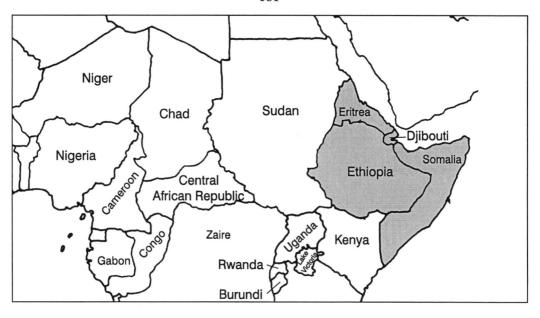

The Horn of Africa

History

One of the oldest countries in the world, Ethiopia traces its roots back to the ancient empire of Axum five centuries before Christ. It survived as an isolated Christian outpost through the Middle Ages, almost disintegrated in the seventeenth and eighteenth centuries, and revived in the middle of the nineteenth. Theodore II started the renewal by reuniting all the petty kingdoms into which the country had fragmented, administering his new domains efficiently, and introducing modern technology. He committed suicide in 1868 when a British punitive expedition sent to rescue imprisoned British citizens captured his capital, but his achievements were maintained by his successors, John IV and Melinik II, who defeated Italian invasions in 1887 and 1896. Melinik actually doubled the size of the empire through conquest, adding considerable territory in the south and in the Somali-populated Ogaden to the east. After he died in 1913, the army, church, and nobility ousted his successor because he had converted to Islam. They placed his daughter Judith on the

throne and named a close relative, Ras Tafari Makonnen, as regent. The two fought over Ras Tafari's modernization schemes, and he gradually increased his power until he became king in 1928. Judith died two years later, and Ras Tafari became Emperor Haile Selassie I.

A few years later, Haile Selassie became a symbol to the world of the plucky underdog. Faced with renewed Italian imperialism under the fascist government of Benito Mussolini in 1934, the Ethiopian emperor made a stirring but vain appeal to the League of Nations for aid. The Italians used airplanes and poison gas to defeat Ethiopia's ill-equipped army in 1936, and Selassie remained in stubborn exile until British victories in World War II enabled him to return in triumph in 1941. Ethiopia joined the Allied coalition in 1942, became a founding member of the United Nations in 1945, and in 1952 was allowed by the UN to make a federation with Italy's former colony of Eritrea, the coastal strip between Ethiopia and the sea.

After World War II, Selassie became more and more autocratic as his renewed modernization efforts generated increasing tensions in Ethiopian society and politics. The system he took over was dominated by a feudal aristocracy whose power rested on control of the peasant majority. In the newly conquered lands, this division between lord and peasant was compounded by ethnic differences dividing the ruling class and the mass of people. The relationship of the members of the aristocracy with the monarchy was ambiguous. They depended on the monarchy's power and benefited from its largesse, but also feared it as a threat to their own domination of society.

Selassie's modernizing programs exacerbated this tension, for economic improvements created new sources of wealth that threatened to overshadow the wealth produced by the nobles' estates. Furthermore, a modern state required a substantial bureaucracy and an army, both staffed by technocrats with modern educations. The old aristocracy feared this new intelligentsia, which in turn resented the aristocracy's complete control of the political system. At the same time, the new middle class created by economic development, along with the older middle class of mostly Moslem merchants, resented the heavy reliance of Selassie's modernization program on foreign investment—a fact that meant foreign firms dominated the modern sectors of the economy.

Added to these tensions within the elite were the complaints of the new urban proletariat, whose wages Selassie's regime kept at a subsistence level in order to attract foreign capital. The peasantry also seethed with dissatisfaction, their traditional complaints about feudal oppression compounded in some areas by anger over expropriations and evictions brought about by the government's promotion of commercial agriculture. The lower classes' dissatisfactions were particularly potent in ethnic minority areas, for cultural ties made a natural bridge between the common people and dissatisfied members of the local elites.

Ethnic tension was particularly acute in the Ogaden and in Eritrea. In the Ogaden, the nomadic populace waged a low-intensity struggle to join their brethren in neighboring Somalia after it became independent in 1960. In Eritrea, the inhabitants, many of them Moslem, never reconciled themselves to Ethiopia's subversion in 1960 of the agreement governing its relationship to the empire. This subversion had transformed Eritrea from an autonomous federated region into an ordinary province. The Eritrean Liberation Front took up arms in 1961 and began an insurgency that bedeviled Ethiopia for the next three decades.

Selassie created a bicameral legislature in 1955 but made no provision for representation of ethnic minorities and gave it little real power. He survived an attempted coup in 1960, but as his regime became increasingly inefficient, corrupt, and autocratic, resistance grew. The international economic recession in the early 1970s caused unemployment that hit both the urban workers and the intelligentsia, and a severe drought between 1972 and 1974 caused a massive famine that claimed over 200,000 victims. The government at first ignored the crisis and then tried to cover it up. In the spring of 1974, strikes and demonstrations convulsed Ethiopia's cities, and peasant revolts swept the countryside. The regime's last hope disappeared when the army, disheartened by decades of inconclusive fighting in remote territories, mutinied. The soldiers, drawn mainly from the peasantry, joined with junior officers, drawn mainly from the intelligensia, and replaced the senior commanders with a coordinating committee. This committee, dubbed the *Dergue* (the Amharic word for "committee"), was composed of 120 members ranging in rank from private to major. The new regime executed 50 members of the old imperial government and at the same time rid itself of its own first leader, General Aman Andom. Haile Selassie was deposed and placed under house arrest; he died in 1975. Major, later Colonel, Mengistu Haile Mariem then engineered a series of bloody purges that gradually transformed the government into a personalized dictatorship.

Taking the lead in the revolution, the *Dergue* dismantled the feudal system and adopted "scientific socialism" as its official ideology. Renaming itself the Provisional Military Administrative Council (PMAC), it took on the role of guide of the "Ethiopian Revolution" and began to transform the country's economy and society. It nationalized land and businesses and organized local governments into urban dweller's associations and rural peasant associations. It resettled over one million farmers from the northwest of the country to the southeast as part of a massive agricultural restructuring that included villagisation and collectivization as well. The regime proclaimed all nationalities and cultures to be equal, officially recognized Islam, allowed broadcasting and publishing in languages other than Amharic, and offered nationalities the options of local self-government and regional autonomy. With Soviet guidance, it created a commission to establish a worker's party (COPWE) in 1979, and in 1983 it began to draw up a constitution for a people's democratic socialist republic that would be run by a single party, the Workers' Party of Ethiopia (WPE). It had a secretary general (Mengistu), an 11-man politburo, and a central committee with 134 full members and 64 alternates. The country officially returned to civilian rule in 1987 under a national assembly that elected Mengistu president of the country and established a series of regional assemblies.

From the beginning, the revolutionary government faced resistance. Partisans of the old regime staged numerous uprisings, most notably an invasion from Sudan by forces of the Ethiopian Democratic Union in 1977. The government easily suppressed these risings because they lacked popular support, but a greater threat was posed by forces on the left. Almost as soon as the military took over, the Confederation of Ethiopian Labor Unions (CELU) staged a general strike to back up demands for a minimum wage and social security legislation. The regime responded by banning it, jailing its leaders, and replacing it with the government-controlled All-Ethiopia Trade Union. Remnants of the old labor union

then joined with radical members of the intelligensia and militant students to launch a campaign of urban guerrilla warfare in 1976 under the rubric of the Ethiopian People's Revolutionary Party (EPRP). The government met this development by organizing the intellectuals who remained loyal into the All-Ethiopia Socialist Movement (MEISON), organizing an armed militia within the urban associations, and empowering special security units to deal summarily with suspected opponents. The "Red Terror" that began in the spring of 1977 intimidated the urban populace with daily executions, mass arrests, and nightly gunbattles with the EPRP. The government gradually secured its position, at which point it turned on MEISON, killing many of its members and forcing the rest underground. It briefly encouraged another autonomous ideological movement called Abiotawi Seded (Revolutionary Flame) in 1979 but abandoned it in favor of its own efforts to organize a political party in the early 1980s.

Nationalist movements posed the gravest threat to the revolutionary regime. The government argued that the revolution had ended the need for secession, offered considerable autonomy, and eventually established an Institute of Nationalities to try to find a solution to the problem they posed. Nevertheless, the existing secessionist movements in the Ogaden and Eritrea intensified their efforts, and new movements appeared in Oromo in the south and Tigre in the north.

The Ogaden conflict moved to the forefront in 1977 when Somalia sent in conventional forces that rapidly seized the region. The Soviet Union, heretofore allied with Somalia, dumped it and sent Ethiopia military advisors and massive quantities of supplies and equipment. Cuba sent 12,000 troops. These helped Ethiopia regain the Ogaden in a lightening campaign, but the Cubans then refused to participate in the counterinsurgency in Eritrea. Soviet advisors and logistical support enabled the government to temporarily regain the initiative there. It was unable to root out the insurgents, however, and the conflict dragged on. Meanwhile, the Tigre People's Liberation Front (TPLF), which had been founded in 1975, began fighting in earnest in 1982. It helped organize the Oromo Liberation Front (OLF) as well as the Ethiopian People's Democratic Movement among the Amahraic people, who formed the core of the country.

Despite drought and debilitating famines, the beleaguered government fought on through the 1980s while reorganizing itself from a military dictatorship into a Soviet-style "people's republic." The collapse of its superpower sponsor, however, undercut its military power and discredited its socioeconomic and political assumptions. The government's opponents, most of whom joined together with the TPLF in the Ethiopian People's Revolutionary Democratic Front (EPRDF), gradually overpowered it. In a coordinated offensive in 1991, the Eritreans won almost complete control of their province, while the TPLF overthrew the Mengistu government in Ethiopia proper.

Having achieved victory, the EPRDF organized a national conference that included representatives of 26 opposition groups. It elected the TPLF's Meles Zenawe as president and adopted a charter establishing a two-year transitional government with an 87-member, multiparty council of representatives. The EPRDF held 32 of the seats, including the TPLF's 10, and various Oromo groups held 26. The conference called for an independent judiciary to be established and human rights to be respected, and the charter recognized the right of ethnic groups to self-determination. The new government accepted that a referendum, which would undoubtedly endorse independence, would be held in Eritrea. It also divided the country into nine ethnically defined provinces—an innovative policy it called "ethnic federalism" that recognized rather than resisted ethnic divisions.

Before the new system could be put to the test, the OLF left the transitional government and began fighting against EPRDF troops. The Afar Liberation Front (ALF) and two Somali organizations took up arms in early 1992 as well, and the violence threatened to prevent scheduled local and regional elections. The EPRDF and OLF managed a reconciliation that allowed the elections to proceed in most of the country, although each manipulated registration and campaigning in the territory it controlled. Since affiliates of the EPRDF dominated far larger areas than the OLF and most opposition groups boycotted the balloting, the election results were overwhelmingly in the government's favor. International observers charged that the scale of irregularities invalidated the results, but Meles' government refused to set them aside.

The government managed to hold the country together, minus Eritrea, and held national elections in May 1995. Most of the opposition parties boycotted them, so Meles' party won by a large margin, but international observers pronounced them free and fair. The opposition charged that the EPRDF continually manipulated the local electoral committees. Since this complaint caused the opposition to remain aloof from the election, the country cannot be considered truly democratic yet. It does, however, allow a vigorous political life, including a large and diverse free press, and the government's use of extrajudicial means against opponents is certainly far less extensive than under Mengistu. Ethnic regions have the right to secede; opponents of the regime have the right to organize parties; and the people have the freedom of worship. The government has reoriented spending from defense to social services and economic development. Although the country remains one of the poorest in Africa, its current economic and political situations and the outlook for the future are far better than they were before. The country's experiment with "ethnic federalism" may well provide a model applicable across Africa.

SOMALIA
Statistical Profile

Capital:	Mogadishu
Area:	246,200 sq. miles

Population Size:	9,800,000 (1994 est.)
Density:	40 people/sq. mile
Growth Rate:	3.2% (1994 est.)
GDP:	$879,000,000
Per Capita Income:	$150
Foreign Debt:	$1,898,000,000
Life Expectancy:	36 (1960), 49 (1992)
Ethnic Groups:	Most Somalis (95%) belong to one ethnic group, subdivided into six major clans: Isa, Isaq, Mijertein, Hawiya, Sab, and Bararetta
Official Language:	Somali; Arabic, English, Italian, and Swahili are also widely spoken
Religion:	Muslim (99%)
Former Colonizers:	Italy, Great Britain
Date of Independence:	1960

History

Kushitic peoples have inhabited the Horn of Africa since they were known as "black Berbers" to the early Greeks and Arabs. The earliest were apparently Galla. The ancestors of the modern Somalis were more recent immigrants who began moving along the seacoast from the northwest around 750 A.D. The great majority of both groups were nomadic pastoralists who wandered the arid landscape looking for pasturage for their herds, although the Somali established some sizable port settlements. Through these they were exposed to Arab influences and eventually converted to Islam. Expanding inland, they gradually pushed the pagan Galla westward into Ethiopia. By the nineteenth century, the Somali had established a cultural unity encompassing the entire desert region in the Horn of Africa.

This cultural unity was not reflected in political unity, however. Before the European intrusion, their townspeople and nomadic clans lived as autonomous units, with the southernmost towns loosely affiliated with Zanzibar. During the scramble for Africa, France took the area around Djibouti at the mouth of the Red Sea. Great Britain got the northern region along the Gulf of Aden and the far south adjacent to Kenya. The Italians took the southeastern coast, and the Ethiopians seized the interior region known as the Ogaden. The tribes in the interior fiercely resisted foreign rule into the 1920s; the inhabitants of the coastal cities sullenly accepted a colonialism that at least made little effort to change their way of life.

The imperial powers rearranged their claims to the territory beginning in the 1930s, when Italy conquered Ethiopia and amalgamated all its territories from Eritrea to Italian Somaliland into a single colony. The reshuffling continued in the 1940s. When British forces defeated the Italians in the area, they restored independence to Ethiopia but did not immediately return the Ogaden and other "reserved territories." Instead, they administered these territories along with their original piece of Somalia and the former Italian colony, giving the Somalis a taste of unification. The British even went so far as to propose creating a single state encompassing all the Somalis, but found no support for this among the other Western powers. They eventually returned the Ogaden and other territories to Ethiopia, and in 1950 the United Nations allowed Italy its part of Somalia for a ten-year trusteeship. However, the events had whetted the Somali appetite for unification.

The Somali Youth League (SYL), founded in 1942, spread rapidly and actively resisted the moves to redivide the country. It also championed independence, which came to the majority in 1960 when the Italian trusteeship ended and the British let go of their portion. The two territories joined together as the Somali Republic. The SYL won elections in both parts of the country in 1964 but proved unable to rule the country effectively. Clan favoritism, corruption, and maladministration led to increasing civil disorder until a chaotic election campaign in 1969 climaxed with the assassination of the president. A few weeks later, Major General Siad Barre led a bloodless coup that installed a military government with himself at its head. He dissolved the old parliament and placed many of the country's former leaders under arrest.

Barre's new government styled itself the Supreme Revolutionary Council (SRC), adopted a socialist philosophy, and renamed the country the Somali Democratic Republic. It established close ties with the Soviet Union; adopted a centralized, state-dominated economic model; and enacted programs to improve social welfare, literacy, and agricultural production. In 1976, the SRC gave way to the Somali Revolutionary Socialist Party (SRSP) and Barre became president in single-party elections. A new constitution that created a people's assembly with representatives elected for five-year terms was promulgated in 1979. They, in turn, elected the president for a six-year term. The elections were duly held, but real power remained in the hands of Siad Barre and the Politburo of the SRSP.

Barre's regime cultivated good relations with the Arab world, joining the Arab League in 1974 and hosting its ministerial summit in 1979, but the country's foremost ties were to the USSR. The Soviets offered the strategically placed country military as well as economic assistance, but as the probability that Somalia would make use of the armaments became greater, the Soviets became less enthusiastic about the relationship. Both the Somalis and the Soviets perceived an opportunity in the collapse of the Ethiopian monarchy, but the opportunities they saw put them at odds. The Soviets saw another potential ally, one that was bigger and more powerful than Somalia. The Somalis saw a chance to regain the Ogaden. They supported the Western Somalia Liberation Front (WSLF) and the Abo Liberation Front in Oromo, even as the Soviets poured in aid to the new Ethiopian regime. The crisis came in 1977 when the Somalis followed up guerrilla successes with a conventional attack and rapidly took control of the entire Ogaden. The Soviets abandoned Somalia and rushed arms, equipment, and advisors to the Ethiopians. They also arranged for the Cubans to contribute 12,000 combat troops, and masterminded a complex counteroffensive that threw the Somalis back into Somalia. Barre angrily broke all ties to the

USSR and turned to the United States, offering use of the port of Berbera as a base in exchange for military and economic aid.

The agreement with the United States did not come in time to affect the outcome of the war, but the fighting did not end. The Ogadenese returned to guerrilla warfare, occasionally supported by the Somali army. The Ethiopians waged a brutal counterinsurgency and launched occasional forays into Somalia. They also began supporting Somali dissidents, who became more and more active against the regime, the core support of which was a clan that included just five percent of the Somali population. The first sign of this discontent was an attempted coup by officers in Mogadishu in April 1978. The government crushed it, executing 17 of the plotters, but it could not deal so easily with dissident groups based abroad. In 1980, the Somali Democratic Salvation Front (SDSF) began broadcasting antigovernment messages from Ethiopia, and in 1981 it attacked and captured two villages on the Ethiopian border. The same year another group, the Somali National Movement (SNM), formed; it was based on the country's largest clan, which predominated in the country's northern region and was almost entirely excluded from power by Barre's regime. The SNM began staging attacks in 1983. By that point, the two opposition groups had already met and forged a common front in October 1982.

Barre responded unsteadily to this growing challenge. In 1979, he declared a three-year state of emergency and revived the Somali Revolutionary Council (SRC), filling it with 17 senior officers. He changed tack in 1981, purging the SRC, and in April 1982 he disbanded it again. A few months later, he arrested seven prominent civilian politicians, and in August, after the first SDSF attacks, he reimposed the state of emergency. He survived an automobile accident in 1986 and was reelected to the presidency for another seven years by the SRSP's central committee.

He was most successful in attacking his enemies indirectly, by undercutting their international support. He made overtures to the Soviet Union in 1983, expressing his discontent with lackluster American support of his regime. In 1984, he divided the SDSF by offering an amnesty that was accepted by 200 members who were frustrated by the movement's domination by Ethiopia and Libya. He signed a border peace pact with Kenya in 1984, defusing long-standing tensions on that front, and in 1988 he achieved his most significant success, a nonaggression pact with Ethiopia. This agreement cut off his opponents from their primary source of support for the small price of abandoning the Ogadenese insurgents, who similarly depended on him.

This triumph of peace came too late, however. The SNM, which had staged a series of powerful raids from Ethiopia before the nonaggression pact, surged into northern Somalia, capturing several large towns and threatening to overrun the entire province. The government responded with ferocity, hiring white mercenary pilots when its own fliers refused to bomb and strafe civilians. Its brutal campaign caused 15,000 deaths and created 300,000 refugees. It was not able to destroy the SNM, however, and in 1989 violent unrest spread to the rest of the country. In June 1990, 100 prominent political and business leaders called on Barre to resign in favor of a transitional government that would be empowered to arrange multiparty elections. Barre responded by arresting 45. He soon released them, and promised to hold a referendum on a new constitution in October 1990 and to hold multiparty elections in February 1991. In September 1989, he dismissed his cabinet and instituted a transitional government. He resigned as secretary-general of the SRSP, and in December 1990 he legalized opposition parties. In the meantime, however, two new opposition factions joined the fight against him—the United Somali Congress (USC) and the Somali Patriotic Movement (SPM). The USC captured Mogadishu at the end of 1990, and Barre fled to his home base in the south. He mounted two unsuccessful attempts to re-

capture the capital during 1991 and went into exile in Kenya in May 1992.

The USC's victory did not end the fighting, however. Although it installed Ali Mahdi Mohamed as temporary president for two years, a faction led by his rival, General Mohamed Farah Aidid, challenged his hold on Mogadishu. The rest of the country splintered into a collection of clan and sub-clan enclaves dominated by petty warlords and their ragged bands of bandit-warriors. The SNM declared the northwestern region to be the independent country of Somaliland in May 1991, and the other, lesser enclaves asserted the informal sovereignty of the gun.

The economy, which had been sagging for more than a decade under the weight of war, refugees, drought, and mismanagement, collapsed entirely. In 1992, fighting, famine, and disease claimed over 300,000 lives, including one of every four children under the age of five. The United Nations reacted slowly, having suspended its relief operations almost entirely by the end of 1991 because of the danger to its personnel from the factional fighting. It was not until May that enough of a cease-fire was worked out for food shipments to resume, and then most of the supplies were seized by militiamen and sold by merchants connected with the dominant clans. Hired security guards often aided in these thefts, so the UN decided to deploy a peacekeeping force to replace them. International wrangling and Somali opposition kept them from entering the country until October, and even then they remained confined to the airport. Meanwhile, televised images of starving children had created an international outcry, and in November 1992, President Bush committed the United States to a major military effort. In December, the first of 28,000 American troops began to arrive.

Originally sent to deliver food, the U.S. troops accepted the collateral assignment of disarming the militias and eventually became embroiled in attempts to kill the intransigent leader of the Somali National Alliance (SNA), Mohammed Farah Aidid. Public support in the

U.S. for the mission waned quickly, and collapsed altogether when 18 members of a small force were killed in an ambush. In 1993, the United States gradually turned the problem over to other UN forces, and pulled out entirely on March 25, 1994. The UN backed off from its confrontational approach to the warring factions and attempted to mediate a cease-fire and the formation of a new national government, but without notable success. Other Western countries pulled out their contingents as the U.S. troops withdrew, and the remaining forces were withdrawn by the end of February 1995.

The country remains a mosaic of hostile enclaves dominated by undisciplined militias led by petty warlords. Somaliland in the northwest has achieved a reasonable degree of internal stability, primarily through a renewal of the conciliatory role of traditional clan elders, but it remains unrecognized by the international community. Elsewhere, democracy and human rights are not even an issue. The country has reverted to the conditions of a medieval frontier territory. Faced with incessant warfare and ever-imminent famine, simple survival is the goal of most of the country's inhabitants.

DJIBOUTI
Statistical Profile

Capital:	Djibouti
Area:	8,494 sq. miles
Population:	600,000 (1994 est.)
Density:	71 people/sq. mile
Growth Rate:	3.0% (1994 est.)
GDP:	$445,000,000
Per Capita Income:	$475
Foreign Debt:	$174,000,000
Life Expectancy:	n.a. (1960), 49 (1992)
Ethnic Groups:	Somali (Issa clan 40%, others 20%); Afars (35%); Arabs; around 12,000 Europeans
Official Languages:	Arabic and French
Religions:	Muslim (94%), Christian (6%)
Former Colonizer:	France
Date of Independence:	1977

History

Djibouti owes its importance to its strategic position at the mouth of the Red Sea. Its original inhabitants were Kushites, but around 500 B.C. a group of Semites crossed from Arabia, settling along the coast to the north and gradually expanding into the northern part of present-day Djibouti. The ethnic division this created—between the Afar in the north and the Somali in the south—continues to dominate the country's politics today.

Before 1000 A.D., the territory lay on the fringe of a series of states oriented toward the Red Sea: first Adulis, then Axum, and finally Abyssinia. In the twelfth century, it assumed a more central place in the Moslem state of Shoa, which brought Islamic influence permanently into the interior before disappearing in the fourteenth century. The territory became an area of loosely administered petty states until the Ottomans arrived in the sixteenth century. They garrisoned the port of Zeila and supported the sultan of Adel with a corps of musketeers that almost enabled him to conquer Abyssinia. The Christian state counterattacked after being saved by the timely arrival of a corps of Portuguese musketeers, but before it could cinch its victory the entire region was overrun by the nomadic Galla. While Abyssinia eventually recovered, Adel did not, and the area of Djibouti returned to its disorganized state.

The Egyptian ruler Ismail incorporated the territory into his empire briefly in the 1870s. The French already had a foothold, having negotiated control of the port of Obok, and in the 1880s they replaced the Egyptians by negotiating a series of protectorates with local sultans. In 1888, they began construction of a new port, which became the city of Djibouti. It became the capital of a consolidated colony, French Somaliland, in 1896. The colony became the official outlet for landlocked Ethiopia's commerce the next year, and the French completed a railroad linking it with Addis Ababa in 1917.

The French granted the colony a local representative council and a representative in the parliament in Paris in 1946, although suffrage was restricted until 1957. An indigenous Somali, Mohamed Harbi, became the colony's representative in 1956, and the next year the representative council became a full-fledged territorial assembly.

The growth of Somali nationalism outpaced French reforms. The first anticolonial demonstrations took place in 1949, following the collapse of the British attempt to forge a "Greater Somalia" that would have included French Somaliland. A decade later, in the referendum of 1958, a quarter of the population voted for independence. Since independence would have meant union with Somalia, Ethiopia, France, and the Djibouti Afar all opposed it. The French allied with the Afar leader Ali Aref, manipulating elections to keep his faction in control of the local government council and suppressing Somali dissenters. Somali nationalism boiled over in riots during a visit by French President de Gaulle in 1966. The French army fired on the demonstrators, and the government drove many Somalis out of the country, so that when another referendum on independence was held in March 1967, 60 percent of the voters favored continued unity with France. Further riots ensued, and several attempts were made to assassinate Aref, but the French increased their military presence, surrounded the city of Djibouti with a barbed wire fence, and granted Aref more power.

In the 1970s, both moderate resistance and armed rebellion increased, as did pressure from the international community. The UN first called for independence following the 1967 riots, but in the 1970s the Arab League and the OAU joined the chorus. In the early 1970s, the predominantly Somali African Popular Union, headed by Hassan Gouled, united with the predominately Afar League for the Future and for Order to make the African People's League for Independence (LPAI), which unsuccessfully contested several elections. The Somali Coast Liberation Front (FLCS) conducted a terrorist campaign, and in 1975 demonstrations against visiting French ministers

shook the regime. Even Ali Aref, who had lost the support of Ethiopia when Haile Selassie fell, came out for independence, but he was too late. In 1976, massive demonstrations in support of the LPAI caused most of Aref's allies in the government to abandon him, and the French forced him to resign. After backing him for a decade, they decided that they'd be better off making their peace with the nationalists and ensuring that the new state would maintain friendly ties.

The French negotiated independence with the LPAI and Aref's former associates, ignoring both more radical Somali groups on the left and anti-independence Afar groups on the right. Legislative elections held in May 1977 established the LPAI as the majority party and made Hassan Gouled the new head of the government. He created an interethnic cabinet containing seven Afars and 13 Issas, as the Somali tribe in Djibouti is known, and the colony became the Republic of Djibouti on June 26, 1977. It signed a series of treaties of cooperation with France solidifying close economic ties and permitting the French to retain a military base. It also strengthened its ties to the Arab world, joining the Arab League and turning increasingly to Saudi Arabia for financial backing.

Soon after independence, Djibouti felt the effects of the Somali attack on Ethiopia in the Ogaden. Influenced by the initial Somali success, Gouled's regime began pushing Afars out of office, and violence between the Issas and the Afar broke out in the streets. By December 1977, 600 Afars had been arrested. When the tide of war in the Ogaden turned, the government moved quickly to reconcile with the Afar. It created a special commission composed of Afars to propose measures to satisfy Afar grievances, released most Afar prisoners, and brought more Afars into the military and the civil service. In February 1978, Gouled reorganized the cabinet to create a careful ethnic balance, and the regime began funneling more economic development money to the north. In 1979, the government divided the country into municipalities to give people more control over local affairs, and Gouled reorganized the LPAI into the Popular Assembly for Progress (RPP) in an attempt to broaden its base.

While Gouled moved to reduce the nation's ethnic tensions, he also gradually tightened his own control on the government. As head of state, he appointed the politburo of the new RPP, and in elections in 1981 he ran unopposed. When opponents organized the Djibouti People's Party (PPD) to contest the legislative elections scheduled for the next year, the government arrested its leaders and made the RPP the sole legal party. The PPD went underground, and in 1983 a wave of violence shook the country, but Gouled's control remained firm. The RPP won another round of legislative elections in 1986, and Gouled won another six-year term in 1987.

In January 1991, the government put down an attempted uprising by frustrated opponents. In March, the RPP convened a conference to consider the calls for multiparty democracy but decided against it. In November the Front for Unity and Democracy (FRUD) launched a guerrilla war by attacking several army posts in northern Djibouti. The government reversed itself and adopted multipartyism, scheduling elections for November 20 and drafting a new constitution allowing for up to four parties. The move was too little and too late, for the opposition resented the lack of consultation, the fact that the new constitution gave the president extensive unchecked powers, and the ruthless repression that accompanied the political reforms. When FRUD continued to fight, the French refused to activate the defensive treaty, calling the struggle an internal affair. French troops sealed the border with Ethiopia, but FRUD soon controlled two-thirds of the country anyway. Nine opposition parties formed a united front in Paris in early 1992 and called for a transitional government and a sovereign national conference, but Gouled refused to negotiate and ignored the guerrilla's unilateral cease-fires. In June, he announced that a referendum on the new constitution would be held in September and released a few of the most prominent political prisoners. The referendum resulted in 96-percent approval from 75 percent of the voters. On September 20, opposition parties became legal. Only two met the stringent qualifications for registration, which included not having a military wing and not representing an ethnic group, and one of them boycotted the legislative elections held on December 18. The RPP won all the seats. Presidential elections were held in May 1993, but all the opposition parties refused to participate, so Gouled won unopposed.

The army mounted a determined offensive two months later and secured control of most of the country. Fighting continued into 1994 but ended with a peace agreement signed by Gouled and Mohamed Daoud of FRUD. The agreement provided for integration of the rebels into the army, fair elections in the future, and immediate participation by FRUD in the government.

Djibouti has a multiparty system, but it does not yet have democracy. The end of the civil war is a tremendous step forward, but the system's most important long-term provisions have not yet been implemented. In the meantime, Gouled has shown increasing favoritism toward his own Mamassan clan in the Issa tribe, a tendency that counteracts the careful ethnic balance he maintains in the cabinet. The judicial system is not independent in political cases, and detention without trial, torture, and extrajudicial execution are all used. The government controls all media, and criticism is not allowed. Freedom of association is restricted, and all unions are part of a government labor federation. Freedom of worship is permitted.

ERITREA
Statistical Profile

Capital:	Asmera
Area:	46,842 sq. miles
Population:	3,500,000 (1994 est.)
Density:	75 people/sq. mile
Growth Rate:	2.6% (1994 est.)
GDP:	n.a.

Per Capita Income:	$115
Foreign Debt:	n.a.
Life Expectancy:	n.a. (1960), 45 (1992)
Ethnic Groups:	Afar, Tigre, Saho, Tigrinya
Official Language:	Amharic
Religions:	Muslim (40%), Coptic Christian (50%)
Former Colonizers:	Italy, Ethiopia
Date of Independence:	1993

History

Eritrea was the first beachhead of the Semitic peoples who migrated from Arabia to Africa around the fifth century B.C. The port of Adulis rose to importance well before the time of Christ as a source of war elephants for the Ptolemaic kingdom of Egypt, and the area formed the nucleus of the mercantile kingdom of Axum in the first centuries after Christ. It remained an important part of Abyssinia for the next 500 years, but the inhabitants along the coast converted to Islam in the eighth and ninth centuries and developed ties with the Arabs. They came under the Mamluks in the fourteenth century, the Ottomans in the sixteenth century, and the Egyptians in the nineteenth century. The Italians took control in the 1880s and ruled until World War II. They did not do much to develop the territory economically, but they did break the power of the old feudal aristocracy.

The British seized the colony in 1941 as part of their East African campaign and ruled it first as a military protectorate and then as a UN trusteeship until 1952, when the United Nations voted to federate the territory with Ethiopia. Eritrea's cosmopolitanism and democratic local administration did not mix well with the feudal and monarchical structures in the rest of Ethiopia. The Ethiopian government systematically subverted the province's autonomy until it was able to engineer its full absorption into the empire in 1962, replacing the UN-mandated provincial autonomy with strict central control.

A significant number of Eritreans resented this high-handed treatment by the Ethiopians

and feared that the province would be economically neglected. Its substantial Moslem minority further feared for their religious rights. Consequently, a rebellion led by the Eritrean Liberation Front (ELF) broke out within a year in the northwestern lowlands. Backed by substantial U.S. military aid (half of all such assistance going to the African continent), the imperial regime was able to keep the rebels in check, but it was not able to defeat them. The endless campaigning eroded the Ethiopian military's morale and thereby contributed to the fall of the monarchy in 1974, but the military regime that replaced it was also unwilling to give up the province.

By now, the Marxist Eritrean People's Liberation Front (EPLF), based in southeastern Eritrea, had beaten the ELF in a bloody confrontation and taken over leadership of the struggle. It rejected Ethiopian offers of autonomy and fought on for another two decades. The tides of war shifted repeatedly, with each side occasionally seizing control of most of the province's territory, but neither was able to knock the other out completely. The EPLF and the ELF fought against each other again in 1982, and in 1985 all the Eritrean opposition groups but the EPLF joined together in the Eritrean Unified National Council (EUNC). The EPLF saw no advantage in cooperating with the other Eritrean factions, but it coordinated with other regional dissidents in Ethiopia that were banded together in the Ethiopian People's Revolutionary Democratic Front (EPRDF). Together they maintained widespread pressure on the regime, which collapsed in May 1991 after Soviet aid dried up. The EPLF cooperated with the transitional government without joining it. A UN-sponsored referendum on the future of the province was held in April 1993. As expected, the overwhelming majority of Eritreans voted for full independence, and Eritrea became Africa's 53rd state on May 24. The struggle had lasted 30 years, cost approximately 200,000 lives, created 500,000 refugees, and left the economy in ruins, but independence had come at last.

The EPLF dominated the country both before and after the referendum. The foundations of its rule had been laid during the decades of revolutionary struggle when it recruited supporters and soldiers through ideological training and political mobilization. As it won territory, it created a governmental structure that reflected its primary dependence on voluntary support. It dropped its Marxist rhetoric in favor of multiparty democracy at a party conference in 1987, and transformed itself into a political party, the People's Front for Democracy and Justice (PFDJ), at another congress held in February 1994. The congress also drafted a charter that stressed national unity and the ongoing role of the party in promoting the country's development. Half of the members of the country's legislature, the National Assembly, are members of the PFDJ's central committee, and the other half are popularly elected delegates. The legislature elects the president, who is currently the party's leader, Isaias Afwerki. He in turn appoints members of the State Council, the country's cabinet, subject to the National Assembly's approval. The PFDJ is attempting to democratize both its own affairs and the country's government, but the transition from revolutionary movement to multiparty democracy is expected to take the rest of the decade.

Local government, in contrast, is already democratic, with elected village committees and councils. At the next level, the country is composed of 10 states in a federal structure. The government recognizes the rights of both Christians and Moslems, although it denied citizenship to Jehovah's Witnesses in March 1995 on the grounds that they refuse to accept the duties of citizenship. A press law allowing freedom of expression is being drafted. The new judiciary is relatively independent, and the government is creating new civil and criminal codes. Women fought alongside men during the rebellion and their status is definitely higher than it was under the old regime, but there are complaints that they have been losing ground since the end of the fighting. Overall, the new government enjoys tremendous goodwill from both its own people and from abroad. The challenge will be to maintain it amid the complexities of peace and the stresses of economic privation.

CHAPTER

Upper South Africa

INTRODUCTION

The nations of Upper South Africa were all "front-line" states during the struggle against white rule to their south. They stretch from Angola on the west coast to Mozambique on the east coast, and include mainly savanna and steppe regions, with some desert along the west coast and tropical forest along the east coast. The three countries in the center—Zambia, Malawi, and Zimbabwe—were ruled by Great Britain, while the two on the coasts were Portuguese colonies. All are currently multiparty democracies, although Angola and Mozambique have recently achieved peace and are still fragile.

ZAMBIA
Statistical Profile

Capital:	Lusaka
Area:	290,583 sq. miles
Population:	9,100,000 (1994 est.)
Density:	31 people/sq. mile
Growth Rate:	2.8% (1994 est.)
GDP:	$3,831,000,000
Per Capita Income:	$290
Foreign Debt:	$4,823,000,000
Life Expectancy:	42 (1960), 48 (1992)
Ethnic Groups:	Primary ethnic groups are Barotse, Bemba, Chewa, and Ngoni
Official Language:	English
Religions:	Christian (75%), Traditional (23%), Muslim (1%), Hindu (1%)
Former Colonizer:	Great Britain
Date of Independence:	1964

History

Human beings have lived in the area of Zambia for at least 200,000 years, but the ancestors of most of today's inhabitants were Bantu-speaking farmers and herders who immigrated in successive waves after the eighth century A.D. By the beginning of the nineteenth century, they lived in a variety of communities that ranged from "stateless societies" to complex kingdoms. The latter arose because of wealth generated by long-distance trade in slaves and ivory with the Swahili cities that grew up along the coast in the thirteenth and fourteenth centuries and with the Portuguese,

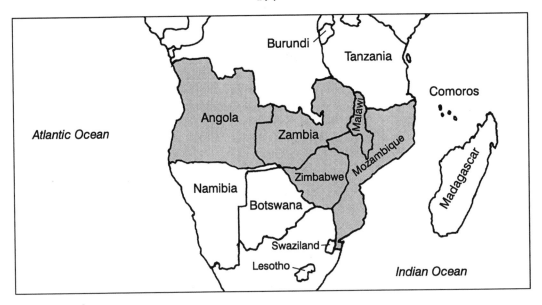

Upper South Africa

who established a colony in Mozambique in the sixteenth century.

The first British intrusion came in the mid-1850s, when the Scottish missionary David Livingstone explored the basin of the Zambeze River. The area came under British domination in 1889, when Cecil Rhodes' British South Africa Company got a royal charter to exploit and rule the territory. Looking for minerals and cheap labor for mines farther south, the company used a combination of persuasion, bribery, trickery, and force to establish its control. Barotseland in the south and west was at first a British protectorate in which Rhodes' company held trading and mineral rights, while in the north and east the company ruled directly. In 1911, Barotseland and the company-ruled territories were merged into Northern Rhodesia under the rule of the British South Africa Company. The British Colonial Office took direct control in 1924 when the territory became a crown colony. In 1953, after decades of white-settler agitation, the territory was federated with Southern Rhodesia and Nyasaland (Malawi).

This move bolstered the settlers' position by linking them with the larger white community to the south. It also generated fierce opposition from African leaders and fueled the growth of modern nationalism. The African National Congress (ANC), the first pan-tribal political organization arose in 1951 to oppose federation. When its leader, Harry Nkumbula, appeared to compromise by agreeing to participate in federal elections in 1958, a group of militants split off to form the United National Independence Party (UNIP). Through a series of mass actions opposing federation and calling for independence, they succeeded in changing the direction of British policy. In 1962, the colonial government held elections in which the UNIP and the ANC together won power from the settlers, and in 1963 the British dissolved the federation. In January 1964, the UNIP won new legislative elections against the ANC, and Kenneth Kaunda, the UNIP's leader, won the presidency in August. On October 24, Zambia became an independent nation.

During its first decade of independence, Zambia remained a democracy, although it was dominated by Kenneth Kaunda and the UNIP. The party retained the aura of leadership it had gained in the independence movement, and Kaunda astutely balanced the interests of the country's different regions to maintain national support. The ANC remained as a rival on the national scene, and a number of regional and ethnic parties also arose. The United Party gained widespread support in Barotseland before it was banned in 1968. Instead of strengthening UNIP's position, the move reduced its popularity; in the 1969 elections, the ANC gained seats in the south and west of the country. In 1971, Kaunda's vice president and closest collaborator, Simon Kapwepwe, resigned in order to found the United Progressive Party, with its base in the northern Copperbelt region. Economic recession undercut the ruling party's popularity, and Kaunda's regime held on mainly because none of its rivals was able to formulate a clear-cut alternative to the UNIP's mildly socialist, nationalist program.

Labeling the opposition as "tribalist," Kaunda moved in the early 1970s to transform Zambia into a one-party state. A new constitution in 1973 abrogated the 1964 charter, established the party as dominant over the state, and made Kaunda dominant over both. UNIP's Central Committee became the supreme policy-making body in the country, and the unicameral National Assembly became one of its subcommittees, made up of docile party nominees. Kaunda, as president of both the party and the nation, was commander-in-chief of the armed forces and gained the power to detain opponents indefinitely. He set the agenda for the party's biannual National Council, and he retained the power to dismiss members of the Central Committee. He brushed aside attempts by rivals to stand for the presidential elections of 1978 and blocked the renomination of outspoken members of the parliament in the legislative elections. He frequently shuffled personnel in the cabinet, the civil service, and the armed forces to prevent his subordinates from establishing stable bases of support.

During the 1970s, foreign affairs bolstered Kaunda's position. As one of the "front-line states" in the struggle against the white supremacist regimes in Rhodesia, Angola, Mozambique, and South Africa, Zambia played a central role in the military and diplomatic struggle. Kaunda steered a careful course between support of African liberation movements and openness to dealing with the whites' leaders. The latter policy drew a certain amount of criticism from more distantly situated African leaders, but they added to Kaunda's stature as a statesman at home and helped blunt the retaliatory inclinations of the powerful whites. Even when the Rhodesians brought economic and eventually military pressure to bear on Zambia in the late 1970s, the effect was to even further justify Kaunda's strong hold on government.

In the longer run, the Rhodesian conflict had a debilitating effect on the Zambian economy that worked to undermine Kaunda's position. Furthermore, declining world prices for Zambian exports, in particular copper, and the overall failure of the government's socialist policies drove down production and the standard of living while fueling corruption and popular discontent. As a consequence, pressure for a return to multiparty democracy mounted throughout the 1980s. In 1980, prominent businessmen called for political reforms, widespread strikes broke out among discontented workers, and the government detained a number of officers and businessmen to quash what it called an attempted coup. More strikes and riots followed in 1981, and the government clashed with the leadership of the Zambian Congress of Trade Unions (ZCTU) that year and in 1982. Another coup attempt was foiled in 1983, and in 1985 and 1986 austerity measures necessitated by the country's dire economic straits provoked more strikes and riots—the most severe since independence.

Although Kaunda backed off from the most stringent of the measures, he only managed to put off the day of reckoning. In late 1989 and 1990, calls for multiparty democracy became stronger, led by the ZCTU and its head, Frederick Chiluba. In June 1990, Kaunda shuffled his cabinet and created a four-man commission to lay the groundwork for a national referendum. Just days later he announced a new austerity plan, needed to obtain loans from the IMF. The move sparked three days of rioting in which 29 people died and more than 100 were wounded in pitched battles with the police. Just as this disturbance was brought under control, a group of dissidents attempted to stage a coup when Kaunda left the capital for a short engagement. While loyal army units quickly crushed the insurrection, Kaunda was shaken enough to set the date for the referendum at October 1990. He later pushed this back to August 1991 at the opposition's request, to give time for preparation of new-voter rolls and national campaigning.

The opposition came together in February 1991 to form the Movement for Multiparty Democracy (MMD). Led by Chiluba, the MMD maintained a united front throughout the spring and summer, when the National Assembly approved a new constitution allowing multiparty elections. Kaunda mounted a spirited campaign in the period leading up to the voting, which was held at the end of October, but the contest ended with a resounding victory for Chiluba. He got 80 percent of the vote for president, while the MMD won 125 of the 150 parliamentary seats. Kaunda accepted defeat gracefully, yielding power with dignity and remaining as the head of UNIP for another year. In 1992, UNIP splintered when a dissident faction led by Enoch Kavindele left to form the United Democratic Party (UDP), and Kaunda retired from politics completely.

Meanwhile, Chiluba took up the reigns of power vigorously, instituting an economic reform plan and moving against corruption. He was criticized, however, for favoring his own financial backers in giving out positions, and his austerity measures, while applauded by the international economic community, precipitated riots in July 1992. The same month, the Committee for National Unity (CNU) left the MMD. Nevertheless, the MMD scored notable gains in local-government elections held in November, which were marred only by the exceptionally low voter turnout of around 20 percent. The government imposed a state of emergency on March 4, 1993, to counteract an alleged coup plot by radical members of UNIP, but lifted it in May. Corruption scandals continued to plague the government, and in 1994 Kenneth Kaunda announced his return to politics. Chiluba described the country's turmoil as "part of the natural progression from dictatorship to democracy."

Zambia today is one of Africa's most striking success stories. It enjoys a new multiparty democracy that has seen a smooth transition between governments; freedom of speech, assembly, worship, and travel; and a judiciary and trade unions that are independent. However, it will doubtless need to deliver a better life to its people for these notable accomplishments to endure.

MALAWI
Statistical Profile

Capital:	Lilongwe
Area:	45,745 sq. miles
Population:	9,500,000 (1994 est.)
Density:	208 people/sq. mile
Growth Rate:	2.7% (1994 est.)
GDP:	$1,671,000,000
Per Capita Income:	$210
Foreign Debt:	$1,557,000,000
Life Expectancy:	38 (1960), 44 (1992)
Ethnic Groups:	Chewa, Yao, Chipoka, Tonga, Tumbuka, Ngonde
Official Languages:	English and Chichewa
Religions:	Christian (75%), Muslim (10%), Traditional (10%)
Former Colonizer:	Great Britain
Date of Independence:	1964

History

The earliest inhabitants of Malawi were related to the Khoisan speakers who presently live in the Kalahari Desert. They were displaced by successive waves of Iron Age Bantu-speaking immigrants, the first of whom appeared in the second or third century after Christ. By the fifteenth century, the Maravi had established an extensive, if loose, empire stretching from the Congo basin to the Indian Ocean. The king derived his income from long-distance trade, and his power rested on his ability to dispense goods to local chiefs and headmen. The king was more a conciliator than a ruler; even his ability to raise troops depended on the agreement of the local communities with the purpose for which the troops were intended.

The Maravi empire declined in the eighteenth century, and in the early nineteenth century the Ngoni and Yao invaded, imposing their rule on the inhabitants and selling many into slavery. In 1859, the Scottish missionary David Livingstone arrived and began working against the slave trade as well as for conversions to Christianity. His exploits played a considerable role in promoting British interest in the area, which led in 1891 to establishment of a British protectorate. A small but influential community of white settlers moved in, setting up plantations on the most favorable land. The government supported them not only by legitimizing this land grab, but also by imposing taxes that forced Africans to look for wage labor. The scale of migrant labor grew steadily, from 6,000 per year in 1900 to 150,000 per year in 1950.

The combination of land seizures and taxation stimulated opposition by the African population. Some traditional states resisted the onset of British influence, but the British crushed them militarily. The same fate befell the armed uprising in 1915 of messianic leader John Chilembwe. The first modern African political organization, the North Nyasa Native Association, appeared in 1912, and it was joined by a number of similar organizations over the next decades. A colonywide association, the Nyasaland African Congress (NAC), appeared in 1944.

The NAC focused on opposing a settler plan for federation of Nyasaland with Northern and Southern Rhodesia, a plan that would greatly strengthen settler influence. However, in 1953 the British government went ahead and federated the three colonies. The older African leadership protested fruitlessly, but

younger leaders aroused the peasants by championing their resistance to government-imposed agricultural policies. They also invited Dr. Hastings Banda, who had been abroad for 40 years, to assume leadership. Banda proved to be a single-minded and effective orator against the federation, so much so that in March 1959 the authorities declared a state of emergency and detained the NAC leaders. When violence ensued, the imperial government reversed its course, bringing Banda to London for a constitutional conference. Banda led his new party, the Malawi Congress Party (MCP), to an overwhelming electoral victory in August 1961. In 1963, the British dissolved the federation, and in 1964 it granted Malawi independence.

Banda dominated the new country from the beginning, and he increased his power steadily. Even before the British left, he gained the power to discipline MCP party members. Soon after independence, bitter controversies arose over the pace of domestic reforms and how to deal with the white regimes in the region. Banda dealt with these disputes by purging the more radical members of the party and government. His former allies attempted to take power in February 1965, but failed and went into exile. The country became a republic in July 1966 with Banda as its president and his MCP as the sole legal party. A more serious uprising in 1967 failed as well, and in 1970 Banda became president for life, with dictatorial powers. He chose who could run for parliament and expelled members at will. Any deputy who voted against the government in a confidence vote automatically lost his seat. Banda determined who could own a business and who could own land, and he intervened frequently in the judicial process, overturning verdicts with which he disagreed. He maintained his power through both legal and extralegal repression: imprisonment and execution of opponents, control and censorship of communications, and cultivation of a network of informers throughout Malawian society. He kept the upper echelons of government in turmoil through cabinet shuffles, purges, and occasionally stronger measures, including, apparently, assassination. He occasionally loosened the reins a little, as in 1977, when he purged two of his most repressive ministers and released many political prisoners. Similarly, in 1978 he allowed internationally supervised, one-party elections. These measures, however, did nothing to undercut his own control of the country.

One of the bulwarks of Banda's rule was support from the leading Western powers. Not only did he pursue conservative social and economic policies within his country, but he also conducted a maverick policy toward Rhodesia and South Africa, which often put him at odds with other African states but ingratiated him to the West. He cultivated good relations with Portugal while it still held Mozambique, established full diplomatic relations with South Africa in 1967, and refused to support the liberation movements in Mozambique and Rhodesia. He met on numerous occasions with South African and Rhodesian leaders and went so far as to support the South African-backed MNR rebels in Mozambique after it became independent.

Foreign support began to wane with the gradual transition from white to majority rule in the region and with the end of the Cold War. These changes were accompanied by a greater emphasis on human rights and democratic reforms on the part of both lender countries and international agencies. Furthermore, they coincided with increasing pressure for multiparty democracy within Malawi. In 1990, the opposition group Lesoma organized a military wing, the People's Liberation Army of Malawi (PLAM), and in mid-1991 the politically oriented United Front for Multiparty Democracy was founded. In the same year, Banda called for debate in both the party and the legislature on creating a multiparty democracy. Both predictably endorsed continued one-party rule, but the pressure intensified rather than subsided. On March 8, 1992, Catholic clergy throughout the country read a pastoral letter denouncing the country's human rights record, an act for which one archbishop and six bishops were arrested. Protests broke out at the University of Malawi on March 16, and the police fired on the demonstrators, wounding a number. In the same month, the underground United Democratic Party (UDP) was founded. On April 6, police arrested the labor leader Chakufwa Chihana at the national airport as he returned from abroad. Workers and political dissidents staged further demonstrations in May that were met with further violence that killed 40 and wounded hundreds. In the same month, the Paris Club of international donors suspended aid because of Malawi's abysmal human rights record. In September, another clandestine party, the Alliance for Democracy (AFORD), was organized.

On October 18, 1992, Banda surprised the country by announcing that a referendum on multiparty democracy would be held. Shortly thereafter, yet another opposition party, the United Democratic Front (UDF), appeared, but late in the month the government arrested hundreds of activists for their membership in the party. Nevertheless, the referendum on multiparty democracy took place on June 14, 1993. The electorate overwhelmingly endorsed change while rejecting the president's life term. Multiparty elections followed in May 1994, and Bakili Muluzi of the UDF replaced Banda as the head of state.

If Malawi's political future looks hopeful, it's economic outlook is discouraging. Despite, or perhaps because of, Banda's conservative economic policies emphasizing capitalism, agricultural development for export, and foreign investment, the country is one of the poorest in the world. In such circumstances, the task of replacing Banda's repressive institutions with a stable liberal government will be a formidable challenge indeed.

ANGOLA
Statistical Profile

Capital:	Luanda
Area:	481,351 sq. miles
Population:	11,200,000

Density:	23 people/sq. mile
Growth Rate:	2.7%
GDP:	$7,700,000,000
Per Capita Income:	$620
Foreign Debt:	$7,628,000,000
Life Expectancy:	33 (1960), 46 (1992)
Ethnic Groups:	Ovimbundu (37%), Mbundu (23%), Kongo (14%), Lunda-Chokwe (9%), Ngangulea (7%); 30,000 Europeans plus *mesticos*, mainly in the cities
Official Language:	Portuguese
Religions:	Catholic (68%), Protestant (20%), Traditional (12%)
Former Colonizer:	Portugal
Date of Independence:	1975

History

Originally home to Khoisan-speaking hunter-gatherers, Angola saw the intrusion of successive waves of Iron Age Bantu-speakers during the first millennium after Christ. By the time the Portuguese arrived in the fifteenth century, the territory contained 8 major ethnic groups and close to 100 smaller ones. Most were organized into "stateless societies" or small chiefdoms, but the Kongo kingdom and a few of its neighbors in the north had attained considerable size and political sophistication. Portuguese influence undermined the older states and kept new ones from rising in their place. Although the Europeans stuck to the coast in small trading enclaves, their insatiable demand for slaves kept the area in a state of turmoil. They did not move to assert control over the interior until the nineteenth century, at first in an attempt to create plantations based on forced labor to compensate for the end of the slave trade, and later to fulfill the conditions required for recognition of territorial claims established at the Berlin Conference in 1884–1885. The pacification campaigns ended officially in 1922, but some enclaves resisted even longer. It was not until after World War II that the whole area came to be securely dominated by Europeans.

In order to both secure their political control and fulfill the colony's economic promise, the Portuguese encouraged white immigration. The number of Portuguese settlers rose from 10,000 in 1900 to 80,000 in 1950 to 350,000 in 1974. Some immigrants were criminals offered the choice of Angola or jail, but most were illiterate peasants looking for a good life of plentiful land and cheap labor. While most settlers ended up staying in the cities to take advantage of opportunities in commerce, the widespread system of forced labor on transportation projects and commercial plantations—the backbone of the colonial economy—embittered the African population and contributed substantially to the rise of postwar nationalism.

Originally fostered by cultural organizations, African political consciousness became radicalized when it ran into implacable opposition from the white settlers and the government. The Portuguese dictator Salazar made the country's colonies into provinces of a unitary, multicontinental dictatorship, and he had no intention of permitting the Africans to participate in politics, let alone create an independent country. Numerous clashes occurred in the 1950s, and in 1961 two large-scale revolts broke out.

The first took place in the capital, Luanda, and was led by intellectuals and labor leaders in the Popular Movement for the Liberation of Angola (MPLA). They had ties to the liberation movements in Portuguese Guinea and Mozambique and were supported by the Soviet Union. They espoused a nationalism opposed to both colonial rule and tribalism and called for social justice as an integral part of national liberation. Their leader was Agostinho Neto.

The second uprising began in the rural areas of the far north, a region called "Bakongo," and was led by the Union of the Populations of Northern Angola (UPNA), which later became the UPA and ultimately the National Front for the Liberation of Angola (FNLA). This movement spread to the eastern and southeastern portions of the country, but in

1966 southern leaders, frustrated by the dominant role played by northern tribes, split off to form the Union for the Total Independence of Angola (UNITA). The FNLA's leader, Holden Roberto, was vehemently anticommunist. His party relied on support from Zaire, which itself relied on support from the CIA. Jonas Savimbi, the leader of UNITA, eschewed a rigid ideology and received support from South Africa, Communist China, and even right-wing Portuguese forces.

During the 1960s and early 1970s, these three factions (the MPLA, the FNLA, and UNITA) were united by their opposition to continued Portuguese rule, which their protracted resistance helped undermine. In 1974, dissident junior officers in Portugal staged a coup that toppled the dictatorship, and the new regime proved anxious to divest the country of its colonial heritage. Most Portuguese settlers left for the home country, while the three African parties formed a transitional coalition government.

The precarious unity did not survive until elections could be held and independence proclaimed, which was scheduled for November 11, 1975. Afraid that the election would bring power to the left-wing MPLA, the United States backed an invasion of northern Angola in March 1975 by the Zairian army on behalf of the FNLA. The South Africans feared that an MPLA-dominated government would support the liberation struggle in Namibia, so in July they attacked in the south in support of UNITA. To help the MPLA, Cuba sent first advisors and then combat troops, who began fighting in November. With their support and Soviet weapons, the MPLA occupied the capital upon independence and expelled the Zairians and South Africans by March 1976.

As it gained control of the country, the MPLA created a socialist government with Neto at its head. He survived an attempted coup by a former interior minister in May 1977, convened a party congress in December that made the country a Marxist-Leninist state, and had the rival position of prime minister abolished in a major governmental reor-

ganization in 1978. He died on September 10, 1979, having created a stable enough government to allow Jose Eduardo dos Santos to succeed him without incident.

With the country in a shambles from a decade of guerrilla warfare, the abrupt withdrawal of the Portuguese, and the recent conventional fighting, the new People's Republic of Angola needed peace and stability above all else. Unfortunately, it remained a battleground in the global struggle between the United States and the Soviet Union and at the same time a front-line state in the struggle against South African apartheid. Neto and dos Santos did what they could to foster good relations, and the aid that flowed from it, with both Western and Communist countries, restoring ties to Portugal in 1978 and signing the Lome Convention with the European Economic Community in 1985. Gulf Oil Company played a major role in developing Angolan oilfields, but the United States, still smarting from the defeat of its proxies, refused to recognize Angola.

Furthermore, Angola continued to host 25,000 Cuban soldiers and supported the Southwest African People's Organization (SWAPO) in its struggle against South Africa. South Africa attacked SWAPO and Angolan forces and supported renewed guerrilla operations by UNITA in retaliation. Discontent over the governments' socialist policies, particularly the collectivization of agriculture, and resentment of the Cuban presence fueled support for the dissident movement.

The combination of guerrilla operations and conventional warfare debilitated the Angolan economy, while the protracted struggle proved a drag on South Africa as well. In the mid-1980s, the United States openly supported UNITA, and at the same time acted as mediator between the warring governments. A basis for compromise appeared in the symmetry between Angola's support for SWAPO and reliance on Cuban troops and South Africa's support for UNITA and UNITA's reliance on South African troops. It took several years of negotiations to hammer out an agreement, but the New York Accord of July 20, 1988, stipulated that Cuban and South African troops would withdraw from Angola, Angola would cease supporting SWAPO, and South Africa would cease backing UNITA and begin steps toward Namibian independence. Over the next several years, the Cubans and South Africans withdrew and Namibia became independent.

As these foreign issues were resolved, the Angolan factions also worked out an internal settlement. With the Soviet Union collapsing and UNITA resurgent despite South Africa's disengagement, the Angolan government moved from single-party socialism to multiparty democracy. In 1990, it renounced Marxist-Leninism and endorsed a multiparty system. It revised the constitution in March 1991 and held peace talks with UNITA that led to a cease-fire at the end of May and an agreement to merge the two armies and to hold elections by the end of 1992. Savimbi ran for president against dos Santos and nine other candidates, and the two leaders agreed to form a coalition government no matter which of them won. In the elections, held September 29, 1992, dos Santos gained 49 percent of the vote and Savimbi won 40 percent. The MPLA won 129 seats in the National Assembly to UNITA's 70, with 31 going to other parties.

Unfortunately, the campaign was marred by increasingly bitter accusations and some violence, and the election itself was marred by allegations of fraud. When UNITA formally protested, the government agreed to a recount and an independent investigation, which declared the results valid. Dos Santos suggested a runoff and formation of the planned government of national unity, but insisted that Savimbi recognize the results of the election and continue the demobilization of his forces. Savimbi refused, and the government cracked down on UNITA supporters in areas it controlled. UNITA boycotted parliament and renewed the civil war in earnest from its bases in the southeastern third of the country. Open warfare lasted from late 1992 to late 1994,

when the two sides signed a new peace accord. Tensions continued into 1995, although Savimbi and dos Santos finally met face to face in May, the same time a force of 7,640 UN peacekeepers began to arrive.

Angola's promising moves toward peace and democracy floundered in 1992, and the return to peace is still fragile. The new parliament passed a series of measures designed to promote human rights, including an end to capital punishment, the institution of the right of *habeus corpus,* a guarantee of independent unions, freedom of assembly, greater freedom of speech, and an independent judiciary. However, both government forces and UNITA were guilty of gross violations of human rights during the war, and until peace is solidly established, the parliament's good intentions are likely to remain just that.

MOZAMBIQUE
Statistical Profile

Capital:	Maputo
Area:	309,494 sq. miles
Population:	15,800,000 (1994 est.)
Density:	51 people/sq. mile
Growth Rate:	2.7% (1994 est.)
GDP:	$965,000,000
Per Capita Income:	$60
Foreign Debt:	$4,153,000,000
Life Expectancy:	37 (1960), 47 (1992)
Ethnic Groups:	Makua-Lomwe (40%), Thonga, Chopi, Tonga, Shona, Makonde
Official Language:	Portuguese
Religions:	Traditional (41%), Christian (32%), Muslim (25%)
Former Colonizer:	Portugal
Date of Independence:	1975

History

Most Mozambicans descend from Bantu-speaking peoples who immigrated into the area from the north and west during the first millennium A.D., although a secondary wave flowed in from the south during the Mfecane upheavals of the 1820s and 1830s. The Portuguese first explored the coastline in the 1490s, and in the sixteenth century they set up coastal trading enclaves and established outposts far up the Zambezi River, close to the source of the gold trade. Some Portuguese entered into private alliances with the paramount chief who controlled the area, a ruler of the Karanga (a branch of the Shona tribe). He rewarded them with grants of land that made them into chiefs in his kingdom, politically independent from Portugal. These land grants made Mozambique the area of greatest European penetration before the nineteenth century. On their lands, these *prazeiros*, or concessionaires, ruled absolutely, combining the traditional powers of African chiefs with European concepts of private ownership and compulsory labor.

The high point of Portuguese influence came in the seventeenth century. The Portuguese crown expanded its formal control by recognizing the monomotapa's land grants and by granting land on its own, bringing both types of *prazeiros* under its rule, at least nominally. In addition, the monomotapa converted to Catholicism in 1628. However, late in the century, an African vassal rebelled, crushed the monomotapa's armies, and then destroyed most of the Portuguese outposts. The *prazeiros* remained as essentially independent rulers through the eighteenth century, while the Portuguese colonial government languished. The crown tried to outlaw the *prazeiros* system in the nineteenth century, but its decrees had little effect, and its authority was further reduced by the Ngoni invasion of the southern half of the colony in 1830. Although the invaders focused more on subduing African than European resistance, and even accepted formal Portuguese overlordship, they dominated the southern interior in practice.

In 1885, the Ngoni sold mineral rights in the area to the British South Africa Company, and in 1894 a vassal attacked a Portuguese outpost. Having finally crushed a 30-year rebellion by *prazeiros* in the Zambezi Valley, the Portuguese turned on the Ngoni kingdom and defeated it. At the same time, Mozambique came under the influence of much larger changes in the surrounding region. The southern part of the colony became a labor reserve for the great mining enterprises in neighboring South Africa, while the port at Maputo became a major outlet for their output. In the north, the Portuguese granted concessions to three foreign firms, giving them virtual free rein over the territory in exchange for regular taxes and the maintenance of order. Following the blueprint of the influential colonial official Antonio Enes, European immigration was encouraged, and Africans in both regions were subjected to onerous forced labor. The Native Assistance Code of 1921 offered the possibility of citizenship, but only through a process of assimilation that was beyond the reach of all but a handful of Africans. Ties between Portugal and the colony strengthened steadily. In 1930, protectionist trade policies bound the two economically. In 1951, Mozambique became an overseas province. In 1972, it became an overseas state.

The last change was a measure of desperation, an attempt to counter a nationalist insurgency that had been growing since 1964. Influenced by the anticolonial movements sweeping through the rest of Africa, concerned by increasing Portuguese settlement and investment since World War II, and frustrated by Portugal's adamant opposition to African political activity, a group of exiles and radical intellectuals founded the Front for the Liberation of Mozambique (Frelimo) in 1962. In 1964, it began a guerrilla campaign that soon brought the northern countryside under its control. At first, the movement's program was narrowly nationalist, but after the assassination of its first leader, Eduardo Mondlane, it adopted a more radical, socialist platform. When a coup by junior officers in 1974 toppled the dictatorship in Portugal, Frelimo negotiated an independence that left it in charge. Samora Machel, the party's leader, became the first president of the People's Republic of Mozambique.

After winning power, Frelimo moved to create an "Afro-Marxist" state. In 1977, its Third

Party Congress formally declared Mozambique to be a "vanguard Marxist-Leninist state," and in the same year Frelimo signed a 20-year treaty of friendship and cooperation with the Soviet Union. The new regime abolished private property, creating people's stores, cooperative factories, and agricultural collectives. It nationalized the banks, industry, most farms, and medical services. It challenged the Catholic Church by officially adopting atheism, and it created people's tribunals to promote popular administration of justice. A total of 27,000 delegates were elected to representative bodies that formed a pyramid from local councils at the bottom to the national Popular Assembly at the top.

These revolutionary social and economic programs inevitably created turmoil and discontent, which came at the same time Mozambique faced other formidable challenges. In the economic sphere, the country was burdened by the legacy of 10 years of civil war, and it was hobbled by the flight of all but about 15,000 of the 230,000 whites. Deprived of their capital and their managerial and business skills, the economy declined after the civil war. As early as 1980, Machel introduced economic reforms aimed at promoting economic recovery by reducing inefficiency and corruption and relaxing socialist policies. In particular, he moved to reduce the government's role in small businesses and to promote foreign investment.

However, before these moderate reforms could have much effect, the country faced a much greater problem in foreign affairs. As a revolutionary government bordering both Rhodesia and South Africa, Mozambique became the most forward of the "front-line states," acting as a base for nationalist forces operating against both countries and cutting its economic ties to them. The economic hardships of this breach cut both ways, and the world community, generous with words against the white regimes, proved stingy with actual aid. Furthermore, the white regimes struck back. Not only did their aircraft and commandos stage raids against their own dis-

sidents, they also attacked Mozambican military and economic targets.

Worse still, the Rhodesian CIA helped Mozambican dissidents form a guerrilla movement called the Mozambican National Resistance (MNR or Renamo), which survived the collapse of the Rhodesian white regime in 1980 and harried the Frelimo government throughout the 1980s. It drew its support not only from South Africa, but also from genuine discontent, particularly among collectivized farmers in the countryside. By 1983, it controlled extensive territory in the rural hinterlands and was carrying out widespread economic sabotage. In 1984, neighboring Zimbabwe sent about 7,000 troops to aid the Frelimo government by guarding the transportation lines that connected it to the sea, while Frelimo signed the Nkomati Accords with South Africa, in which each agreed not to support the other's dissidents. MNR activity continued, however, and the economy continued to deteriorate.

In 1986, Machel was killed in an airplane crash when his plane went radically off course and hit a mountain. Rumors suggested that the South Africans had used electronic warfare to confuse the plane's instruments, but an international inquiry concluded that it was an accident. Nevertheless, Mozambicans ransacked the Malawi embassy in Maputo in retaliation for its rumored involvement in the affair. On November 4, the party's central committee elected Joaquim Chissano to be the new head of the party and the state, and he redoubled the efforts against the MNR. His efforts proved vain, however, and by 1989 the insurgents had virtually brought the economy to its knees. In early 1990, a new force entered the fray, as civil servants, doctors, nurses, and teachers went on strike, fed up with demands for austerity. The government met the unprecedented wave of strikes with reforms, both by conceding better salaries and working conditions to the strikers and by introducing a new constitution guaranteeing direct elections by secret ballot to national offices, the right to strike, the right to own property, and an end to capital punishment.

The concessions ended the strikes, but not the calls for reform. In March 1990, former Frelimo soldiers petitioned for multiparty elections. In the same month, exiles meeting in Cologne, Germany, issued a manifesto calling for a cease-fire and a government of national unity. Both Frelimo and the MNR voiced their readiness to discuss an end to the fighting, but the talks dragged on through 1991. They finally resulted in three accords in which the MNR recognized the Frelimo government, the rules governing party registration were established, and free private media was legalized. A cease-fire agreement capped the talks in October 1992 and was accompanied by a commitment to hold multiparty elections within one year. Afonso Dhlakama, the leader of the MNR, announced that he would stand as a candidate against Chissano, and altogether 15 parties were formed. Nevertheless, Chissano and Frelimo won the elections in October 1994. The MNR did well enough to hope for a cabinet seat and governorships in its strongholds, but it did not get either when appointments were announced in late 1994 and early 1995. Nevertheless, the country remained relatively peaceful, and the new political process appears to have worked.

The two sides agreed to integrate their opposing armies into a single national army, and the people's tribunals have been replaced by an independent judiciary. Some human rights abuses continue, however. By the end of the war, over 600,000 people had been killed, about 1.5 million had fled as refugees, and six million Mozambicans remained on the verge of starvation. In the mid-1990s, the government continues to face formidable problems.

ZIMBABWE
Statistical Profile

Capital:	Harare
Area:	150,803 sq. miles
Population:	11,200,000 (1994 est.)
Density:	74 people/sq. mile
Growth Rate:	3.0% (1994 est.)

GDP:	$5,543,000,000
Per Capita Income:	$570
Foreign Debt:	$3,085,000,000
Life Expectancy:	45 (1960), 60 (1992)
Ethnic Groups:	Shona (80%), Ndebele (19%), several thousand Europeans
Official Language:	English
Religions:	Traditional (50%), Christian (24%), Muslim (24%)
Former Colonizer:	Great Britain
Date of Independence:	1965, 1980

History

Zimbabwe's original inhabitants were Khoisan speakers, but Bantu speakers from the north gradually absorbed or displaced them during the first millennium A.D. These people began trading gold with the peoples along the coast before the year 1000, and this lucrative activity was continued and expanded by the second wave of Bantu speakers who moved in a few centuries later. These people, the Shona, established the first significant civilizations in Africa south of the equator: the Mutapa Empire, which rose in the fourteenth century, peaked in the fifteenth, and declined in the sixteenth; and the Changamire Empire, which replaced the Mutapa Empire in the seventeenth century and lasted until the Ndebele invasion that resulted from the Mfecane disturbances in the 1840s. The core group of the Ndebele, Ngoni speakers who had mastered the Zulu's revolutionary military techniques, established themselves as the ruling caste; Sotho speakers who traveled with them formed a middle stratum. The native Shona formed the lower class.

The Portuguese in Mozambique established outposts near Zimbabwe's eastern border in the sixteenth century but the Europeans remained a peripheral presence until the end of the nineteenth century, when the discovery of diamonds and gold nearby in South Africa stimulated Cecil Rhodes' interest. In 1888, his agents obtained the deceitful Rudd Concession, which the Ndebele king, Lobengula, thought ceded mineral rights but which

Rhodes claimed gave him sovereignty. This concession became the basis for British rule. In 1890, a "pioneer column" established a settlement at Salisbury (Harare). In 1893, the English defeated the Ndebele in battle, and by 1897 had crushed a rebellion involving both the Ndebele and the Shona.

After the defeat of this first *chimurenga*, or war of liberation, the number of whites in "Rhodesia" increased steadily, rising from 12,000 in 1904 to 24,000 in 1911 to well over 200,000 in 1960. At first, the whites were administered by Rhodes' British South Africa Company, but in 1922 they gained self-rule. The franchise was theoretically open to anybody, but property qualifications restricted it in practice to whites, and they gradually established a stranglehold on the African population. The 1930 Land Apportionment Act gave them the better half of the colony's land even though they comprised less than 10 percent of its population, and it prohibited Africans from growing cash crops in competition with them. The 1934 Industrial Conciliation Act barred Africans from skilled occupations in industry. The two acts together made the Africans into a vast impoverished labor pool forced to supplement their inadequate farm output with wage labor at subsistence levels for the Europeans.

The consolidation of settler rule culminated in 1953 with the creation of the Central African Federation. Combining Rhodesia's thriving farms and factories with Northern Rhodesia's minerals and Nyasaland's teeming population, the Federation gave the settlers the basis for a powerful state.

However, this consolidation galvanized African nationalism, which had gained strength only slowly in the preceding decades. Ndebele in the colony had formed the Rhodesian Bantu Voters' Association and Shona had formed the Rhodesian Native Association as early as the 1920s. In 1934, a short-lived African National Congress (ANC) was formed. After World War II, unions took the lead, staging a successful railroad strike in 1945 and a general strike in 1948, but African political consciousness really emerged in the early 1950s. Joshua Nkomo became the president of the anti-federation All-African Convention in 1952, but the convention declined after federation and was replaced in 1955 by the militant City Youth League. In 1957, a new ANC formed, but the government banned it in 1959. When its organizers re-formed as the National Democratic Party (NDP), the government banned it at the end of 1961. The African nationalists then formed the Zimbabwe African People's Union (ZAPU), which was duly banned in 1962. This time, while some members re-formed as the People's Caretaker Council within Rhodesia, Nkomo maintained ZAPU in exile. The next year a militant splinter group led by Ndabaningi Sithole formed the Zimbabwe African National Union (ZANU) and began training in Communist China for guerrilla war.

Amid the growing tension, even some settlers leaders began to see a need for concessions to the African majority. However, the majority of settlers opposed all such moves as a threat to their privileged socio-economic position. In 1958, when Prime Minister Garfield Todd attempted to satisfy some African demands, they replaced him with Edgar Whitehead. In 1961, the settlers approved a new constitution that proposed eventual parity between blacks and whites, but they did so only because it seemed to promise independence from Great Britain long before such parity could be achieved. In 1963, the year the British dissolved the Federation, the Rhodesian electorate dumped Whitehead for being too soft and voted in the right-wing Rhodesian Front (RF). In the face of Great Britain's refusal to grant independence until the colony made some concessions to black political interests, Ian Smith took over as RF party leader and the colony's prime minister, cracked down on both ZAPU and ZANU, and held a referendum that showed overwhelming white support for a unilateral declaration of independence (UDI). In elections in May 1965, the RF won all 50 upper roll seats, and Smith's government declared independence unilaterally on November 11.

Great Britain responded to the UDI by imposing mild sanctions, which were strengthened and made mandatory by the United Nations in 1968, although the Western powers (including Great Britain) honored them only intermittently. The British attempted to negotiate a settlement with Smith's government in 1966, 1968, and 1971. The Rhodesians rejected the British proposals in the first two instances, and the agreement reached by the two sides in the third failed when the British insisted that it be acceptable to all Rhodesians. Bishop Abel Muzorewa organized a new party, the African National Council, that mobilized African opinion against the agreement. Meanwhile, the Rhodesians adopted a new constitution in 1969 that gave 85,000 whites and 7,465 blacks the vote. In 1970, Rhodesia declared itself a republic.

While the British talked, the Africans in ZANU and then ZAPU gradually formed guerrilla armies. They launched an armed struggle in 1966. The first battles ended in African defeats, but by the early 1970s they began to do better. Moreover, they were able to open a new front by cooperating with the Frelimo rebels fighting the Portuguese in Mozambique to the east.

Events in the Portuguese colonies took on even greater importance in the mid-1970s, for the collapse of the Portuguese empire inspired the Western powers, in particular the United States, to reconsider the support they had been giving the Rhodesians. With the insurgents' power so effectively demonstrated, the U.S. reversed course and began to press the white government to make some accommodations. Even the South African government had adopted a policy at least ostensibly promoting stability. Under international pressure, the Smith government began negotiations with Muzorewa's party, which became the "United" ANC, or UANC. When these talks broke down, Smith switched to negotiations with Nkomo, but these, too, soon proved fruitless. American Secretary of State Henry Kissinger met with Smith personally in 1976 and de-

manded that he agree to majority rule within two years, albeit with conditions that guaranteed indefinite white control of the government. Smith agreed to that demand and also agreed to attend a conference in Geneva with the UANC, ZAPU, and both factions of a recently divided ZANU, which were led by Sithole and Robert Mugabe. Mugabe and Nkomo (ZAPU) formed the Patriotic Front (PF) for the negotiations, but could not get Sithole and Muzorewa to join. When the talks broke down, the latter two participants returned to Salisbury, while the PF continued the armed struggle.

Despite the failure of the conference, Smith's agreement to negotiate caused a right-wing rebellion in his party, but he realized that the pressure of the guerrilla war and the international economic sanctions made some sort of resolution imperative. Smith held elections in mid-1977 to get a mandate to negotiate an "internal settlement," which he won. After brushing aside another Anglo-American proposal, which the PF also rejected, he embarked in December 1977 on talks with Muzorewa and Sithole. These talks produced an agreement by March 1978 that created a transitional government that would write a new constitution and hold elections that included the African majority. But the agreement also contained provisions that essentially guaranteed continued white dominance during the transition and under the new government.

The agreement failed to end either the guerrilla war or the international sanctions, so in August 1978 Smith attempted to split the PF by negotiating secretly with Nkomo. When these talks yielded nothing but the animosity of the betrayed partners on both sides, Smith attempted to improve his international standing through a visit to the United States that was sponsored by conservative senators. Once again his efforts bore little fruit.

In January 1979, the white electorate approved the new constitution in a referendum, and elections in April made Bishop Muzorewa the first black head of state. The election was widely denounced as a fraud, and the government it produced still could not end the sanctions or the war. Therefore, just five months after the implementation of this internal settlement, the government agreed to a new round of negotiations intended to create a genuine and lasting settlement.

Conceived at a Commonwealth meeting by British Prime Minister Margaret Thatcher, Zambia's President Kenneth Kaunda, and Tanzania's President Julius Nyerere, these negotiations were held at Lancaster House in London in the fall of 1979. With Thatcher pressuring the Rhodesians and the others pressuring the PF, the two sides agreed to a plan in which the country briefly would revert to colonial status under Great Britain. During this time, the two sides would stop fighting, lay down their arms, and hold an election; then the new government would take its place in the community of nations. Amazingly, this is precisely what happened. The fighting stopped. The guerrillas and soldiers reported to their assembly points, laid down their weapons, and began to form a new, national army. A free and fair election was held, which was won by Mugabe's ZANU, and on April 18, 1980, just four months after the signing of the agreement, the British governor-general turned over administration to the newly elected prime minister. Rhodesia had become Zimbabwe.

The happy transition did not, however, guarantee a happy ending. Mugabe made genuine efforts to conciliate not only the whites but also his rivals, and he proved more pragmatist than ideologue in his economic policies. Many whites stayed on, and Nkomo took an important post in the government, but after a honeymoon period, economic and political problems began to grow. Shortly after independence, whites were dismayed when a black cabinet official was acquitted in the killing of a white farmer under an antiterrorist law that had previously given white officials immunity after killing blacks. The

government discovered and forestalled an alleged coup plot involving a white member of parliament in December 1981. In May 1982, it arrested other whites for stockpiling arms and planning acts of sabotage. In July 1982, white airforce officers in league with South Africa blew up planes at an air base, and in the years that followed, emigration by skilled whites became a serious drain on the economy.

The government's relations with ZAPU also deteriorated. Activists from the two parties fought a number of street battles in 1980, and ZANU party offices were blown up in December 1981. In early 1982, Mugabe dismissed Nkomo from the cabinet because huge caches of arms had been found on property belonging to him and his followers, and in March the government arrested two former ZAPU commanders. In June, dissidents attacked Mugabe's own home. Violence in Matebeleland, ZAPU's heartland, grew steadily worse during the year, and in early 1983 Mugabe's government cracked down. Fearful of allowing a rebel movement that could be manipulated by the South Africans like they had manipulated the MNR in neighboring Mozambique, it sent in the Fifth Army Brigade, an elite unit composed of ethnic Shona who had been trained by the North Koreans. The brigade moved ruthlessly to suppress the dissidents, killing numerous civilians in the process. Over a thousand people died, but by the middle of 1983 the nascent rebellion had been crushed. Fighting between ZANU and ZAPU activists created such turmoil that the vote scheduled for June 1985 had to be pushed back a full year.

Amid this continued turmoil, Mugabe retained and expanded the emergency powers originally enacted by Smith's government. At the first ZANU party congress in 20 years, held in August 1984, Mugabe strengthened his control over the party, while the party endorsed his plan to make the country into a one-party state. The voters endorsed this program; they gave ZANU an overwhelming victory when the elections were finally held in

July 1986. In September 1987, the government abolished the reserved seats and separate elections for whites that had been established in 1980 (despite the fact that no changes to the constitution were supposed to take place for 10 years). In October, it created an executive presidency with broad powers, including those previously held by the prime minister and those heretofore covered by the perennially renewed emergency legislation. Mugabe continued his drive for power in December 1989 when he arranged a long-discussed merger of ZANU with ZAPU to form ZANU-PF, with ZANU definitely the senior partner. He also changed the legislature into a unicameral body in which 20 of the 150 seats would be appointed by him and 10 would go automatically to leaders loyal to him.

He did not attain his goal of a one-party state, however. Four parties disputed the March 1990 elections with his ZANU-PF: the Zimbabwe Unity Movement (ZUM), ZANU-Ndonga, the UANC, and the National Democratic Union (NDU). Mugabe and his party carried the election by a landslide once again, but they faced strikes and increasing criticism of the country's human rights record. A controversy over a government land redistribution program that involved forced sales by whites of large commercial farms dominated Zimbabwian politics in 1993 and 1994, but the controversy was handled through the legal system and the measure did not disrupt the country's rapidy expanding economy. ZANU-PF won legislative elections again in April 1995 with 118 of the 120 elected seats; ZANU-Ndonga gained the other two. Mugabe won the presidency again in April 1996 in an election that was uncontested after his two opponents, Muzorewa and Sithole, withdrew.

Zimbabwe remains a multiparty democracy despite ZANU's domination of the political scene. The judiciary is relatively independent, although recent legislation has curtailed the scope of judicial review and the Law and Order Maintenance Act gives the country's Central Intelligence Organization wide powers. The press is dominated by state-controlled media, but small private papers are allowed. The right of assembly is not constitutionally guaranteed but is generally respected, and unions are permitted with some restrictions. Freedom of religion and travel are respected. In the late 1980s, Zimbabwe seemed destined to become a one-party dictatorship, but the movement for multiparty democracy now appears to have won out.

CHAPTER

Lower South Africa

INTRODUCTION

Lower South Africa contains two countries with large territories but small populations, Namibia and Botswana; two countries that are tiny enclaves within South Africa, Swaziland and Lesotho; and the large, populous nation of South Africa. The ecologies of these countries range from arid desert to fertile prairies to tropical forests, and their economies range from hunting and gathering to modern industry. All but Namibia were ruled by Great Britain at one point; Namibia passed from German to South African control before independence. All are currently democracies, although Lesotho has a parliamentary system without parties. South Africa is the most prominent country in the area both because of its economic power and because of its recent spectacular transition from white rule to black majority rule and the accompanying transition from apartheid to integration and affirmative action.

BOTSWANA
Statistical Profile

Capital:	Gaborone
Area:	231,803 sq. miles
Population:	1,400,000 (1994 est.)
Density:	6 people/sq. mile
Growth Rate:	2.7% (1994 est.)
GDP:	$3,700,000,000
Per Capita Income:	$2,790
Foreign Debt:	$538,000,000
Life Expectancy:	46 (1960), 68 (1992)
Ethnic Groups:	Majority are Tswana, divided into eight major groups: Banangwato (35%); Khoisan-speaking Sarwa and the related Bakalahari; and a small number of Europeans
Official Language:	English
Religions:	Traditional (67%), Christian (30%), Muslim (3%)
Former Colonizer:	Great Britain
Date of Independence:	1966

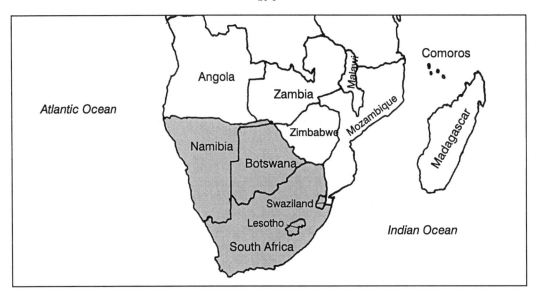

Lower South Africa

History

Only Khoisan-speaking hunter-gatherers inhabited Botswana until the eighteenth century, when Tswana Sotho speakers moved into the most fertile region in the southeast. The newcomers organized small kingdoms in which the royal family and a narrow aristocracy dominated the majority of commoners and serfs by virtue of their wealth in cattle, their right to tribute labor, and their right to appoint headmen. The headmen, in turn, allocated land to the others. The Tswana lived in sizable towns (their capital had 30,000 people) and satellite villages. As the nineteenth century progressed, the wealthier among them became increasingly involved in the region's burgeoning economy. They sold grain, cattle, and oxen to travelers and invested the profits in plows and wagons. Khama III, king of the Ngwato, even organized a state-owned trading company.

The area's growing economic ties to the outside were accompanied by growing dangers from outside as well. In the 1830s, the Kololo and Ndebele devastated the area while passing through on their way north, and by the 1870s pressure came from both Afrikaners and Cecil Rhodes' British South Africa Company.

The Tswana kings turned to the British government for help, and in 1885 the northern portion of their kingdom became the protectorate of Bechuanaland, while the southern portion became a crown colony. The southern colony disappeared into the Cape Colony a decade later, but the protectorate remained autonomous, administered by a commissioner responsible to the colonial office and advised by three councils: one of African chiefs, one of European businessmen and farmers, and one of delegates from both of the others. Most of the inhabitants of Bechuanaland suffered from economic changes in the twentieth century that made it essentially a labor pool for South Africa, but the upper class managed to profit from economic change and stood ready to take over when the British withdrew. In 1960, a new constitution introduced a legislative council, but its special provisions for whites provoked vehement African opposition. In 1965, the constitution was replaced by another providing for nonracial elections to a national assembly, an advisory house of chiefs, and a president elected by the Assembly. In 1966, Bechuanaland became the Republic of Botswana.

The first president of the new nation was Seretse Khama, grandson of Khama III and head of the Botswana Democratic Party (BDP), which had won 28 of 31 seats in the pre-independence elections. The BDP drew its strength from the rural masses, which gave it an advantage over both the narrowly based traditional rulers and the more radical parties, which represented the intelligentsia and urban workers. The party followed a conservative modernizing course, remaining sensitive to the hopes and fears of the peasant majority while promoting foreign investment and planned development. Blessed with diamond mines that opened in the late 1960s and remarkably unencumbered by both the corruption and the overly ambitious investment that were so rampant elsewhere on the continent, the country's GDP grew by 14.5 percent per year in the 1970s and 9.8 percent per year in the 1980s, a record exceeding every other African nation by far and even bettering such Asian dynamos as Korea, Hong Kong, and Singapore. The country was one of the 20 poorest in the world at independence, and is now one of the richest in Africa. Both contributing to and benefiting from this growth has been the political stability that kept Seretse Khama in office until his death in 1980 and his successor Quett Masire in power since then.

The growing wealth did not benefit all sections of the country equally, however, and socio-political tensions did exist. The vast majority of the people remained subsistence farmers, and employment opportunities for urban workers did not grow as fast as their numbers. Opposition parties therefore continued to exist. The Botswana People's Party (BPP) advanced a moderate socialist program, while the Botswana National Front (BNF) attempted to link urban radicalism and rural populism. In the late 1970s, the BDP launched an offensive against them, labeling the BPP's socialism "subversive" and calling the BNF a potential terrorist threat, but the parties continued to operate, and the BNF actually registered gains in the 1984 elections.

The country's biggest challenge in the late 1970s and the 1980s was weathering the storms over Rhodesia and South Africa. Botswana opposed the whites' racist policies and counted itself among the "front-line" states, but both geography and political philosophy led it to tread carefully. It adopted a policy of accepting black exiles and refugees but refusing to allow them to use Botswana as a military base. The most dangerous confrontation with Rhodesia actually came after the whites were defeated, when fighters from ZAPU tried to rally in Botswana after their suppression by the ZANU-dominated government. The two governments eventually defused this crisis, but the conflict between South Africa and the insurgent African National Congress (ANC) proved harder to contain. The weak Botswanan army could exercise little control along the lengthy South African border, so ANC fighters and South African commandos crossed it with increasing disregard for Botswanan sovereignty. A security pact between the two countries signed in February 1986 did little to stop the raids, and only the coming of peace to South Africa restored peace to Botswana.

In 1991, the opposition parties formed a coalition calling for reforms to the political system, which contains a number of features favorable to the ruling BDP that help account for its permanent domination of Botswanan politics. On the one hand, rules barring chiefs from running for the assembly hindered political activity by traditionalists. On the other hand, the lack of absentee ballots for the 20 percent of the population who are migrant workers and the gerrymandering of urban electoral districts to contain 70 percent more people than the rural ones combined to minimize the political clout of the left.

The reformist efforts did not bear fruit, but Botswana nevertheless can be counted among Africa's true multiparty democracies. In elections in October 1994, the opposition scored unexpected gains, although the BDP retained a majority. The judiciary is independent, and there are no restrictions on religion, travel, or association, including the right to join unions. The press is free and vigorous; in 1992 it helped expose a land scandal involving top government officials. The government does have extensive potential powers under security laws, but these remain theoretical. Botswana is an example of an African country that has managed to remain a multiparty democracy while making remarkable economic strides.

NAMIBIA
Statistical Profile

Capital:	Windhoek
Area:	318,259 sq. miles
Population:	1,600,000 (1994 est.)
Density:	5 people/sq. mile
Growth Rate:	3.3% (1994 est.)
GDP:	$2,106,000,000
Per Capita Income:	$1,610
Debt:	$27,000,000
Life Expectancy:	42 (1960), 58 (1992)
Ethnic Groups:	Ovambo (50%), Damara, Herero, Kavango, Lozi, Tswana, Nama, Orlam, Afrikaners (4%), other Europeans (2%)
Official Languages:	English, German, and Afrikaans
Religions:	Christian (90%), Traditional (10%)
Former Colonizers:	Germany, South Africa
Date of Independence:	1990

History

Khoisan-speaking San and Nama hunter-gatherers were the first inhabitants of Namibia, and they were joined in the distant past by the Damara. Bantu-speaking Herero immigrated in the sixteenth and seventeenth centuries, establishing small "stateless societies," while the Ovambo settled in the north and established larger-scale kingdoms. In the early nineteenth century, Orlams moved in from the south, pushed off their land by Afrikaners migrating out of South Africa. In the middle of the century, Afrikaners set up a loose state around Windhoek which collapsed

in the 1860s. In 1878, the British claimed Walvis Bay for the Cape Colony, and in 1884 the Germans laid claim to the rest of the territory. The Germans suppressed an uprising by the Herero and Nama between 1904 and 1909 with extreme savagery, exterminating 75–80 percent of the Herero and following up their victory with a brutal forced-labor program.

In 1915, during World War I, South Africa invaded the territory and replaced German rule with its own. After the war, a League of Nations mandate formalized this arrangement on the condition that the South Africans would promote the welfare and development of the indigenous inhabitants. The League exercised little oversight and had no mechanism for enforcement, however, so South Africa ruled the territory essentially as a colony.

The South Africans applied repeatedly for permission to formally annex the territory, but this the League denied. The United Nations, which replaced the League after World War II, similarly refused to sanction outright annexation. Conversely, the South Africans refused to accept the transformation of the old mandate into a UN trusteeship, despite numerous resolutions passed by the UN General Assembly urging it to comply. Faced with this stubborn opposition and the failure of an attempt by Ethiopia and Liberia to have the International Court of Justice declare South African rule illegal, the General Assembly revoked the mandate on October 27, 1966. The next spring the UN created the Council for Namibia to act as a transitional government, and in 1969 the UN Security Council passed its first resolution calling for South African withdrawal. When this failed to bring action, the council passed several resolutions calling on member states to bring pressure on South Africa, and in 1973 the United Nations recognized the South West African People's Organization (SWAPO) as the "authentic" representative of the Namibian people.

SWAPO was the latest and most militant expression of indigenous opposition to South African rule. Tribal leaders had kept the flames of opposition alive between 1915 and the 1950s by leading passive resistance to land removals and, after World War II, by publicizing South African malpractices. Eventually, they petitioned the United Nations to revoke the old mandate. In the 1950s, two new movements superseded the tribal leaders. The first, the South West African National Union (SWANU), was founded in 1955 and was made up of students, intellectuals, and other educated city-dwellers. The second, the lineal ancestor of SWAPO, began as a movement among migrant contract workers. They staged spontaneous demonstrations in Ovamboland in the mid-1950s and organized the Ovamboland People's Organization (OPO) in 1957. In 1959, OPO cooperated with SWANU and the older Chief's Council to oppose the imposition of apartheid in Windhoek, but when the police reacted with deadly force, the three movements parted company. OPO realized that improvements for the contract workers depended on larger political changes, so in 1960 it reconstituted itself as a national liberation movement, SWAPO. It pursued a three-tiered strategy of international lobbying, political agitation, and, eventually, military operations. After holding back a full six years until the International Court of Justice rendered its decision and the United Nations itself lost patience, SWAPO began its war of liberation in August 1966. In December 1969, it formally created the People's Liberation Army of Namibia (PLAN).

Thereafter, South Africa used all means at its disposal to delay or derail international efforts to reach a solution while energetically pursuing an internal settlement that would leave it in control. Its chief weapon on the international front was the strong sympathy of the leading Western powers, for whom South Africa was both an ally in the Cold War and an important trading partner. The International Court of Justice validated the United Nations' sovereignty over Namibia, ending any legal basis for support of South African rule, and in 1973 the UN appointed a commissioner for Namibia. Real progress did not

occur, however, until the collapse of Portuguese control in Angola convinced the Western powers that they, and South Africa, would have to make accommodation with nationalist forces throughout southern Africa. The United States finally backed a UN peace plan in 1976. When the South Africans rejected it, the U.S. in 1978 supported Resolution 435 calling for UN-supervised elections. The United States also organized the "contact group," including itself, Great Britain, France, West Germany, and Canada. The contact group at times protected South Africa from UN efforts and at times also brought pressure to bear for a solution. The South Africans played on Western ambivalence to create interminable delays by variously agreeing to talk, throwing up obstacles to agreement, and launching initiatives touted as an "internal solution."

Within Namibia, South Africa pursued policies that alternately pulled it directly under South African control and pushed it towards some sort of autonomy. In 1969, South Africa proclaimed the territory its fifth province, transforming native reserves into Bantustans, supposedly autonomous tribal "homelands." In 1973, it conducted Bantustan elections while suppressing SWAPO political activities. In 1974, it announced a constitutional conference at which "all options" would be open. However, almost as soon as the results of what was called the "Turnhalle Convention" appeared in 1977, South Africa decided to impose direct rule through an administrator-general. He set up "internal" elections held in December 1978, which were won, as expected, by the South African-backed Democratic Turnhalle Alliance (DTA). The elections led to the creation of an "interim government" consisting of a national assembly (1979) and a council of ministers with a chairman who was effectively prime minister (1980). This government fell apart in 1983, which led to a new administrator-general, a new "multiparty conference" that never got off the ground, and yet another "interim" government in 1985.

The real solution to the Namibian situation was achieved rather obliquely, through linkage with the Angolan civil war. Since 1974, South Africa had been fighting Angolan and Cuban forces in Angola, and in the early 1980s the United States promoted the idea of linking the withdrawal of the Cubans to disengagement by the South Africans. Furthermore, the end of South African support for UNITA in Angola and the end of Angolan support for SWAPO's war in Namibia fit together nicely, but the Angolan government would agree only if South Africa consented to set Namibia on the road to true independence. In 1988, drained by decades of warfare and facing greater challenges at home, the South African government agreed. On April 15, 1989, the UN Transitional Assistance Group arrived, and it oversaw elections in November. SWAPO won 41 of 75 seats in parliament. Because this total was short of the two-thirds majority necessary for SWAPO to write its own constitution, representatives of all seven parties drafted a constitution. It established a multiparty democracy with an executive president assisted by a prime minister and cabinet, a bicameral legislature, an independent judiciary, and guarantees of civil and human rights. The country became independent on March 21, 1990, with Sam Nujoma, leader of SWAPO, as the first president.

Since independence, Namibia has enjoyed relative political stability, although the economy's performance is lackluster. The country continues to be dominated economically by South Africa, whose corporations own most of the major businesses, and which retained control of the country's major port at Walvis Bay for several years. However, the transition in South Africa to black majority rule has taken much of the sting out of the former, and the latter ended in 1994. SWAPO continues to hold the people's political allegiance, as demonstrated by its victories in 38 of 47 local elections and 9 out of 13 regional elections in 1992. Representatives to the legislature's upper house (which gives each region equal representation, like the U.S. Senate) were elected in 1992, while delegates to the lower house (based on proportional representation, like the U.S. House of Representatives) were chosen in December 1994. The press is free, although the government owns broadcast media and the state subsidizes SWAPO's weekly newspaper. Unions operate freely. Racial violence between black strikers and white policemen broke out in March 1992, but in general Namibia appears to be one of Africa's brighter political lights. The 1994 elections gave SWAPO the two-thirds majority it needs to amend the constitution however it wants, but President Nujoma promised that any such changes would be submitted to a referendum.

SOUTH AFRICA
Statistical Profile

Capital:	Pretoria
Area:	471,444 sq. miles
Population:	41,200,000 (1994 est.)
Density:	87 people/sq. mile
Growth Rate:	2.6% (1994 est.)
GDP:	$103,651,000,000
Per Capita Income:	$2,670
Debt:	$20,600,000,000
Life Expectancy:	49 (1960), 63 (1992)
Ethnic Groups:	Afrikaners, English-speaking whites, Zulu (18.8%), Xhosa (18.3%), Tswana, Sotho, Shangaan, Swazi, Ndebele, Venda, Coloreds, and Asians (principally Indians)
Official Languages:	Afrikaans and English
Religions:	Christian majority; Hindu, Muslim, Jewish, and Traditional minorities
Former Colonizers:	Holland, Great Britain
Date of Independence:	1910

History

When South Africa gained independence in 1910 as a dominion in the British Commonwealth of Nations, it was a complex society incorporating Afrikaners and Englishmen, mixed-race "coloreds" and Indians, "Bushmen" and "Bantus" (see Chapter 2). While the last-named group made up the overwhelming majority, the first two groups—the whites—controlled the government and the economy. The relationship of the white groups with each other dominated politics in the early years of independence. Afrikaners outnumbered the English two to one, and so their party, the South African Party (SAP), took power upon independence, but the prime minister, Louis Botha, was a moderate Afrikaner who strove to reconcile the two groups and to foster good relations with Great Britain. His moderation alienated some Afrikaners. In 1914, General James Hertzog founded the Afrikaner National Party (NP), and General Christiaan De Wet led an uprising when Botha brought South Africa into the First World War on the British side.

Jan Smuts, the defense minister, became prime minister when Botha died in 1919, but because the war and a postwar depression had heightened discontent among Afrikaners, the SAP did not gain a majority in elections in 1920. Smuts amalgamated the SAP with the English-speaking Unionist Party, but after the government used troops to crush a massive strike by white mine workers in 1922, the NP was able to form the government with the English-speaking Labor Party in 1924. The new "Pact" government enacted the "civilized labor policy," which recognized white unions and reserved skilled jobs for whites, a racially defined privilege that cemented the alliance of Afrikaner nationalists and ordinary whites that remained the foundation of South African politics until 1989. The Pact government also began the enactment of social legislation, like the Immorality Act prohibiting interracial sex outside of marriage, that both reflected and fostered the cultural and psychological dimensions of racism.

White South Africans' growing concern about their position reflected in part the growing power of black activists, who formed the African National Congress (ANC) in 1912 and the African People's Organization (APO) and the Industrial and Commercial Workers' Union (ICU) in 1919. In 1920, 70,000 black mine workers struck in the Witwatersrand, and by 1927 the ICU was able to claim 100,000 members. The government responded with the Native Administration Act and the Riotous Assemblies Act, which gave the police broad powers against African organizations. While South Africa's industrial sector grew markedly during the 1920s, the position of black workers declined. The Great Depression made it still worse, pitting worker against worker in the scramble for scarce jobs. Economic desperation inspired some to radical activity, but by the early 1930s the ICU had collapsed and the ANC was moribund.

The Great Depression also heightened competition between poor whites and blacks as the demand for skilled labor declined and Afrikaner farmers lost their land and moved to the cities. In order to deal with the unprecedented economic crisis, Smuts offered to fuse the SAP with Hertzog's NP to create the United Party (UP) in 1933–1934, accepting the post of deputy prime minister, and also accepting a plan to disenfranchise Cape Province "coloreds" while expanding the size and role of the African "reserves" that had been first established in 1913. His government had first instituted pass laws and urban residential segregation in 1923, and he now cooperated in expanding these policies as part of a sweeping institutionalization of segregation. By the end of the 1930s, almost all schools and churches were divided by race, and whites had their own health, welfare, and even penal systems.

The UP presided over a dramatic economic recovery and then expansion in the late 1930s and 1940s, but the party came under increasing pressure from the nationalist right. Even as the NP and the SAP came together in the early 1930s, a group led by Daniel Malan had broken away to form a purified National Party. The new NP advocated more strident

Casting being made at Vecor, Vanderbijlpark, near Vereeniging in South Africa. South Africa has the only modern industrial economy in Africa. Courtesy of South African Consulate General (New York).

Afrikaner nationalism and stricter racial segregation, and it opposed helping Great Britain during the Second World War. South Africa's fascists went farther and came out in favor of the Axis, but by the end of the war they were discredited.

At the same time, the needs of the wartime economy and then the postwar economic boom pushed wages up and made it difficult to keep strict controls on people's movement and activity. This had the effect of eroding segregation and emboldening African activists. Between 1939 and 1945, blacks staged almost twice as many strikes as between 1924 and 1939, and in 1946, 76,000 black miners walked off the job.

South Africa stood at a crossroads. Liberals and some business interests advocated reforms that would free up the labor market, recognition of black unions, and regularization of the blacks' position in urban affairs. Afrikaner nationalists and other businessmen called for a renewal and extension of the segregationist policies that shored up the whites' material and psychological privileges while keeping the black majority as an ultracheap labor pool. Smuts' UP wavered, while the NP stood squarely for the second path. In the 1948 election, the privileged white electorate had no trouble deciding between them.

Once in power, the NP moved quickly to enact its program, which it called apartheid, or "separateness." It first enacted the Prohibition of Mixed Marriages Act of 1949 and followed up with the Immorality Act of 1950, which outlawed all interracial intercourse. The Population Registration Act of 1950 laid the foundation for a racist society by classifying everyone according to race; the Group Areas Act of the same year strictly divided where people could live and own businesses. To control the movement of blacks, the Pass Laws were applied nationally to men in 1952 and women in 1956. In 1957, police arrested over 350,000 people under these laws. In 1959, the Bantu Self-Government Act transformed the African reserves into "self-governing tribal homelands" that would eventually become "independent." With virtually all blacks assigned to one tribe or another, 75 percent of the country's people were theoretically consigned to 13 percent of its land. In reality, they were transformed into foreigners with no rights in the communities where they actually lived.

To support this unprecedented intrusion into the lives of the people, the nationalist government passed a series of increasingly stringent security laws: the broadly defined Suppression of Communism Act of 1950, the Criminal Laws Amendment Act of 1953, the Public Safety Act of 1953, and the Riotous Assemblies Act of 1956. In later years, these acts were reinforced by the Unlawful Organizations Act of 1960, the General Law Amendment Act (the "sabotage" act) of 1962, and the Terrorism Act of 1967.

The black leadership at first met this assault with nonviolent resistance. The ANC called a general strike on June 26, 1950, Freedom Day, and launched the Campaign for the Defiance of Unjust Laws in conjunction with the Indian Congress in 1952. This campaign ended with the arrest of 8,000 people and the passage of the two security acts of 1953. In 1955, the ANC brought together an array of organizations, including the white Congress of Democrats, to proclaim the Freedom Charter, which pledged them to aim for an end to apartheid and a redivision of the country's wealth as the basis for a just and democratic government. In 1956, three women were shot during an ANC-led protest against the pass laws, and in 1958 a group broke away from the ANC to form the Pan African Congress (PAC), with a more militant program that deemphasized interracial cooperation in favor of exclusively black activism. In 1960, the PAC launched a defiance campaign against the Pass Laws, which climaxed at Sharpeville when police shot into a crowd, killing 67 and wounding hundreds. Demonstrations broke out across South Africa, leading to thousands of arrests.

The Sharpeville massacre marked a turning point in the campaign against apartheid. The government banned both the PAC and the ANC, and in 1961 both turned away from legal protests and civil disobedience to launch armed struggles, with the ANC forming the Umkhonto we Sizwe (Spear of the Nation) and the PAC forming Poqo. Even the white Liberal Party formed the Armed Resistance Movement (ARM). All aimed to destabilize the state by attacking symbolic and economic targets and accepting but not seeking civilian casualties. For the next two years, they conducted numerous acts of sabotage that rocked the nation.

The police caught up with the leaders in 1963, and many, including Nelson Mandela, were sentenced to prison for life. Most of the surviving militants went into exile to begin the long, slow process of organizing an externally based guerrilla movement. But with the Portuguese in control of Angola and Mozambique, a white-settler government in control of Rhodesia (Zimbabwe), South Africa in control of Southwest Africa (Namibia), and Botswana, Lesotho, and Swaziland both militarily and economically weak, it was clear that their struggle would have to wait for the collapse of white rule to the north of South Africa.

During the 1960s, white South Africa enjoyed a deceptive calm. Protests were muffled, the economy grew, and trouble seemed a long way off. In 1963, the Bantustan policy of creating homelands for the different Bantu peoples got under way with the formation of Transkei for the Xhosa. Abroad, South Africa projected an image of a developed Western country that stood as a bulwark against communism by defending the crucial sealanes connecting Europe and America to the oil-rich Middle East. The country had to drop out of the British Commonwealth in 1961 because of Commonwealth opposition to apartheid, but the government was able to co-opt enough black leaders and build enough bridges to conservative groups abroad that its position seemed secure.

Beneath the surface, however, tensions were building. Influenced by the anticolonial struggles to the north and the Black Power movement in the United States, students led by Stephen Biko began the Black Consciousness movement, which aimed to free blacks from the psychological bonds of apartheid. Originally a cultural movement, it was pulled into the political vacuum and became more militant in the early 1970s. Simultaneously, the worldwide recession of the early 1970s sent black unemployment soaring, which led to a wave of strikes that began in Natal in 1973 and to violence that broke out among miners in 1974. In 1976, students in Soweto, a huge black slum outside of Johannesburg, demonstrated against a new regulation that half their courses had to be taught in Afrikaans, the language of the oppressor. After the police fired on the schoolchildren, killing and wounding many, demonstrations and rioting spread throughout the country. Over the next few months, hundreds of people were killed, thousands wounded, and thousands more arrested. South Africa's long period of calm was shattered.

The government reacted to the school boycott movement with a two-pronged strategy. On the one hand, it folded the Department for Bantu Education into a broader Department of Education, introduced the new Education and Training Bill in place of the Bantu Education Act, and appointed a separate minister of education. On the other hand, the police arrested Biko. He died in their custody in 1977, a victim of their brutality. Despite renewed protests and an international outcry over his death, most of the black consciousness organizations were banned, and by September 1978 the national school boycott movement died away.

Partial boycotts continued to occur, however, and other forms of rebellion flared up across the country. Black workers staged widespread strikes in 1978 and a bomb destroyed the chambers of the collaborationist Soweto Council in December. Guerrillas machinegunned a police station in April 1979 and fought pitched battles with security forces in January and November in Bophuthatswana, near Johannesburg. In 1980 and 1981, strikes, demonstrations, and riots continued, while numerous armed attacks occurred. Guerrillas sabotaged power plants, machine-gunned police stations, planted bombs in government offices, and raided banks. Perhaps most serious of all, violence against individual black collaborators—councilors, policemen, and suspected informers—became endemic in black townships, an anarchy that for all its security apparatus, the government was powerless to control.

The disintegration of governmental authority in the face of the blacks' multifaceted, persistent, and implacable rejection of the apartheid regime stimulated contradictory responses in the white community. On the one hand, there was the visceral urge to crack down, to intensify repression in the hopes that the blacks would give up. In the years after Soweto, the government increased its spending on defense and security forces tremendously and used them freely. Already involved in Angola after the fall of the Portuguese empire in 1974, South African forces invaded repeatedly and supported the rebel UNITA faction in order to counter Cuban support for the MPLA and to strike back at SWAPO guerrillas fighting from there to free Namibia. On the other side of the continent, South Africa supported the MNR dissidents fighting the leftist government of Mozambique. South African forces periodically raided that country as well as Botswana, Zimbabwe (after the fall of the white government in 1980), Lesotho, Swaziland, and even Zambia. The attacks kept the exiled insurgents off-balance and succeeded in compelling several neighboring states to accept nonaggression pacts, but the fighting dragged down the country's economy and sapped its morale. Similarly, the government's clandestine effort to keep up its image in the West by spying on antiapartheid organizations, bribing British politicians, contributing to U.S. conservative politicians' election campaigns, buying up newspapers, and starting a new political party in Norway helped generate support for the country in the short run. In the long run, the exposure of these ploys embarrassed it abroad and caused a ma-

jor political scandal at home. The controversy became the focal point of the struggle between the *verlegte* (reformist) and *verkrampte* (conservative) wings of the National Party and resulted in the choice of a leader of the former faction, P. W. Botha, as prime minister.

The other white response to the interminable disorders was to offer reforms in the hope of placating a critical mass of opponents without having to give up the essential levers of white power. Shortly after the killings in Soweto, a group of white businessmen joined with black businessmen and professionals to create the Urban Foundation to funnel money for improvements into the townships, in particular for housing. The government supported this move in 1979 by relaxing the Group Areas Act to allow "qualified" blacks to buy homes in urban areas. The government also legalized black labor unions in 1979, albeit with criteria for registration so stringent that many could not meet them, and it removed limits on the number of blacks that could be employed at industrial concerns. It tried to draw in community leaders in the townships by creating urban and regional councils, although these became the focal points of intense hostility and generally failed to defuse antigovernment agitation.

A similar reaction greeted the long-promised granting of "independence" to the Bantustans—first to the Transkei and Bophuthatswana in 1976 and then to Venda in 1979 and the Ciskei in 1981. Not one foreign country recognized these fragmented, economically impossible territories as independent states, and most black South Africans considered their "independence" a fraud. As with the township governments, a few blacks collaborated for their own ends and others tried to make the best of a bad situation, but the great majority regarded acceptance of limited self-government within the apartheid system as a betrayal of the larger cause.

In 1983, Botha tried to forge an alliance between the whites, the Asians, and the coloreds by offering each race a chamber in a new, tricameral parliament. He ignored the blacks because as far as he was concerned they were represented by their homelands. What he offered the Asians and the coloreds, however, was only a junior partnership. White representatives would outnumber the combined total in the other two chambers, and whites would control the new state presidency that would replace the current combination of ceremonial president plus executive prime minister. His proposal met stiff opposition in both the colored and the Asian communities, but two-thirds of the whites voted for it in a referendum in November. Elections were held in August 1984, and the new government took over on September 5, with Botha as president.

Over the next year, Botha's government tried to maintain the momentum of limited reform by dismantling "petty apartheid." In April 1985, it repealed the laws against interracial marriage and sex, and in September it rescinded the laws requiring segregated trains, restaurants, and other public facilities. In the same month, it replaced the blacks' hated pass books with national identity cards issued to everyone, and it agreed to let some blacks who lived permanently in the townships apply for South African citizenship.

Botha's cosmetic reforms failed to defuse the situation; if anything, they added to discontent. Over 600 organizations came together in the multiracial United Democratic Front (UDF) to oppose the new constitution, and they succeeded in persuading the majority of Asian and colored voters to boycott the elections. Only 60 percent of the eligible coloreds registered, and only 29 percent of them voted. Almost 80 percent of the Asians registered, but a mere 20 percent cast ballots. Violence marred the elections and continued after they were over. In the seven months following the elections over 300 people were killed and 1,500 were wounded, and by the end of 1985 the death toll rose to over 1,000. Most of the casualties were caused by the police, but violence against black collaborators intensified as well.

With police losing all semblance of control in the townships, Botha declared a state of emergency in July 1985, giving the police and military sweeping authority to arrest, search, and detain in three regions of the country. Still the violence continued. In June 1986, Botha imposed a new, more draconian state of emergency. The violence continued unabated. One hundred fifty people were killed each month from 1986 to 1988.

Faced with the steady erosion of white privileges and the chronic violence in the townships, conservative and fascist Afrikaner groups grew in strength in the late 1970s and 1980s. Extremists conducted their own acts of violence, such as bombings and shootings, while more restrained elements challenged the National Party politically. They steadily rose in power, and reduced the NP government's majority dramatically in elections in 1987 and 1989.

Even more ominous for the government was the deterioration of the country's economy as the decade came to a close. In part this resulted from the internal disorders, and in part it reflected the effects of international sanctions. In response to the incessant social upheaval in South Africa, international banks had by the mid-1980s begun to withhold credit, some international corporations pulled out, and Western governments got serious about sanctions. In October 1985, the heads of government of the Commonwealth decided to send a delegation of seven eminent persons to try to work out a solution with the South African government. But just as they seemed to have worked out a basis for negotiations in 1986, violence by right-wing Afrikaners scared Botha into taking a hard line. Canada, India, Australia, Zambia, and the Bahamas imposed sanctions. Later in the year, the European Economic Community and Japan halted new investment and banned South African iron, steel, and gold. The United States banned new investment and bank loans and prohibited imports of South African uranium, coal, steel, textiles, military vehicles, and agricultural products. In the wake of these moves, even more banks and businesses pulled out: Great Britain's Barclays Bank, General Motors, IBM,

Coca Cola, Exxon, and a host of smaller U.S. companies. The sanctions were far from a complete economic blockade, but they gradually took a toll. Combined with internal disruption, security costs, and worldwide recession, they dragged the South African economy steadily downward.

As South Africa lurched toward crisis, fate intervened. In January 1989, Botha suffered a stroke and F. W. de Klerk assumed leadership of the NP. In August, Botha resigned the presidency, and de Klerk campaigned on the platform of a "new plan of action" that promised to bring blacks into the government in a limited way. He won the election in September and inaugurated a period of dramatic reforms. He permitted multiracial demonstrations against apartheid, fully desegregated many public facilities, and permitted certain neighborhoods to be designated multiracial. He strengthened political control over the national security apparatus, and in December 1989 he released eight leading black political prisoners. Two months later he released Nelson Mandela and removed the ban on the ANC. In January 1991, the government took the first steps toward integrating the schools, and in June parliament repealed the Land Acts of 1913 and 1936 and the Group Areas Act of 1966. It also repealed the Population Registration Act of 1950, thereby removing the government's ability to divide the population into racial groups.

De Klerk's initiatives made possible the opening of a dialogue with black leaders, and South Africa was fortunate that he found his complement in Nelson Mandela. Mandela assumed leadership of the ANC upon his release, and by mid-1991 the organization had ceased its armed struggle. Around the same time, the UDF disbanded, and the government accepted a UN-supervised plan enabling political exiles to return. Formal negotiations to end white minority rule, conducted in a forum called "the Convention for a Democratic South Africa" (Codesa), began in 1991, attended by the ANC and 18 other parties. Its first session ended on an optimistic note in

December, and de Klerk received a decisive endorsement from the white electorate in an extraordinary referendum on reform in March 1992. International economic sanctions were lifted, sporting and cultural ties were resumed, and South African companies began entering African markets.

Unfortunately, the second round of talks, Codesa II, broke down almost immediately upon opening in May 1992. The formal sticking points were minority veto power and the percentages needed to ratify the new constitution, but the larger issue was the nature of the new state—whether it would be a strongly centralized state, as favored by the ANC (which could expect to dominate it), or a loosely organized federation of regions, as favored by the whites and the smaller black parties like the Zulu Inkatha Freedom Party (IFP). The disagreements became intractable because of spiraling violence and the government's inability, or unwillingness, to bring it under control. Violence by white extremists was to be expected, and did occur, but the main problem was the dismaying escalation of violence by blacks against other blacks: the IFP against the ANC, Xhosa against Zulu, migrant laborers against settled town dwellers. Violence became so bad in Natal that in April 1991 de Klerk sent in security troops with Mandela's approval. When the violence continued, Mandela became increasingly critical of the security forces and de Klerk's government, pointing to evidence that some security officials were not simply failing to prevent the violence, but were actively encouraging it. De Klerk demoted his defense and law and order ministers, but Inkatha leader Mangosuthu Buthelezi drew increasingly close to Afrikaner conservatives, and fighting between IFP and ANC supporters continued. The most dramatic incident took place on June 17, 1992, when IFP members, supported by the police, went on a rampage and massacred 39 people.

The ANC conducted a mass-action campaign of rallies and marches over the summer to press for renewed progress. This campaign culminated in a general strike on August 3 and a march on parliament led by Mandela himself. The NP, for its part, organized a pro-federation summit on September 7, including representatives of the white Conservative Party, the IFP, and several of the homelands. The ANC marched on the Ciskei on the same day to protest this alliance, and when Ciskeian troops fired into the crowd, killing 25 and wounding 200, the prospects for further progress seemed dim.

Surprisingly, Mandela and de Klerk broke the logjam only weeks later in bilateral talks on September 27, 1992. They signed the Record of Agreement, which stated that an elected constituent assembly (CA) would create a new constitution, a multiparty transitional executive council (TEC) would be created alongside the CA, and a government of national unity would be elected after the new constitution was adopted. Despite opposition from Inkatha, conservative whites, and homeland leaders, reform regained momentum. In November 1992, the ANC stated its willingness to share power with the government and other parties after the adoption of a new constitution. De Klerk set out a timetable in which multilateral talks would resume in the spring of 1993, the Transitional Executive Council would be created in June, and elections for the Constituent Assembly would be held in April 1994. The parliament approved an interim constitution in December 1993 that abolished the homelands, divided the country into nine new regions, established a bicameral legislature with a lower house based on proportional representation and an upper house based on equal regional representation, created an independent judiciary, and included a bill of rights. Right-wing violence jeopardized the elections scheduled for April 27, 1994, and conservatives threatened a boycott. But when the historic day arrived, the voters came out in huge numbers, and there was a minimum of violence. The ANC won 63 percent of the votes, a solid majority but not enough to allow it to write the new constitution without the support of other parties.

The NP came in second with 20 percent. The IFP won 10 percent, and a coalition of right-wing groups gained 2 percent. Nelson Mandela became president on May 10, with de Klerk as one of two deputy presidents. The ANC selected 17 of the 27 cabinet officers, while the NP and IFP chose the rest. The new government has until April 1999 to work out a permanent constitution.

Even before the conclusion of the transition, South Africa began reorienting its foreign policy away from its earlier confrontational stance. The end of the Cold War in 1989 deflated the South African argument that it was a bastion of Western democracy besieged by communist insurgencies directed from Moscow. Botha's government had concluded arrangements for Namibian independence in the late 1980s as part of a larger deal to remove Cubans from Angola and end the ongoing guerrilla wars. De Klerk's government presided over the final withdrawal from Namibia in 1990, and instead of the feared controversy, the whites seemed to issue a collective sigh of relief. The government signed a peace accord with Angola in 1991 and with Mozambique in 1992. In 1994, South Africa granted sovereignty over Walvis Bay to Namibia, and in June of that year it joined the Organization of African Unity (OAU). In the summer of 1995, South Africa announced that it would join the African Development Bank.

From being an international pariah, South Africa has rapidly become an influential participant in regional affairs and a much sought-after source of capital investment for the rest of Africa.

SWAZILAND
Statistical Profile

Capital:	Mbabdne
Area:	6,703 sq. miles
Population:	800,000 (1994 est.)
Density:	119 people/sq. mile
Growth Rate:	3.2% (1994 est.)
GDP:	$883,000,000
Per Capita Income:	$1,080

Foreign Debt:	$233,000,000
Life Expectancy:	n.a. (1960), 57 (1992)
Ethnic Groups:	Swazi (90%), Zulu, Tonga, Shangaan, European
Official Languages:	English and siSwati
Religions:	Christian (56%), Traditional (43%), Muslim (0.5%)
Former Colonizer:	Great Britain
Date of Independence:	1968

History

Swaziland's roots go back to the eighteenth century, when the Swazi Dlamini clan crossed the Lubombo Mountains and subdued the clans living on the far side. In the early nineteenth century, King Sobhuza I conquered an area approximately twice the size of present-day Swaziland. After he died in 1839, his successor, Mswati I, transformed the conquest state, which consisted of armed encampments amidst a restive populace, into a strong centralized monarchy based on military service and tribute labor exacted from the subject peasantry.

At the same time that the Swazi king was consolidating his hold on the state, he began to lose parts of it to the Transvaal Boers. By 1880, they had taken half his domains, and the kingdom might have disappeared altogether were it not for the competing interest of the British. In 1894, the British and the Boers agreed to incorporate the remainder of the Swazi territory into the Transvaal, but after the Boer War, it passed to the control of the British high commissioner for South Africa.

Under the British, the king's jurisdiction was restricted to local civil affairs. In 1907, the Concessions Partitions Proclamation gave 25 percent of the land to concessionaires, who had flocked in since gold had been discovered in 1879; over 33 percent to the British crown, which sold most of it to white settlers; and only 38 percent to the Swazi themselves. The king who took office in 1921, Sobhuza II, refused to recognize British limits on his authority, however, and used his income from taxes

to gradually buy back another 20 percent of the country's land.

The British did little to develop Swaziland when they ruled it, so its social and economic base remained relatively unchanged and Sobhuza was able to retain firm control of its political affairs. He ruled through appointed chiefs and headmen, who were organized into district councils under the Swazi National Council (SNC). Originally opposed to political parties, he organized the Imbokodvo (Grindstone) National Movement to contest elections organized by the British in 1964. After Imbokodvo won a sweeping victory, Sobhuza gained full recognition from the British as the nation's leader. Imbokodvo swept another election in 1967, and in September 1968 the British granted the country independence as a constitutional monarchy. The constitution formally invested executive power in a cabinet with a prime minister, and legislative power in a bicameral parliament with a majority of delegates elected and a minority appointed by the king. In reality, the king controlled the government almost completely.

Even before independence, urban-based reformist parties led by educated and entrepreneurial elites who looked for support to the working class challenged the monarchy's hold on the country. Unfortunately for this opposition, it never really coalesced; most parties failed to support a strike by the workers in 1963. Only the Ngwane National Liberatory Congress (NNLC) secured the backing of the workers and union organizers through its support of their strike; it was able to go from 12 percent of the vote in 1963 to 20 percent in 1964. In 1972, it won one of eight three-member constituencies. When the monarchy tried to disqualify one of the party's three representatives, a constitutional crisis ensued, which Sobhuza resolved by abrogating the constitution, dissolving all political parties, declaring a state of emergency, and, after a major strike, restricting the activities of trade unions.

Sobhuza ruled arbitrarily for the next few years, and in October 1978 instituted a new constitution. He did not allow details of the new document to be published, however, and no campaigning was allowed for the elections that followed (the names of the nominees were not even announced until the day of the elections). The chief's committee from each tribal group selected two members to an 80-person electoral college, which in turn selected 40 delegates to the House of Assembly. The king appointed 10 more delegates, and the House then selected 10 of 20 senators, with the monarch appointing the remainder. The new legislature, which opened on January 19, 1979, had to submit all legislation to the king, who delegated much authority to his hand-picked advisors on the Central Committee. This new constitution basically created an absolute monarchy.

The new constitution gave the king control of the government, but it could not eliminate discontent. Workers and educated professionals staged strikes and demonstrations, and in 1979 the radicals among them organized the militant Swazi Liberation Movement (Swalimo) in exile. In response, the monarchy made liberal use of its power to detain opponents incommunicado for 60 days (a term that could be renewed indefinitely), and it increased the numbers and powers of the security forces. These forces included 5,000 regular army troops, thousands of irregulars, the Police Mobile Unit, and the security police. The army troops generated considerable discontent by shaking down and roughing up travelers at their numerous roadblocks, while the security police gained notoriety for cooperating energetically with their counterparts from South Africa.

During the late 1970s and 1980s, Swaziland became increasingly embroiled in the conflict between South Africa, Mozambique, and the insurgent African National Congress. The kingdom, which depended heavily on South Africa economically, barely tolerated the presence of exiles from South Africa and readily cooperated in curbing and even suppressing their activities. This collaboration culminated in 1982 with a secret security pact between the two countries, which reportedly was sweet-ened for Swaziland by South Africa's willingness to cede territory along their border. This deal fell through in the face of strong international pressure and the opposition of the affected communities. Despite the pact, South African commandos staged repeated raids into Swazi territory in the late 1980s.

Sobhuza died in 1982. One of his senior wives, Dzelwe, became regent, and a regency council, the Liqoqo, chose one of Sobhuza's hundreds of children, a 15-year-old son, as his successor. The regent and her prime minister opposed the land deal and favored a progressive program in general, which brought them into conflict with traditionalists on the Liqoqo. They forced the prime minister to resign in March 1983, replaced Dzelwe with the heir's mother, Ntombi, and purged all the progressives from the cabinet in November 1983. These moves did not end the power struggle, and in June 1984 a number of officials were dismissed for allegedly plotting a coup. They were arrested along with others later in the year and in early 1985. Before they were tried, however, the police arrested two senior members of the Liqoqo for "defeating the ends of Swazi justice." Those who had been arrested were released, and the two who had been behind the false accusations against them were eventually imprisoned.

On April 25, 1986, the new king was crowned as Mswati III. He dissolved the Liqoqo, reshuffled the cabinet, and replaced the prime minister, establishing himself firmly in control. In 1990, he responded to criticisms of the inherited constitutional order by announcing a review committee, which began meeting in September 1991 and reported to him in February 1992. The committee reported widespread discontent about the indefinite terms of the members of the Central Committee, corruption among members of parliament, and the 60-day detention law. The opposition continued to call for an interim government to set up multiparty elections, and Mswati established a second review committee to draw up recommendations. While it was working, the regime relaxed its repression of illegal parties. The Swaziland Youth Congress obtained permission to march to "raise funds," while the underground People's United Democratic Movement (Pudemo) went public. Smaller parties soon followed suit, and the king announced that parliamentary elections would take place in the near future. The second review committee reported in October 1992, recommending an end to the 60-day detention law as well as other reforms. But it recommended the direct election of candidates as individuals rather than true multiparty democracy.

Despite criticism of the plan by opposition parties, it became the basis for a new constitution, and elections were held in September and October 1993. In addition to their new right to elect representatives directly, the Swazi now enjoy a relatively independent judiciary, relatively free speech, and freedom of assembly (including the right to form unions). The state is still dominated by its traditional aristocracy and it is not a multiparty democracy, but Mswati III appears to have started it in a new direction.

LESOTHO
Statistical Profile

Capital:	Maseru
Area:	11,718 sq. miles
Population:	1,900,000 (1994 est.)
Density:	162 people/sq. mile
Growth Rate:	1.9% (1994 est.)
GDP:	$536,000,000
Per Capita Income:	$590
Foreign Debt:	$442,000,000
Life Expectancy:	42 (1960), 60 (1992)
Ethnic Group:	Basotho (100%)
Official Languages:	English and Sesotho
Religions:	Christian (90%), Traditional (10%)
Former Colonizer:	Great Britain
Date of Independence:	1966

History

Bantu-speaking immigrants first joined Lesotho's original Khoisan-speaking inhabitants in the seventeenth century. In the early nineteenth century, a lesser chief used careful diplomacy and military conquest to forge a powerful kingdom, which included considerable territory in the fertile plains as well as the country's present-day mountainous territory. Moshoeshoe I went on to consolidate his rule by creating a federal structure in which the diverse peoples he had drawn together retained control of their local affairs while participating in his national government, which included a consultative national assembly. Pressure from the Boer's Orange Free State in the 1850s and 1860s forced him to look to the British for protection, however, which came after the loss of the country's most fertile territory to the Boers.

The British took Lesotho, which they called Basutoland, under their wing in 1868, administering it first through the Cape Colony and after 1884 as a protectorate under the same high commissioner who oversaw Bechuanaland and Swaziland. Early on, the British gave the Africans a forum for political expression, setting up an informal council in 1903 and formalizing it as the Basutoland National Council (BNC) in 1910. The fact that the king appointed all members of the council contributed to a growing authoritarianism in Lesotho society, as did the chief's control of land and cattle as the growing population put increasing pressure on the resources of the small country. Consequently, even though the British made some seats in the BNC elective and gradually increased its influence in policymaking, political discontent in Basutoland increased over the years.

Activity in reformist politics among the Africans was centered in the Progressive Association, founded by traders and clerks in 1907; the more populist League of the Common Man, founded about a decade later; and then a wide range of unions, professional associations, and other quasi-political bodies founded in the succeeding decades. In 1952, Ntsu Mokhehle founded the Basutoland African Congress (later the Basutoland Congress Party, or BCP). The new party affiliated itself with the South African Pan-African Congress and advocated first self-rule and then total independence. In response, traditionalists organized the Marema-Tlou Party (MTP) in 1957, and in 1958 Chief Leabua Jonathan organized lower chiefs and headmen into the Basutoland National Party (BNP), which opposed both the MTP's royalism and the BCP's radicalism. With the backing of the Catholic Church, South Africa, and eventually the British (who really favored the MTP), the BNP overcame the BCP's early dominance. The BCP won 20 of 30 seats with 36 percent of the vote in the first elections, held in 1960. But in the crucial pre-independence elections in 1965, it gained only 25 of 60 seats, while the BNP won 31 (and gained through defections most of the 8 won by the MTP). On October 4, 1966, Great Britain granted Lesotho independence, with Jonathan as the new country's first prime minister.

Jonathan moved quickly to increase his power, abolishing elective district councils in 1966 to enhance the power of his chiefly supporters and reducing the king to a figurehead in 1967. When the BCP appeared to be winning the election of January 1970, Jonathan declared a state of emergency, abrogated the constitution, arrested opposition leaders, banned their parties, and ruled by decree. He released the prisoners over the next two years on the condition they abstain from politics. He also convened a national assembly to create a new constitution in 1973, but since he appointed its members, it was essentially a cover for his personal rule.

During the 1970s and early 1980s, Jonathan pursued a two-pronged strategy toward his opponents. On the one hand, he attempted to reconcile with them, holding secret negotiations between 1975 and 1978 that succeeded in drawing some BCP members into the government but failed to create the basis for a compromise with the BCP leadership. On the other hand, even before the failure of these negotiations, he began to lay the groundwork for a one-party state. After the opposition launched scattered attacks on police stations in January 1974, he promulgated a new security law that allowed for 60-day detentions without trial and created a BNP militia, which carried out a ruthless campaign against BCP supporters. In 1975, he formally banned the BCP, but Mokhehle created the Lesotho Liberation Army (LLA) to carry out an armed struggle. In 1979, the LLA launched an offensive, setting off bombs, fighting with the paramilitary Police Mobile Unit (PMU), and attempting to assassinate Jonathan's associates. The government responded with renewed repression of BCP supporters, increased security at the borders, and greater powers for the police The attacks intensified in the early 1980s.

The LLA's campaign was able to mount in intensity because it was receiving increasing support from South Africa. Initially, the white regime had supported Jonathan's BNP and opposed the BCP, but after the mid-1970s Jonathan moved away from his cooperative attitude with South Africa toward a more confrontational posture. After the Soweto uprising of 1976, Jonathan used the increased international hostility toward South Africa to gain greater Western aid and political support. He came out in favor of the liberation struggle, denounced apartheid, and refused to recognize the "independence" South Africa "granted" to the Transkei. The new "nation" responded by closing its border with Lesotho; the United Nations sent a mission to study the situation and the Western powers gave increased aid. Lesotho also concluded trade and cultural treaties with Mozambique in 1979; established relations with Cuba, North Korea, and the Soviet Union in 1982; and allowed the insurgent African National Congress (ANC) to operate within and across its borders. South Africa conducted retaliatory airstrikes and commando operations against Lesothan economic targets as well as against insurgent bases, and in 1983 imposed a partial economic blockade, which compelled Lesotho to airlift ANC members to Mozambique and Tanzania. Tension between the two countries continued to build until January 1986, when South Africa demanded that Lesotho close the communist embassies and hand over all members of the ANC. When Jonathan refused, South Africa imposed a total blockade, and within a week the commander of the Lesotho Paramilitary Force, Justinus Lekhanya, ousted Jonathan in a coup.

Lekhanya moved swiftly to improve relations with South Africa, closing the communist embassies and signing a security pact that committed each of the two countries to preventing "terrorists" from operating against the other. He also revamped the national government, restoring legislative and executive authority to King Moshoeshoe and creating a six-member military council and 18-member cabinet to assist him. Unfortunately, relations between Lekhanya and the king soured; when Lekhanya dismissed two of the king's relatives from the military council in February 1990, the king refused to accept the move and went into exile. Lekhanya invited him to return, but deposed the king when he spurned the invitation. In consultation with the principal chiefs, Lekhanya selected Moshoeshoe's eldest son to become King Letsie III, on terms that made him a mere figurehead.

In the same month, Lekhanya announced that the country would return to civilian rule by June 1992, and in April he created a 109-member constituent assembly made up of politicians and officials to be appointed by him,

local government officials, traditional chiefs, and representatives of the police. Political activity, however, was still banned, and the opposition refused to participate. In April 1991, Colonel Phitsoane Ramaema ousted Lekhanya in another coup; he legalized political parties in May. After several delays, elections took place in March 1993, and the BCP won every seat. In August 1994, Letsie III suspended the constitution and dismissed the government, claiming the BCP was unpopular. Within a month Botswana, South Africa, and Zimbabwe pressured him into backing down. He also agreed to abdicate in favor of his father Moshoeshoe, whose return was actually one of his objectives. Moshoeshoe reigned until February 1996, when he was killed in an auto accident. Letsie then returned to the throne.

With the 1993 elections and reinstatement of the government in 1994, Lesotho has become a parliamentary state, if not exactly a democratic one. The government can detain people without charge, but otherwise the judicial system is independent. A private press exists alongside government-controlled media, and the people are free to travel, worship, and associate freely, although unions are subject to some restrictions. Fighting in the capital in early 1994 indicated that this new democracy is still unstable, but the country has clearly taken a step in a democratic direction.

CHAPTER

13

Indian Ocean Islands

INTRODUCTION

The Indian Ocean Islands are considered part of Africa mainly for the convenience of geographers, for they do not have much in common with most African states or with each other. Madagascar is a large, relatively populous island whose people are descended from a mix of Malay-Polynesians and Africans. The other nations covered in this chapter are groups of tiny islands with equally tiny populations. The Comoros Islands are strongly Arabic. Mauritius is dominated by people of Indian descent. The population of the Seychelles includes both South Asians and Africans. Madagascar and the Comoros were ruled by France; Great Britain controlled Mauritius and the Seychelles. The people of Mauritius and the Seychelles enjoy some of the highest per capita incomes in Africa; the citizens of Madagascar and the Comoros have among the lowest. Madagascar, Mauritius, and the Seychelles are currently multiparty democracies, although the government of the Seychelles retains strong repressive powers. The Comoros have recently experienced their third coup by mer-

cenaries led by Bob Denard. It is still unclear what type of regime will emerge.

MADAGASCAR
Statistical Profile

Capital:	Antananarivo
Area:	226,656 sq. miles
Population:	13,700,000 (1994 est.)
Density:	60 people/sq. mile
Growth Rate:	3.3% (1994 est.)
GDP:	$2,767,000,000
Per Capita Income:	$230
Foreign Debt:	$3,805,000,000
Life Expectancy:	41 (1960), 51 (1992)
Ethnic Groups:	Malagasy are divided into 18 main "clans," including Merina, Betsileo, Sakalava, Antankarana, Betsimisaraka, Antaimoro, Antasaka, Antanosy, Antandroy, Bara, Mahafaly, Vezo
Official Languages:	Malagasy and French
Religions:	Traditional (50%), Christian (43%), Muslim (7%)

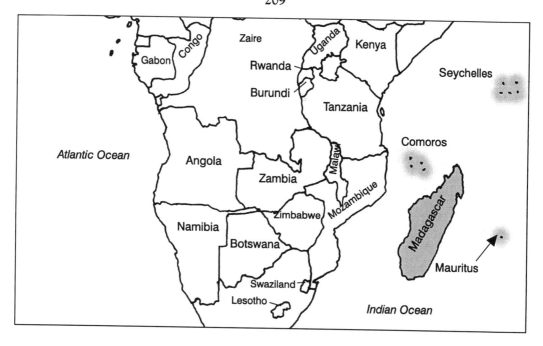

Indian Ocean Islands

Former Colonizer: France
Date of Independence: 1960

History

Madagascar was uninhabited until early in the first millennium A.D., when Indonesian sea-farers arrived, probably by way of southern India and the East African coast. African immigrants followed in the next centuries, and the island formed a peripheral part of the Swahili trading system that developed along the East African coast after 1000 A.D. Portu-guese explorers visited the island in the early fifteenth century, and the French set up a trad-ing post in 1643. However, European influ-ence remained marginal until the king of Merina used English military assistance in the early nineteenth century to unify the entire island under his rule by overcoming the two states that had been dominant since the 1600s—Menabe and Boina. He and his suc-cessors built a state based on fiefdoms and vassalage but held together by a modern army and bureaucracy. They also actively promoted

education and cultural development. None of this helped, however, when France declared a protectorate in 1895. Widespread resistance to this takeover forced the French to spend 20 years establishing full control over the is-land, but they gradually transformed it into an outpost of their empire, using forced labor to build roads and railroads and to work on the coffee plantations that formed the basis of the colonial economy. Politically, they ruled through existing institutions except at the top, but they resisted calls for equality, autonomy, and independence. Increasing resistance cul-minated in a rebellion in 1947 that was sup-pressed at the cost of over 50,000 lives. A decade later, during the period that France was disengaging from its colonial empire generally, the people of Madagascar voted to accept in-dependence as an autonomous republic within the French Community.

Philibert Tsiranana became president of the new Malagasy Republic on June 26, 1960. He embarked on a conservative course, maintain-ing close economic, military, and diplomatic ties with France while emphasizing the unity of the new nation. A few large French companies continued to dominate commercial life, French forces remained in army and naval bases, and the republic supported French foreign policy, refusing contacts with communist countries and engaging in "dialogue" with South Africa. In return, France made the republic its biggest aid recipient south of the Sahara, and the country's GDP grew at 2.9 percent per year. Unfortunately, the population grew at 2.8 percent per year. The consequent stagnation of living standards undercut Tsiranana's program of "anticommunist socialism," in which the state promoted development, allowed private enterprises to grow unfettered, and attempted to equalize economic conditions between the more advanced area around the capital and the less developed areas along the coast. Tsiranana did not attempt to create a dictatorship or one-party state, but his Social Democratic Party (PSD) developed into the only truly national political organization, and he became increasingly resistant to criticism.

In 1971, rebellion broke out in the arid and perennially poor south. The government crushed it with particular brutality. Early in 1972, 100,000 students went on strike in Antananarivo, the capital. They demanded nationalization of foreign companies, replacement of all 50,000 foreign personnel by Malagasy citizens, and far-reaching social reforms. The government suppressed the strike, but in May 1972 more rioting broke out in the capital and other major towns. Tsiranana resigned in favor of a military government headed by General Batriel Ramanantsoa, ending Madagascar's "first republic."

Ramanantsoa formed an "apolitical" government of soldiers and technocrats and changed the country's course dramatically. The new government renegotiated the terms of aid from France, closed the French military bases, and removed the country from the Franc Zone. It severed its ties to South Africa, Israel, and Taiwan, and established relations with the Soviet Union, China, and leftist regimes in Africa. It also embarked on a radical restructuring of local government. Dissension within the government grew, however, culminating in an attempted coup in early 1975. After it was suppressed, Ramanantsoa turned the government over to Colonel Ratsimandrava, but six days later he was assassinated. In June, a military directorate gave Commander Didier Ratsiraka power, and in December the people voted to confirm him as president and head of state.

Ratsiraka appointed the Supreme Revolutionary Council (SRC) to act as his cabinet, and changed the country's name to the "Democratic Republic of Madagascar." He declared his intention to transform the country into a socialist society by the year 2000. His "Charter of the Malagasy Revolution," or "Red Book," became the basis for the new regime, Madagascar's "second republic." In 1976, Ratsiraka formed a party, Vanguard of the Malagasy Revolution (AREMA). He also organized an umbrella organization, the National Front for the Defense of the Revolution (FNDR), which included all parties that endorsed the revolutionary charter. When elections to the advisory National Assembly were held in June 1977, only members of parties in FNDR were eligible. Local and regional elections to fill out the other levels of government took place in the same year, and in 1978 the government created a supreme court to rule on constitutional questions, rounding out Ratsiraka's governmental reforms.

Ratsiraka's government also inaugurated broad social programs. It nationalized all foreign businesses and created state corporations to coordinate food production and supply. It set up a regional development program to focus effort on the poorer coastal regions, and it instituted a crash building program to provide an elementary school for every village and a high school for every district. It made education free, offered free health care, and subsidized rice, the national staple. Abroad, Ratsiraka's government continued the military government's policy of non-alignment, and challenged France over some small islands that lay within Madagascar's territorial waters. As French aid declined, Madagascar turned to the Soviet Union and China.

Unfortunately, Madagascar's chief exports—coffee, vanilla, and cloves—competed in saturated markets, so the country could not sustain these ambitious programs. By the late 1970s, the country was in serious economic trouble, which translated into increasing social and political trouble. The government claimed to have uncovered coup attempts in 1980, 1982, and 1983, and Ratsiraka steered an erratic course politically. In 1980, he arrested the opposition leader, Monja Jaona. When this arrest sparked demonstrations and riots, he switched to a policy of reconciliation, pardoning the leaders of the disturbances and actually bringing Jaona into the government. In 1982, he changed course again and expelled moderates from the government. In 1983, he permitted Jaona to challenge him for the presidency but then rigged the elections. The police suppressed the demonstrations that followed, and Ratsiraka dismissed Jaona from the SRC and later had him arrested.

In 1984, security forces crushed the Kung Fu cult, which had approximately 10,000 members drawn from disaffected urban youth. Security forces used artillery to suppress a riot by the Kung Fu rank and file and then killed the leaders while assaulting their headquarters.

The next year, Manandafy Rakotonirina's Maoist MFM challenged Ratsiraka's government in elections and gained three seats in the assembly, and Rakotonirina sat in the SRC. In 1986, cuts in the number of workers employed in the country's biggest port sparked new rioting. In 1987, students struck to protest a plan to reduce their number by 20 percent. Ratsiraka stuck to his economic course, devaluing the Malagasy franc by 40 percent and increasing fuel prices by 50 percent in the same year.

Ratsiraka's economic course was actually the International Monetary Fund's course, for

Ratsiraka proved as flexible in his socioeconomic policies as he was in his political tactics. He continued to espouse socialism and kept leftist politicians in the government, but he accepted an IMF structural adjustment agreement in 1982 that required his government to roll back the social programs it had initiated and gradually return to a free-market economy. He quickly gained a favorable reputation among international bankers for the determination with which he implemented the IMF's program, slashing social spending and imports while cranking up exports. The World Bank qualified the country for money from its Special Fund for Africa, and France and the United States increased their flow of aid. The price of this largesse was a precipitous decline in the Malagasy standard of living; the GDP grew at the rate of just 0.2 percent per year in the early 1980s, and the average yearly income fell from $360 in 1978 to $240 in 1987. Eighty percent of households could not afford to buy the food that would provide the minimum calorie requirements. Malnutrition became the leading cause of death, and infant mortality doubled. Economic crisis underlay the country's political dissatisfaction and social turmoil.

Although international aid helped stave off even greater economic disaster in the 1980s, political discontent remained. In 1987, a near-successful assassination attempt was made on one of the leaders of the government. In 1989, Ratsiraka won another election, but his hold on power began to slip. Later in the year, a small group seized a radio station and announced a fictitious coup to point up dissatisfaction; they repeated the stunt in 1990. In the same year, a supreme court ruling led to the legalization of opposition parties outside the FNDR framework. In June 1991, hundreds of thousands of supporters of the opposition coalition called "Active Forces" staged major protests around the country, demanding a new constitution, a sovereign national conference, and the resignation of Ratsiraka. In October, Ratsiraka agreed to replace the SRC and the National Assembly with the transitional High

State Authority, which would oversee the drafting of a new constitution during 1992. Albert Zafy was selected to lead the new body, but Ratsiraka remained as president. Cabinet positions were divided equally between Ratsiraka's supporters and his opponents.

A "national forum" convened to draw up the document in February 1992, and despite attempts to disrupt the process with violence, the constitution was approved in a referendum on August 19. Two rounds of elections concluded in February 1993 with a decisive victory for Zafy over Ratsiraka, and the new president took office in March. Madagascar had already enjoyed an independent judiciary; a free press; freedom of religion, movement, and assembly; and unions with the right to strike. With the elections of 1993, it joined the ranks of the fully democratic states of Africa.

COMOROS
Statistical Profile

Capital:	Moroni
Area:	719 sq. miles
Population:	500,000 (1994 est.)
Density:	695 people/sq. mile
Growth Rate:	3.5% (1994 est.)
GDP:	$245,000,000
Per Capita Income:	$510
Foreign Debt:	$165,000,000
Life Expectancy:	n.a. (1960), 56 (1992)
Ethnic Groups:	Comorans (no major subdivisions)
Official Languages:	French and Arabic; the people speak a local variant of Kiswahili
Religions:	Muslim (99%), Mohore has significant Catholic minority
Former Colonizer:	France
Date of Independence:	1975

History

Malayo-Polynesians settled the Comoros Islands by the sixth century A.D., and they were joined by Africans and Arabs in the eighth. Thereafter, a dozen sultanates established by religious refugees from the Arab world dominated the islands. European explorers first visited them in the sixteenth century, but it was not until 1842 that one island, Mayotte, first came under French rule. The rest of the islands followed by 1886, and the French imposed such absolute control that the islands were isolated until the 1960s. In 1961, France granted the islands internal autonomy, and in 1968 a student strike provoked such vicious repression that virtually the entire population rose in revolt. The French permitted the formation of political parties, and the next five years saw growing agitation for independence. Pro-independence parties won the great majority of seats in the local Chamber of Deputies in elections in December 1972 and immediately passed a "resolution for independence." The French tried to delay the transition by five more years and, knowing that anti-independence forces were particularly strong on Mayotte, also insisted on an island-by-island referendum. In December 1974, a referendum endorsed independence by 96 percent overall, but Mayotte voted 64 percent against it. Unwilling to accept a partition of the island group on any basis and tiring of the delays, President Ahmed Abdallah issued a unilateral declaration of independence on July 6, 1975.

Mayotte's five deputies immediately cabled France, rejecting independence and appealing for French protection. The United Nations admitted the Comoros as an integrated territory in November 1975, and the government appealed to France and to the people of Mayotte, but that island remained under French control. In a referendum on February 6, 1976, the people of Mayotte endorsed continued association with France by a wide margin, and on December 18 the French Senate voted to make it a "territorial community" within the French Republic. In 1981, French President François Mitterrand agreed to review Mayotte's status every five years, but the material benefits of the French connection virtually ensure that the island will not reunite voluntarily.

Meanwhile, on the other islands, President Abdullah's rule lasted only a few weeks before European mercenaries, led by the Frenchman Bob Denard, staged a coup and installed Ali Soilih, who appeared to be more conciliatory toward France. Once in power, however, Soilih embarked on a program of radical reform. He unveiled women, abolished the traditional costly "grand marriages" and funerals, and attacked the system of prestige based on ancestry. In April 1977, the "Black Period," he dismissed all civil servants, destroyed all government records, and even resigned himself. Called back by the "Revolutionary Youth" he had left in charge, he recalled the government officials on the basis of a new constitution that emphasized local control and decentralized economic and political life. When he undertook these reforms, France withdrew all aid and recalled its technicians, sending the economy into a tailspin. Opposition to Soilih's rule increased, and on May 13, 1978, he was ousted by white mercenaries again led by Denard, who was now working for Ahmed Abdallah.

The mercenaries reportedly cost Abdallah $2 million, and they stayed on to act as his bodyguards—for another $3 million per year. The Organization of African Unity expelled the Comoros for part of a year because of the mercenaries, but the financial and military support Abdallah received from France more than compensated for this. Furthermore, conservative Arab states sent considerable aid to the country, now renamed the Federal Islamic Republic of the Comoros, to finance roads, an airport, a harbor, new power plants, and a telephone system. Abdallah had another benefactor as well, South Africa, which paid for his bodyguards in exchange for help in funneling arms to rebels in Mozambique. So close did the clandestine relationship become that by the late 1980s Denard was jokingly referred to as South Africa's "governor-general" in the Comoros.

After Soilih's reign, Comorians welcomed Abdallah and his mercenaries as liberators. Abdallah ruled initially as co-president with another opposition leader, Muhammad Ahmed. They set up a people's assembly and submitted a new constitution to a referendum. Within hours of its approval, however, Muhammad Ahmed resigned, and the new regime became increasingly corrupt and dictatorial. Supporters of the old government were punished, Abdallah was elected president unopposed, and political parties were banned for 12 years. The opposition in exile formed a party in 1981, and in 1983 the first of several coup attempts took place. Abdallah won another unopposed election in 1984 and his party won rigged elections in 1987. In 1989, he was assassinated by members of the army.

For a brief time, Denard ran the country almost openly, but the French forced him out, and elections were held in March 1990. The acting president, Said Mohamed Djohar, won with 55 percent of the vote. The election was tarnished by allegations of fraud, and Djohar experienced considerable trouble governing. He accused his defeated rival of complicity in a coup attempt in 1991, but just months later invited him into the government and organized a national reconciliation conference. In mid-1992, the conference created a new constitution that reduced the power of the executive. Legislative elections were held in November; they were marred by irregularities and failed to produce a majority party. After half a year of instability, Djohar dissolved the assembly so that new elections could be held; these gave his government a majority. On the surface, Comorian politics settled down, but discontent remained. In September 1995, Bob Denard staged yet another coup. French troops forced him out within days, but Djohar was out as well.

Until the coup, the country seemed to be moving, even if haltingly, toward democracy. In all likelihood, another somewhat democratic regime will emerge. However, with a relatively independent judiciary, free speech, freedom of worship, and the right to organize unions and to strike, Comorians enjoy extensive, even if imperfect, civil rights. Whether their political rights will be stronger or weaker because of the coup remains to be seen.

MAURITIUS
Statistical Profile

Capital:	Port Louis
Area:	718 sq. miles
Population:	1,100,000 1994 est.
Density:	1,532 people/sq. mile
Growth Rate:	1.5% (1994 est.)
GDP:	$2,566,000,000
Per Capita Income:	$2,700
Foreign Debt:	$936,000,000
Life Expectancy:	59 (1960), 70 (1992)
Ethnic Groups:	Hindu of Indian descent (22%); Muslims from India (19%), Creoles (29%), Chinese, and Franco-Mauritanian "Europeans"
Official Languages:	English and French
Religions:	Hindu (51%), Christian (31%), Muslim, Buddhist
Former Colonizers:	France, Great Britain
Date of Independence:	1968

History

Mauritius remained uninhabited until the late sixteenth century, although Arab, Malay, and Portuguese mariners had all visited it. The Dutch first settled in 1598 and remained until 1710. In 1715, the French took over, establishing sugar plantations worked by slaves from the mainland. Great Britain took the island in 1810. In 1833, the British abolished slavery despite fierce resistance from French planters. Indentured Indian workers took the place of slaves, and by 1860 they comprised two-thirds of the island's 300,000 inhabitants. The planters gained representation equal to that of colonial officials in the Council of Government in the early 1800s, and by the early 1900s Creoles and poor whites were politically active. Indian laborers first organized protests against their working conditions in 1909. In 1936, the Labour Party (LP) was formed. At first it represented mainly Creoles in the towns, but between 1948 and 1953 Seewoosagur Ramgoolam, leader of a rural-based Hindu faction, took over leadership. The party became the dominant member of a pro-independence alliance that included a smaller Hindu party and a Moslem party, while the Creoles shifted to the anti-independence Mauritian Social Democratic Party (PMSD). Ramgoolam's alliance won the general election of 1967, and Mauritius became independent on March 12, 1968.

The new country's government was a constitutional monarchy under the British crown. The legislative body was a unicameral national assembly, with 62 elected seats and 8 seats reserved for the "best losers" (selected by a special committee). The governor-general appointed a prime minister from the majority party or coalition, who then chose a council of ministers. The judiciary included a supreme court, a court of assizes, and inferior courts. The Mauritius government is the the the only African parliamentary democracy to survive and function—from independence to today—as a truly multiparty system. The only significant change was in 1992, when the island became a republic, and the governor-general was replaced by a president elected by a majority in the National Assembly.

In the early years, this stability was not apparent. In 1969, Ramgoolam drew the PMSD into the government, shifting the balance of forces to the right. With a wage freeze in effect and 25 percent unemployment, unrest among workers grew until they staged a series of strikes in 1971 and formed the Militant Mauritian Movement (MMM). The government reacted with repression, postponing the 1972 elections for four years, abolishing by-elections, and adopting the Public Order Act and the Industrial Relations Act. The LP-PMSD coalition broke down in 1973, however, and the MMM won 34 seats in the 1976 election. Although Ramgoolam was able to retain control of the government by reviving the LP-PMSD coalition, its hold on power was shaky. As the economy weakened in the late 1970s, opposition grew stronger. In 1982, a coalition of the MMM and the Mauritian Socialist Party (PSM) took 60 seats, and Anerood Jugnauth became prime minister.

The new government did not last long, for the MMM split on the question of whether to accept IMF-mandated austerity measures. Jugnauth rebounded by forming the Militant Socialist Movement (MSM) and winning new elections in 1983 in coalition with the old Labor Party. His government survived a scandal in 1985 involving drug-smuggling by members of parliament, and he won the 1987 elections by broadening the coalition to include the PMSD. He then led the MSM to victory again in 1991 by breaking with the LP and PMSD and forging a new coalition with the MMM. Although there were allegations of electoral irregularities, the Supreme Court validated the election.

Mauritius is a model African democracy. The press is free, having survived an attempt by Jugnauth to curb it in 1984, and the people enjoy freedom of assembly, association, worship, and travel. Unions are active and exercise their right to strike. The GDP per head is one of the highest in Africa, and the GDP is rising by over 6 percent per year. The unemployment rate is just 2.1 percent, and inflation is only 5 percent per year. The economy is diversifying beyond sugar cultivation to textile manufacturing, tourism, and finance, and the government is putting a social welfare program into place. Mauritius is a small but bright spot on the eastern edge of Africa.

SEYCHELLES
Statistical Profile

Capital:	Victoria
Area:	176 sq. miles
Population:	100,000 (1994 est.)
Density:	568 people/sq. mile
Growth Rate:	1.5% (1994 est.)
GDP:	$343,000,000
Per Capita Income:	$5,480
Foreign Debt:	$147,000,000
Life Expectancy:	n.a. (1960), 71 (1992)
Ethnic Groups:	Creole, with a small number of Indians, Chinese, and Europeans
Official Languages:	English and French
Religions:	Catholic (90%), Anglican (8%)

Former Colonizers:	France, Great Britain
Date of Independence:	1976

History

First seen by Europeans in 1502, the Seychelles Islands remained unexplored until 1742 and uninhabited until the 1770s, when French planters imported African slaves to raise sugar. The British seized the islands in 1810 and ruled them from Mauritius until 1888. They became a crown colony in 1903 with nominated executive and legislative councils, and the first elections with even limited suffrage did not take place until 1948. The plantation owners' Seychelles Tax Payers Association dominated this limited system until 1964, when the Seychelles Democratic Party (SDP) and the Seychelles People's United Party (SPUP) were formed. The first, led by James Mancham, advanced association with Great Britain; the second, led by France-Albert Rene, called for independence. The two parties tied in the elections of 1967. The SDP won in 1970, but Great Britain did not favor association. By 1974, Mancham had switched to supporting independence, and he won a bitterly disputed election. A constitutional conference the next year laid the groundwork for independence in 1976, with Mancham as president and Rene as prime minister.

Within a year, Rene staged a coup while Mancham was away. Over the next years, haunted by fears of a countercoup, he steadily increased his own powers. He used a rumored mercenary plot in Kenya to justify passage of the Preservation of Public Security (Emergency Powers) Regulations, under which he declared a state of emergency and ruled by decree. In June 1978, he changed the name of his party to the Seychelles People's Progressive Front (SPPF) and created an affiliated labor organization, the National Workers' Union (NWU). In 1979, a new constitution made the SPPF the country's sole party, and Rene won the presidency in an unopposed election. He organized an army, the Seychelles People's Liberation Army, and set up a people's militia as well, both of which were trained by

Tanzanians. In 1979, Tanzania and Madagascar each sent 300 soldiers and Madagascar sent 2 warships for joint maneuvers intended to ward off any prospective mercenary invaders.

Despite these strong measures, the government was shaken by a series of threats. In October 1979, a proposal to institute national youth service sparked violent protests, which Rene then linked to another alleged plot to overthrow him the next month. A third and more serious coup attempt took place in November 1981, when mercenaries from South Africa disguised as tourists flew in. Customs officials foiled the attempt after a shootout, capturing seven and forcing the others to fly away. In 1982, a group of soldiers mutinied and were put down only with Tanzanian help. In 1983, another less serious coup attempt took place, and was also foiled.

The SPPF conducted single-party elections in 1983 and 1987. Rene won reelection in unopposed contests in 1984 and 1989, but Mancham continued to mobilize opposition from exile. In 1984, the Seychelles National Movement (SNM) replaced the Movement for Resistance (MPR) and two other politicians took over leadership, but in 1985 one of them was machine-gunned in front of his house in London. In 1989, Mancham and the other, Paul Chow, formed a new Democratic Party (DP). In 1990, Mancham challenged Rene to test his popularity in a multiparty election, and in late 1991 Rene accepted the challenge. He set out a three-step process involving elections to a constitution commission, a referendum, and elections to form a new government. He legalized opposition parties, and eight emerged to contest the first election in July 1992. The SPPF won 58 percent of the vote and 14 of 22 seats on the commission; the DP won 33 percent and most of the remaining eight. In a surprise move, the electorate rejected the proposed constitution in November because it favored the SPPF, so Rene postponed the elections and reconvened the commission. The second draft passed. It created a 33-member national assembly—with 22 elected directly and 11 selected proportionally—and a five-year presidency limited to three terms. Rene and the SPPF beat Mancham and the DP handily in elections in 1993.

Seychelles has returned to multiparty democracy, but it remains only partially free as a society. Freedom of the press, religion, and travel is generally respected. But the right of workers to strike is inhibited by ties between the unions and the ruling party and by regulations. The government maintains a network of spies in every village, and uses force and manipulation of the judicial system against political opponents. Still, the broadening of freedoms in the early 1990s may complete the transition to democracy in the latter part of the decade.

PART

3

CONTINENTAL PERSPECTIVES

Introduction to Part 3

Although a discussion of each African country reveals the particularities of its development, the international dimensions of politics and government can best be understood in terms of the continent as a whole. Furthermore, despite the tremendous diversity of countries and governments in Africa, certain common themes can best be illuminated by a continental perspective. Part 3 contains two chapters. The first examines Africa's international relations, both among African countries and between Africa and the rest of the world. The second explores the common themes in the politics and government of the African nations, the common economic and social trends underlying political developments, and the common features of those developments themselves.

CHAPTER

14

International Relations

The three major issues in Africa's international affairs are war and peace, intra-African cooperation, and Africa's external economic relations. Until recently, the first of these seemed the most compelling, but the end of the Cold War and the demise of South Africa's apartheid regime have contributed to the resolution of many of the continent's armed conflicts. Cooperation within the continent, both on the political level of the Organization of African Unity and on the economic level of regional economic communities, is more prominent in Africa than elsewhere in the developing world, but as time has passed, this corporation has come to look increasingly impotent.

The most important aspect of African international relations in the mid-1990s is the continent's external economic relations. Around 1980, most African economies began experiencing increasing difficulties. Their income from exports dwindled, and their expenses—for imported goods and the interest on their debts—mounted. Aid from international agencies and wealthy countries has been helpful, but the long-term solution—internal

development—became increasingly difficult to implement as foreign investors began to pull out of Africa in order to invest in other, more promising regions of the world. The International Monetary Fund and the World Bank became central to Africa's economic survival, but the price was high: structural adjustment that cut imports to the bone, promoted the highest possible level of exports, and required reductions in government subsidies and services that left the majority of people increasingly worse off.

Eventually, the international economic agencies realized that structural adjustment would have to include political reform, and in the late 1980s they became an important force pushing for democratization. In this, their goals dovetailed with the desires of most Africans, but their stringent economic policies made questionable the long-term viability of the democratic regimes they were promoting.

WAR AND PEACE

Africa has experienced a considerable amount of warfare since 1960, but relatively little of it has involved conventional combat between regular armies of opposing states. Furthermore, most of the conventional confrontations that have occurred were brief border skirmishes. The bulk of organized violence in independent Africa has been in civil wars and guerrilla conflicts pitting a regular army on one side against irregular forces on the other.

The most significant small-scale border wars, in which conventional forces clashed briefly in disputes over frontier territory, were between Morocco and Algeria in 1963, Egypt and Libya in 1977, Mali and Burkina Faso (the Upper Volta) in 1974 and 1985, and Senegal and Mauritania in 1989. The conflicts that came closest to being major wars between nation states were the Somali attempt to seize the Ogaden from Ethiopia in 1977 and the Tanzanian campaign that brought down Ugandan dictator Idi Amin in 1978. Two other conflicts that involved large-scale operations by competing conventional forces were Libya's 1986 invasion of northern Chad using helicopters and tanks, which was defeated only with the help of French aircraft and paratroopers, and South Africa's repeated incursions into Angola from the mid-1970s, which fought Cuban army units, Angolan army units, and SWAPO guerrillas.

South Africa's operations in Angola represented the largest-scale component of a much broader military campaign it waged against the "front-line" states in the 1970s and 1980s. South African forces carried out attacks against SWAPO and ANC guerrillas in Mozambique, Zimbabwe, Botswana, Swaziland, and Lesotho, as well as in Angola. They also launched commando operations against guerrilla bases. Furthermore, South Africa staged commando operations against military and economic targets—and it supported guerrilla and dissident political movements—of the countries themselves. The white Rhodesian government conducted the same sort of warfare before it fell, attacking both insurgent and neighboring government targets with its own ground and air forces and also supporting antigovernment forces operating within hostile neighbors.

The white regimes of southern Africa were not the only African governments to intervene militarily in other countries. The Ethiopian army conducted hot pursuits into Sudan and the Angolan army did the same into Zaire. In two cases, African countries committed forces in attempts to influence the outcome of fighting after a regime collapsed. In 1975, Zaire invaded northern Angola in an attempt to help the FNLA against the MPLA as the Portuguese left. In 1990, Economic Community of West African States (ECOWAS) members Nigeria, Ghana, Guinea, Gambia, and Sierra Leone sent troops into Liberia to prevent Charles Taylor's NPFL from taking Monrovia.

In three other instances, African governments sent their troops to support established governments. Senegal sent troops into Gambia to suppress an uprising there in 1981. Zaire sent troops into the Central African Empire in 1978 to support Emperor Bokassa. Morocco, along with French and Belgian troops, sent a contingent to Zaire in 1978 to ward off Katangan rebels attacking out of northern Angola.

The Shaba invasions of 1977 and 1978, in which rebels attacked from Angola into Zaire, are examples of the most common form of military involvement by African states in each others' affairs—support for guerrilla movements. Roughly half the countries in Africa have experienced at least one major internal conflict since independence, and in almost every case the insurgents received some support from neighboring states. In southern Africa, the front-line states actively supported guerrilla movements fighting the apartheid regime until the early 1990s. Zaire and Angola harbored each other's insurgents until 1985; Ethiopia and Somalia also supported each other's antigovernment forces. Ethiopia also supported insurgents against Djibouti until 1991. Libya definitely supported factions in the civil wars in Chad and Sudan, and may have helped Islamic radicals in Algeria and Egypt. Charles Taylor's insurgency in Liberia started from bases in the Ivory Coast, and the Liberian insurgents in turn supported guerrillas operating against the governments of Sierra Leone and Gambia. Senegal claims that Mauritania also supported the rebels in Gambia, and Algeria has supported the Polisario in the Western Sahara.

The Moroccan struggle against the Polisario for control of the Western Sahara is an unusual case. This war pits the Moroccan army against the Polisario's guerrilla forces, which is typical of an internal war. But in this case, Morocco is asserting its sovereignty over a territory that never belonged to it—a territory claimed by an indigenous group that has won recognition from over 35 countries. Yet the Sahraoui Arab Democratic Republic has never controlled the Western Sahara, and Morocco does. Perhaps this conflict is most analogous to the pacification campaigns that followed the European scramble for Africa.

There are several reasons why independent Africa has experienced so few conventional wars relative to the total amount of fighting. For one thing, African leaders early established that the boundaries inherited from the colonial period would be maintained. They recognized that the alternative was an anarchy in which almost every state had as much to lose as to gain. Their realism was reinforced by the probability that open aggression would provoke international sanctions or even intervention by the Western powers.

Another reason is that African leaders have shown exemplary energy in acting as mediators in interstate conflicts. Whether it is because of cultural traditions or because of an overriding interest in stability, mediation is a well-established tradition among African heads of state and has played a role in bringing many smaller conflicts to a speedy end.

A third reason is that most African armies are essentially incapable of conducting a foreign war: they lack the logistical services to sustain combat operations beyond their borders, and they have little training for or experience with large-scale conventional combat. A final, and related, reason is the severe limits most African economies place on military ambitions. Tanzania's attack on Uganda, for example, strained Tanzania severely, and even South Africa found it impossible to sustain its war effort. Only superpower backing allowed most African countries to sustain conventional operations for any length of time.

Consequently, the end of the Cold War has helped defuse many of Africa's conflicts, and the transition to majority rule in South Africa has dampened many more. The ending of conflict between South Africa and Angola led to the end of the insurgency in Namibia and stopped South African raids on its other neighbors. In the Horn of Africa, the collapse of the Marxist government ended the war in Eritrea as well as Ethiopian support for insurgents in Somalia and Sudan. In late summer 1995 the combatants in Liberia readied an agreement to end that war, although renewed fighting erupted in April 1996. Other major armed conflicts continuing in 1996 include ethnic fighting in Rwanda and Burundi, the anarchy in Somalia, the interminable civil war in Sudan, and the Islamic uprising in Algeria, but the level of armed conflict on the continent in mid 1996 was at its lowest point since the 1960s. Because total arms expenditures by African countries declined from the 1980s to the 1990s, much of Africa should enjoy a real "peace dividend" in the later part of the decade.

REFUGEES

Because of the mobility of Africa's subsistence-level rural population as well as the multiplicity of problems besetting it, Africa has contributed a disproportionate share of people to the world's refugee problem: almost 30 percent of the world's refugees against 11 percent of world population. Since southern Africa and the Horn of Africa were the two main sources of recent refugees, the end of apartheid and the defeat of the Megistu regime has led to some decline in the number. On the other hand, Sierra Leone, Liberia, Somalia, and Sudan remain in turmoil; Algeria faces mounting civil insurrection; and the latest round of ethnic fighting in Rwanda and Burundi has created another two million refugees. Because political oppression, ethnic conflict, economic distress, and civil and international wars all displace populations, refugees will be an issue in African international relations well into the future.

Refugees are an obvious economic problem because they need food, shelter, and other support, a burden that falls by default on the host country; but they pose other problems as well. The international agencies that come to their aid have their own administrations and agendas and can seriously compromise the sovereignty of the host country. Furthermore, if the relief effort is particularly successful, it can actually make the refugees better off than the local population, inverting the more usual sources of tension. The refugees themselves can also pose a political as well as an economic burden because wittingly or unwittingly they can carry into the host country the conflicts that forced them to flee. Insurgent groups routinely use refugee camps as recruiting grounds and base camps. Host governments are not supposed to allow this sort of activity, but they often lack the power to suppress it. At the least, the issue clouds relations between the host and source countries, exacerbating what may already be a tense situation. At worst, citizens of the host country can become caught in the crossfire between guerrillas and foreign forces, and the conflict may even escalate into open war.

Despite the problems posed by refugees, the nations of Africa have developed one of the more enlightened policies in the world. The United Nations Convention Relating to the Status of Refugees, drafted in 1951, defined refugees narrowly as people who have fled persecution because of their social group or political opinions. In 1969, the Organization of African States enacted the Refugee Convention, which defines refugees much more broadly, as anyone fleeing external aggression, occupation, foreign domination, or events seriously disturbing public order. The Convention requires that refugees be settled well away from the frontier of the source country and that they refrain from using the host country as a base for subversive activities against their homeland. These provisions have proved dif-

ficult to enforce. Hosts have also had difficulty determining who gets the status of refugee and when the conditions in the home country justifying that status have been corrected. In general, African countries lack the power to enforce such determinations, not only because of their military weakness, but also because attempts to expel refugees would almost certainly alienate aid-providing international agencies and foreign governments.

Aid for refugees comes from a wide variety of sources, mainly Western governments and international relief agencies, but most of the funds are funneled through the United Nations High Commissioner for Refugees (UNHCR). The office was established in 1951 to protect refugees, but the force of circumstance expanded its mission dramatically to include providing assistance. It can work only with the permission of the host government, but generally does not work through that government. Instead, the UNHCR prefers to deliver aid directly to the refugees, ostensibly to avoid overloading the host country's administration, but in reality because it fears that too much will otherwise be lost to corruption.

Although the UNHCR has provided invaluable assistance to innumerable African refugees, it does not always receive an invitation to help. Sometimes the host government fears the intrusion of international agencies, as Sudan did in 1983 when it discovered that U.S. and Israeli covert agencies had been sneaking Falasha refugees from Ethiopia out of Sudan to Israel. In other cases, the host may not want to acknowledge refugees in deference to the source country. Burundi, for example, declined to publicize the presence of refugees from Rwanda before the holocaust in 1994. The Ivory Coast did the same in regard to refugees from independent Guinea.

Yet another reason a host country may not invite international relief is because it plans to absorb the refugees. As the history of the United States shows, refugees can be a source of enrichment, bringing needed skills and labor. Sierra Leone, for example, absorbed tens of thousands of refugees from Guinea during the rule of Sekou Toure. Overall, only about 40 percent of African refugees have needed the help of international relief agencies; the other 60 percent have "spontaneously settled" in the host countries (in the parlance of the UNHCR). For a continent burdened by poverty and underdevelopment, this is a remarkable achievement.

Refugees who do not "spontaneously settle" wait for a change of conditions in the source country so that they can return home. Fortunately, in many cases the reasons they uprooted are relatively transitory: an oppressive but unstable regime, a drought, or a short-lived insurgency. As a consequence, being a refugee has not been so interminable a condition for Africans as it was for East Europeans and Palestinians displaced in the 1940s. Perhaps because many live as subsistence farmers in communities that have only weak ties to the larger polities, Africans have proved quick to move when conditions got bad. They have also proved quick to settle where they can or to return when conditions improve. The sufferings of African refugees and the difficulties they create for their host countries should not be minimized, but they have generally not evolved into the kind of unappeasable diaspora found elsewhere in the world.

THE ORGANIZATION OF AFRICAN UNITY

On May 25, 1963, the heads of 30 independent African states signed the charter for a new international organization intended to bring the beginnings of unity to a continent that had heretofore been divided by vast sociocultural differences and rival colonial empires. Two of Africa's three remaining independent countries, Morocco and Togo, joined shortly thereafter, and all colonies that subsequently gained their freedom joined as well. Only South Africa remained outside the organization until 1994, when the white regime that made the country anathema to the rest of the continent gave way to black majority rule.

The organization that began its life in 1963 fulfilled a pan-African vision that went back to the nineteenth century. A product of the black diaspora in the United States and the Caribbean as much as of Africa itself, the pan-African movement spawned a series of five pan-African conferences between 1901 and 1945 that brought together black leaders from both sides of the Atlantic and inspired anticolonial agitation as well as dreams of continental unification. After the black anticolonial movement first bore fruit with the independence of Ghana in 1957, the new nation's leader, Kwame Nkrumah, invited the heads of eight of the nine then-independent African states (all but South Africa) to Accra to attend the first Conference of Independent African States in April 1958.

Thereafter, the movement splintered into several groups before coming together to form the OAU. Nkrumah and the other "radicals" drafted a charter for a "Union of African States" in November 1958, which they adopted at a conference in Casablanca in January 1961. Leaders of Francophone states in the "Brazzaville" group formed several different organizations as these countries became independent, most notably the Afro-Malagasy Union (UAM) in September 1961. Liberia's William Tubman invited a group of more conservative leaders to a series of meetings between 1959 and 1961 in Liberia and Nigeria at which they drafted a charter for an association of sovereign states that did not involve political integration. Ethiopia's Haile Selassie managed to persuade the members of all these groups to convene in Addis Ababa, where they overcame their differences and created the OAU.

The charter drafted by the founders of the OAU laid down the principles and set out the structure of the organization, which, with a few modifications, have lasted over 30 years. The organization's basic principles include (1) the equality of member states; (2) noninterference in the internal affairs of member states; (3) acceptance of the borders inherited from colonialism; (4) promotion of cooperation for the common good; and (5) peaceful resolution of disputes between states. Its structure includes an assembly of heads of state that meets annually, a council of ministers composed of cabinet-level representatives of each state that meets twice a year, and a general secretariat headed by a secretary-general to oversee the organization's day-to-day operations. The charter also set up a commission of mediation, conciliation, and arbitration to settle disputes between members, and five other specialized agencies to deal with economic and social issues; educational and cultural matters; health, sanitation, and nutrition; scientific and technical research; and defense. Chairmanship of the Assembly of Heads of State rotates annually, and by tradition the chairman's country hosts the convocation that year.

Like other international organizations composed of sovereign states, the OAU has suffered from a fundamental weakness—it can only deal with issues its members want to act on, and the need to maintain unity often precludes taking an aggressive stance. Thus, the principle of noninterference in internal affairs kept it from even acknowledging the gross violations of human rights by Idi Amin, "Emperor" Bokassa, and Macias Nguema, among others. Similarly, the organization's rigid acceptance of inherited boundaries made it difficult for its mediation commission to actually mediate border disputes because all it could do was defend the status quo. The danger of fragmentation kept the organization from addressing some of the continent's toughest international problems, such as the war between Ethiopia and Somalia, and its one attempt to deploy a peacekeeping force—to Chad in 1981—ended quickly in failure. The organization suffers from a serious financial deficit because of the failure of many of its members to pay their dues; yet many of these same members manage to put on a lavish display when it is their turn to host the summit, with newly constructed convention halls, hotels, and other facilities that generally go unused once the delegates have left. Even some African heads of state despair of the organization: President Bongo of Gabon once remarked, "These summits are a waste of time

. . . . Sometimes, sitting there, listening to all the talk, I think I will scream."

Nevertheless, the OAU has managed to score some notable successes. Its survival as a symbol of continental unity and a potential forum for debate and action is an achievement in itself. Moreover, it has been able to help achieve some of the goals that its founders set. It helped launch the mediation efforts that ended the border war between Morocco and Algeria in 1963, and it was instrumental in bringing the border wars between Mali and Burkina Faso (then Upper Volta) to an end as well. It played a strong role in coordinating African policy toward South Africa, decisively rejecting the accommodationist approach advocated by some countries in the early 1960s and sticking to an implacable opposition that helped finally bring the apartheid regime to its knees. Along the way it supported a series of anticolonial struggles, and it opposed Morocco's annexation of the Western Sahara. It admitted the Sahraoui Arab Democratic Republic as a member in 1982, a decision it stuck to even though Morocco then withdrew. Furthermore, the dispute, coupled with the distaste of many members for the imperious radicalism of the year's chairman, Muammar Gaddafy, led to the cancellation of the annual meeting that was to have been held in Tripoli. In 1987, the OAU formally responded to criticism of its doctrine of nonintervention by adopting the African Charter of People's and Human Rights, thereby establishing a standard that can potentially supersede the doctrine of noninterference.

The OAU has been even more vigorous in the economic sphere. It began to deal with Africa's growing economic difficulties in 1978 by bringing together the continent's agriculture ministers to create a plan giving priority to food production. The heads of state adopted this "Lagos Plan" in 1980, and at the same time resolved to create an African Common Market by the year 2000. In 1985, the organization adopted the African Economic Recovery Program to deal with the continent's economic problems, and African leaders worked together to get a special session of the

UN General Assembly to discuss the plan and get pledges of support from the developed countries of the world. The success of this effort is hard to measure because of the formidable economic problems dragging the continent down, but good intent and energetic action were there.

Finally, there can be no question of the benefits of the more mundane cooperative development ventures the OAU's specialized commissions have fostered over the years, things like the creation of the Trans-Saharan Highway, the establishment of direct telephone links between African capitals, and the coordination of joint programs in preventive health and technological research. It is easy to fault international organizations like the OAU for their inability to solve the great problems of the day, but it is equally easy to overlook the myriad contributions they make to long-term efforts to solve the less visible problems that bedevil humankind.

REGIONAL ORGANIZATIONS

Since independence, the countries of Africa have created over 200 intergovernmental organizations, the most extensive network of international linkages of any region in the developing world. In part, this pattern reflects the continent's colonial heritage, for the colonizers organized many aspects of government and economy on a regional basis. The French administered their colonies as two regional blocs until the eve of independence and deliberately frustrated African attempts to maintain them during the transition in order to keep the new states politically weak. At the same time, they encouraged the new states to maintain economic ties that linked them to France. The British did not develop regionalism to the same extent when they ruled, but in several cases they did try to integrate neighboring colonies. The ill-fated Central African Federation united Nyasaland (Malawi) and the two Rhodesias (Zambia and Zimbabwe) for the decade before independence, although the federation collapsed because the Africans feared that it would insure settler domination.

Farther north, the East African Common Services Organization, embracing Kenya, Tanzania, and Uganda, survived independence to become the basis for the East Africa Union, one of the earliest and most extensive attempts at economic integration.

The other basis for Africa's enthusiastic internationalism is the small size and poverty of most African states. Most of the intergovernmental organizations are economic in nature, ranging from research and professional organizations to development banks and customs unions. Their primary reason for being is to create economies of scale and avoid duplication of effort. Five countries faced with persistent drought might not be able individually to afford studies of the climate needed for long-range planning, for example. Even if they could, they would end up paying for the same information five times. By pooling their resources, they can afford things they could not obtain alone and avoid wasting precious resources on things their neighbors are also doing. Similarly, any one country might not have enough people to justify investment in a cement plant or hydroelectric dam, but a half dozen countries would.

An important reason that Africa's regional organizations tend to be economic is that the existence of the Organization of African Unity discourages the formation of smaller political groupings. Only the Francophone states have bucked this trend, encouraged by France, which works to maintain its dominance over them even in independence. The then conservative West African states of the Ivory Coast, Mali, Dahomey, and Upper Volta formed the Entente Council in 1959, and in 1965 most of the former French colonies came together in the Common African and Malagasy Organization (OCAM). The latter organization expanded to include countries not historically linked to France. The organization itself is not very effectual, but the member states continue to hold biannual summit meetings at sites alternating between Africa and France.

The only other political organization rivaling the OAU is the Arab League, which includes the five North African states plus Sudan and Somalia. However, the two organizations have tended to support rather than oppose each other. In 1973, the Arab League created the Arab Bank for Economic Development in Africa to help offset the damage done to African states by rises in the price of oil, and African countries generally support the Arabs diplomatically in their struggle against Israel.

The African Development Bank (ADB) is a continental organization that is purely economic in orientation. It was formed in 1964 under the aegis of the UN's Economic Commission for Africa (ECA), with 32 members. Its membership has expanded as more countries have become independent, reaching 51 African states in 1994. In the same year, it had 26 non-African members as well, mainly Western and Arab states, for membership was opened to them in 1974. This move brought in a substantial infusion of capital, and the bank has played a crucial role not only in financing development projects, but also in helping states through the structural adjustments mandated by the IMF and the World Bank in the 1980s.

At the other end of the spectrum from these broadly defined continental institutions are a host of organizations with specialized purposes. These are too numerous to discuss individually, but the mention of five conveys something of their tenor. One is the African Center for Monetary Studies, which researches economic issues. Another is the West African Rice Development Association, which is dedicated to making the region self-sufficient in rice. The purpose of the Organization for Coordination in the Fight against Epidemic Diseases in Central Africa (OCEAC) is clear from its title. The Club of the Sahel brings countries in this drought-stricken region together with potential aid donors. The Permanent Inter-State Committee on Drought Control in the Sahel (CILSS) works with the UN Sudano-Sahelian office and brings together the heads of state and a council of ministers to deal with drought problems. Like the specialized bodies of the OAU, these organizations, and dozens of oth-

ers like them, perform a myriad of prosaic but vital services for the people of Africa.

The most prominent regional organizations are the ones promoting wide-ranging regional economic integration. These range from organizations focused on a single geographic area, most often a river basin, to massive groupings embracing entire sections of the continent. Most of the former are located in West Africa and include the Mano River Union, the Niger Basin Authority, the Organization for the Development of the Senegal River (OMVS), and the Liptako-Gourma Integrated Development Authority. The only similar association in Central Africa is the Economic Community of the Great Lake Countries (CEPGL), joining Rwanda and Burundi to Zaire.

Southern Africa has no organization tied to a specific geographical feature, but it does have two economic unions that were outgrowths of the racial confrontation between blacks and whites. The Southern African Customs Union (SACU) dates back to 1910 and was reorganized in 1969 and again in 1976. Its original purpose was to institutionalize white South Africa's economic domination of Botswana, Lesotho, and Swaziland. It forbade them from concluding any trade agreements without South African consent and bound them in a common market. The Southern African Development Coordination Conference (SADCC) was formed by the black states of the region in 1980 with the explicit purpose of reducing their dependence on South Africa. The group solicited and apportioned aid from outside donors to compensate for direct and indirect costs of the struggle against apartheid, and it coordinated the economic activities of its members. Mozambique focused on transport and communications, for example, while Zimbabwe specialized in food production and Tanzania took the lead in industrial development. The end of apartheid in South Africa has ended the political reasons for these organizations, but the region's economic problems mean that they will probably remain, although undoubtedly in modified form.

The most ambitious regional groupings are two sets of economic unions, one in West and the other in Central Africa. The older members of each set were outgrowths of the French regional administrations during colonial times. In West Africa, the Customs Union of West Africa (UDAO), founded in 1959, was expanded into the Economic and Customs Union of West Africa (UDEAO) in 1965. In Central Africa, the Equatorial Customs Union, also founded in 1959, grew into the Economic and Customs Union of Central Africa (UDEAC). The UDEAO collapsed in 1969 due to its failure to promote the interests of its poorer members, but a new organization, the Economic Community of West Africa (CEAO), took its place in 1973. The UDEAC developed without interruption into a successor organization, the Economic Community of Central African States (ECCAS), which was founded in 1983.

In West and Central Africa, each of the Francophone economic communities has an associated central bank that issues CFA (African Financial Community) francs tied to the French franc. CFA francs are used as a common currency by the member states. Each also has an associated development bank that helps arrange and finance development projects. The two regions differ in that Central Africa has no organization to parallel the West African Monetary Union (UMAO).

Both of these associations of French-speaking countries exist within larger, more recently established economic unions that arose from a very different impetus. Since its inception in 1958, the UN Economic Commission for Africa (ECA) has promoted regional integration schemes that draw together all states into organizations without ties to former colonial masters. In the early 1970s, Nigeria adopted the idea in order to foster its own burgeoning economy and embarked on a diplomatic campaign that led to the founding of the Economic Community of West African States (ECOWAS) in 1975. This organization of 16 states includes an assembly of heads of state that meets annually, a council of ministers that meets semiannually, a permanent secretariat, a development bank, and a currency clearing house to facilitate intraregional trade. Member states committed themselves to a three-stage transition process over a 15-year period that would begin with a freeze on tariffs and end with the creation of a free-trade zone and a common external tariff. Poorer members are compensated for their losses under the arrangement; a "rules of origin" provision benefits locally owned (mainly Nigerian) industries while penalizing foreign-owned (mainly Francophone) ones.

In 1980, the ECA scored another success when the OAU, meeting in Nigeria, adopted the Lagos Plan of Action (LPA). The LPA called for the creation of a single continental common market by the year 2000 through a two-step process in which a number of regional unions would be created as a transitional measure and then merged. ECOWAS and the Arab Maghreb Union of North Africa already existed, but associations for the rest of the continent were needed. The Preferential Trade Area of East and Southern Africa (PTA) was established in 1981 and had 20 members in 1995, while the Economic Community of Central African States (ECCAS) followed in 1983 and had 10. Both are modeled on ECOWAS, although the PTA has no compensation mechanism and a more sophisticated mechanism to deal with foreign ownership, and the ECCAS made little progress toward defining a common policy or creating common institutions in its first decade.

Despite their ambitious programs, these economic unions have failed to produce results. Member states typically implement few of the plans they so enthusiastically approve at the annual summits because the costs are immediate and measurable while the benefits are long-term and uncertain. The unions have not generated much additional investment. This is so because Africa, with its poverty and political instability, is a less attractive opportunity than other areas of the world; because even the unified markets are relatively small; and because the specific provisions penalizing foreign ownership in the LPA unions discourages the very thing the groups are intended to promote (Africans having relatively little capital to invest themselves). The actual amount of trade among the member states has remained static at roughly 5 percent of their total foreign trade, owing in part to confusion between the overlapping Francophone and LPA units, but mainly to the simple fact that these countries have little their neighbors need.

Ironically, the main potential of the regional unions is political and diplomatic rather than economic. The French consciously promote Francophone associations to maintain their neocolonial influence on the continent. ECOWAS has been most successful as a forum for regional diplomacy and peacekeeping. Its members signed a formal defense protocol in 1981, and its most notable accomplishment to date has been the organizing of a peacekeeping force to intervene in the Liberian civil war. ECOWAS also provided a site for reconciling Senegal and Mauritania in 1989. The PTA has not been as successful as a diplomatic forum, perhaps because it is too big. ECCAS has had trouble attracting heads of state to its meetings at all. These reasons account for the unimpressive records of these two organizations.

Because most African states are small and poor and need to pool their resources, it is unlikely that they will cease trying to establish regional intergovernmental organizations. Unless and until a number of regional powers emerge to lead the way to broad unity, as Nigeria did during the formative stages of ECOWAS, the most consequential institutions in African affairs will actually be the innumerable, anonymous specialized bodies. The more visible regional unions will be mostly for show.

AFRICA AND EUROPE

Europeans have been involved with Africa since the fifteenth century. The collapse of their short-lived empires did not destroy the much more deeply rooted economic relationships, and colonialism itself left a legacy of diplomatic, cultural, and, in the case of France, military ties.

Of the former colonial powers, France has maintained the strongest links to the continent. The CFA monetary zone and the network of regional organizations that bind the French-speaking African countries directly to each other and indirectly to France are just one element of its aggressively neocolonial policy, which includes economic, political, diplomatic, and military elements. Through these, France has not only maintained strong ties to its former colonies, but it has expanded its influence to include other African countries as well.

In the economic sphere, France maintains direct, bilateral economic ties to most of its former colonies. It holds exclusive or preferential rights to a variety of strategic raw materials like uranium and oil, ensuring steady access to these crucial commodities. It channels most of its foreign aid to Africa, and that aid makes it the single biggest donor to the continent, although 70 percent of the funds end up paying for French products and helping support more than 7,000 French technical personnel stationed on the continent. The former colonizer and the former colonies maintain a trade relationship in which the latter supply mainly raw materials while the former returns manufactured goods, perpetuating the colonial division of labor.

In the political sphere, France exercises a shadowy influence on the affairs of its independent former African colonies, manipulating their policies through a combination of incentives, pressures, and dirty tricks. Its methods have ranged from vetting potential African leaders and involving them in lucrative business deals to maintaining "special action" bureaus in their capitals and even assassinating public figures deemed hostile.

Diplomatically, France has been more open, posing as a friend of Africa in international forums while asserting its primacy in the area against other world powers. France's independent-minded foreign policy during the Cold

War made its pro-Third World stance ring true, although the certainty that the other Western powers would insist on a conservative course meant that it seldom had to live up to its rhetoric. Its overriding concern was the defense of its own interests against both outside encroachments and African assertions of independence. As former president Valery Giscard d'Estang once put it, "I am dealing with African affairs, namely with France's interests in Africa."

The teeth of France's African policy are the ongoing military relationships it maintains with a variety of countries. France has technical assistance agreements with 23 countries, to which it provides a total of 960 advisors. It has full defense agreements with eight countries, and stations a total of 8,650 troops in seven. To back these up, it maintains a rapid deployment force of 44,500 men. In the 30 years from 1963 to 1993, it intervened in Africa a total of 30 times, or an average of one intervention per year. Its military role serves the triple purpose of defending France's own interests, making France the West's "gendarme" in Africa, and making manifest France's claim to the status of a world power.

World power has its costs as well as its benefits, and in the 1980s and 1990s France began to stagger under its burden. In the 1980s, French private investors reacted to Africa's growing economic distress by disinvesting, reducing the overall flow of French capital to the continent from 5,800 million francs in 1985 to just 300 million francs in 1990. The French government tried to ignore the declining profitability of its informal empire, but in 1990 a government report concluded that "Sub-Saharan Africa is . . . not suffering from a temporary crisis nor from a passing slump . . . but from a lasting inability to make itself part of the world economy." In that same year, France refused to intervene on behalf of a government in a country where it had troops, when it allowed Idriss Deby's army to take over Chad. The next year, it similarly declined to fight for the government of Djibouti.

In 1994, in the most crucial development, France devalued the CFA franc by 50 percent, thereby admitting that it could no longer afford the burden of supporting the overvalued currency and the underdeveloped countries that used it. "France alone cannot solve all the economic and financial problems of all the African countries," explained Prime Minister Balladur, and his government announced that it would tie new aid to prior agreements with the IMF and the World Bank. The consequence will be sharp reductions in the standards of living of the affected countries. It may also have the effect, as Albert Bourgi observed, of "mentally decolonizing the African leaders . . . finally cutting the umbilical cord that, for more than three decades, has tied them to their former metropole."

France's turn away from its neocolonial policy moves it in the direction the other former imperial powers have long taken. When France was more aggressive, Spain was happy to see Equatorial Guinea gravitate into the French orbit. Republican Portugal restored good relations with its former possessions, but it was too poor to keep them from similarly gravitating toward France. Belgium maintains strong ties to its old possessions, particularly Zaire, but it did not resist when France established its primacy there as well. With these countries linked to its former colonies, France could claim leadership not just of Francophonic Africa, but of a Latin Africa, which it championed against the Anglophonic influences of Great Britain and the United States.

In contrast to France's aggressive neocolonialism, Great Britain maintains thin political ties to its former colonies, and its economic interest in them has steadily shrunk. The new states joined the Commonwealth, which provides a forum for informal cooperation and played a crucial role in the transformation of Rhodesia into Zimbabwe in 1979. In the 1980s, however, it was seriously strained by the schism between Great Britain, which opposed sanctions against South Africa, and the rest of the members, which favored them. Great Britain's attitude toward the Commonwealth in the 1990s was signaled by its decision in 1993 to cease funding the Commonwealth Institute in 1996.

Great Britain's waning interest in the Commonwealth parallels its waning interest in Africa in general. The continent receives scant attention in the popular British press, and British political circles generally regard it with a mixture of impatience and disappointment. The Conservative government cut aid programs by more than 20 percent in the early 1980s; its contribution has been lower than Japan's since 1986 and Italy, the Netherlands, and Sweden each gave more in 1990. It refused to support the World Bank's Special Facility for Africa until 1985, and in 1993 it refused to help finance loans to countries engaged in IMF-mandated structural adjustment programs. The programs Great Britain does fund are increasingly oriented towards furthering its own interests—large construction projects, for example, which in the past have proved of limited value in promoting economic development, but which generate lucrative contracts for British multinationals.

British businesses, however, have generally lost interest in Africa even more than the government has. Imports from sub-Saharan Africa made up 7.2 percent of British imports in 1965 but only 1 percent in 1992. Similarly, Great Britain sent 6.4 percent of its exports to sub-Saharan Africa in 1965 but only 1.6 percent in 1992. The growth of alternative sources of raw materials and opportunities for investment account for these declines to some degree, but Africa's economic malaise is the primary reason. In 1992, for example, the cumulative cost to the British Treasury of honoring export credit guarantees on loans to Nigeria that had gone bad was approximately $4 billion, four times the total value of British exports to Nigeria in the previous year.

One African country with which Great Britain has maintained close economic and diplomatic ties is South Africa. In 1985, British imports from and exports to South Africa were almost equal to British trade with all 46 of the other sub-Saharan countries. Before

majority rule, this was a real blemish on the British record, but when South Africa's political situation changed, it gave Great Britain a unique opportunity to help with one of Africa's most promising developments.

The former colonial powers' disengagement from Africa in the 1980s and 1990s is symptomatic of a broader change in the relationship between the two continents. Since the formation of the European Common Market, Africa has enjoyed a privileged economic relationship with its northern neighbor, for France insisted that its African colonies receive preferential treatment under the Treaty of Rome. In 1963, the Yaounde Convention modified this relationship to reflect the Francophone countries' new independence. In 1973, the Lome Convention broadened the relationship to include all of Africa and islands in the Caribbean and Pacific to accommodate British interests when the country joined the Common Market. The basis for the relationship was the concept of "Eur-afrique," the supposed complementarity of Africa as a resource producer and Europe as a manufacturer of finished goods. Even though this was the same old relationship that had worked to Africa's disadvantage since the sixteenth century, it was touted as a partnership of equals. Coming at a time when the world's less-developed countries were demanding a "new international economic order" that would benefit them (and when the 1973 oil embargo made the industrial countries fear for their access to raw materials), the Lome Convention offered Africa special access to European markets, stabilized prices, and a generous helping of aid. The agreement was renewed three times at five-year intervals, with the last installment due to last for 10 years, but its future thereafter is in doubt. It has lost appeal for the European countries because not only have raw material prices remained low for decades, but raw materials have declined in importance for Europe as it shifts from an industrial to a service economy. Furthermore, other, more stable, areas—Eastern Europe, the Far East, and even Latin America—have emerged as sources of the raw materials that are needed and as markets for manufactured goods. Africa's contribution to Europe's imports has fallen from 8.9 percent in 1965 to 3.2 percent in 1992. The percentage of exports from Europe to the continent has dropped from 8.2 percent in 1965 to 3.7 percent in 1992. Europe's ties to Africa are becoming inconsequential to the Europeans.

Africans have reasons to question the Lome Conventions as well, for in practice they have failed to stabilize prices, failed to promote industrial development, and helped perpetuate the continent's economic dependency on Europe. Unfortunately, Africa remains far more dependent on Europe than Europe does on it. Europe's share of African imports and exports has declined since 1960, but only from above 60 percent of each in 1960 to about 45 percent of each in 1992; Africa receives about the same proportion of its aid from Europe. Africa may be marginal to Europe's economy, but Europe is central to Africa's.

Ironically, Europe's economic withdrawal from Africa, which was most pronounced in the 1980s, contributed to Africa's democratization movements in two complementary ways. First, by contributing to the economic crisis afflicting the continent, it fueled the discontent that shook many of the existing authoritarian governments. Second, European governments increasingly put conditions on further aid, making it dependent on political reforms. The French have proved unwilling to follow up their tough talk about connecting aid to reforms with tough action. In fact, they have stepped up internal security training to counter pro-democracy agitation in their most important (and despotic) clients. Other European countries, however, have stuck to their guns, and insisted on evidence of reforms before extending further aid. Some have gone beyond this crude economic coercion to promote democracy through positive programs of political training and civic education. The real question is whether European governments and businesses will try to help reverse the current economic trends for the political purpose of helping newly democratic governments weather the storms that lie ahead.

THE UNITED STATES, THE SOVIET UNION, AND THE COLD WAR

Ties between the United States and Africa go back almost to the founding of the first American colony. In 1618, two years before the sailing of the *Mayflower*, the first African slaves landed in Jamestown, itself founded just 11 years before. Over the next two centuries, European and American slavers brought millions of Africans to the New World; African-Americans today comprise more than 10 percent of the U.S. population. One of the first commercial treaties the young republic signed was with Morocco, in 1786, and 15 years later it fought its first overseas war on the shores of Tripoli. In 1799, the United States established its first sub-Saharan consulate (in Cape Town). This consulate was followed in the next decade by others in the Cape Verde Islands, Gambia, and Zanzibar. In 1816, the American Colonization Society began organizing the reverse migration that brought the first ex-slaves to Liberia in 1821. Americans participated in the exploration of Africa, and American missionaries went to teach the gospel, but the country held back from Europe's partition of the continent. In the late nineteenth century, black-American interest in African affairs increased steadily, culminating in Marcus Garvey's United Negro Improvement Association, which sought to promote racial pride and a "back-to-Africa" movement. By 1930, the United States had full diplomatic missions in Addis Ababa, Monrovia, and Pretoria, and consulates in seven other towns. During World War II, President Roosevelt criticized European colonialism on numerous occasions and insisted that the Atlantic Charter applied to Africans and Asians as well as to Europeans. After the war, the American government pushed for inclusion of Ethiopia and Liberia in the new United Nations, but with Europe's far stronger ties to Africa and the American need for European support in the Cold War, the United States let the Europeans take the lead in Africa through the late 1950s.

American policy changed when European and American blundering pushed Egypt into the arms of the Soviet Union. The USSR had never had a strong interest in Africa, but the Soviets saw the colonial world as a natural source of allies and were always on the lookout for targets of opportunity. When the United States blocked funding of the Aswan High Dam and the British and French invaded in reaction to Nasser's subsequent nationalization of the Suez Canal, Egypt turned to the USSR. The Soviets poured in technical assistance and military equipment, and Cairo became a center for African liberation movements.

The Soviet-Egyptian alliance lasted for over 10 years, but it broke down in the early 1970s when Anwar Sadat expelled the Soviets and invited in the Americans. The Soviets had supplied plenty of arms and advice, but relatively little money for development, and the Egyptians decided that they could get a better deal from the West. This pattern was repeated elsewhere in Africa when newly liberated countries turned to the Soviets as an alternative to the Western powers only to find that they could be just as racist and that they were eager to supply arms and advisors but were niggardly with cash. What aid they did provide was often ludicrously inappropriate, and everything seemed to come at a heavy price. The first development aid the USSR sent to newly independent Guinea consisted of two snowplows and 10,000 toilet seats. A Soviet-financed meat-packing plant in Somalia sent the bulk of its output to the Soviet Union at discount prices. Ethiopia had to mortgage its coffee crop for 10 years to pay for the $1 billion in Soviet military aid sent in 1977, and when drought hit Ethiopia a short time later, Soviet humanitarian aid came to nothing. The Soviets became the continent's largest arms supplier, sending 11 times more weapons than the United States and four times

more than France, but they contributed little to the continent's economic development. From the 1950s to the 1970s, the Soviet Union remained popular in Africa because of its support for liberation movements, and many Africans who received their education in Moscow retain strong ties to the USSR. Its support for the repressive Ethiopian regime's war in Eritrea in the 1980s, however, soured many Africans toward it.

Aside from a larger budget for economic aid, the United States generally pursued an equally short-sighted and self-serving policy in Africa. Deferential to the economic interests of its European allies and inclined to view every local power struggle as an extension of the Cold War, the United States frequently ended up supporting corrupt dictators who espoused anticommunism simply to secure American backing while terrorizing their people and impoverishing their countries. The top six recipients of American aid between 1962 and 1988—imperial Ethiopia, Kenya, Liberia, Somalia, Sudan, and Zaire—were all dominated by authoritarian leaders. Five of the six experienced civil wars, and four of the six finally overthrew their U.S.-backed leaders.

Two issues particularly troubled American relations with Africa during the Cold War. The first was the preference most African states showed for a policy of nonalignment over explicit ties to the West. To Africans, this policy was attractive both because they could play the two sides off against each other and because they hoped to avoid being drawn into conflicts over issues that really didn't matter to them. The United States, however, interpreted nonalignment as hostility and adopted a belligerent stance that made the U.S. fear into a self-fulfilling prophesy.

The second issue that troubled African-American relations was white rule in southern Africa. For one thing, U.S. businesses had considerable investments in the region. Also, southern Africa was a source of important minerals found in few other places on earth, it lay along the route that supertankers used to carry oil from the Persian Gulf to Europe, and it was run by people who looked a lot more like the great majority of policymakers in Washington than did the leaders of other African countries. Consequently, while American public opinion generally disapproved of white rule, the American government proved reluctant to do anything about it. President Kennedy encouraged American diplomats to flout South Africa's segregation laws___ 'resident Carter promoted human___ as elsewhere, but overall th___ the whites from the ·___ that it professe___ most pror___ dent Reaga___ gagement"___ community wa___ ever, both Amer___ the economic impact___ ___tion in international sanctic___ ___uted to South Africa's dramatic ref___ ___s.

At just the same historical moment, the Soviet Union became much more cooperative towards the United States, and when it broke apart, the Russian state that succeeded it was so far reduced in power that it ceased to be a factor in African affairs altogether. The United States no longer had to tolerate corrupt dictators in the name of global strategy. It continued to tolerate some in the name of economic expediency, but it also began to promote peace and democracy more vigorously in the early 1990s. Soviet-American cooperation played a vital role in resolving the Angolan and Namibian situations in the late 1980s. Since 1990, the United States has worked for peace negotiations in Sudan, Mozambique, Angola, Liberia, and Somalia. Most often the United States uses a combination of financial incentives and economic penalties to influence the parties, but in Somalia in 1992 it went so far as to send 28,000 troops to ensure delivery of food supplies, disarm warring factions, and lay the foundations for a stable government. It was able to accomplish only the first of these goals, just as it has been able to help bring about peace agreements in only some of Africa's other trouble spots, but there is no question that the world's remaining superpower has been using its influence to dampen the continent's brushfire wars.

In countries plagued by corrupt dictatorships, the United States is using its considerable resources to promote democratic reforms. By 1990, the United States Agency for International Development (U.S. AID) had adopted a policy of making democratic reforms an explicit consideration in its disbursements. In 1993, the Clinton administration announced that it was sending substantial sums to South Africa, Mozambique, and Ethiopia, which were making great strides toward democracy, and nothing to Zaire, Liberia, and Sudan, which were not. In the same year, the U.S. offered to forgive at least half the debt of about 18 low-income African countries on the condition that they adhere to economic liberalization policies, and it suspended aid to Nigeria when the military derailed that country's democratization process.

A final contribution by the United States to Africa's democratization movement in the 1990s is a series of programs aimed at fostering democratic values and techniques among African peoples. Run mainly by the government-funded National Endowment for Democracy (NED), which includes institutes run by the Democratic Party, the Republican Party, the AFL-CIO, and the U.S. Chamber of Commerce, these programs include training in party organization, electioneering, judicial procedures, union organization, and entrepreneurship; monitoring election procedures and human rights; and publicizing democratic concepts. The programs attempt to move beyond throwing money at Africa's problems to creating the political culture in which they can be solved.

THE UNITED NATIONS

The United Nations consists of six principal organs and 16 affiliated organizations. Only three independent African countries existed to join the United Nations when it was founded, but over the next quarter century the continent came to comprise over 25 percent of the organization's members. As African and other "emerging" nations came to predominate, the UN's concerns broadened from its original focus on collective security and postwar recovery to long-term economic development and social welfare. Consequently, the United Nations has become one of the foremost external influences on the African nations.

The United Nations' six principal organs include the Security Council, the General Assembly, the Secretariat, the Trusteeship Council, the International Court of Justice (ICJ), and the United Nations Economic and Social Council (ECOSOC). African states have been influenced by all six.

The Security Council consists of five permanent members that hold veto power and ten nonpermanent members that do not. It bears prime responsibility for maintaining international peace and security. None of the permanent members is African, so no African nation has veto power, but African nations serve regularly as nonpermanent members, which can give them considerable influence in world affairs. Actions directed by the Security Council have had considerable influence in African affairs—from the ill-fated intervention in the Congo in 1960 through the successful shepherding of Namibia to independence in 1989.

Every country in the United Nations is represented in the General Assembly, and each has one vote. Consequently, the sheer number of African countries gives a strong influence to the continent. Since African interests often correspond to those of Latin America and South Asia, the less developed countries can generally determine the General Assembly's policies. Unfortunately for them, the body can pass only nonbinding resolutions and therefore has little real power, but it serves as an important forum in which issues can be raised, options discussed, and the consensus of world opinion expressed. It does not give the small and poor countries of Africa control over world affairs, but it gives them an opportunity for influence they would not otherwise enjoy.

The Secretariat runs day-to-day affairs. The secretary-general heads it, supported by a staff of 14,000 international civil servants. In 1996, the Secretary-General is Boutros Boutros-Ghali of Egypt, the first African to hold the position. Both he and the second secretary-general, Dag Hammarskjold of Sweden, asserted their leadership in ways that had a significant impact on Africa. Hammarskjold played a prominent role in organizing the UN intervention in the Congo, and Boutros-Ghali exercised considerable influence on the UN intervention in Somalia. Otherwise, the main influence on Africa of the Secretariat, aside from administering decisions by other organs, has been as a training ground for African diplomats, since staff positions are allocated in part on the basis of geographic distribution.

The Trusteeship Council played an important role in the transition of now-independent African countries from colonialism. Trust territories inherited from the League of Nations, like the Cameroon, and those created after World War II, like Somalia, were not colonies destined to perpetual subordination, but temporary dependents that were to be prepared for eventual independence. This difference affected not only the trust territories themselves, but also the colonies, for if the trusts were capable of eventual self-rule, then it was harder to justify holding neighboring colonies in perpetuity. The Trusteeship Council also played a role in resisting South African designs on Namibia by maintaining a commissioner for the territory once the International Court of Justice affirmed UN sovereignty over the area in 1973. With Namibian independence, the work of the Council in Africa was done.

Both through its own agencies and through its oversight of almost all the UN's affiliated institutions, the Economic and Social Council is the arm of the United Nations with the greatest influence over African affairs. Its regional Economic Commission for Africa

(ECA) has played an important role in formulating African development strategies, most notably the Lagos Plan of Action of 1980. It has other commissions that deal with statistics, population problems, social welfare, human rights, and science and technology. All of these are particularly important to the less-developed countries because they would not be able to afford to focus on these issues on their own.

Similarly, the autonomous agencies ECOSOC oversees contribute in a variety of ways to the economic and social development of African countries. One of the most important agencies is the International Labor Organization (ILO), which focuses on improved working conditions but encourages improved living standards and economic stability as well. Another is the Food and Agriculture Organization (FAO), which promotes agricultural improvements in order to raise nutrition and living standards in the less-developed world. The World Health Organization (WHO) promotes both disease control and improved health services, with an inevitable emphasis on less-developed countries. Its most notable accomplishment was the eradication of smallpox, having tracked down the last known cases of it in Ethiopia. Other agencies specialize in areas like communications, meteorology, and civil aviation, which, while of less specific concern to African countries, still benefit them in particular because they could not otherwise afford them at all.

THE INTERNATIONAL MONETARY FUND AND THE WORLD BANK

Two of the United Nations' affiliated organizations have come to play a decisive role in African politics since the mid-1980s. Ironically, both are essentially economic institutions: the International Monetary Fund (IMF) and the World Bank. How they have come to influence the continent's politics so enormously reveals much about the condition of contemporary Africa.

Both the IMF and the World Bank originated at the 1945 Bretton Woods Conference. Originally called the International Bank for Reconstruction and Development, the World Bank first focused on helping with the reconstruction of war-ravaged Europe, but it soon branched out into loans to promote development. It gets its capital from subscriptions by its members, who vote in proportion to their contributions, and from the sale of securities to private investors and central banks. As a consequence, the Bank follows extremely cautious loan policies, in part because of the influence of the dominant "Group of Five" (the United States, Japan, Germany, Great Britain, and France) and in part because of its need to maintain the confidence of its investors. Therefore, it channels most of its regular loans to higher-income developing countries.

In order to help poorer, riskier countries, the Bank established the International Finance Corporation (IFC) in 1956. This branch makes both loans and equity investments in concert with other agencies in order to act as a catalyst for development. In 1960, the Bank set up a soft-loan subsidiary, the International Development Association (IDA), which offers almost concessional assistance to poor countries. In 1988, it created the Multilateral Investment Guarantee Agency (MIGA) which guarantees loans to minimize risks due to political actions like war, revolution, and nationalization.

Through these various agencies, the World Bank funneled money in three phases to Africa, and other less-developed regions. In the first phase, from the 1950s through the 1960s, the Bank focused on big-ticket infrastructure development projects like dams, highways, railways, power plants, and telecommunications facilities. In the 1970s, it switched its emphasis to grass-roots rural development and social welfare, funding programs to promote agricultural improvements, population planning, public health, and small-scale business enterprises. Neither of these approaches succeeded in sparking self-sustaining development in Africa, so they were followed by the third phase in the 1980s. The Bank began pushing structural adjustment, or the restructuring of countries' economies to emphasize free enterprise and maximum participation in the international economy. It was in this phase that the Bank's activities began overlapping those of the IMF.

The Bretton Woods system gave the IMF the role of maintaining orderly currency relations in the international economy, which included loaning money to help countries cope with short-term balance of payments problems. The Fund acts essentially as a credit union. Members make contributions in proportion to their financial resources, and they can draw out money in times of need. Its government, like the World Bank's, is based on financial contributions, so it is effectively controlled by the Group of Five plus Saudi Arabia. Each country's potential draw is divided into four portions, which are increasingly more difficult to access. In the Fund's first years, loans were strictly limited in both amount and duration, but over time the potential amounts were increased, particularly for primary producers like most African countries, and the repayment periods were extended. The Fund recognized that problems originally seen as transitory were in reality structural.

The IMF's involvement with developing countries grew over the course of the 1970s as it was increasingly called upon to help with their balance-of-payments problems due to skyrocketing oil prices and declining prices for other commodities. In 1982, when Mexico threatened to default on its massive debt and thereby brought the international economy to the brink of catastrophe, the IMF became the key player in defusing the crisis. It helped Mexico and other debtors renegotiate terms and obtain financing, providing the latter itself when necessary but only if the recipient agreed to radical measures to cut imports, increase exports, and reduce inefficiencies caused by government intervention in the economy. At this point, the IMF's policies converged with those of the World Bank, confronting distressed nations with a uniform pressure for fiscal conservatism.

The debt crisis hit Africa particularly hard. In 1974, Africa's total debt amounted to about $15 billion; in 1992, it had climbed to almost $185 billion, about 109 percent of Africa's total GNP. The root of the problem was a combination of ambitious and ill-conceived development projects undertaken with borrowed money and declining prices for the mineral and agricultural exports that were supposed to pay for them. The consequence was a dramatic increase in the number of African countries beholden to the IMF, from two in 1978 to 28 in 1990. In the 1970s, African nations accounted for less than 20 percent of the IMF's assistance programs, but in 1990 they accounted for about 60 percent. African countries also have the highest repeat rate in the world. Over 75 percent of sub-Saharan countries received some form of assistance from the IMF during the 1980s, and most of them also had agreements with the World Bank.

The extent of Africa's reliance on the IMF and the World Bank has had not only severe economic consequences for the continent, but social and political ones as well. To some extent, these consequences are outgrowths of the economic impact, for reduced imports and government spending mean fewer luxuries for the well-to-do and fewer social programs for the poor. Increased exports often mean decreased food production, as land and labor are used to grow commercial crops. All these economic strains mean heightened social tensions and eventually political unrest.

The IMF and the World Bank have also had a far more direct influence on African politics. During the late 1980s, these bodies expanded the concept of structural adjustment beyond the economic sphere to encompass political reform as well. Disillusioned with the economic performance of the corrupt dictatorships Western aid had long supported, the two institutions began to insist on political reforms as part of structural adjustment. The change was codified in the World Bank's 1989 publication, *Sub-Saharan Africa: From Crisis to Sustainable Growth*, which emphasized the need for political accountability, freedom of the press, and political pluralism—in other words, multiparty democracy. As with the earlier economically oriented strategy, the IMF became the principal architect of the structural adjustment programs. IMF approval came to be a precondition not only for its own assistance and that of the World Bank, but for assistance from other international agencies and individual countries as well.

By a conjunction of historical circumstances, the most conservative Western economic institutions began pushing for the same goals as Africa's leading reformers at a time when the end of the Cold War made political experimentation possible. As a result of this conjunction of circumstances, in early 1996 roughly half of Africa's 53 nations could be considered either democratic or well on their way to becoming democratic. The IMF's and the World Bank's programs have helped shape not only the policies but the very nature of African governments in recent years.

CHAPTER

15

Common Challenges

Today the nations of Africa confront three sets of challenges. The first set of challenges is economic. Africa's population is the fastest growing in the world, while its economy is the slowest. All the prescriptions from the 1960s and 1970s have failed, leaving most African countries impoverished debtors staggering under the burden of externally imposed austerity programs. These programs have proved extremely painful, and their success is far from assured. One way or another, either African economies must grow faster or African populations must grow slower. Otherwise, the people's standard of living will continue to deteriorate, leading to an accelerating succession of crises and a chronic state of human degradation. The most hopeful scenario is that political reforms will lead to administrative reform that will unlock the continent's economic potential. The vibrant and extensive black markets in most African countries suggest that the potential is there, but to realize that potential Africans will face formidable obstacles in vested interests and established practices.

The second set of challenges is social. Every African country contains diverse groups divided by economic interests and ethnic affiliations. They must find ways to live together, or else their societies will be torn apart. The forms of social decay range from crime through civil war, but all entail human misery and inhibit economic development and human progress. The most important thing that must be recognized about the social divisions, however, is that they are not caused by some sort of human failing in Africans, as many Americans seem to assume. Rather, these divisions represent reasonable adaptations to the continent's economic and political realities. In particular, the ethnic affiliations misleadingly labeled "tribalism" are not throwbacks to the primitive past, but instead are modern social structures that meet people's economic, social, and cultural needs. Rather than ignoring or repressing them, a successful solution will have to find some way to accommodate them or to fulfill their functions better.

The third set of challenges is political. Virtually all the parliamentary structures set up at the point of decolonization collapsed within a decade and were replaced by authoritarian regimes that proved to be both inefficient and corrupt. African public affairs came to be dominated by complex patronage networks in which individuals used resources obtained legally and illegally through their official positions. Within this almost feudal structure, fiefdoms were defined sometimes geographically and more often bureaucratically. Local patrons dispensed favors to their clients, and were clients in turn to more powerful patrons located closer to the centers of power. In most cases, the ultimate source of wealth, and hence power, was control over the flow of external resources into the country from overseas, so the upper levels of the civil and military bureaucracy came to form Africa's real ruling class. The human embodiment of this patronage network was the president/head of the party at its apex. Its political face was the all-embracing official party, behind which wealth and power could be dispensed and used outside of public scrutiny. Its social underpinnings were the ethnic relationships that defined the channels of patronage and clientage linking the center to the country at large.

Since the late 1980s, this situation has changed as domestic and foreign pressures push for multiparty democracy. The external pressure comes from donor countries and institutions convinced that their economic stake in the continent can only be secured through political reforms. The internal pressure reflects the frustration of a growing number of people with a system that is increasingly incapable of delivering a better life because of inefficiency and corruption radiating down from the top. Democratization has met with success in some countries, but in others the established powers have found ways to block or co-opt it. Even where the transition has been accomplished, the tide can turn at any time. Democracy in Africa remains on the upswing, but its hold on peoples' imaginations is still fragile. It will have to clearly accomplish the purposes for which it was created—promoting economic development and ending profiteering by select social groups—if it is to endure.

POPULATION PRESSURES AND HEALTH

Population growth and economic decay have caught most African nations in a squeeze play. They must get a handle on one or the other, or preferably both, if they are to break out of the downward spiral in which they are trapped.

Africa's population is growing at the fastest rate of any region in the world today. In 1800, there were 70 million people in Africa. By 1960, the number had tripled to 210 million. It tripled again to 660 million in just 30 more years, by 1990, and it is expected to double to 1.2 billion by 2015. The annual rise was 2.9 percent in 1994, almost twice the 1.6 percent of the world's average and almost a third higher than the 2 percent for developing countries overall. Africans made up just 7.8 percent of the human population in 1950; by 2000 they will make up 14.2 percent.

The primary cause of this rapid increase is high fertility rates (number of babies born per thousand people in one year) combined with a modest decline in mortality (number of people out of a thousand who die each year). Premodern societies around the world had high fertility rates, but they had correspondingly high mortality rates. Africans continue to reproduce at premodern levels, with 46 children born per 1,000 people each year, in contrast to 27 per 1,000 in the world as a whole. Meanwhile, improvements in health have reduced the reported death rate to 16 per thousand, which is still higher than the world average of 11. In some African countries the acknowledged rate reaches 20 per thousand and it may be closer to this overall because of under-reporting of infant mortality, but even this figure is only about half the death rate of premodern societies. While the exact numbers are not certain, there can be no doubt that markedly fewer deaths plus a steady birth rate make for a rapidly expanding population.

In most parts of the world, this disjunction between birth rates and death rates brought spurts of population growth similar to Africa's, until people adapted to the new health situation by having fewer babies. Western countries went through this transition in the nineteenth century. Asian and Latin American countries, still in Africa's situation in 1960, have dropped their birth rates markedly over the last 30 years (from 41 per thousand in Latin America to 31 and from 42 per thousand in Asia to 22). Africa's birth rate, however, has remained the same.

Africa's fertility rate has remained high for a variety of reasons. Two factors among women—the high rate of marriage and an early average age of marriage—play an important role, for the proportion of women marrying affects the proportion having children, and the earlier a woman begins bearing children the more she is likely to have. The number of children can, of course, be controlled through contraception, but the rate of usage is particularly low in Africa. Only four countries south of the Sahara reported that 25 percent or more of married women practiced family planning in the mid-1980s. The reason is in part low levels of literacy and education among Africa's rural poor, but even many relatively educated women living in cities exhibit a striking desire for a large family. Many African societies still place great emphasis on a woman's ability to have children, and a man's status is also affected by the number of his offspring. Furthermore, parents expect children to take care of them in their old age, and in a society where social services are uncertain at best, children constitute the most reliable form of social security. African governments, run in some cases by men whose children numbered in the dozens, generally exhibited little interest in family planning programs until the 1980s. As a result, African women continue to have an average of six or seven children each.

Ironically, while Africa has the highest population growth rate in the world, it has the highest mortality rate as well. As a consequence, the average life expectancy is about 20 years lower than it is in the developed countries, 50 years instead of almost 70. The main causes of this difference are the appallingly high infant and childhood mortality rates. One baby in eight dies before its first birthday, in contrast to one in 65 in Europe. Diseases like measles, dysentery, polio, lockjaw, and gastroenteritis, which are easily controlled through sanitation or medicines, carry off innumerable children under five. The rate of immunization against serious diseases did go from less than 20 percent in 1980 to almost 60 percent in 1990, but less than half of the Africans south of the Sahara have regular access to health care and nearly two-thirds lack a source of safe drinking water. There was one physician for every 580 people in Europe in the early 1980s, but there was only one for every 25,600 people in Kenya and one for every 92,000 in Burkina Faso. Furthermore, most doctors in African countries live and practice in the cities, so their availability to the rural majority is in fact far less than these proportions would indicate. Finally, training and compensation structures for doctors orient them away from knowledge of the infectious diseases that afflict the majority of Africans toward the chronic illnesses, such as those associated with old age, that are the major problem not only of Western peoples but also of the small African elite who can afford to pay for medical care.

The general level of health care in Africa is thus just high enough to fuel the population explosion but low enough that it does not prevent widespread misery. The emergence of AIDS threatens to tip the balance toward high mortality rates again. Twenty-nine African countries had reported cases of AIDS by the late 1980s, and the list has continued to grow. The total number of known cases was 14,000, but the actual number was estimated at 10 times that figure, and estimates of the number of people infected by the HIV virus range up to 5 million. East and Central Africa have been particularly hard hit, with 8 to 10 percent of city dwellers infected, 30 percent of long-distance truck drivers testing positive, and up to 80 percent of prostitutes carrying the disease. Some countries have begun AIDS-prevention campaigns, but they face an uphill battle against illiteracy, resistance to condoms, inadequate sterilization of needles at underfinanced and overworked clinics, and the inability to afford the cost of screening blood transfusions. At the least, detecting and caring for the victims places a significant new burden on Africa's already inadequate health services. At the worst, AIDS may prove to be a demographic disaster, halting or perhaps even reversing Africa's rate of population growth.

ECONOMIC DEVELOPMENT

The purpose of the colonial economic systems was to transfer wealth from the colonies to the metropolitan countries. The colonies provided raw materials in exchange for manufactured goods on terms that overwhelmingly benefited the colonial powers. The raw materials themselves were often produced or extracted through compulsory labor, were transported to the coast on roads and railroads built by forced labor, and were handled by European firms that enjoyed formal and informal privileges and that funneled most of the profits back to Europe. Transported aboard European-owned ships, the products were processed in European plants and then resold to the Europeans' profit. If destined for Africa, the finished goods were transported aboard European ships once more and sold in protected markets. At best, colonialism generated far more wealth for the metropolitan country than for the colony. At worst, and overall, it drained wealth from Africa in the form of uncompensated labor, expatriated profits, undervalued exports (relative to world markets), and overpriced imports (relative to the same). The net effect was to fuel Europe's economic development and hinder Africa's.

In the early 1960s, when the majority of African countries became independent, they faced a choice between two prevailing economic theories on how they should develop. The first approach, "modernization" theory, which was prevalent among Western development experts, held that the new nations should continue to focus on exporting raw

materials to the industrial countries. By exploiting their comparative advantage at producing certain products, they could build up capital and invest it in infrastructure and technological improvements. These investments would in turn stimulate expanded production and enhanced productivity, generating further profits that could eventually be channeled into other, more advanced economic activities.

The other approach advocated rapid industrialization in order to create a modern manufacturing sector. Some radicals advocated an extreme version in which the new countries were to become industrial juggernauts within the span of a decade or two. Inspired by the successes of the Soviet Union in the 1930s, they envisioned the rapid development of basic industries within a socialist structure of central planning. Some Western economists and moderate African leaders embraced a more moderate version, known as the "import substitution" strategy, in which industrial development was to start by replacing imported consumer goods with local manufactures. In both cases, tariffs, subsidies, and other preferential treatment would be needed to protect the infant industries, and in both cases the goal was to create an industrial sector that could act as the engine drawing the rest of the country forward economically and socially. This approach would at the least free the country from the disadvantaged position of raw-materials supplier and might turn it eventually into a regional powerhouse stimulating (and profiting from) development in neighboring countries.

During the 1970s, both of these strategies began to be seriously called into question. At first, the criticisms were essentially theoretical, perhaps best exemplified by Edward Schumacher's book *Small Is Beautiful*. The new view rejected both large-scale agricultural projects and massive industrial projects in favor of small-scale programs designed and implemented by or in close consultation with local communities. These programs would create incremental improvements that would build almost imperceptibly toward an eventual transformation of society. Essentially a demand-oriented approach in contrast to the supply orientation of the others, it inspired a new focus on rural development programs and underlay the World Bank's "basic human needs" strategy in the 1970s that targeted the poor and oppressed in cities as well as on farms. If the other strategies reflected a "trickle down" approach, this new strategy aimed for a tidal effect by which the entire economy would be lifted from below.

A far more serious challenge to the dominant development strategies came in the late 1970s and 1980s: the recognition that they had failed to deliver development. The roots of this failure were already apparent in the early 1970s, when the Third World nations began calling for a "new international economic order." This effort collapsed in the face of the First World's implacable resistance, and the international economic climate went from bad to worse. The first shock was the dramatic rise in oil prices after the Yom Kippur War in 1973, followed by further rises in 1978 and 1979. In 1970, Africa paid 10 percent of its export earnings for oil; a decade later the figure was 22 percent. The rise in oil prices benefited the lucky few African countries that had significant reserves, but the collapse in prices in the 1980s hit them severely and did not come in time to help the rest significantly.

The dramatic fluctuations in energy prices alone would have been enough to devastate Africa's development efforts, but other problems beset both agriculture and industry. One major problem was the emphasis on cash crops for export at the expense of food production, a problem that was compounded by a series of droughts and the steady desertification caused by deforestation, overgrazing, and farming of marginal land by the continent's burgeoning population. In some cases, warfare has added to the misery, disrupting both production and distribution. As a result of all these factors, food production declined from 353 pounds per person in 1970 to 220 pounds per person in 1984; output increased only 1.5 percent per year while the population increased at double

that rate. As a consequence, cereal imports rose from four million tons in 1965 to 20 million tons in 1980. Despite the imports, almost 40 percent of the population suffered from chronic malnutrition by the mid-1980s, and almost 10 percent were on the verge of starvation. Ironically, Africa, the world's most agricultural continent, depends for its food on imports from the world's most industrialized ones.

Unfortunately, the emphasis on export crops at the expense of food crops did not result in increased production of the export crops. On the contrary, after increasing by 1.9 percent per year in the 1960s, agricultural exports declined in the 1970s at the same rate. As a consequence, they were no greater in 1980 than in 1960, even though overall world trade in the commodities had grown by 1.8 percent in volume and 3.3 percent in value (constant prices) each year during these two decades. Africa's share of the world market fell from 80 percent to 65 percent for cocoa, from 54 to 27 percent for peanuts, and from 21 percent to 3 percent for palm oil. Commercial farming suffered from all the problems that bedeviled food production: drought, desertification, and the disruptions of war. Furthermore, many African governments pursued economic policies that hurt export production. They tended to keep currency values too high, which hurt competitiveness, and they deprived farmers of the full world-price value of their crops. In theory, this was to divert the surplus into other development programs, but all too often it just supported a corrupt managerial class while reducing the farmers' incentive to produce and their ability to invest in the technological improvements they needed to remain competitive.

African agriculture was also hurt by declining terms of trade, especially late in the 1970s. One ton of cocoa was worth $23,400 in 1975 and could buy 148 barrels of oil, but in 1980 it was worth just $10,200 and could buy just 63 barrels of oil. Similarly, cotton went from $18,400 per ton, or 119 barrels of oil per ton, to $9,600, or 60 barrels of oil.

African mineral exports, which make up twice as much of the continent's output as do agricultural products, were hit by declining terms of trade at least as hard. Copper, for example, fell from $17,800 or 115 barrels of oil per ton in 1975 to $9,500 or 58 barrels of oil in 1980. Oil-exporting countries did not suffer from these forces in the 1970s, but they were hit by steeply declining prices in the mid-1980s.

Overall, commodities prices have remained low since the early 1970s due to changes in industry and the opening of competing sources in other parts of the world. Meanwhile, the costs of manufactured goods, Africa's chief imports, have increased consistently, rising as much as 14 percent in the single year 1985–1986.

Another source of stagnation in the export sectors is inefficiency and corruption in government and business, which causes misallocations of resources. These misallocations demoralize producers and reduce competitiveness in the global marketplace. This problem played an even bigger role in the overall failure of Africa's industrialization efforts. All too often, industrial enterprises were run by parastatial corporations, semipublic companies that served as sources of patronage and opportunities for bribes more often than as entrepreneurial organizations aggressively holding down costs while seeking market opportunities. Hothouse industrialization would have been difficult in any case given the small size of many African countries' markets, the small pool of technically trained personnel, the difficulty of keeping up with advances in manufacturing technologies and techniques, and the complacency that always threatens businesses protected by government from competitive pressures. Combined with the rampant corruption, lackadaisical work routines, and administrative confusion that bedeviled much of independent Africa, the failure of most African industrial enterprises was almost certain. Of all the countries on the continent, only South Africa has succeeded in industrializing. Only a handful of others—

Nigeria, Kenya, Senegal, Ghana, the Ivory Coast, Mauritius, Swaziland, and Zimbabwe—have significant industrial sectors at all, and only in the last two listed did manufacturing contribute more than 20 percent of the GDP in 1980.

While Africa's economic performance between 1960 and 1980 was lackluster at best, it virtually collapsed during the 1980s. During the first two decades of independence, the per capita GDP grew at an average rate of 1.6 percent per year for the continent as a whole. During the first five years of the 1980s, in contrast, the per capita GDP *fell* at the rate of 4 percent per year, for a decline of almost 20 percent in the standard of living between 1980 and 1985. Looked at another way, 80 percent of African countries improved their standard of living between 1960 and 1980, but in the early 1980s, 75 percent saw their standard of living fall. Elsewhere in the world, per capita GDPs generally increased despite economic hard times, even in other less developed regions like South Asia and Latin America. Africa will require 40 years of moderate growth to regain the per capita GDP it had in mid-1970s.

This dismal economic record both caused and reflected the IMF-imposed structural adjustment programs discussed in the previous chapter. In brief, African countries, like other less developed nations, borrowed from commercial lenders during the 1970s but found themselves increasingly strapped as the world's economic climate and their own internal economic policies turned bad. The IMF and the World Bank worked together to define conditions for loans that emphasized reductions in the state sector, an end to consumer subsidies, increased exports, and decreased imports. The goal was to improve the balance of payments, and not only IMF and World Bank loans, but loans from almost all sources, came to depend on adoption of the prescribed policies.

The austerity programs proved bitter pills for society in the short run, have generally failed to produce the desired results in the medium run, and have had a severe impact on the outlook for the long run by curtailing investment in economic and social development. IMF programs have sparked rioting and rebellion in some countries and generate resentment everywhere. They have added to the daily hardships of an already-pressed populace, punishing the poor and powerless in particular for programs that seldom benefited them, or did so marginally at best. The daily misery of the poor and powerless translates directly into long-term debility for their societies as a whole. Malnutrition has been so exacerbated that 40 percent of African children in the mid-1980s went through a period of deprivation that caused permanent mental or physical damage. Their suffering was thus not just their personal tragedy, but also a long-term legacy that will affect the economic performance of the next generation. Similarly, reductions in health care result not only in immediate discomfort for the afflicted, but in long-term disabilities that will ultimately cost far more than their prevention or timely cure. Cuts in education similarly undercut one of the areas vital for the future, while decaying infrastructures and deferred investments will cost sorely as time goes by. Africa has the lowest rate of nourishment, health care, literacy, and investment in the world, and the IMF and the World Bank, established to inject capital to alleviate balance of payments problems and foster development, have found themselves in the ironic position of drawing capital out of the continent and pursuing policies that endanger long-term development.

Worst of all, the structural adjustment programs achieved uncertain gains at best. Between 1980 and 1990, half the IMF programs in Africa broke down, while two-thirds of the Bank's failed as well. By their own reckoning, only one of 26 countries did well in 1990–1991, 14 did fair, and 11 did poorly. The democratization movement of the early 1990s that the two institutions have helped promote may prove more effective at creating conditions for economic development, but there is no real basis in experience to expect it. Both East Asian and Latin American economic suc-

cesses have generally been achieved under authoritarian regimes. The failure of Africa's authoritarian governments to promote economic development proves that authoritarian rule is not a sufficient condition for development of a less-developed country, but it does not prove that democratic government will fare any better. Democracy is worth promoting for its political value in any case, but its economic value remains to be seen.

Of course, it is unfair to lay all Africa's economic woes at the feet of the IMF and the World Bank, for they did not originate them, and no coherent alternative to their prescriptions has been put forward. As Ghana's Kwesi Botchwey has said, "Structural adjustment is very painful, but structural maladjustment is much worse." Without the intervention of these institutions, Africa's position might well be far worse. In the decades after independence, Africans worried about the continuing role of Western multinational corporations in their economic affairs, going so far as to fully or partially nationalize them in order to reduce their power. Since the late 1980s, however, African leaders have begun to worry that the multinationals will go away. Disinvestment from Africa is the dominant trend among international businesses, which are disillusioned with the instability, corruption, and inefficiency, and which see better opportunities elsewhere. B.A. Kiplagat, a senior African diplomat, observed recently that "Eastern Europe is the most sexy beautiful girl, and we are an old tattered lady. People are tired of Africa. So many countries, so many wars." An executive in a multinational company put it even more bluntly in a confidential interview with Thomas Callaghy, head of the University of Pennsylvania's Political Science Department: "Who cares about Africa? It's not important to us. Leave it to the IMF and the World Bank." Under these circumstances, the international agencies either are the only source of funding, or their imprimatur is the only thing that makes other sources willing to lend.

Africa's economic outlook is currently bleak. A few countries are attempting to establish export-processing zones in imitation of the East Asian success stories and Mexico, but these have met with little interest in the international business community. Until recently, the dominant theory of Africa's status in the world was known as "dependency theory," which held that African states, along with other less developed countries, occupied a peripheral position in the world economy that condemned them to perpetual servitude to the industrialized core countries. Africa's experience gives some validity to dependency theory, but the emergence of the newly industrialized countries of the Pacific Rim has challenged it by demonstrating that peripheral countries can under some circumstances industrialize, just as earlier modernization theory predicted. The current trends in Africa challenge dependency theory in another way. African countries are now in danger of complete marginalization both politically and economically. Since the end of the Cold War, they have ceased to have much geopolitical significance, and their economic decline means that their economic importance is on the wane as well. As foreign investment dries up, they will be hard put to meet their growing populations' most basic needs. If present trends continue, much of Africa may cease to play even a peripheral role in the world economy. There is a real danger that sections of the continent will collapse into an economic black hole, with resultant human misery on an unprecented scale.

On the other hand, the official economic data may be so inaccurate that Africa will prove to actually have a relatively robust economy that is being deliberately hidden from the predatory view of the state. Regional studies indicate that a tremendous amount of economic activity goes unrecorded, from unpaid labor and moonlighting to massive smuggling operations that involve millions of dollars and thousands of people. Corruption and inefficiency may actually mask necessary and beneficial activities impossible within formal institutions of state, just as smuggling tramples on the artificial borders left by colonialism to re-establish natural routes of trade and commerce. Unfortunately, the magnitude of the underground economy is by definition impossible to measure, since its whole purpose is to avoid the costs and inefficiencies imposed by official institutions. It could make up a large fraction, or even a low multiple, of the official economy. If this is the case, then more representative and rational political structures could well release pent-up potential by removing at least some of the inefficiencies in the black market created by having to operate illicitly and at least some of the obstacles to legitimate commerce created by the existence of a parallel economy.

To some extent, the democratization movement may reflect the frustration of urban middle-class people who participate in the illicit system because it is necessary for their survival in a cash economy, but who are aware of and resent the costs that it imposes. The really successful people can afford necessities, luxuries, and the private guards needed to protect them, and have no interest in reform. People of more modest means would benefit enormously from a system free of the inefficiencies created by official corruption and illicit operations. Transformation of Africa's dual economy into a single legitimate system would both reveal heretofore uncounted resources and yield tremendous savings.

URBANIZATION AND CLASS CONFLICT

By the end of the colonial period, African society had been thoroughly disrupted. Since the continent remained predominantly rural, significant aspects of traditional social relations survived to varying degrees in different countries, but in most areas the changes were more significant than the continuities. Similarly, while precolonial Africa had sizable urban centers, particularly in the north and west, the cities that emerged under colonialism and continued to grow apace after independence had far greater differences than similarities to the precolonial centers. In town and countryside alike, the new economic interest groups and the new networks of social relations that arose under colonialism continued to grow after, and were joined by new groups and relationships arising from independence.

In the countryside, colonial rule and the process of decolonization generally undercut the traditional status of the upper classes. In most cases, the traditional rulers' power was based on control of taxes and labor rather than on ownership of the land itself. When the colonial administrations usurped these governmental powers, traditional rulers had no residual property rights to sustain their social predominance. Where the colonizers ruled through them or included them in colonial councils, their interests put them at odds with nationalist movements, and the nationalists tarred them as collaborators. In some colonies, elements of the traditional ruling class allied with or even gained leadership over the independence movements, and in a larger number they continued to exercise considerable influence over rural society after independence. However, in most cases this reflected their ability to capitalize on the vestiges of traditional power to gain a modern education, organize a modern political party, or engage in modern business enterprises. Like aristocracies elsewhere, the extent to which Africa's precolonial elite maintained its social status depended on the extent to which it was able to adapt to new economic and political realities.

Among the rural masses, processes begun and relationships formed under colonialism usually continued. In some countries, like Tanzania and Mozambique, land reform programs attempted to impose collectivist, state-controlled agriculture, but these generally met with widespread resistance and little economic success. More often agriculture continued to combine widespread near-subsistence farming by the majority of people with pockets of commercial farming. In some places, peasants grew commercial crops on farms they owned themselves, perhaps assisted by landless wage laborers or neighbors supplementing their

subsistence farms with paid work. In other places, export crops were grown by wage laborers on plantations that were either still owned by foreign multinationals or had been nationalized and were now run as state agencies or parastatal corporations. In these conditions, a small group of peasants have emerged as entrepreneurial farmers, while the vast majority have languished as subsistence cultivators, have struggled to eke out a living combining some farming with wage labor, or have given up farming to seek survival through wage labor in agriculture, in mining, or, most commonly, in employment in one of the continent's burgeoning urban centers.

As a consequence of the flight from the farms, Africa's cities have continued to grow at an unbridled pace since independence. The population of Cairo, the continent's largest city, increased five times between 1940 and 1990, and Johannesburg doubled in the same period. Lagos increased 10 times from 300,000 in 1970 to 3 million in 1985; Nouakchott, Mauritania, grew 50 times, from 5,000 to 250,000, between 1965 and 1985. Overall, the continent's urban population in 1950 was 32 million people, less than 15 percent of the total population. By 1985, it had swelled to 170 million people, or over 30 percent of the total. By the end of the century, it is expected to reach 350 million people and make up 40 percent of the continent's population.

Most of the increase has been in a relatively small number of large cities. In 1950, the continent had just one city over 500,000, but in 1985 it had 10. Five of these had populations of 2 million or more. By the end of the century the number is expected to rise to 29.

Many of the largest cities are national capitals; others are important regional administrative centers. These connections have heightened the bias of most African governments against rural interests in favor of urban ones—the single most important social fissure in Africa today. Just as the colonial powers used the surplus from African agriculture to support administration and development, independent African governments have seen agricultural wealth as the source of funding for industrial and other urban-oriented development. Furthermore, political considerations have made it more urgent to please city dwellers, who live near the centers of government, than to please peasants, who live far away. Finally, the influential members of the government have themselves lived in cities and have aspired to a modern middle- to upper-middle-class lifestyle.

As a consequence of all these considerations, African governments have used various means to divert profits from agriculture to the cities. These means have ranged from marketing boards that pay below-world prices for commodities to protectionist tariffs that keep the cost of finished goods artificially high to currency policies that overvalue exports and undervalue imports. Profits from agriculture have provided the collateral for loans and the direct source of funds for investment and social welfare programs benefiting urban dwellers, rich and poor alike.

The interest that urban dwellers share in regard to the rural masses does not, of course, preclude important differences among them. The great bulk of the urban population consists of impoverished migrants from the hinterland hoping for a better life. Lacking modern education and skills in most cases, and competing in all cases for a limited number of jobs, they settle in shantytowns on the outskirts of the towns. Their housing ranges from tumble-down buildings to sheet metal and cardboard lean-tos. Clean water is a luxury, food is scarce, sewers are nonexistent, and health services are rare. Most people live on the margin of subsistence, sustained by occasional labor, private or government handouts, and illicit activities. To some extent, the latter involve ordinary goods and services that are illicit only because they are provided out of sight of the state in order to avoid taxes or other restrictions. To a considerable degree, however, they involve more genuinely criminal activities: violence, theft, and prostitution. Most African cities suffer from extraordinarily high crime rates as individuals and gangs ranging up to 100 people engage in street robberies, burglaries, carjackings, extortion, and, in ports, even piracy. The police are not infrequently part of the problem, and when they aren't they are generally overwhelmed. Occasional crackdowns by national governments achieve transitory successes at best.

In this context, Africans with steady blue-collar jobs form a privileged stratum of urban society. In 1985, wage earners typically comprised about 10 percent of the total work force in most West African states, and in none did they make up more than 15 percent. Their privileged status is strictly relative, however, for their situation has in many ways worsened since independence. As the economy has deteriorated, so too has their standard of living. An International Labor Organization study in 1984 found that the real value of the minimum wage in the Ivory Coast had declined by more than 18 percent in the previous few years, while the wages of low-income earners in Liberia dropped by 17 percent in 1983 alone.

Unfortunately, workers who continued to receive even their depleted paychecks were the lucky ones, for economic decline led to massive layoffs in numerous countries. Nigeria, for example, laid off a million workers between 1981 and 1983, and Ghana terminated a proportionally larger total of 30,000 government workers in 1983 alone. IMF and World Bank austerity measures have compounded labor's worsening material position, forcing governments to lay off tens of thousands more workers, reduce fringe benefits, eliminate subsidies for staple foods and transportation, and end low-cost health and education services that had particularly benefited the working poor. Reduced demand for labor has also enabled employers to tighten up workplace discipline.

About the only bright spot for the working class has been the improved position of labor unions as a result of the democratization movement that has swept the continent since the late 1980s. Unions played an important role in the anticolonial movements in many colonies, but after independence they found themselves increasingly restricted by governments jealous of any autonomous institutions. Just as they suppressed or absorbed rival political parties, governments also suppressed or absorbed independent labor unions. The unions became patronage machines and mechanisms for forcing labor's obedience to government policies rather than representatives of the true interests of the working class. More recently, however, they have regained their autonomy in many countries and are able to elect their own officials, voice their real concerns, and strike to enforce their demands. How meaningful this autonomy will prove to be in the face of the continent's continuing economic weakness is open to question, but it may enable them to improve their conditions.

Above the working class in the urban hierarchy are the groups that make up the middle class. These include mainly businesspeople, professionals, and government officials.

In keeping with the continent's economic weakness, Africa's business community remains relatively underdeveloped. Many men and women own the innumerable small businesses ranging from stores and restaurants to trucking companies and small plants producing consumer commodities that service local communities, and some substantial owners control sizable networks of such enterprises. However, their fortunes are precarious due not only to the continent's general economic problems but also to the uncertainty of the political environment and their relative powerlessness in the global business game. Almost no Africans control businesses in the league of the great multinational corporations. Not one of the world's top 500 companies and only 18 of the top 500 banks are African (of which 10 are North African and five are South African). Just four of the top 382 transnational corporations are African, with three based in South Africa and the other in Zambia. In general, the highest positions Africans attain in the world business community are important positions in local subsidiaries of multinational corporations. Entrepreneurs and managers

play an influential role in African politics, with the best-off comfortable with the status quo and the less well situated more interested in reform. In most cases, they cannot play a dominant role since the economy is ultimately controlled by actors above and beyond them.

The professional occupations include medicine, teaching, law, and engineering. They require completion of a specific academic curriculum and certification, which thereby confers a certain social status and income potential. During the colonial period, Africans were drawn to these professions because entrance depended on educational qualifications, and practitioners were assured a relatively secure income and generally enjoyed the respect of the colonial administrators.

After independence, however, the status of professionals declined somewhat. While professionals organized many of the first nationalist parties and most nationalist leaders came from their ranks, the rise of mass politics toward the end of colonialism made them suspect both because of their relative wealth and their cultural ties to the metropolitan countries. With the transition from multiparty to single-party states, professionals often continued to play a leadership role as individuals, but their opportunities for collective political action were reduced as their parties disappeared and even their occupational associations came under governmental control. In some countries, they became the objects of persecution, and in many more they suffered particularly under more generalized repression because their educations encouraged them to take a visible role in society and politics. Finally, the general economic decline reduced their standard of living, and the decay of modern infrastructure in many countries demoralized them. The result has been a "brain drain" of significant proportions as professionals leave Africa in search of political freedom, better pay, and more stimulating working conditions elsewhere. The current wave of democratization holds out the promise of removing at least one reason for this emigration, and it may create an environment in which professionals feel free to participate in political discourse once again. As people of modest means dependent on the cash nexus, they are probably an important source of support for the democratization movement.

Government officials make up the third major element of the middle class. Because the educational requirements for entering government service were considerably less than those for the professions, and because they at the same time offered social status, job security, licit and illicit sources of income, and the opportunity to dispense patronage, government work was the goal for many Africans during the colonial period. Independence only increased the desirability of government service because Africans could now hope to reach the top. The continent's economic malaise has made it even more attractive. Government officials act as the gatekeepers for both the external companies and agencies that bring wealth to African countries and the mass of inhabitants who depend on government approvals and services for their survival and success. Higher civil servants and military officers thus effectively constitute the ruling class in most African countries, the group with control over the wealth and coercive power needed to buy or compel the obedience of the rest of society. They form a politico-managerial elite similar to the one that ruled the Eastern bloc countries under communism; the power of this elite is based not on individual ownership of the means of production but on collective control of the economic and military resources of the state. They form the apex of the patronage networks that constitute the true sinews of most African states.

The objective validity of this group's dominance was demonstrated repeatedly during the three decades after 1960. Whenever a revolutionary party or enlisted men's conspiracy overthrew the established order, the new leadership rapidly evolved into a new elite. Whatever ideological and humanitarian differences they might have had with the regime they replaced, the new rulers ended up drawing their power from the same economic base and gov-

erning society through a similar sort of patronage system. Overall, the democratization movement poses a threat to this privileged position, although, as in the former Eastern bloc countries, the economy has deteriorated in many countries to the point that the lower ranks feel the pinch, and thus they are ready to support reform.

ETHNIC DIVISIONS

For more than a century, racial differences constituted the most important social division in Africa. White Europeans conquered both Arab/Berber and black Africa and imposed themselves as a privileged elite. Setting themselves apart by where they lived, how they lived, what they did, and how they related to those around them, they proclaimed themselves a racially superior form of human being. On most of the continent, their pretensions collapsed with their empires, and the last bastions of white supremacy slowly gave way in the 1970s and 1980s in southern Africa. With the election of Nelson Mandela as president of South Africa in 1994, the long struggle was over. Animosity between blacks and whites ceased to be a predominant aspect of African affairs.

Of course, the end of colonialism and the collapse of white rule did not remove all whites from Africa. In South Africa, affirmative action has replaced apartheid as the new government attempts to dismantle the structures of white privilege without destroying the country's economy. Farther north, smaller white-settler populations were successfully integrated into Zimbabwe and Kenya after independence. In the summer of 1995, President Moi of Kenya attempted to exploit reverse racism against Richard Leakey, a prominent white leader of a new opposition party, but on the whole the 75,000 whites who reside there and the 135,000 in Zimbabwe have found that their economic contribution insures them a secure place in the nation. Africans in general have exhibited remarkably little hostility toward the whites who once lorded over them. Black South Africans in particular have exhibited truly remarkable restraint considering the depths of their debasement under white rule and the costs of the struggle needed to win their basic human rights.

Outside these three countries, whites continue to have a significant presence as skilled workers and managers who generally come for tours lasting a few years. In the mid-1980s, there were more than 250,000 of them, including 20,000 Americans. A majority were French, with 50,000 in the Ivory Coast alone. Given Africa's continuing technological backwardness, the services they perform are valuable, but their presence generates a certain amount of resentment. First and foremost, Africans complain that they take jobs that Africans should fill. Secondly, they complain that expatriates live as a privileged class, commanding extraordinary salaries in relation to those earned by Africans. Thirdly, Africans gripe that many are second-rate professionals in their own countries who pass themselves off as experts in Africa. Fourthly, some allege that the expatriates deliberately sabotage the economy in order to maintain their jobs. There is undoubtedly some substance to all these complaints except the last, but they are definitely a lesser issue than colonialism and apartheid were in their day.

Another conflict often portrayed in American accounts as a form of racism is that existing between "Arabs" and "blacks" in the Sahel. In reality, as discussed in the introduction to Chapter 5, the division is less racial than a complex split between ethnic groups and economically defined life-styles. Arabic-speaking northern elites in Mauritania and Sudan definitely oppress non-Arabic Southerners in their countries, denying them political rights and even enslaving them. In Mauritania, democratization has proved to be a sham, and the southern population bears the brunt of continued repression. Even worse, although slavery was formally outlawed in 1980, the United Nations Human Rights Commission has estimated that 100,000 people remain enslaved there, working without pay and subject to torture and even death at the whim of their owners. Similarly, in Sudan, Northerners enslave members of the Dinka tribe, and the northern-controlled government has used starvation, concentration camps, and poison gas as weapons in its war on the Southerners.

The situation in the Sahel is also complicated by religion. Africans created a multitude of animist belief systems on their own, and they have also been influenced by both Christianity and Islam since the earliest years of both faiths. During the colonial period, both Christianity and Islam grew dramatically in the countries of the Sahel, and they have continued to grow since independence. Christianity naturally expanded under European rule, but it has continued to gain converts afterwards. Islam grew substantially under colonial rule, and it has spread tremendously afterwards. By the mid-1990s, approximately 260 million of the continent's 660 million people, about 40 percent, were Christian; 235 million, or about 35 percent, were Moslem; and the remaining 165 million, or 25 percent, adhered to traditional animist beliefs.

Religious diversity has given rise to two types of important conflicts. First of all, while the animists are generally willing to live and let live, both the major religions claim exclusivity, and their adherents naturally clash. Secondly, Islam is in the midst of a fundamentalist revival. The first type of conflict has contributed to a series of struggles in the Sahel and the Horn of Africa, including the civil wars in Chad and the Sudan, the Eritrean war of independence, and the Ethiopian war with Somalia. It also played a role in the Nigerian civil war. The second has generated a number of crises in North Africa, most notably massive civil disorder in Algeria and Egypt and a campaign of repression in Tunisia. Furthermore, fundamentalists led a series of uprisings in Nigeria that resulted in over 8,000 deaths. Islam continues to gain ground in sub-Saharan Africa, and Christian fundamentalists have taken the initiative within the Christian community, so religious competition between and within the faiths will undoubtedly continue to be a source of unrest in Africa well into the future.

The most significant type of social divide in Africa is between ethnic groups, communities defined by a combination of language, culture, mode of economic life, and, in some cases, political traditions. Approximately 2,000 of these ethnic units are found in Africa, far more than on any other continent. These groups speak 750 different languages and over 1,000 dialects. Despite the formation of ostensibly national states during decolonization, there is little prospect that the number of ethnic groups will decline rapidly. The languages of the ex-colonial powers are generally used for official business, so education does not reinforce a predominant national language, but creates a bilingual situation in which people speak their traditional tongue at home. An awareness of the nation can co-exist with ethnic identity, but it will need to be tied to compelling influences in peoples' lives before it will displace the older type of identification.

The term "tribalism" has often been used to describe these ethnic groups, but it is not really accurate. Derived from Greek and Roman descriptions of the uncivilized peoples to their north, the term "tribe" refers to self-contained, autonomous groups based on kinship, practicing subsistence economy, and governed by chiefs and elders. Many African peoples before the twentieth century existed in groups that roughly fit this description, but many did not. Some lived in smaller groups with less internal definition; others lived in much larger groups—kingdoms and empires—with elaborate feudal or bureaucratic hierarchies and complex political and economic relationships with neighboring peoples. The "tribalism" referred to in modern politics is more properly the ethnic differentiation and consolidation that occurred under colonialism when suddenly mobile people discovered, or were told, that they had more in common with some people than with others. In most cases, "tribes" emerged from the process by which fairly large

cultural-linguistic groups distinguished themselves from each other and some smaller groups joined together. The ethnic groups had existed for a long time; what was new was the idea that the commonalities within them and differences between them were important. The process was encouraged by the colonial powers—as a version of divide and rule among the larger groups and an expedient to consolidate and rule the smaller ones—but it also reflected the Africans' need to redefine their identities to reflect the new dimensions of their social world.

Ethnic tensions generally increased after independence, for several reasons. First, the new nations' boundaries, which were based on the old colonial boundaries, divided some ethnic groups and lumped others together. The European nation-state had been designed expressly to avoid this situation by including only members of one ethnic group, so why anyone expected the new African states to succeed as nations is something of a mystery. Of course, African leaders were supposed to engage in "nation-building," but what was forgotten in the enthusiasm of decolonization was that nation-building in Europe was a long-term process that relied heavily on pogroms, purges, crusades, civil and foreign wars, internal colonization, and cultural imperialism. Small wonder that African leaders have not been able to peacefully forge viable nations from their disparate ethnic groups in one generation.

However, the strength of "tribalism" in contemporary Africa reflects more than the weakness of nationalism. Ethnic identification plays such an important role because it works. It works for African leaders, and it works for ordinary Africans. African culture emphasizes the individual's responsibility to share success with the group, and in modern Africa the group is the family, then the clan, and then the tribe or ethnic group. This set of relationships defines the lines of patronage for both leaders and citizens. Leaders know that they already owe a special obligation to certain people over the rest, and they know that they are linked to them by bonds stronger than simple expediency. Ordinary citizens know which leaders should be receptive to them and on what basis they can approach them. In a system characterized by acute lack of, and therefore fierce competition for, resources of all types, it is small wonder that Africans exploit traditional ties to obtain maximum advantage in the struggle for survival. The theoretical alternative of a disinterested bureaucracy dispensing services according to rigid criteria defined by distant committees offers little to recommend it to any particular individual, no matter how much sense it may make to Westerners.

Despite the loosening of traditional ties in modern sectors of African society, tribalism gives a cultural underpinning to the patronage system run by the *apparatchiki* that was lacking in the amoral individualism of the Soviet Union. Consequently, it is likely to prove much more resilient in the face of democratization. In fact, it may well turn out that democratization simply widens access to the source of patronage, enabling different groups to feed at the trough at different times (or working out some division of the spoils), with the voters deciding when they have gotten enough. As was the case in Western countries in the nineteenth century, if each major group can be assured reasonable access to the public purse, then all will be content to retain the status quo. The crucial question, of course, is how this rosy scenario can transpire amid acute economic scarcity.

NEW SOCIAL ISSUES

As Africa moves into its second generation of independence, a number of new social issues have emerged that affect African politics in various ways. They include the demographic ascendancy of young people, the declining quality of the environment, the status of women, and rising levels of education and communication.

The ascendancy of young people is a simple outgrowth of Africa's rapid population growth. While only about 20 percent of Europe's population is under 15 years of age, almost 45 percent of Africa's is, and in Kenya the number exceeds 50 percent. At the other end of the age range, about 13 percent of Europe's population is 65 or older, while only 3 percent of Africa's is. The distribution of adults in between is correspondingly skewed toward the young end of the range in Africa relative to Europe.

This age distribution has serveral consequences for African politics. For one thing, despite the fact that children help with child care and farm work, the ratio of dependents to productive workers is relatively high in Africa, which compounds the continent's other economic problems. As children grow up, they pose another economic problem: they need land and jobs, both of which are in increasingly short supply. The large number of landless and unemployed young men poses a particular problem, for this is the group most likely to take to crime or take up arms. As a consequence, the continent is plagued by both rampant street crime in the cities and disturbances in the countryside that range from simple banditry to guerrilla warfare.

A final political consequence of the youthful age structure is the relative lack of connection most Africans have with the recent past. Only a distinct minority of Africans alive in 1996 experienced colonialism and the struggle for independence, even in the Portuguese-speaking countries that gained their freedom in the early 1970s. Most were not alive or were just babies when Rhodesia became Zimbabwe. For them, the great problems and proposed solutions that were so defining to the generation that brought Africa into independence are relics of history. The young can have no direct appreciation for the obstacles faced and accomplishments achieved by their fathers and grandfathers, and correspondingly they have only a limited attachment to their polities and programs. This situation may prove to be a source of particular innovation or particular instability, or both, as Africa moves into its future.

Environmental issues form a second new concern in African affairs. Unlike in the industrialized countries, pollution of the air and water are local problems by and large, concentrated in mining areas, off-shore oil fields, the cities, and South Africa's industrial zones. Desertification—the transformation of thousands of square miles of grassland into desert each year—is the continent's biggest environmental problem, afflicting countries in North Africa, the Sahel, the Horn of Africa, East Africa, and Southern Africa. It results from the overgrazing of herds and inappropriate agricultural techniques, and it is a major cause of declining food production and periodic famines.

Deforestation is another major environmental problem. Destruction of forest cover contributes to the process of desertification and also creates a growing shortage of wood for fuel. Destruction of the rainforests represents a particular problem. Along with the rainforests of Latin America and Southeast Asia, Africa's tropical forests contribute to both global climatic balance and the world's biological diversity. Rainforests contain between one-half and two-thirds of the plant and animal species on earth, and if the forests disappear, so too will the associated forms of life. Africa loses over 3 million acres of rainforest a year, and the Ivory Coast alone has lost 70 percent of its forest cover since 1900.

Forest creatures are not the only endangered animal species in Africa. A century ago the savannas teemed with wildlife; today dozens of species are facing extinction. Farmers compete with wild animals for land, herders covet the grass for their cattle, and poachers hunt them for profit. Conservationists and tourist dollars have made African governments aware of the value of wildlife. In some areas, game wardens and poachers are essentially at war, but the problem presents Africans with a dilemma. As with the destruction of the rainforest and even the causes of desertification, long-term wisdom competes with short-term needs. As the leader of the Zimbabwean peasant union put it, "Why should my cattle die to save some wild animals for Europeans who never come look at them anyway?" Elephants, magnificent as they appear on TV, are a terrifying threat when they stampede through a village. Lions and leopards will eat a herders' cows as a convenient alternative to hunting wild antelope. From a political point of view, wildlife conservation, like environmentalism in general, presents African governments with hard choices between the immediate needs of their hard-pressed people and the long-term interests of Africa and humanity.

A third social issue of growing importance is the status of women. In traditional society, which still holds sway in most of rural Africa, women are juridically subordinate to men, responsible for bearing and rearing children and for a considerable amount of agricultural labor. Women in matrilineal societies, in which a person's primary identification is with the mother's family rather than the father's, tend to have more rights and freedom than women in patrilineal ones, and some African societies exhibit an easy acceptance of women who take on male roles. Overall, however, women traditionally have been subordinate to men.

In the cities, women have escaped traditional constraints, but they continue to occupy a subordinate position. Poor women in shantytowns, struggling to raise children amid unbelievable squalor, make up the most downtrodden segment of urban society. Educational and job opportunities for women are far fewer than for men, and even women with skills and education find their options limited. Most work in the service sector, and on average earn considerably less than men. Nevertheless, some women have managed to succeed as entrepreneurs, and a few have managed to gain high government and professional positions. African women have participated widely in demonstrations and strikes supporting democratization, and numerous representatives attended the United Nations conference on women in Beijing in August 1995. Women are already a factor in African politics, and as their role in society and their awareness of their situation evolves, both they and their concerns will undoubtedly play an increasing part.

A fourth significant new development in African society is concerned with the rising levels of education and communication. Since colonial times, Africans have placed great stock in education as a means of promoting social mobility. Independent African governments have promoted it for political and economic reasons as well, to reinforce nationalism and in some countries socialism, and to impart skills needed for development. Expenditures for education represent about one-fifth of most countries' budgets, the single largest category except, in certain countries, the military.

Because of its colonial heritage and continuing poverty, Africa remains the least educated continent, but the money spent on education has bought considerable progress. In 1960, fewer than 20 percent of adults in sub-Saharan Africa could read and write. In 1985, over 45 percent could. About the same percentage of young people in 1960 were enrolled in school. By 1982, the percentage had risen to 44 percent. Some countries have achieved universal primary education, and secondary school enrollment has risen from five to 25 percent. Only a small percentage of age-eligible Africans go on to higher education overall, although 21 percent of Egyptians, 11 percent of Libyans, and 8 percent of Moroccans do.

The rising level of education influences African life in a number of ways. Education is associated with improved family nutrition, lower infant mortality, smaller family size, higher earning capacity, and, in rural areas, greater productivity. Combined with improved methods of communication, particularly electronic communication, education has expanded the politically aware, and thus potentially engaged, population considerably. The "mass" parties of the 1950s and 1960s were generally not mass parties at all, but populist factions able to mobilize large demonstrations on occasion. In the 1960s and 1970s, most governments attempted to politi-

cize the people through party organizations as well as public schools; but even where conscious politicization was not pursued, education, exposure, and, frequently, the intrusion of armed conflicts drew people into political life. At independence, national politics were for the great majority of Africans a distant and occasional concern, reported through word-of-mouth and requiring at most a trip or two to a polling place. By the late 1980s, however, most Africans were aware of national politics, many had been caught up in national affairs in one way or another, and a good number followed the news and took an ongoing interest. So long as corrupt dictators dominated the government, cynicism or fear kept most people from working for improvements, but as the democratization movement gained steam, many took heart and joined in. The quantitative change in the level of education achieved by Africans has led to a qualitative change in the social milieu of African politics.

DEMOCRATIZATION

The nations of Africa have gone through three general phases of political life since independence. The first phase, which was relatively brief in most cases, was a period of parliamentary democracy based on the institutions bequeathed by the departing colonial powers. The second, and longest, phase was a period of authoritarian rule by governments ranging from strong presidents leading one-party systems to maniacal dictators ruling through the military and secret police. The third phase, which began in the late 1980s, is dominated by the democratization movement. Although it is too soon to tell what its ultimate impact will be, by the mid-1990s virtually every country on the continent had been influenced by the movement to some extent. Even if it ultimately fails, its status as a distinct phase of continental history seems assured.

For a number of reasons, the first parliamentary phase lasted only a few years in most countries. To begin with, colonialism had ill prepared Africans for democracy. Colonial government itself was a dictatorial regime, with authority emanating from the metropolitan government through the colonial governor to district officers and ultimately to local officials, whether European or African. In most cases, the African people had little or no preparation for participation in democratic politics; they had only a decade or two of experience in forming opposition parties and had participated in just a handful of elections and referenda. The colonial experience taught them at most how to oppose the government, but it had not taught them how to run it.

More fundamentally, Africa at independence lacked many of the social and economic underpinnings of European parliamentary democracy. Most of the people were illiterate, and communications were rudimentary. Perfectly capable of running their own local affairs, they were ill equipped to participate in national politics, a situation that was exactly the reverse of what the centralized parliamentary governments required of them. Furthermore, African society was not divided into two dominant urban classes, capitalists and workers, whose parties advocated alternative programs as solutions to common national problems. Instead, the vast majority of Africans were peasants at the margins of national politics, and the parties represented competing factions within the elite that wrangled over control of power and patronage.

Finally socialism existed as an alternative to parliamentary democracy. Untainted by connections to the colonial past and apparently validated by the Soviet Union's economic success between the two world wars, a one-party state with a centrally planned economy seemed a way to avoid the petty bickering and lingering dependence associated with the Western model. At the time, even Western economists generally foresaw an extensive role for the state in developing countries, while many political scientists assumed that authoritarian institutions might be necessary to implement the difficult decisions required for development. Few African countries fully adopted Soviet-style communism, but most energetically pushed the state into the center of the economy. Almost all rejected parliamentary institutions in favor of more-or-less authoritarian political structures.

The authoritarian regimes adopted by African countries ranged in character from relatively benign strongman presidencies like Houphouet-Bolgny's in the Ivory Coast and Kenneth Kaunda's in Zambia to ruthless dictatorships like Idi Amin's in Uganda and Francisco Macias Nguema's in Equitorial Guinea. In some cases, the transition from parliamentarianism involved a gradual evolution away from multipartyism to a single-party system, and from a democratically elected national leadership to a *de facto* or *de jure* presidency-for-life. In other cases, a military coup abruptly ended the rule of law and inaugurated rule by force. In only a few cases did the initial deviation from parliamentary democracy endure. Far more often, a succession of civilian strongmen and military dictators ruled, and there were even occasional attempts to restore multiparty democracy.

In its more benign form, authoritarianism meant monopolization of public affairs by a single party led by a charismatic leader with the general support of the country's population. The strongmen justified single-party rule by the need to maintain national unity. They claimed that reconcilation of competing interests through consensual means within the party structure would be less divisive than competition between parties. These single-party systems often worked as much by co-opting opponents as by suppressing them. Many allowed a significant amount of internal democracy, and some fielded competing candidates in elections that gave the public at large a real, if limited, choice. Overall, the parties enabled the ruling group to mobilize the masses when useful, to channel patronage to the politically powerful segments of society, and to manage the important aspects of government behind the scenes, beyond the more formal mechanisms of public institutions.

At the other end of the spectrum, authoritarianism meant despotic rule by a ruthless military dictator through ubiquitous supervision of public and private life, murderous repression of opponents real and imagined, and unbridled corruption to the profit of the leader and his allies.

Although the differences between these regimes and the more mild ones were significant, particularly to the lives of their people, both rested ultimately on the same institutional structure. In some cases, there was even a gradual evolution from the more benign to the less benign type, particularly as the top man got older. Controlled movement in the opposite direction also took place, as military juntas transformed themselves into political parties or handed power over to civilian cabinets. In other cases, the transition was more traumatic—as when military coups overthrew corrupt civilian governments or when ruthless dictatorships collapsed as a result of popular resistance and belated foreign renunciation.

What came afterwards was usually better, but it was seldom democracy. All shades of authoritarianism curbed people's political and human rights to a greater or lesser extent, eviscerating elections, curbing free speech and freedom of the press, limiting freedom of assembly, outlawing opposition parties, manipulating the judicial system, conducting extrajudicial trials and punishments, and subordinating or suppressing labor unions and denying the right to strike. Some benign regimes, like the one in Tanzania, were able to maintain their relatively mild policies, and only a minority descended into utter despotism. But in the absence of effective institutional safeguards, most found it difficult to resist the temptation or pressure to gradually increase their reliance on repression.

Throughout the 1970s and early 1980s, occasional attempts to restore multiparty democracy punctuated Africa's political life, most notably Nigeria's unsuccessful experiment in 1980. The real resurgence of multipartyism did not come until the late 1980s, however, and generally it came not from African governments themselves but from outside and from below. The external impetus came both from the examples of democratization in Latin America and, later, Eastern Europe, and from the conditions attached to structural adjustment loans by the IMF and the World Bank. The internal impetus came from the demands of the people as expressed through support of opposition figures, organization of new opposition parties, circulation of unauthorized newspapers, and demonstrations, strikes, and riots.

The African supporters of democratization took their inspiration from African traditions of resistance to tyrants as well as from events overseas, and their actions were precipitated by the boiling over of frustration with the inability of their governments to deliver on their promise of a better life within a civil society. Africa in the 1980s was in a classic prerevolutionary situation, like France before the revolution of 1789. After decades of modest development, people's rising expectations were frustrated by the onset of economic hard times, attributable more than anything to the corruption and mismanagement of the ruling class. Even deeper, the swelling of the population, like the demographic situations of revolutionary France and Central Europe in the 1930s, created an inexorable pressure to develop or die. Millions of Africans just coming of age were clamoring to survive and to prosper, and the democratization movement may be just the first in a series of upheavals fueled by their needs.

By the mid-1990s, the democratization movement had engendered five types of transition, two of which represented a real triumph of democracy. Of the three that didn't, the least hopeful outcome was the total frustration by the ruling military autocrats—through deceit, manipulation, and fraud—of an attempted transition to democracy, as happened in Nigeria, Zaire, and Togo. Somewhat more hopeful, but still far from complete, were transitions in which the military managed to retain control over the process, thereby insuring a favorable outcome for its own interests. Burkina Faso, Ghana, Guinea, and Mauritania were examples of this. Similarly, in Cameroon, the Ivory Coast, Ethiopia, Gabon, Kenya, and Senegal, incumbent civilian presidents allowed multiparty elections but were able to retain power through dominance of the media, control of the electoral administration, alliances with powerful patronage networks, and deep pockets. In Malawi and the Central Africa Republic, the attempted manipulations didn't work, and the strongman ended up losing. In the successful transitions, in Benin, Congo, Mali, and Niger, broad coalitions of social groups assumed sovereign powers, appointed a transitional administration, and organized elections that brought in a new, democratic government.

While the completely successful efforts are in the minority, so too are the complete failures, and the pressure for multiparty democracy remains strong. How many more successful transitions will take place in the future, and how durable their outcomes will be, cannot be known in advance, but the forces militating for and against long-term success can be delineated.

So long as the IMF and other external donors tie their aid to democratic reforms, even governments with no desire to really comply will continue to put up a front, and there is always the chance that their insincere concessions will give the opposition the leverage it needs to force true changes. It is uncertain, however, how long foreigners will continue to care about Africa's internal affairs or attempt to influence them.

Furthermore, the aid and loans to which external donors tie conditions actually reinforce the status quo by continuing to funnel wealth through central governments and thus perpetuating their role as fonts of patronage. External threats and sanctions against nondemocratic regimes unquestionably play a useful role in promoting democratization, but even more useful would be programs and pronouncements that positively reinforce Africa's internal democratic tendencies. Efforts like the American National Endowment for Democracy (described in Chapter 14), financial aid

to nongovernmental organizations monitoring African political affairs, and direct economic links to private African enterprises can do much to help Africa evolve away from its excessively centralized administrations.

External manipulations, however, can at most help positive trends and hinder negative ones; they cannot determine the ultimate direction of African politics. Only the efforts of Africans themselves will do this, and they will have to find their own way. A few factors that will influence the outcome can be discerned from afar, however. First and foremost, democratic reforms must go below the surface of constitutional arrangements and political forms to affect the social and economic underpinnings of the status quo. It was not a coincidence that parliamentary democracy failed the first time around and that earlier attempts at reform almost always collapsed into renewed authoritarianism. So long as the national government is the dominant source of economic and political power, it will continue to be a prize to be won.

Many commentators point to the prevalence of checks and balances in precolonial African governments as evidence of some sort of predisposition among Africans to curb executive power. What this analysis overlooks, however, is that these checks and balances were grounded in the reality that the executive ultimately lacked the power to coerce obedience. Either the king's soldiers were balanced by soldiers controlled by others, as in a feudal empire, or else the people could just move away. Similarly, checks and balances will work only if they rest on real balances of institutional power. Some of these institutions may be internal to the government, like competing branches of the armed forces; firmly separated executive, legislative, and judicial branches; and federal and local levels of government with their own incomes and budgets. Others may be entirely separate from the government yet capable of acting against abuses, like an independent press, organized interest groups, religious groups, free labor unions, and even privately owned businesses. Only by rooting the concept of checks and balances in institutional and economic reality are those curbs likely to endure.

From this point of view, perhaps the most hopeful experiment of 1996 is underway in Ethiopia, where the government is working to decentralize itself, giving regional groups the opportunity to withdraw from the national union entirely, and, assuming they opt to stay, offering them wide-ranging autonomy. By facing up to the central political role played by ethnic identification, this approach promises to yield a nation based on the consent of its real constituent parts. Furthermore, by decentralizing the economic aspects of government, it will allow parallel networks of patronage to operate, independent of the interests of any one ethnic group. The arrangement may seem regressive from a Eurocentric point of view, but it seems well advised in light of African realities.

CONCLUSION

Africa today is in deep distress. As of the middle of 1996, Rwanda remains riven by ethnic hatreds and Somalia is still splintered by warring clans. Zaire continues to languish under the deadening hand of "Messiah" Mobutu, and General Abacha retains his iron grip on Nigeria. South Africa is a bright spot of hopeful transformation, but poverty and decay seem to dominate the rest of the continent.

The roots of this sorry situation can be traced back deep into the past, back to the first depravations by Portuguese raiders during the European Renaissance. They stretch through the slave trade to the colonial period, when Europe's impact evolved from an incidental to a deliberate subordination of Africa to the emerging European-dominated world economic system. This subordination survived the transition to political independence, when geopolitical and neocolonial machinations and shifts in the world economy helped thwart Africa's clumsy attempts to develop autonomously.

In the 1990s, Africa's neocolonial period may be coming to an end, as Europe's economic interest and the United States' strategic interest in the continent wane. Unfortunately, this development may further diminish rather than improve Africa's prospects. The continent may soon find itself in a position analogous to an urban ghetto, but on a global scale: producing little of value to the outside, sustained by international welfare, ruled by corrupt strongmen, rife with crime and violence, and burdened by the despair of a generation born into economic hopelessness. The situation of many African countries has caused some observers to suggest that the Third World is splitting off a Fourth and even a Fifth World, with the lower layers trapped in a quagmire of economic marginality.

However, developments in the 1990s present opportunities as well as dangers. Conventional wisdom holds that democracy requires economic prosperity and social stability to flower, yet Africa is enjoying a resurgence of democracy despite its economic distress, and indeed because of it. Fed up with the inefficiency and corruption of the authoritarian governments, both international agencies and Africans themselves are agitating for representative institutions and the rule of law. Not every movement has been successful, but some have succeeded, and others are persevering in the face of obstructionism and repression. Collectively, they have transformed the terms of African politics, raising aspirations that all governments have found they must take account of, even if only to attempt to deny them. And where democratization succeeds, it opens up the possibility not only of improving governance and respect for human rights, but also of unleashing the pent up potential of the economy. Reconciling Africa's official and illicit economies by creating a single legitimate system would both reveal heretofore uncounted resources and yield tremendous economies in business activities. It is here, in Africa's own local enterprises, that the continent's best hopes may be found.

If these hopeful possibilities appear unrealistic, it is important to remember that 10 years ago the collapse of the Soviet Union, the end of the Cold War, peace between Israel and the PLO, and the end of apartheid appeared unrealistic as well. Realization of all these unlikely events reflected both the committed work of idealistic people and changes in the underlying economic and social realities that had kept the status quo in place. There is certainly no lack of committed and idealistic people in Africa today, and it appears that the decay of the continent's economy has created conditions favorable to continued reform. These reforms, in turn, could provide the key to economic improvement. To realize this potential, governments will need to be based on real balances of power, and to foster real economic activity. Upon their success at this depends the long-term viability of democracy in Africa, and the ultimate well-being of the African people.

GLOSSARY

In general, unusual or specialized terms are explained where they occur, but inevitably in a work that will be used as a reference some recur in a way that makes it impractical to define them at each occurrence. The most commonly used of these are explained here.

Apartheid: The system of extreme racial segregation that the Afrikaner Nationalist Party imposed on South Africa between the late 1940s and the early 1990s. The basis of the system was the classification of all South Africans into racial groups, which included whites, Asians, mixed-race coloreds, and blacks. Furthermore, members of the black majority were assigned to tribal groups that were given ostensibly independent homelands, making them foreigners within the rest of South Africa, where most actually worked and lived. The system required an extensive array of security laws to enforce, and its purpose was to insure permanent white dominance of South Africa.

Anglophone: English-speaking. Most African states retain their former colonizer's tongue as an official language because it provides a common means of communication for peoples who speak different local languages. The term is often used to designate former British colonies (as well as Liberia, which was long dominated by an English-speaking elite).

CFA Franc: African Financial Community Franc. A currency issued by the central banks of the Francophone West and Central African economic communities for use by member states as a common currency. Its value is tied to the French franc, which helped to support the economies of the countries using it until the French government declared in 1994 that it could no longer afford to carry the burden and announced a 50 percent devaluation.

Francophone: French-speaking. Most African states retain their former colonizer's tongue as an official language because it provides a common means of communication for peoples who speak different local languages. The term is often used to designate former French colonies, which for most indicates continued close ties to France and to each other.

GDP: Gross Domestic Product. The market value of all a country's goods and services produced in a year, excluding its exports and imports. The GDP is the most commonly used measure of national economic activity.

Horn of Africa: The region of east Africa that includes Somalia, Djibouti, Ethiopia, and Eritrea. Its name comes from its appearance on the map; the region appears to jut out into the Indian Ocean.

IMF: International Monetary Fund. An agency of the United Nations originally created to help stabilize currency relations by loaning money to help countries cope with short-term balance of payments problems. In the 1970s, these loans grew in size, and the repayment periods lengthened as the problems of less-developed countries mounted, and the IMF's role gradually evolved to include prescribing long-term economic reforms designed to improve the recipient's financial standing.

Loi-cadre: A legislative act in 1956 in which the French government reoriented its policy toward its African colonies. It abandoned its attempt to assimilate them into a unified central government including metropolitan France and all its overseas territories. Instead, it created a form of association in which the colonies became autonomous, self-governing members of a federal system in which they had extensive control over local affairs while the government in Paris retained control of foreign affairs and had a final say in other matters. At the same time, the importance of the two major territorial divisions (French West Africa and French Equatorial Africa) was reduced in favor of direct relations between France and the individual colonies.

Lusophone: Portuguese-speaking. Most African states retain their former colonizer's tongue as an official language because it provides a common means of communication for

peoples who speak different local languages. The term can thus be used to designate former Portuguese colonies.

Maghrib: The region of northwest Africa roughly corresponding to present-day Morocco, Algeria, and Tunisia.

OAU: The Organization of African Unity. Founded in 1963, it set the groundwork and created a forum for inter-African diplomacy over the next three decades. It contains every African country except Morocco, which withdrew in 1985 to protest admission of the Western Sahara.

Parastatial Corporation: A business enterprise that is owned 50 percent or more by a national government, which therefore controls it. In general, parastatials exist because their activities are deemed to be in a broader public interest than private ownership will be able to serve. However, nonprofit government services like fire departments and armies are not parastatials.

Pastoralists: People whose way of life is based on tending migrating herds of animals. In Africa, these are typically cattle. Prominent pastoralist peoples include the Fulani of northern Africa and the Masai of east Africa.

Sahel: The steppe region immediately to the south of the Sahara desert and west of the upper Nile. Historically the home of nomadic pastoralists, today it is plagued by rapid desertification due to climatic shifts, overgrazing, and ill-conceived agricultural projects.

Savanna: In general, regions of tropical and subtropical grassland with scattered shrubs and trees that experience a heavy wet season and a dry season each year. In African history, the strip of savanna south of the Sahel and north of the coastal forests in West Africa played a particularly important role as the home of the first sub-Saharan civilizations.

Structural Adjustment Programs: Economic reform programs imposed by the IMF and the World Bank that involve reducing public spending, boosting the private sector, cutting social welfare programs, and emphasizing export-oriented businesses.

Swahili: A Bantu language with a heavy admixture of Arabic that developed due to extensive contact between the original speakers and Arab traders. Swahili became the language of commerce in east Africa and now serves as a common language in the whole region.

World Bank: An agency of the United Nations originally created to finance the reconstruction of war-ravaged Europe that soon branched out into loans to promote economic development. Over the years, it established several subsidiaries that specialize in loans to low income countries, which has given it a prominent role in African affairs. In the 1950s and 1960s, it focused on big-ticket projects like hydro-electric dams. In the 1970s, it switched to funding grass-roots rural development and social welfare programs. In the 1980s, the World Bank changed course again, imposing structural adjustment programs that cut public spending on social programs in favor of export-oriented private enterprise.

BIBLIOGRAPHY

Africa in World Politics: Post-Cold War Challanges, 2nd edition. Harbeson, John, and Rothchild, Donald., eds. Boulder: Westview Press, 1995.

Ayittey, George. *Africa Betrayed*. New York: St. Martin's Press, 1992.

Crowder, Michael. *West Africa Under Colonial Rule*. Evanston: Northwestern University Press, 1968.

Current History. May 1994.

Davidson, Basil. *Africa in History: Themes and Outlines*. New York: Macmillan, 1991.

Davidson, Basil. *The Black Man's Burden: Africa and the Curse of the Nation State*. New York: Random House, 1992.

Davidson, Basil. *Modern Africa: A Social and Political History*, 3rd edition. London: Longman, 1994.

Dunnigan, James, and Bay, Austin. *A Quick and Dirty Guide to War*, revised edition. New York: William Morrow, 1991.

Economist Intelligence Unit. *EIU Country Monitor*, various. New York: Economist, 1995.

Financial Times.

Freedom in the World: The Annual Survey of Political Rights and Civil Liberties, 1992–1993. New York: Freedom House, 1993.

Freund, Bill. *The Making of Contemporary Africa: The Development of African Society since 1800*. Bloomington: Indiana University Press, 1984.

Handbooks to the Modern World: Africa, 2 vol. Moroney, Sean, ed. New York: Facts on File, 1989.

Hourani, Albert. *A History of the Arab Peoples*. Cambridge, Mass.: Belknap Press of Harvard University Press, 1991.

July, Robert. *A History of the African People*. New York: Charles Schribner's Sons, 1970.

Keesing's Record of World Events, vol. 40 (1994) and vol. 41 (1995). Avenel, N.J.: Cartermill Publishing.

Kidron, Michael, and Segal, Ronald. *The New State of the World Atlas*. New York: Simon and Schuster, 1987.

Kidron, Michael, and Smith, Dan. *The War Atlas*. New York: Simon and Schuster, 1983.

de Kiewiet, C. W. *A History of South Africa: Social and Economic*. London: Oxford University Press, 1957.

Kwitny, Jonathan. *Endless Enemies: The Making of an Unfriendly World*. New York: Penguin, 1986.

Lamb, David. *The Africans*. New York: Vintage Books, 1987.

Lands and Peoples: Africa. Danbury, Conn.: Grolier, 1995.

McEvedy, Colin. *The Penguin Atlas of African History*. London: Penguin, 1980.

Naipaul, Shiva. *North of South: An African Journey*. London: Penguin, 1979.

New African Yearbook, 1993–94. Edited by Linda Van Buren. London: IC Publications, 1994.

New York Times.

Oliver, Roland. *The African Experience*. New York, HarperCollins, 1991.

Oxford Companion to Politics of the Modern World. Krieger, Joel, ed. New York: Oxford University Press, 1993.

Polk, William. *The Arab World*, 4th edition. Cambridge, Mass.: Harvard University Press, 1980.

Rosenblum, Mort, and Williamson, Doug. *Squandering Eden: Africa at the Edge*. San Diego: Harcourt Brace Jovanovich, 1987.

Rosberg, Carl, and Nottingham, John. *The Myth of "Mau Mau": Nationalism in Kenya*. Chicago: Meridian, 1966.

Spence, J. E., ed. *Change in South Africa*. London: Pinter, 1994.

Times Atlas of World History. Barraclough, Geoffrey, ed. London: Times Books, 1980.

Unger, Sanford. *Africa: The People and Politics of an Emerging Continent*. New York: Simon and Schuster, 1986.

Wall Street Journal.

INDEX

. . . .

by Kay Banning